MW00334494

POISON IVY

Also by Evan Mandery

Nonfiction

A Wild Justice: The Death and Resurrection of Capital Punishment in America

Capital Punishment:
A Balanced Examination

The Campaign: Rudy Giuliani, Ruth Messinger, Al Sharpton, and the Race to Be Mayor of New York City

Fiction

The Professional

Q

First Contact (Or, It's Later Than You Think)

Dreaming of Gwen Stefani

POISON IVY

HOW ELITE COLLEGES DIVIDE US

EVAN MANDERY

LIBRARY OF
CONGRESS
SURPLUS
DUPLICATE

THE
NEW
PRESS

NEW YORK
LONDON

© 2022 by Evan Mandery
All rights reserved.
No part of this book may be reproduced, in any form, without written permission from the publisher.
Requests for permission to reproduce selections from this book should be made through our website:
https://thenewpress.com/contact.

Published in the United States by The New Press, New York, 2022
Distributed by Two Rivers Distribution

ISBN 978-1-62097-695-1 (hc)
ISBN 978-1-62097-722-4 (ebook)
CIP data is available

The New Press publishes books that promote and enrich public discussion and understanding of
the issues vital to our democracy and to a more equitable world. These books are made possible
by the enthusiasm of our readers; the support of a committed group of donors, large and small;
the collaboration of our many partners in the independent media and the not-for-profit sector;
booksellers, who often hand-sell New Press books; librarians; and above all by our authors.

www.thenewpress.com

Book design and composition by Bookbright Media
This book was set in Minion Pro and News Gothic

Printed in the United States of America

10 9 8 7 6 5 4 3 2 1

For Mattie

Sorry.

I want you to make a difference . . .
Until you do, who will?

President John F. Kennedy to the leaders of five major universities, including Harvard and Yale (Fall 1962)

CONTENTS

AUTHOR'S NOTE

The colleges and universities discussed in this book are inconsistent in their use of racial and ethnic terminology. For example, Harvard identifies the percentage of its students who are "African American" and "Asian American," while Princeton classifies students as "Black" and "Asian." In most instances, I use the terminology employed by the college being discussed at the time.

INTRODUCTION

Each morning for nine years, between 2012 and the start of the pandemic in 2020, I took a train between two worlds. At one end was an affluent suburb, Manhasset, where my family had landed for complicated reasons. We put all our money into our house and lived month to month, among the poorer people in a community where 70 percent of the population is white and the average family income is nearly $300,000 per year. At the other terminus was John Jay College of Criminal Justice, part of CUNY—the City University of New York—where I've taught for more than twenty years. At John Jay, 18 percent of the students are white and the average family income is $42,000 per year.

This train ride is an apt metaphor for my life, most of which I've spent in schools, traversing class boundaries. I attended elementary school in Brooklyn, where my father worked as a public high school math teacher and, later, a principal. When I was twelve, my family moved to a middle-class suburb in Long Island, where my mom began teaching junior high school Spanish. Both of my parents attended CUNY, but with their support I made it to Harvard. Over holidays, while my friends jetted off to exotic places, I went home to East Meadow to bowl and play basketball.

I stayed at Harvard for law school and then worked as an attorney until I realized my dream of becoming a teacher myself and landed at CUNY. This experience reshaped my view of opportunity in America. At John Jay, I met thousands of brilliant, hard-working young people who faced almost insurmountable obstacles in trying to achieve their dreams. You'll meet many of them in the pages that follow. Inevitably, I began to think about the chasm that separated my students' lives and fortunes from those with whom I'd gone to school and now lived. This chasm is massive. Almost no one who attends or has graduated from John Jay lives in the suburbs. Almost no one from Manhasset will attend a college like John Jay.

At first blush, my metaphor may seem strained or mixed. Manhasset is a residential community. John Jay is a college. In fact, these universes are deeply interconnected. Manhasset, and thousands of white suburbs like it, are defined by class anxiety. The author and social critic Barbara Ehrenreich says the angst that affluent, suburban parents feel about passing on their status—what she calls the "fear of falling"—is palpable. The surest pathway to keep from falling is to get your kid into an elite college. "This knowledge, however tacit," says UCLA professor Patricia McDonough, "is a bone-chilling wind blowing through suburbia."

Admission to an elite college is indeed a near-perfect protection from falling. At Harvard, nearly 100 percent of the students graduate, and their average salary by their tenth reunion is almost $200,000 per year. At CUNY, about half of entering students never finish their degrees, and about 10 percent of those who do will be living in poverty in their early thirties. Nationally, the dropout rate for poor college students is almost 90 percent. Yet, private colleges lavish more and more resources upon their students while investment in public education dwindles. Harvard, aided by massive tax subsidies, spends nearly $120,000 per student per year. At CUNY, the figure is $15,000.

Schools like CUNY are precisely what affluent, suburban parents don't want. Manhasset High School students joke that if you don't do better you're going to go to Binghamton, the flagship of SUNY, the New York State university system. No one even mentions CUNY. Parents in these communities organize to do everything within their power to land their children at an elite college. They hire tutors and private admissions counselors and make massive investments in sports that most of my students have never heard of, like fencing, crew, and lacrosse.

We're going to be talking a lot about lacrosse.

This book emerged from a dinner bet with a college friend. He and I had much in common. We'd each been raised by teachers in a middle-class Long Island suburb. We shared the same politics. We both worried about growing income inequality in America. Likely you know this data. Income inequality in the United States has never been higher. The richest 1 percent earns nearly twice as much as the bottom 50 percent. Since 1980, almost all of the economic growth in America has gone to the top 10 percent. The median income has remained stagnant.

The American Dream is fading. More than 90 percent of children born in 1940 went on to earn more than their parents. By 1985, this was true for less than half of people. In a global ranking of social mobility, the United States ranks twenty-seventh, just ahead of the Russian Federation but behind Lithuania and Estonia. Of American children born into the lowest income quintile, 43 percent remain in the bottom quintile as adults, while only 30 percent make it to the middle quintile or higher. For Black Americans, it's worse. Fifty-three percent remain in the bottom quintile. Only 26 percent make it to the middle quintile or higher. My friend and I recognized the risks in these data. Social scientists had linked declines in social mobility with drops in social capital and trust, with higher mortality rates, and to increases in violent crime.

We diverged on our view of how much responsibility our alma mater bore. Like many graduates of elite colleges that I'd spoken with over the years, my friend argued that Harvard was a good actor. After all, they allowed anyone whose family made under $65,000 to attend for free. This begged the question, I said. How many kids at Harvard came from families making less than $65,000 a year? So, we bet dinner. In 2013, the median household income in the U.S. was $52,000. This meant that more than half of Americans would qualify for free tuition. If anywhere close to 50 percent of Harvard students came from families making less than $52,000, or even $65,000 per year, I said I'd buy.

It wasn't even close.

Less than 20 percent of Harvard students came from families earning under $65,000 per year. More came from families in the top 1 percent than the bottom 50 percent. We settled our bet using data from an annual survey of freshmen taken by the *Harvard Crimson*. Soon our understanding of opportunity in higher education would be immeasurably enriched by a groundbreaking study based on millions of tax filings and tuition records. The picture painted by the economists Raj Chetty and John Friedman, whom you'll soon meet, was worse than anyone imagined. The average family income of a Harvard student in the class of 2013 was $505,000 per year. As many students came from families in the top one-tenth of 1 percent as from the bottom 20. This, Chetty and Friedman found, was the story at all elite colleges. Thirty-eight colleges had more students from the top 1 percent than the bottom 60 percent. At the most competitive colleges, kids from the top income quintile outnumbered kids from the bottom income quintile by an average of fourteen to one.

Economic disparities effectively dictated where a child would go to college. For kids born into the bottom income quintile, the prospects could hardly have been bleaker. Less than half of 1 percent would attend an elite college. More than 60 percent wouldn't attend any college at all. Meanwhile, kids born into families in the top 1 percent had it made. Virtually all would attend one of the top one thousand schools in Barron's selectivity ranking. About a quarter would go on to attend an elite college.

The story Harvard, Yale, and Princeton tell is that these data are a reflection of the underlying inequities in American society. Extreme income inequality and residential segregation create massive educational disparities that shape who is qualified and willing to attend these schools. Elite colleges look the way they do, they say, because America looks the way it does.

What if the causal chain is reversed?

What if America looks the way it does because elite colleges look the way they do?

The Harvard Financial Aid Initiative, and other programs like it, are a central part of a story that elite colleges have long told: Given the existing inequality in America, elite colleges are a force for good. Almost every element of this story is a myth. It's as misleading as those television commercials from Shell and other energy giants that advertise their commitment to developing clean energy alternatives—not a lie, exactly, but fundamentally misleading. They tout the pittance they spend on gravity lights and bio-beans to deflect attention from the hundreds of millions they spend every year lobbying to defend their right to emit as many billions of tons of carbon dioxide as they can.

It's the same with elite colleges. They do promote some upward mobility. About 3 percent of Harvard students come from families in the bottom income quintile. We could quibble about how many of them "deserve" to get in on their "merits." I'll argue that the concepts of desert and merit are meaningless in connection with college admissions. But it's certainly true that no student from a family in the bottom quintile—meaning less than about $20,000 annually—could afford tuition at an elite college. It's also true that more than half of these students will ascend to the top income quintile after graduation.

Harvard touts its "affordable" and "transformative" education on the homepage of its website. All elite colleges do. This masks their core mission. Twenty times more Harvard students come from the top income quintile as the bottom. For every poor student Harvard promotes to affluence, it will help ten affluent students remain affluent. The story is the same at every elite college. Their core business isn't lifting poor kids out of poverty. It's keeping rich kids rich.

Of course, it wouldn't do to say this explicitly any more than it would have done to admit that the foundation of the modern admissions system—with its emphasis on character, athletic ability, and preference for the children of their graduates, so-called "legacies"—evolved in the early twentieth century as a mechanism to legitimize the exclusion of Jews. This would be a public relations disaster. It would also undermine the rationale for the tax exemption—ostensibly for nonprofits that serve the public interest—upon which elite colleges have built their massive endowments. So, they defend their admissions policies in the name of "diversity" and place value on "objective" metrics, despite abundant evidence that most have little, if any, relationship to college performance and all are correlated with class.

These policies don't exist in a vacuum. The emphasis that elite colleges place upon academic peacocking, athletic prowess, and extrinsic measures of character shapes society. In response, suburban communities build state-of-the-art athletic facilities, mount dozens of Advanced

Placement courses, and fund traveling Model United Nations teams. Out of fear of falling, affluent white parents seek out these communities precisely because they help their children develop the kinds of narratives that elite colleges choose to value. These expensive programs fuel residential segregation, which elite colleges reward, creating a vicious cycle of competition that almost entirely excludes the poor.

It would be one thing if elite colleges turned affluent high school graduates into do-gooders. They do the opposite. They steer them into careers in finance and consulting, further exacerbating inequality. Elite colleges are essentially the only means of access to the most elite jobs—at Goldman Sachs, McKinsey, and the like. More than 21 percent of Harvard graduates will end up as 1 percenters. Elite colleges deny the reality that they shape career preferences. More damningly, they deny the reality that their degrees are almost always awarded to people based on accidents of birth. Rather, they perpetuate the notion that their students are the best and the brightest, and shower them with opportunities that help them to develop an upper-class way of being—a habitus—that makes living in community with ordinary people almost impossible and fuels resentment of elites.

What's so confusing is that elite colleges are populated almost exclusively by liberals. Yet these institutions are conservative in every sense of the word—their policies favor rich white people, and they have invested a fortune in protecting the status quo. Over the pages that follow you'll meet many social scientists who have carefully chronicled and explained the mechanisms that fuel inequality in American education. Most of them work at these schools. Yet almost none have called out their colleges as bad actors. The same is true of most alumni of these schools, like my friend, and perhaps even you. They're surely falling prey to a human tendency to justify the system to which one belongs. This requires a sort of willful blindness. I'm here to open your eyes.

The United States maintains an apartheid educational system.

To this point, elite colleges have received a pass for the central role they play.

It's time for them to account.

POISON IVY

PART I

The Shopping Mall

1

Going Up

Shortly after his ninth birthday, Abdoulaye Djiba Diallo's parents found themselves in conflict. A classroom had opened at the two-room schoolhouse in Hafia, the small village in Guinea's Labé region where Diallos had lived for hundreds of years. This presented a rare opportunity. The school admitted new students only every few years, when it had a free room. If the family passed, Abdoulaye would be too old to enroll the next time seats became available.

Nevertheless, Abdoulaye's mother, Djiba, was against it. In their family debates, she emphasized the school's rampant corruption. Alhassane, the fourth of her seven children, had attended the school for two years and gotten nothing out of it. Amadoury, her fifth son and the one closest in age to Abdoulaye, had spent the bulk of his days working for the teachers. As Djiba saw it, attending school effectively constituted a form of indentured servitude. If a student didn't work hard enough, they'd be beaten. Graduates of the school didn't seem to do well enough to justify the mistreatment.

Most people in the community shared Djiba's reservations about the school. Abdoulaye's best friend, Thierno, came from one of the wealthiest families in the village. Thierno's father mined a highly valued type of sand that was commonly used to build houses. Their family could afford things that others couldn't. They owned two huts instead of the usual one, regularly ate fresh bread, and while most kids played with a makeshift ball made of sap, they had a real soccer ball. Still, Thierno's parents didn't send him to the school because of their fear that he'd be exploited. Today, Thierno lives in Abidjan, the largest city in Ivory Coast, where he sells watches at traffic lights.

Abdoulaye says this easily could be him. Instead, with a preternatural maturity and sense of his own best interests, Abdoulaye prevailed upon his father, Mamadou, to allow him to attend the school and thereby changed his own fate. Mamadou Diallo possessed no formal education himself. He made a modest living selling trinkets and farming some inherited land, but he nevertheless loved learning. Abdoulaye's father spent his weekends teaching the Qur'an to villagers, and he admired the elites who manned the bureaucracy in the prefecture, all of whom had gone to school. Mamadou had a more favorable impression of the École Primaire de Hafia Centre than his wife did. He had three wives, and one of his other sons—Abdoulaye's half-brother—had finished the primary school. Though he still lived in the village, he knew how to write well. Most importantly, Mamadou saw a fiery combination of intelligence and motivation in his youngest son. Abdoulaye wanted to go.

So he went.

Many of Djiba's fears for her son proved to be well founded. One cold January morning, the wind howling down from the Fouta Mountains to the north, Abdoulaye was beaten for being late. Thirty years later, he remembers the sting of his teacher's wooden stick. During Ramadan, the teacher—Cherif Diallo—punished a group of students by making them run the length of Hafia's main street. When Abdoulaye took a shortcut, Cherif made Abdoulaye run the entire route again.

But Abdoulaye fell in love with learning. In his little classroom, he saw a map for the first time—more accurately, *une carte*, as all the classes were in French. He didn't know it was a map. But he saw the names of cities, and Abdoulaye conceived, for the first time, that there might be a world beyond his village. So, he willingly did the teachers' chores, collecting water in the evening from the village's single well, which ran down to a creek, and applied himself to his lessons. These mostly involved rote memorization in history, arithmetic, and his favorite subject, geography. Every Wednesday they discussed ethics, which Abdoulaye liked right away and made him more determined to graduate. Each year more than a quarter of the class would drop out of the École Primaire. Of the approximately seventy-five people who started with Abdoulaye, only a handful would ultimately finish. But Abdoulaye persevered, and he distinguished himself as one of the top students in his class.

His family took notice. After fourth grade, Abdoulaye's brothers urged his parents to allow Abdoulaye to join them in Guinea's capital, Conakry, where the schools were better. This caused far less controversy than the initial decision to attend the Hafia primary school. Pretty much everyone moved to Conakry around their thirteenth birthday. That's where all the jobs were. Abdoulaye's brothers had worked while they attended school in the capital, but they resolved to allow Abdoulaye to study full time. They wanted him to have the opportunity that they'd been denied.

Abdoulaye made the most of it. At the end of tenth grade, Conakry winnows its student population with a brutal exam. Those with the top scores go on to high school. The others are tracked into a vocational program. Abdoulaye received one of the highest scores in the region. At the end of thirteenth grade, an even more brutal, content-based test further pared down the student body, determining the select few who would go on to university. Abdoulaye's brothers paid for him to hire a tutor. He scored high enough to get his pick of schools, selecting the University of Conakry's campus in Kindia, where they had a program in law and economics.

For the first time, Abdoulaye enjoyed a measure of economic self-sufficiency. University tuition was free, and the government paid the students a small stipend. But Abdoulaye soon learned that even the university in Guinea was a dead end. Only the government had jobs for lawyers. More than 80 percent of graduates found themselves unable to get work.

Once again, Abdoulaye's family came to the rescue. Three years earlier, Abdoulaye's brother, Alhassane, and a friend's brother, Mouctar, had moved to the United States. Mouctar nominally enrolled Abdoulaye at Mercer University, which qualified him for a student visa, and

Alhassane, who drove a cab, sent Abdoulaye money for a plane ticket and offered him a place to live in the Bronx. On October 4, 2001, after a layover in Brussels and sixteen hours of flying, Abdoulaye arrived at JFK Airport—not part of a huddled, yearning mass but just as surely in pursuit of the American Dream.

As he stood in line to enter the country, clutching his passport and visa, he glanced anxiously at the portrait of George W. Bush. Barely three weeks had passed since 9/11, and Abdoulaye worried that something would go wrong. When he cleared customs, he breathed a giant sigh of relief.

Now the hard work began. Abdoulaye took a job as a messenger and enrolled in English classes at the Spanish-American Institute in Times Square. The courier gig paid him $3 per parcel. In a good week, he made about fifty deliveries, which meant he collected approximately $150, of which he spent $50 on his language lessons. The rest he saved for college. One day he delivered a package to John Jay College of Criminal Justice. He took the admission information packet, thought it was a law school, and decided that's where he wanted to go.

All of Abdoulaye's Guinean schooling had been conducted in French—he didn't speak a word of English when he landed in New York, but within eighteen months, Abdoulaye had progressed enough to take the TOEFL—the Test of English as a Foreign Language—which qualifies international students for admission to CUNY. John Jay required a score of 500 for admission. Abdoulaye got a 577. But he failed the writing portion of the exam, which meant he had to take—and pass— a one-credit remedial English course. He felt enormous pressure—not because of the difficulty of the class, but because of the expense. A credit cost $400, about a fifth of what he had in the bank. As Abdoulaye remembered, "Everything was about money."

He got an A.

Enrolling at John Jay, which cost about $4,500 a year, represented another huge gamble. CUNY's community colleges charged about half as much in annual tuition as the four-year colleges, and Abdoulaye only had about $2,000 remaining after paying for the writing course. He took the plunge anyway. "I just knew that I had to get started," Abdoulaye told me. He continued working as a messenger—now earning $9 per hour, studied day and night on the buses and trains of the city, and made straight As.

At the end of the year, Abdoulaye applied for a scholarship for outstanding freshmen. Going into the interview, he felt confident. Based on his grades, he should have been a shoo-in. And he would have been—if only he'd had a green card. Abdoulaye felt deflated, but the two women who administered the program couldn't help but be impressed by him. One helped Abdoulaye find work as a tutor in the writing center. The other recommended him for the college's honors program.

Admission to the honors program meant some additional resources. It also meant that Abdoulaye would have to take a required course on Friday mornings. To that point, he'd worked his class schedule around his messenger gig. One of his colleagues told him that cutting his hours would be too big a risk. But after everything he'd done, Abdoulaye wasn't about to start playing it safe.

So it came to pass that Abdoulaye ended up in my classroom—in an honors section of a course that I'd modeled on Harvard professor Michael Sandel's Justice course, which I'd loved in college, and that I still teach to this day. I vividly remember where Abdoulaye sat—front of the room, stage left. The course pairs readings in classical philosophy with modern-day ethical dilemmas. On the second week, I assigned the class an excerpt from Immanuel Kant's *Grounding for the Metaphysics of Morals* to spark a conversation about the death penalty.

Abdoulaye read the entire book.

Thus began one of the most fulfilling friendships of my life. Abdoulaye has taught me far more than I could ever teach him, and, in return, I've had his back. I wrote his letters of recommendation, including one for a fellowship run by the Steamboat Foundation that paid for a year and a half of tuition, and, later, for law school. When I became chairperson of my department, I got him a job as an academic advisor, which allowed him to apply for a green card. When his brother moved to Indiana, leaving Abdoulaye without a place to live, he moved in with our family. It's the sort of cushion that every rich white kid takes for granted, with two notable differences. When we moved to

Manhasset, we discussed whether Abdoulaye should check in with the police, and when I peeked into his room, just before he moved out two years later, his modest belongings and prayer mat were folded neatly in the corner.

Still—with the support of me, my wife, and his brothers, who'd devoted their collective will to seeing their youngest sibling reach his fullest potential—even with all of that, Abdoulaye almost got knocked out. Getting a permanent work visa can take years. While waiting for his green card, Abdoulaye needed to remain in school. The only practical option was John Jay's master's program in criminal justice. It'd be a piece of cake for him academically, but the program cost $12,000 a year. I found a course that Abdoulaye could teach, which would qualify him for a tuition discount. To get appointed as an adjunct professor, however, he'd need his official transcript, which the college refused to release until he paid what he owed for his last undergraduate semester. Again, it took a Guinean village. Abdoulaye's friend Billo, who worked as a tourist guide on buses while he attended CUNY, loaned him $6,000. Abdoulaye got his transcript, got his teaching job, and, finally, got his green card.

Today, he's a graduate of Fordham Law School. He has a brilliant and beautiful wife, Fatimatou, a nurse who is also a transplanted Guinean, and an even more beautiful baby boy, Ahmadou. He works for the Phillips Black Project, a public interest law firm that represents people living under sentences of death, and owns a two-family home in Mount Vernon, which will give him some income and build equity so that Ahmadou doesn't have to go through a similar ordeal to his own.

I consider it a privilege to have witnessed Abdoulaye's story firsthand. It's heartwarming and remarkable in many respects. For one, it's close to the theoretical maximum of upward mobility. Abdoulaye started at the very bottom—in Credit Suisse's ranking of countries by total wealth, Guinea comes in 128th. More than half of the nation's population lives below the poverty line, as his own family did.

In this sense, Abdoulaye's story is the embodiment of the American Dream. Indeed, in nefarious hands it might be used to illustrate what's right about college in America, in the way that *Homeless to Harvard*, the triple Emmy-nominated, made-for-TV movie about Liz Murray's improbable journey from the foster care system to Harvard's freshman class, is used to promote a narrative of equal access to a meritocratic institution of excellence. Instead, I offer Abdoulaye's story as a cautionary tale and draw your attention to three aspects of it that illustrate the precarious nature of social mobility through higher education in America.

One, it happened at CUNY, not at an elite college.

Two, at no interim point in the story was Abdoulaye's success even remotely assured.

Three, he didn't quite reach the top.

We're going to need a metaphor.

Imagine a shopping mall with one hundred floors. Life gets better as you move toward the top. At the bottom, the shoppers struggle to make ends meet. Many are homeless. The upper floors are opulent, the stores adorned by brazen, ostentatious displays of wealth. At the food court, they serve Kobe beef sliders, truffle fries, and other delicacies of great delight.

Linking the floors are an array of escalators of varying length and speed. There's a set of staircases in the back, to be used in case of fire, near that place behind the double doors where the employees have their bathrooms. It's very dodgy and you never know where you'll come out, so most people are focused on the escalators.

Not all escalators are built the same. They're grouped in a category called "college"—in the same way that my place and Bill Gates's are both called "homes." These escalators differ dramatically in length and width. Some lift people as many as dozens of floors. Some produce more uncertain outcomes. Some—notably, "for-profit" colleges—make many of their students' lives worse. Some carry lots of people. Others very few. Some are really hard to get onto. Some will let pretty much anyone aboard.

It's long been understood that these escalators lifted people higher than they otherwise would reach, but precisely how far was anyone's guess. Everyone had a sense that the fancy escalators—elite colleges—elevated students higher and more reliably than the others, but no one had ever proved that with hard data. Moreover, the demographics of whom these escalators carried, and whether they worked as well for poor people as for the rich, were open questions. Did *Homeless to Harvard* represent what Ivy League colleges regularly did or was it an exceptional case? And did the Ivy League escalator work as well for the Liz Murrays who managed to get in as it did for the Bushes and Roosevelts? No one really knew.

In 1967, Peter Blau, an Austrian sociologist who spent the bulk of his career at the University of Chicago, and Otis Duncan, an itinerant Texan who ended up at the University of California at Santa Barbara, published the first major quantitative study of how parents transmitted their social standing to their children, particularly by affecting their education. They based their findings on a survey of approximately twenty thousand men between the ages of twenty and sixty-four, which they appended to the U.S. Census Bureau's population study.

By the standards of the time, Blau and Duncan's "Survey of Occupational Changes in a Generation" was a huge data set, and their use of sophisticated statistical regression techniques represented a quantum leap forward for social science, but surveys are notoriously unreliable. Furthermore, Blau and Duncan didn't ask about income, so they were left to draw inferences about the magnitude of social mobility based on a ranking of occupations that they constructed based on average salaries, educational achievement, and prestige.

Nearly forty years later, methods hadn't gotten much better. Social scientists studying mobility still only had surveys and small samples to draw upon. Some European countries had databases that tracked people over the course of their lives, but the U.S. had almost nothing. And no one had even begun to crack the question of what value college added in and of itself.

Then, a pair of enterprising young economists spotted an ad in the *National Tax Journal* and everything changed.

In the spring of 2009, John Friedman got an email from his friend, Raj Chetty, saying that the IRS was soliciting outside contractors to help manage its databases. Friedman, a Bostonian, and Chetty, an Indian immigrant, had vastly different backgrounds, but they shared a passion for using big data to understand inequality, and this was the mother lode of data on economic mobility—tax returns and Social Security numbers that linked people across generations. The IRS also collected a form from each tuition-paying college student that contained their Social Security number and an identifier for the college they were attending. Friedman immediately saw the potential.

"Yeah," he replied, "That would be amazing."

Friedman was seemingly born to be an economist. His father, Benjamin, holds an endowed chair in economics at Harvard. His mother managed a mutual fund. He attended Buckingham Browne & Nichols, a private school in Cambridge, through ninth grade, then transferred to Andover. At Harvard, he won the top undergraduate prize in economics and graduated summa cum laude.

Despite his relatively privileged background, Friedman traces his interest in social mobility to his roots. "Boston was a recovering post-industrial city, which didn't look all that different from Buffalo or Cleveland," Friedman told me. "Cambridge," he added, "was a manufacturing town." When Berkeley's Emmanuel Saez, Oxford's Tony Atkinson, and Thomas Piketty of the London School of Economics started writing about income inequality as a growing problem, Friedman was drawn to the issue. "I'm a data-driven person," he said.

It was thus only natural that Friedman would gravitate to Chetty, who was preternaturally precocious with data. Chetty would win a MacArthur genius grant in 2012, and, a year later, the John Bates Clark Medal for the top American economist under the age of forty. As an undergraduate, Friedman tracked down Chetty, who was two years ahead of him at Harvard. The two had lunch one summer day at Spices, a Thai restaurant on Holyoke Street in Cambridge.

So began a friendship, which solidified years later when they worked on problem sets together as graduate students, from sunset to sunrise. "You bond over something like that," Friedman recalled. In the late 2000s, the duo reunited at Berkeley, when Chetty, then a young professor, emailed Friedman, who was on a post doc.

Despite his enthusiasm, Friedman was skeptical they'd get the job. They had to get on a list of approved federal contractors, which took some doing. Friedman remembered filling out a giant binder of OSHA compliance documents that they had to deliver in triplicate hard copies. Rather than fly from California, they paid for Friedman's brother to take a cab to IRS headquarters on Constitution Avenue and submit the application package. "It was kind of duct tape and baling wire back in the day," Friedman recalled.

But their price was right—zero—for the assistance of a couple of Harvard PhDs and the final addition to their team, Saez, the MIT PhD-turned-Berkeley professor, whose groundbreaking work on inequality had inspired them in the first place.

They got the job.

Chetty and Friedman's work, originally published as a working paper at the National Bureau of Economic Research, transformed our understanding of how escalators work.

To make their findings accessible, Chetty and Friedman created "mobility report cards," grading institutions on their "mobility rate," which they operationalized as the product of *access*—the percentage of students coming from the bottom quintile, and *success*—the percentage of students admitted from the bottom who made it to the top. So, for example, if a college admitted 5 percent of its student body from the bottom income quintile, and half of those students made it to the top quintile, it would have a mobility rate of 2.5 percent.

Turns out, the "Ivy-Plus" colleges—which Chetty and Friedman defined as the eight Ivy League colleges, University of Chicago, Stanford, MIT, and Duke—produced great results for the Liz Murrays of the world.* Nationally, kids who were born rich ended up an average

---

* Chetty and Friedman divided colleges into five tiers using data from Barron's 2009 index of selectivity. The first tier was the Ivy-Plus colleges. The second tier, "elite," included the sixty-five colleges in Barron's Tier 1, such as Middlebury, Amherst, and Wesleyan. The third tier, "highly selective," included the ninety-nine colleges in Barron's Tier 2. Examples of these schools include Boston University, Wheaton College, and Skidmore. The fourth tier, "selective," included the 1,003 colleges in Barron's Tiers 3, 4, and 5. All of the remaining colleges were classified as "non-selective." Each category subsumes the ones below. For example, 176 colleges would qualify as highly selective: the ninety colleges in Tier 2, the sixty-five elite colleges in Tier 1, and the twelve Ivy-Plus schools.

of about thirty income percentiles higher as adults than children who were born poor. For poor children who attended an elite college, the gap was just seven percentiles. Elite colleges closed more than three-fourths of the gap between rich and poor. In dollar terms, rich Ivy-Plus graduates had average salaries of about $88,000 as young adults. Poor kids who graduated from Ivy-Plus schools made almost as much, about $76,000.

The problem is that elite colleges don't let many poor kids in. This had been suggested before in other research. Chetty and Friedman laid out the inequities of access in graphic detail. The IRS data showed that at the Ivy-Plus schools more students came from families in the top 1 percent than the entire bottom half of the income distribution. Let that sink in. Only 3.8 percent of students came from the bottom income quintile. A kid born into a top 1 percent family had a seventy-seven times greater chance at attending an Ivy-Plus college than a kid born into the bottom quintile.

Examining the data more closely, it's hard not to see American education as an apartheid system. My commitment to you, dear reader, is to make my case with only a dozen charts. I'm going to use up four of my allotment in this chapter to graphically illustrate the extremity of these access disparities.

Table 1 lays out the colleges with the smallest percentage of low-income students, both nationally and among the Ivy-Plus schools. Washington and Lee, the grand dame of Lexington, Virginia, holds the ignominious distinction of admitting the smallest percentage of poor students. Just 1 percent of Generals come from families in the bottom income quintile. The Ivy-Plus colleges do only slightly better. The percentages range from a low of 2.04 percent at Princeton to a high of 5.11 percent at MIT.

Looking at it from the other end of the spectrum, many colleges overwhelmingly serve the poor. More accurately, many private and public for-profit colleges serve the poor. Table 2 sets out the colleges with the highest percentage of low socioeconomic status (SES) students. Nationally, about a third of students at four-year public colleges are either in or near poverty. At public community colleges, it's half. At John Jay, more

TABLE 1. SCHOOLS WITH LOWEST
PERCENTAGE OF STUDENTS FROM
FAMILIES IN LOWEST INCOME QUINTILE

AT ALL COLLEGES (low to high)		AT IVY-PLUS COLLEGES (low to high)	
Washington and Lee	1.12%	Princeton	2.04%
Mary Washington	1.27%	Dartmouth	2.77%
William & Mary	1.35%	Brown	2.92%
Davidson	1.38%	Harvard	3.05%
Notre Dame	1.44%	Duke	3.18%
Colby	1.49%	University of Pennsylvania	3.54%
Hampden Sydney	1.64%	Stanford	3.58%
Loyola Maryland	1.69%	Yale	3.63%
Stonehill	1.72%	University of Chicago	4.30%
Richmond	1.74%	Cornell	4.90%
Saint John's of Minnesota	1.74%	Columbia	5.02%
Dayton	1.77%	MIT	5.11%
Wake Forest	1.79%		
Bates	1.84%		
St. Olaf	1.85%		

than a quarter of our students come from the lowest income quintile. Overall at CUNY, about a third do. Chetty and Friedman's gold stars went to a relatively narrow range of schools. Among schools with more than five thousand students, eight of the top twelve schools in a ranking of overall mobility came from CUNY. They're listed in Table 3. Pace, with campuses in Lower Manhattan and Westchester, was the only private nonprofit college on the list.

A clear picture emerged from Chetty and Friedman's research: public institutions were producing the lion's share of upward mobility. Some of these escalators looked quite different from one another. "Many different types of institutions produce high levels of mobility

TABLE 2. SCHOOLS WITH HIGHEST
PERCENTAGE OF STUDENTS FROM
FAMILIES IN LOWEST INCOME QUINTILE

ALL COLLEGES (high to low)		CUNY FOUR-YEAR COLLEGES	
United Talmudical Seminary	61.0%	Lehman	36.7%
South Texas College	52.4%	City College of Technology	35.3%
Southern Careers Institute	47.1%	City College	32.5%
Boricua	46.7%	York	30.7%
Moultrie Technical College	46.4%	Medgar Evers	30.5%
CUNY—Hostos	45.8%	Baruch	27.6%
Mississippi Valley State	45.5%	John Jay	27.1%
Albany Technical College	44.5%	Brooklyn	23.2%
Plaza College	44.5%	Hunter	21.2%
ASA Institute Of Business & Computer Technology	44.4%	Queens	20.1%
Western Technical College of El Paso	43.7%	Staten Island	14.3%

rates," Friedman explained to me. Some did it by running less selective programs. Many community colleges and open-access four-year programs generated high mobility. Other schools generated mobility in a more selective way. At SUNY Stony Brook, for example, only 16 percent of students came from the lowest income quintile, but the school's success rate in promoting poor kids to the top income quintile was so high—51.2 percent—that they cracked the top ten in overall mobility. "Lots of different models seem to work for this broad measure of mobility," Friedman said.

But the Ivy-Plus schools weren't part of the conversation. Their mobility rates—listed in Table 4—averaged 2.2 percent. It wasn't that the schools couldn't get the job done. Of students from the bottom income quintile who were admitted to Harvard, an impressive 57.7 percent

TABLE 3. TOP MOBILITY RATES

CUNY—Baruch College	12.9%
CUNY—City College	11.7%
CUNY—Lehman College	10.2%
Cal State—Los Angeles	9.9%
CUNY—John Jay College	9.7%
Pace University	8.4%
SUNY—Stony Brook	8.4%
CUNY—City Tech	8.3%
Texas A&M International University	8.1%
CUNY—Brooklyn College	8.1%
CUNY—Hunter College	7.5%
CUNY—Queens College	7.1%

TABLE 4. MOBILITY RATES AT IVY-PLUS COLLEGES

MIT	3.40%
Columbia	3.07%
Cornell	2.91%
Stanford	2.25%
Yale	2.08%
University of Pennsylvania	2.05%
University of Chicago	1.94%
Harvard	1.76%
Duke	1.60%
Brown	1.55%
Dartmouth	1.38%
Princeton	1.35%

made it to the top income quintile by their early thirties. Elite colleges simply didn't let in enough low-income students to produce significant upward mobility. In Chetty and Friedman's overall ranking, Harvard came in just below Contra Costa Community College in San Francisco, and just ahead of Bates—not the fancy liberal arts college in Maine, but rather the technical college in Seattle, Washington.

MIT topped the Ivy-Plus colleges in overall mobility. It came in 1,288th.

Homeless to Harvard is inspiring. But it might give you the mistaken impression that Harvard produces a lot of stories like Murray's—or that Abdoulaye's path is the rule rather than exception.

Elite colleges engage in a lot of impression management of this kind. They produce glossy brochures showing idyllic diversity, trumpet the hundreds of millions of dollars they spend on financial aid, and, most nefariously, compare themselves to one another. In the *New York Times'* presentation of the Chetty data, the default screen ranks Harvard among the Ivy-Plus colleges. By this sort of comparison, they don't look so bad. They do more for low-socioeconomic students than the prestigious liberal arts colleges of the New England Small College Athletic Conference, like Williams and Amherst, and other would-be Ivies, like Washington University in St. Louis, where the economic diversity numbers are horrifying. But this creates a false competition to be the best of the worst, and it deflects attention from the plain truth that elite colleges promote precious few people out of poverty. In fact, their core function is almost exactly the opposite: keep a lot of rich people rich. To understand how, we need to understand how people at the mall fall off the escalators.

2

Falling Off

Junior year of college, I made my first rich friend. Statistically speaking, it's certain that I'd interacted with other super-wealthy people before that, but I'd never gotten close enough to see how one actually lived. My friend—let's call him Alistair Sinclair—had F.U. money. Al was the only teenager I knew who had his own car. His parents had a lavish vacation home. On the weekends, he took flying lessons.

Al had plenty going for him—oodles of charm, a good sense of humor, and that car. But he wasn't very good at math. When you go to Harvard, you get a different sense of what it means to be "good at math." In high school, I'd thought I was—my dad was a math teacher, after all. My senior year, I scored a 93—out of 150—on a tough exam offered every year by the Mathematical Association of America. If you got a 95, you qualified for an even tougher, fifteen-question exam. Though I'd missed the cutoff, my dad and I took it for kicks. We scored one and zero, respectively. Freshman year, I met a kid who answered all fifteen correctly.

Against that baseline of talent, Al's struggle with the precalculus math requirement seemed conspicuous. It also would have put him at risk for dropping out of most colleges. Not Harvard. The college poured resources into struggling students: peer tutoring, academic coaching, even extra help in the residence halls. Add in a fair dose of grade inflation. Despite not having the best work ethic, Al never came close to falling off the escalator. Almost no one at Harvard ever does.

Today, this is even more true than when we were there. Harvard's six-year graduation rate is 98 percent. At Yale, it's 97 percent. These statistics are close to the theoretical maximum. In the same way that unemployment will never be zero because of shifts in the economy and inefficient job searches, retention can never be perfect—students get sick or travel or go to work. If you get your kid into Harvard, it's virtually certain that they're going to finish unless they leave to start the next Google.

CUNY is another world entirely.

During a stint as a speechwriter for the president of Georgetown University, Christina Ciocca Eller had two epiphanies. The first concerned the amount of power that rich universities possess. As a Georgetown graduate herself—valedictorian of the class of 2005, thank you very much—she understood how elite colleges shaped the lives of their students and faculty. She understood, too, that Georgetown's administration and faculty influenced national and international affairs. What she hadn't realized was that Georgetown's reach also extended into local matters, even zoning issues. Writing the words of Georgetown's leader fascinated Ciocca Eller, and the experience whet her appetite to say things in her own voice.

The second epiphany stemmed from her interactions with an intern in the president's office—a brilliant, first-generation student of Mexican descent who'd threaded the eye of the needle in making it to Georgetown. Ciocca Eller had enjoyed a relatively privileged upbringing in Connecticut, but she was blown away by this young man's perseverance and wanted to make kids like him the focus of her life's work. The problem was that students like her intern were, as she puts it, "only, like, 5 to 10 percent of the Ivy League." If she wanted to understand the lives of people like him, she'd have to study an institution quite different from Georgetown.

Shortly after she began graduate school at Columbia, Ciocca Eller offered her services as a data analyst to CUNY for free. This may sound like an unusual career move for a budding sociologist, but Ciocca Eller knew that examining the data of the largest public university system in the United States would be invaluable, and so she told CUNY that she'd do whatever they needed. Ciocca Eller has some serious quant skills. Soon, she proved herself indispensable and earned access to CUNY's treasure trove of data. In 2019, Ciocca Eller completed one of the most comprehensive studies of public university students ever undertaken.

The first thing Ciocca Eller noticed is that CUNY, like many other public universities, is plagued by high dropout rates. Only about half of students who start out at one of CUNY's four-year colleges get their degree within ten years. (Nationally, the ten-year completion rate is approximately 62 percent, but that aggregate average includes the tony privates.) At the community colleges, the numbers are lower still. CUNY-wide, about 38 percent of students who start an associate degree finish within ten years.

The second thing Ciocca Eller found was that each CUNY college performed differently for different kinds of students. This may seem obvious, but, to that point, almost no research had been done on the value that colleges actually add. Retention rates tell you almost nothing. Any college can graduate rich kids, as Yale and Harvard do, and any college would struggle if it let in armies of low-SES, first-generation college students, as CUNY does. Using institutional data, Ciocca Eller controlled for income, parental support, and other factors that predict graduation rates.

She found that where you went to school mattered a great deal. Entering CUNY students don't generally do much comparison shopping, but picking the right college as much as tripled their odds of graduating. Different colleges did better for students of different races and ethnicities. Across the board, seeing administrators and faculty who looked like you had a beneficial effect. The single best thing, other than being really smart, was having a good advisor or mentor. These findings in and of themselves would have been noteworthy.

But Ciocca Eller further strengthened her study by doing something that many social scientists disdain: she talked to her subjects. Ciocca Eller is just the right sort of person to get a student's story. After experiencing bullying, she'd found refuge in high school theatre. During college, she acted professionally, and even performed in the London premiere of *The Laramie Project*. Ultimately, Ciocca Eller drifted away from the stage because she didn't like the gaps it left in her days, but the skill set never left her. "At its core, acting is just about empathy," she told me. Ciocca Eller has this in abundance. In an online forum about the sociology job market, filled with mostly smarmy comments, Ciocca Eller's rivals openly rooted for her.

It was thus hardly surprising that CUNY students opened up to Ciocca Eller. What was surprising were the commonalities among their stories. Despite the massive dropout rate, none of the sixty or so young men and women Ciocca Eller spoke to believed that they would fail. "Even if they had empathy and understanding about dropping out, none of them thought it would ever apply to them," she told me. "They would say, 'It's never going to be me.' But obviously it is them, because it's 60 percent of them."

Ciocca Eller calls the stories students told her "narratives of hope." At the outset of their careers, the students have enormous expectations. "They come in with these huge dreams about what's going to happen," she explained. "For an elite audience, it's like it's just a degree from CUNY—it's just any BA, but for them it's the only BA. For them, it might as well be Harvard. It's a way to get this American credential of excellence. They're so shiny when they start and just ready to go for it."

When Ciocca Eller spoke to them just a year later, the students' stories had changed dramatically. "Their hopes and dreams and aspirations are just ground out of them," she said. "Bit by bit, red tape by red tape, academic failing by academic failing, lack of support and attention, bureaucracy—just so many hurdles—some expected, some completely unexpected." Students with extremely strong academics did fine. So did the tiny fraction who had a strong network or financial resources to draw upon. Almost everyone else became jaded.

"Man," Ciocca Eller said, "the story of how the shininess becomes dull. I see it so clearly over and over again. It's heartbreaking."

We both laughed when I asked Ciocca Eller whether she perceived a difference between the students she studied at CUNY and the students she teaches at Harvard, where she's now on the faculty. Ciocca Eller kept a straight face just long enough to give me a professorial answer. "It really is quite different," she said, "when you have as many safety nets as the average Harvard student has underneath them, both borne out of their lives, but also provided by the college itself."

Ciocca Eller's work demands that we refine our metaphor. The upward escalators don't vary in just their length and carrying capacity, they also differ in the very quality of their construction. The Ivy-Plus escalator is broad and exquisitely well maintained with high guardrails. It's like a ride at Disney World—buying tickets will break your bank account, the lines are really long, but once you finally climb aboard, the view is nice and it's hard to fall off even if you try. The CUNY escalator, by contrast, is narrow with almost nothing on the side to keep you from plummeting to your death—like the giant centrifuge at one of those traveling fairs where half the fun is wondering if the carnies adequately tightened the bolts. But it's cheap and they'll let on pretty much anyone.

America's disinvestment in public universities is a major part of the problem. The Center on Budget and Policy Priorities found that, after adjusting for inflation, states cumulatively spent $6.6 billion less on two- and four-year colleges in 2018 than they had a decade earlier. That translates to a decline of $1,220 per student. Public universities are left with a cruel choice between making up the shortfall by cutting services or raising tuition.

Meanwhile the escalators at elite colleges have become more and more lavish. This is also part of the problem. Student support costs money, and the Ivies spend a lot of it on the emotional and physical well-being of their undergraduates. Yale spends more money than any other college on student services—about $23,500 per student in the most recent year for which data is available. At John Jay, that figure is $2,764. Overall, Yale's annual instructional cost per student is an astonishing $182,000.

Spending more on instruction and student services makes it harder for students to fall off the escalator, but it also increases the marginal cost of admitting a new student. In practical terms, it becomes more expensive to subsidize someone with financial aid. From a utilitarian standpoint, the question is whether it's ethical to spend money to increase the graduation rate of cohorts of students who, given their demographics, are overwhelmingly likely to succeed. "Harvard and Yale do add a good amount of value," Ciocca Eller explained, "but the base is already high." So why do they do it?

The answer is to maintain their *U.S. News & World Report* ranking. But we'll get to that later.

Another important part of Al's story is that he's thriving today. He works as an investment advisor.

I'm confident that none of his clients have any sense that he's not so hot at math. They just know that he has a degree from Harvard and that he lives in an affluent suburb. For Al, his Harvard degree had an immunizing effect—an inoculation against the dreaded affliction of downward mobility.

In terms of our metaphor, one might think of the top floors as being surrounded by a series of thickly woven nets that would catch even the most determined jumper. For someone at the top of the mall— especially someone at the top with an elite college degree—it's almost impossible to slip through the gaps in these webs. To fall far, something must go seriously wrong—like drug use, crime, or mental illness.

When people think about social mobility, they tend to talk about who goes up rather than who goes down. Virtually all the coverage surrounding the publication of the Chetty-Friedman data focused on upward mobility. I'd argue that the data is most important for what it says about downward mobility. Elite college admissions are a massive insurance policy against falling. If you're at the top, a variety of mechanisms make it likely that your children will remain there. The most important of these is elite college degrees. They are the net. Heretofore, this truth has been almost entirely untold.

An important component of this truth is that elite colleges let in lots of rich kids. You might have guessed this, but just because elite colleges don't let in many poor kids doesn't necessarily mean they're filling the rest of the class with rich kids. They could be filling their remaining seats with middle-class students. They're not. At Harvard, 70 percent of the class comes from the top income quintile. At John Jay, the figure is 11.6 percent. That's in New York, where the $100,000 or so it takes to make the top quintile doesn't go very far.

As you ascend the scale, the disparities become even more extreme. Over 15 percent of Harvard's entering class comes from families in the top 1 percent, meaning they have annual incomes exceeding $630,000. Fully 3 percent come from families in the top tenth of 1 percent, meaning they make more than about $2.8 million per year. At John Jay, less than one in one thousand come from families in the top 1 percent. None come from families in the top tenth of the top percentile. Table 5 presents a ranking of American colleges by highest percentage of students admitted from families in the top income quintile, the top 1 percent, and the top one-tenth of 1 percent.

TABLE 5. COLLEGES RANKED BY WEALTHY STUDENTS ADMITTED

SHARE OF STUDENTS FROM FAMILIES IN . . .

TOP INCOME QUINTILE		TOP 1%		TOP 0.1%	
Washington and Lee	81.3%	Vanderbilt	21.9%	Lynn	3.5%
Davidson	77.2%	Middlebury	21.1%	SMU	3.5%
Princeton	76.8%	SMU	20.8%	Princeton	3.2%
Middlebury	75.8%	Princeton	20.1%	Duke	3.2%
Colby	74.6%	Colgate	19.8%	Brown	3.2%
Richmond	74.2%	Trinity	19.2%	Colgate	3.1%
Wake Forest	73.9%	Duke	19.2%	Williams	3.1%
Brown	73.6%	Brown	18.9%	Harvard	3.0%
Yale	73.2%	Colby	18.3%	Middlebury	2.9%
Colgate	73.1%	Williams	17.9%	Vanderbilt	2.9%
Harvard	*70.3%*	*Harvard*	*15.4%*		
John Jay	*11.6%*	*John Jay*	*.098%*	*John Jay*	*0.0%*

If you look at the data prospectively, family wealth almost perfectly predicts where a child will go to school. For kids born into the lowest income quintile, the picture is bleak. Less than half will make it to college. Those who do are most likely to attend either a two-year or a non-selective, four-year college. Less than 10 percent attend a highly selective, four-year college. The odds of making it to an Ivy are about one hundred-to-one against. For the wealthy, the picture is reversed. Almost everyone attends college and the vast majority attend a selective four-year school. More than 80 percent of kids born into the top 1 percent go on to attend a selective, four-year college. About 10 percent make it to an Ivy-Plus. A kid born into the top 1 percent has about a seventy-seven times greater chance of landing at an Ivy than one born into the bottom income quintile.

These disparities are only growing worse over time. The earliest available data on the socioeconomic status of college students comes from a 1927 book by the historian Ora Edgar Reynolds. Relying on survey data, Reynolds found that 47 percent of Yale students and 68 percent of Williams students came from families making more than $10,000 a year—right around the cutoff to make the top income quintile. (At the time, the median income was approximately $2,100 per year.) As Bryn Mawr's David Karen shows, the influence of parental income as a predictor of admissions to prestigious colleges doubled during the 1980s and 1990s. Today, 73 percent of Yale students and 70 percent of Williams students come from the top income quintile. It's a simple history, really: elite colleges have always been, and increasingly are, the domain of the rich, while public colleges remain almost exclusively reserved for the poor.

Chetty and Friedman's key statistic, the mobility rate, was a measure of upward movement—a function of the number of poor students let in and the institution's success at promoting them out of poverty. Ivy-Plus schools did very poorly by this metric because they let in so few poor students. If we look instead at what I call the *stability rate*—the product of the percentage of rich kids an institution admits and its success at keep them rich—a very different picture emerges.

Elite colleges are exceptionally good at keeping rich kids rich. Recall that Harvard successfully promoted 57.7 percent of the poor kids it admitted out of poverty. By contrast, 67.3 percent of Harvard students from the top income quintile remained there as adults. MIT tops the Ivy-Plus colleges with a success rate of 73.5 percent.

When it comes to preventing rich students from falling into poverty, elite colleges are near perfect. At Harvard, only about 8 percent of students from families in the top income quintile end up in the bottom quintile. This includes people who make voluntary choices to forego income by, say, teaching at a public university. As Friedman puts it, "Very few people from elite institutions end up in a position of serious economic insecurity through something other than their own choices."

Table 6 presents a ranking of schools by stability index. The mobility rate table looked like the *U.S. News* ranking of colleges with the best bang for the buck. By contrast, this list looks like the Ivy League with a sprinkling of elite Catholic, Patriot League, and liberal arts colleges.

John Jay is an afterthought on this list, but not for the reason you might think. My college succeeds about half the time in keeping kids in the top income quintile. It just doesn't admit enough of them to keep up with elite colleges. No college could. In terms of income mobility, about half of what elite colleges do is keep rich kids rich. Princeton, you'll recall, had an upward mobility rate of 1.3 percent. Roughly speaking, for every poor kid Princeton promotes out of poverty, it keeps forty kids rich.

One might reasonably ask whether college is the entire story here. In other words, are there other pathways to class mobility? The answer is none are nearly so powerful. Chetty and Friedman's research dramatically illustrates this. The gist of the picture they paint is that if you're born rich and attend college—as almost every rich kid does—you're overwhelmingly likely to remain rich and virtually certain not to become poor. If you're born rich and don't go to college, you're more likely to be poor than to remain rich. On the other side of the equation, if you're born poor and attend college, you have about an equal chance of becoming rich as remaining poor. If you're born poor and don't go to

TABLE 6. STABILITY INDEX TOP 20

Princeton	54.2%
Washington and Lee	52.6%
Georgetown	51.5%
Duke	50.8%
University of Pennsylvania	49.9%
Notre Dame	49.6%
Villanova	48.4%
Stanford	48.0%
Holy Cross	47.3%
Yale	47.3%
Harvard	47.3%
Colgate	47.2%
Dartmouth	47.1%
Babson	46.8%
Richmond	46.4%
Wake Forest	46.3%
Lafayette	46.0%
MIT	45.8%
Boston College	45.8%
Tufts	45.3%
John Jay	*5.8%*

college, you've overwhelmingly likely to remain poor and have virtually no chance of becoming rich. Across the board, the most likely outcome is remaining where you started.

The true story of American social mobility is stagnation. "An individual's relative income," writes the author and historian Richard Rothstein, "is remarkably similar to how his or her parents' incomes compared to others in their generation." Stagnation requires two conditions: The first is that it's hard for people at the bottom to move up. It has long been understood that this is difficult in America and that college is the principal pathway to success. The second condition is that it's hard for people at the top to fall down. This has been almost entirely ignored, but it's true nevertheless, and college is again the principal mechanism that prevents falling.

In reality, there are two versions of the American Dream. The first is Abdoulaye's—not quite a rags-to-riches story, but a rags-to-upper-middle-class story in which elite colleges occasionally but rarely play a role. The overwhelming majority of students who rise from the lower floors do so at a public college. The second is Al's—you make enough money to get your kid a top degree and thereby ensure that their class standing is protected. Elite colleges' participation in this second version of the dream dwarfs their participation in the first. In fact, they are the main player.

Still, damning as all this is, it's not the full story. There's a secret top floor we haven't talked about yet. And pretty much the only way to get in is through an elite college.

3

The Top Floor and the Iron Ceiling

After Jorge Montano fled El Salvador during its civil war in the early 1980s, he started a Spanish-speaking construction company in Suffern, a white, upper-middle-class suburb of New York near the base of the Ramapo Mountains in Rockland County. There he met Myrian, an Argentinian immigrant, and started a family. Over time, they had two children—a daughter, Gabriela, and a son named Nico.

It would have been natural for the Montanos to live in Suffern, a picturesque town where George Washington had often stayed during the Revolutionary War, but because of redlining, they couldn't get approved for a mortgage. Instead, they settled in nearby Spring Valley, a less affluent community of some 32,000 people, about two-thirds of whom were Black. Spring Valley is part of the East Ramapo Central School District, a mishmash of seven districts, including New Square, an all-Hasidic village with the highest poverty rate in New York State.

East Ramapo schools are underfunded. Not just underfunded in the way schools in many lower-middle-class communities are underfunded, but, rather, spectacularly and famously underfunded. The district is the subject of a riveting episode of *This American Life*. The story goes that the Orthodox Jewish community wanted both lower taxes and for special education students to receive services within the yeshiva, instead of the public schools, even though this violated state and federal law. Frustrated by their inability to get what they wanted, the Hasidim broke a longstanding, unspoken détente and, starting around 2007, fought a war for control of the school board. Spoiler: the kids lost. The new, all-Hasidic board sold off two buildings to yeshivas at submarket prices. It also cut AP courses, elementary music, and pretty much everything else in the school system. So Gabriela and Nico Montano had baptisms of fire in the inequities of American education.

After graduating from East Ramapo High, Gabriela enrolled at John Jay. Two years later, Nico followed her there, despite having scored a 1400 on the SAT. Looking back, Nico sees that he could have shot for an elite college, but you'd be hard pressed to imagine someone who got more out of a CUNY degree than he did. Nico designed his own major on the psychology of juvenile delinquency, was chosen to participate in a Latino leadership program run by the Harvard Kennedy School, and maintained a GPA of 3.997. In his senior year, he did something almost unthinkable and won a Marshall Scholarship.

Founded in the early 1950s as a tribute to Secretary of State George Marshall and the Marshall Plan, the program grants winners two years of study at any British university. While its main competitor, the Rhodes, was historically focused on well-roundedness and athleticism, the Marshall has always been about academics. Its alumni include *New York Times* columnist Thomas Friedman, Supreme Court justices Stephen Breyer and Neil Gorsuch, and Angela Duckworth, the University of Pennsylvania psychologist whose pioneering research on grit earned her a MacArthur Fellowship. Twelve Marshall winners have gone on to win genius grants. Perhaps unsurprisingly, the overwhelming majority of winners come from private colleges. Of the 2,138 brilliant young men and women who have won a Marshall, only eight have come from CUNY. Nico is the only winner ever from John Jay.

In England, Nico took a master's in research methods at the University of Liverpool and a second master's in gender, media, and culture at the London School of Economics. He also had his first real brushes with wealth. Nico had helped his mother clean the homes of many affluent people, but this was different. He met Prince Charles and spent a weekend—with the entire Marshall and Rhodes crews—on an estate that had been in the family of a former Rhodes scholar since the eighteenth century. Another weekend, a group of his classmates jetted off to Monaco. During recruiting season, Nico was courted by investment banks and consulting firms that would have never come within a light-year of CUNY—in the metaphorical sense, that is. The worldwide headquarters of McKinsey & Company, which flew all the Marshalls to Austria, are just half a mile from the Borough of Manhattan Community College campus. "It was like—astounding—the level of access people had," Nico recalled.

The experience strengthened Nico. "There was nothing intrinsically different in the other Marshalls' level of intelligence," he realized. Over time, Nico came to feel like he could hold his own. He became comfortable admitting if he didn't know something. When he returned to the U.S., Nico took a job as an analyst at a think tank that focused on criminal justice issues, where he'd interned as an undergraduate, and became active in efforts to diversify the Marshall program.

Things are marginally better today, but in 2013, when Nico started his Marshall, only seven of the forty Marshall scholars were women. None were women of color, and Nico was the only Latino. In 2018, Nico joined a new commission that reached out to underrepresented schools in the hope of expanding the program's reach. He also became a reader of scholarship applications.

During his first year on the selection committee, Nico got paired with an old-school banking type. He and Nico gave candidates almost opposite scores. "I was taken aback by the things he valued in an education," Nico told me. Case in point: an applicant from the University of Chicago who said she'd been in the choir. This hadn't scored any points with Nico, but it did with his partner. "She'll do well," the banker said. "She's been in one of the best choirs and will be in one of the best choirs in the U.K." Meanwhile, Nico had ranked an applicant from CUNY's Baruch College at the top of his list. The banker dismissed her. "There's no academic rigor at CUNY," he said. Nico revealed that he'd gone to CUNY, but his partner offered no apology and brooked no dissent.

Around the same time, Nico landed a long-shot $750,000 grant from the National Institute of Justice to study the effects of a novel intervention aimed at reducing violence among young prisoners. The program uses well-behaved lifers as mentors, allows the young inmates to shape their experience, and generally treats them with dignity. Shortly after receiving the incredible news, Nico attended a meeting where his supervisor openly discussed the type of person they were thinking of hiring to run the grant. Nico felt blindsided. He'd always presumed he'd run the grant himself. Little comments had filtered back to him over the years—whispers of unprofessionalism. It's almost impossible to imagine that this is the right word—Nico radiates intelligence, but he does wear his hair long and openly identifies himself as queer. If you were looking for a conformist, he wouldn't be your guy. But this was a left-leaning think tank studying a radical reentry program modeled on the German prison system.

Nico said that he'd written the grant with the idea that he'd run it.

"I don't see it that way," his supervisor replied.

The think tank hired someone from NYU, and Nico left to work at Columbia.

"Did you see this as a sort of institutional snobbery?" I asked Nico some time later.

"Fuck yes," he replied.

He didn't know it at the time, but Nico had bumped his head on the iron ceiling.

Over the years, I've taught many students who are outstanding by any imaginable metric of excellence. Maybe you've heretofore shared Nico's banker friend's prejudice that CUNY and other public universities don't attract strong students and aren't academically rigorous. I'd like to disavow you of this. It just isn't true. Lots of my students have high SAT scores. At CUNY's Macaulay Honors College, which has a campus at John Jay, the mean SAT score is consistently above 1400. Last year, I taught a kid who got a 1550. Grade inflation has turned Ivy League transcripts into Monopoly money, but there's none of it at John Jay. Many of my students, from within the honors college and without, have gone on to top PhD programs and law schools. A young woman I mentored is in her first year at University of Pennsylvania Law School as I'm writing this. You'll meet her later in the book. She's the second of my students to attend Penn Law in the past five years.

What is true, though, is that none of these superstars have ever cracked the highest echelon. The ones who make it to top law schools get very good jobs, as Abdoulaye did, but none have made it to Cravath, Swaine & Moore, Sullivan & Cromwell, or any of the super-elite white-shoe firms. Ultimately, they all have some version of Nico's experience.

This might be dismissed as anecdotal evidence were it not so resoundingly confirmed by the Chetty-Friedman data. Another less told story of their findings is the special role that elite colleges play in promoting—or, one might say, limiting—access to the very highest-paying jobs. Chetty and Friedman found that graduates of Ivy-Plus colleges have about a one in five chance of landing in the top 1 percent by their mid-thirties. Graduates of Barron's sixty-two Tier 1 colleges have about a one in eleven chance of making it. For community college graduates, the chance is about one in three hundred. If you don't go to college at all, it's about one in a thousand.

Earlier, when we sorted colleges by mobility rate—success in promoting poor students out of poverty—the resulting list looked like promotional material for CUNY. It certainly didn't resemble anyone's list of the top colleges in America. Later, when we sorted by the stability rate—success in keeping rich kids rich—the resulting list looked more familiar but still contained several outliers like Washington and Lee and Holy Cross—excellent schools, but not conventionally at the top of any rankings.

When we look at access to the top 1 percent, however, a more familiar pattern emerges. Table 7 arranges colleges by *top-mobility rate*, which I've defined as the product of *access*—the percentage of students admitted from the top income quintile, and *success*—the percentage of these students who make it to the top 1 percent. The resulting list looks like a slightly reshuffled version of the *U.S. News & World Report* ranking of best universities.

A shorthand way to think of this data would be that if you attended a Princeton reunion, about one-fifth of the alumni you'd meet would be students who started out wealthy and ended up wealthier. Almost a

TABLE 7. TOP-MOBILITY RATES

COLLEGE	TOP-MOBILITY RATE	SHARE OF GRADS IN TOP 1%
Princeton	19.3%	23.2%
University of Pennsylvania	17.1%	22.5%
Stanford	15.9%	20.9%
Harvard	15.9%	21.1%
Duke	15.8%	20.4%
Yale	14.7%	18.5%
MIT	14.0%	20.4%
Georgetown	13.8%	17.5%
Dartmouth	13.5%	17.7%
Columbia	12.5%	16.6%
John Jay	*0.01%*	*0.36%*

quarter of Princeton graduates end up as top 1 percenters. University of Pennsylvania and Harvard grads trail close behind. My college is a blip on this list. Overall, about three John Jay graduates in a thousand will make it to the top 1 percent. It's just not what public colleges do.

It is, however, the very essence of what elite colleges do. Elite colleges are very good at promoting kids out of poverty—they just don't do very much of it and other colleges do it almost as well. They're excellent at keeping wealthy kids wealthy. When it comes to promoting people into the stratosphere of wealth, elite colleges are light-years better than any others. Friedman was quick to point out to me that lots of different types of colleges were successful at promoting poor kids out of poverty. Access to extreme affluence was another story. Friedman said, "For top-end mobility, which we're measuring as entry into high-paying jobs and elite positions in society, whether they be defined by income or political leadership or some other thing, the very elite schools seem to be the only game in town."

This necessitates the final modification to our metaphor. Many escalators don't quite reach the top. To reach the presidential suite, where they stock white pearl albino caviar, matsutake mushrooms, and the 1947 Château Cheval-Blanc—for that, you're going to need a special key that's only available from the concierge at elite colleges. While other (perhaps not quite so direct) routes to extreme affluence exist, for access to certain professions, the odds of landing a job are slim without an elite college degree on your résumé.

For Friedman, this fact justifies the attention that's paid to elite colleges. "I think it's very important to think about mobility at these very elite schools, even though from the grand scheme of things, there are not an enormous number of students," Friedman says. "You're not going to solve intergenerational mobility for all of the nation focusing only on schools that, even with an expansive definition, are serving only 100,000 students per year."

"But," Friedman continues, "that's where many of the leaders in society come from, and I think that those individuals have a lot of influence on societal norms and policy making. So, making sure that people have access in however probabilistic a way to that elite—making sure that no matter where you're coming from—making sure that you have a shot—I think that's very important both in an economic sense and a social and political sense."

You might reasonably ask: why doesn't everyone have a shot right now? Brilliant young people can be found in all walks of life and at all kinds of colleges. Why is the principal route to the type of influence and elite job that Friedman is talking about solely through a handful of elite colleges, accessible principally to the rich? We don't have to speculate as to the answer. We know why because the elites have told us themselves.

In April of 2009, the late Supreme Court justice Antonin Scalia delivered the keynote address at a conference hosted by American University's Washington College of Law. The subject was an obscure doctrine relating to whether a federal court must follow an administrative agency's interpretation of an ambiguous law. The policy is known as "*Chevron* deference," after a 1984 case in which the corporate energy giant attempted to evade a provision of the Clean Air Act. I highly doubt many students had much interest in *Chevron* deference, a dull topic even by the standards of C-SPAN, which was covering the event, but this was Scalia. The place was packed, and when he opened with his big line, "Administrative law is not for sissies," the audience responded with ample nervous laughter.

After he finished his speech, the dean announced that Scalia had agreed to answer a few questions. They were supposed to relate to administrative law, but that didn't last for long. A first-year student named Christina Stutt asked what she described as "a more general question." Stutt was obviously and understandably nervous—she was a 1L talking to a sitting Supreme Court justice, after all, but her question went to the heart of the nature of opportunity in America. Stutt asked, "Part of the American ethos is that our society is a meritocracy where hard work and talent lead to success, but there are other important factors like connections and elite degrees and I'm wondering, other than grades and journal, what do smart, hardworking WCL students with strong writing skills need to do to be *outrageously* successful in the law?"

Stutt's choice of, and emphasis on, "outrageously" got laughs from the crowd, and Scalia was smiling even before he began his response. "Work hard," Scalia said, "and be very good." This prompted more laughter, and the moment might have passed unremarkably had the exchange ended here, but Scalia had the heart of a performer, and he felt the moment.

"You know," he expounded, "by and large, unless I have a professor on the faculty who's a good friend, and preferably a former law clerk of mine whose judgment I can *trust*." Scalia hit "trust" even harder than Stutt had hit "outrageously." "I'm going to be picking for Supreme Court law clerks," he continued. "I can't afford a miss. I just can't. So, I'm going to be picking from the law schools that, basically, are the hardest to get into. They admit the best and the brightest and they may not teach very well, but you can't make a sow's ear out of a silk purse. And if they come in the best and the brightest, they're probably going to leave the best and the brightest."

C-SPAN doesn't do audience reaction shots, but you can feel the jaws of the law students drop and the pit rise in their collective stomach.

Forget the many flaws in Scalia's reasoning. Would hiring someone from a school that wasn't among the hardest to get into really constitute a mistake? Scalia went on to acknowledge that the best clerk he'd ever had—someone he inherited after Lewis Powell retired, and who now sits on the Sixth Circuit Court of Appeals—was someone he never would have hired himself. "For God's sake," Scalia said, "He went to Ohio State."

And could he really not afford a mistake? Scalia famously picked a liberal law clerk every year, just so he'd have someone to argue with. He believed in this version of diversity. His tolerance just didn't extend to diversity of law schools. Scalia had gone to Harvard Law School, as had four of his colleagues. Three others had gone to Yale. The only justice who hadn't gone to an Ivy League school, John Paul Stevens, went to Northwestern Law School and did his undergraduate work at the University of Chicago.

Scalia's message came through so loudly and clearly that he might just as well have said it explicitly to the stunned audience of law students who couldn't help but reconsider the mammoth debts they were incurring: "Sorry Christina Stutt, if you ain't from Harvard Law School, I ain't picking you."

During the late 2000s, Lauren Rivera, a PhD student in sociology at Harvard, set out to study how people got chosen for elite jobs. She interviewed 120 professionals involved in hiring at consulting, banking, and law firms, and another 32 job candidates from highly selective schools. To really get under the hood, Rivera spent an additional year working in the human resources department of an unidentified New York City consulting firm, which she calls Holt Halliday. Before entering graduate school, Rivera had worked in management consulting at the Monitor Group—now Monitor Deloitte. Perhaps as a result, Holt Halliday trusted her enough to put her on the recruitment team for an elite school.

At Harvard, Rivera studied under Michèle Lamont, an eminent sociologist of inequality. Initially, Rivera planned on studying the influence of gender in hiring, but when she began her fieldwork, she immediately saw the outsized role that culture and socioeconomic status played in the hiring process and made that the focus of her study. The resulting 2015 book, *Pedigree: How Elite Students Get Elite Jobs*, is wonderfully written, thoroughly engaging, and just about the most depressing book you'll ever read.

Rivera, today a professor at Northwestern's School of Management, found that when it came to getting your foot in the door, where you went to college hardly could have mattered more. "Number one people go to number one schools," an attorney named Jasmine told Rivera succinctly. Recruiting generally focused on three to five "core" schools. These lists generally included Harvard, Yale, Columbia, and when it came to hiring MBAs, the Wharton School of the University of Pennsylvania. Firms without large West Coast offices often didn't even visit Stanford. "It's just too far," said a banker named Bill.

Of course, not every Harvard and Yale student can get a job at Goldman Sachs. Rivera found that when it came to deciding which elite students to pick for elite jobs, people involved in the hiring process overwhelmingly relied upon factors that perpetuated class inequality. Interviewers preferred people who looked like them and who'd shared similar experiences, in much the way that Nico's partner on the Marshall selection panel favored the candidate who'd sung in a choir. They wanted to hire someone who could "actually be your friend," as a consultant named Amit told Rivera—someone with whom they could imagine being drinking buddies or who'd shared a formative athletic experience, like lacrosse.

A few people valued diversity. Generally, these were people who were not themselves the product of a privileged background. People who hadn't gone to fancy colleges were more open to candidates who hadn't gone to fancy colleges. But, by the very nature of the system, they were outliers. As at the elite colleges whose graduates they favored, hiring at elite firms served principally to perpetuate inequality.

Where you went meant—and means—just about everything. When Scalia answered Christina Stutt, he might as well have been speaking for the entire legal profession, and for investment banking and consulting, too.

*   *   *

In the same year that *Pedigree* came out, Frank Bruni's *Where You Go Is Not Who You'll Be: An Antidote to the College Admissions Mania* hit the *New York Times* bestsellers list and held a moment in the zeitgeist. In the book, the longstanding *Times* columnist makes, effectively, three arguments. The first is that the college admissions process cannot and should not define who someone is as a person. It's almost impossible to argue with this humane position. College admissions are arbitrary in the extreme. Where one gets in can hardly be considered a referendum on much of anything. And attending college is about so much more than the name that's on the diploma. It's about becoming a learner, encountering diversity, and engaging in self-reflection.

Bruni's second argument is that the significance of elite colleges is dramatically overblown. Less than 1 percent of college students attends an Ivy-Plus school, and yet, Bruni notes, more is written about Harvard than all community colleges combined. If the media wanted to write about the issues that affect the most students, the focus would be on the defunding of public universities. The focus on Harvard seems more justifiable given Lauren Rivera's research on the extent to which elite colleges act as a funnel to elite jobs, but Bruni's point is fair enough.

His third point is way more problematic. Colleges, Bruni argues, are not deterministic of economic outcomes. To support this, he cites many examples of business leaders and scientists who succeeded despite the handicap of being deprived a super-elite education. His argument is based entirely on such anecdotes and scans of Fortune 500-type lists. Notably, these lists do not include the personnel directories of elite law firms, investment banks, and consultancies.

In the most literal, trivial sense, what Bruni says is true. College admissions are not *purely* deterministic. Where you go is not *necessarily* who you'll be. But if Bruni had written his book based on data, the feel-good stories of former Citigroup chairman Dick Parsons and secretary of state Condoleezza Rice, people of color who overcame the disadvantage of being deprived of an Ivy League degree to become outrageously successful, would be followed by hundreds of pages of stories of rich, mostly white teenagers who solidified and legitimized their class position by going to Harvard or Yale.

At bottom, Bruni is arguing that people should calm down. I'd argue that they aren't agitated enough. When one looks at Chetty and Friedman's data in the aggregate, the maniacal, obsessive focus on college admissions is entirely rational. An elite college degree is the single best insurance policy against downward mobility and, for certain types of super-elite careers like investment banking and consulting, the sole pathway to success. Rich and upper-middle-class families accurately perceive this empirical reality, even if Bruni does not.

The problem is that poor people, especially poor people of color, don't accurately perceive it either. That's because they've been sold a bill of goods, which exaggerates the role that elite colleges play in promoting upward mobility and ignores entirely the role they play in preventing downward mobility and promoting access to the elite. The bill comes in part from books like Bruni's. In larger part, it comes from the colleges themselves, which want the focus to remain on upward mobility.

Understanding the lesser-told stories of Chetty and Friedman's research is central to understanding the increasing severity of income inequality in America. More deeply, it's central to understanding America itself. Affluent whites move through the nation seeking resources for their children and attempt to construct the narratives that elite colleges choose to value, such as athleticism and well-roundedness. In so doing, they change the communities in which they choose to live—almost inevitably for the worse.

PART II

How Elite Colleges Distort Communities

4

Finding the Escalator

After they got married, Michael Petrilli and his wife settled in Takoma Park, Maryland, just over the northeastern border of Washington, DC, not far from Silver Spring. Petrilli worked at the Department of Education under George W. Bush. He wanted to live in or near DC to be able to ride his bike to work, and so that he and his wife could remain in contact with their friends. Takoma Park fit the bill perfectly. In 2003, they bought a cottage bungalow on Woodland Avenue. At just over 1,100 square feet, it contained about as much living space as a medium-sized apartment, but it had a wooden deck and a porch swing, and you could walk to the Metro in less than twenty minutes. The Petrillis loved it.

Takoma Park is exceptionally diverse. About 35 percent of the population is Black and another 12 percent identify themselves as Latinx. Less than half of the population is white. It's socioeconomically diverse, too. Most of the inhabitants rent apartments, many of which rise alongside Sligo Creek, a tributary of the Anacostia River. Perhaps not surprisingly, it's also super-lefty. The city hosts annual folk, jazz, and film festivals. In 2013, it became the first American city to lower the voting age in municipal elections to sixteen. Residents affectionately refer to it as the Berkeley of the East or, perhaps less affectionately, as The People's Republic of Takoma Park. Petrilli, who grew up outside St. Louis, is politically moderate, but his wife is liberal, as are pretty much all their friends, and they fit right in.

Then they had kids, and everything changed. Suddenly they weren't sure Takoma Park was right for them long-term. Maybe, they thought, the suburbs would be a better environment in which to raise their two sons. Petrilli, who today is president of the Thomas B. Fordham Institute, an education think tank, was unusually public about the deliberations that ensued. He published them in a small book, *The Diverse Schools Dilemma: A Parent's Guide to Socioeconomically Mixed Public Schools*.

"Mainly, we were concerned about the schools," Petrilli wrote. "They had a mixed reputation and lackluster test scores, largely due to their diverse population of students." On the other hand, he and his wife valued the diversity in Takoma Park. Petrilli agonized enough that he drew up charts comparing the test scores, as well as the socioeconomic and racial diversity, of the various schools and communities they were considering as alternatives.

"It really could have gone either way," Petrilli told me. In the end, they bought a house in Bethesda—the best educated city in the United States and just about the opposite of diverse. Eighty-six percent of the population is white. The average annual family income is approximately $160,000. At Wood Acres, the elementary school for which their new home was zoned, almost none of the students came from low-income families.

I asked Petrilli what he thought about the decision in retrospect.

"It's worked out well for the kids," he replied.

Petrilli's story isn't unusual. In fact, according to Cornell University demography professor Dan Lichter, it's the prototypical life course of a white family. "Kids and young adults start out living in the city," Lichter says. "Then they find a spouse, have kids, and move to the suburbs."

Lichter has spent his entire professional career thinking about the relationship between geographical and social mobility. He's pretty much always seen the world in terms of haves and have-nots. Growing up in Mitchell, South Dakota, about seventy-five miles west of Sioux Falls, Lichter was a have-not. Mitchell, with a population around 15,000, is best known as home to the World's Only Corn Palace. The palace isn't actually made of corn, but the exterior murals are. They're redesigned every year—using approximately 325,000 ears of corn and 1.5 million nails—a massive demonstration of the arability of South Dakotan soil. The highlight of the year is the Corn Palace Festival, held around harvest time. It's a draw for top talent. When Lichter was a kid, they got Lawrence Welk, Guy Lombardo, and Andy Williams.

You may laugh—Lichter does—but growing up, he regarded himself as an urban kid. Even in the smallest of cities, though, there's a right and wrong side of the tracks. In the case of Mitchell, the tracks were I-90. The federal superhighway crossed the town just south of the Lichters' modest home. The fancier homes were to the north, near Lake Mitchell.

The Lichter family worked hard to make ends meet. Dan's father, Tom, was an electrician. His mom, Alice, worked odds jobs, including at a Dairy Queen, until she finally landed a gig in the accounting department of a hospital. Neither went to college, but Tom and Alice invested their kids with an ethic that suffused their lives. "My parents emphasized hard work," Lichter recalled. All eleven Lichter children got part-time jobs as soon as they were able. In high school, Dan delivered newspapers and performed odd tasks, often working as much as sixty hours per week during the summer.

The work ethic became central to his identity and led to some clashes at the Holy Spirit Catholic Church, where Dan attended school. "We went toe-to-toe with the rich kids," Lichter told me. "We were the working-class kids. We'd show up in extramurals resentful and bitter of status differences. We thought the nuns favored the rich kids," he said, adding with a smile, "I wasn't respectful of the nuns." He describes himself as having been a middling student—strong at math but terrible at reading comprehension. Lichter says he never gave a thought to going anywhere other than South Dakota State University, through which he paid his own way. In sociology class, a light went on. "It opened up a whole new way of thinking," Lichter told me, and he became interested in "how we think about the structure of society."

One of Lichter's insights is to change the way demographers conceptualize that structure. Census data is traditionally aggregated in units called "tracts," the brainchild of Walter Laidlaw, a Presbyterian

minister who, in 1895, became director of the New York Federation of
Churches and Christian Workers. Laidlaw had a PhD and a passion for
statistics, and he wanted to understand the social and economic needs
of New Yorkers. The problem was the state and federal censuses didn't
mesh. The federal data was compiled in years ending in "0," using city
council wards. The state data was collected in years ending in "5," using
state assembly districts, which were routinely redrawn. Drawing upon
the "section" system, which had been used in the eighteenth century to
survey and sell undeveloped land in the American West, Laidlaw proposed collecting census data by permanent "quarter-section blocks" of
approximately 160 acres. Over time, the Census Bureau has reduced the
size of these blocks and re-termed them "tracts," but Laidlaw's innovation remains the basis for how population data is collected.

When one looks at U.S. demographic data by tract, it's possible to find
a basis for optimism. By some measures, especially in urban environ-
ments, Black-white segregation has declined, and that's the story many
demographers tell. But Lichter says this conceptualizes space the wrong
way. Political units—places—drive neighborhood change and segregation. Local politicians and economic elites are the ones who compete
for affluent taxpayers and differentiate housing markets.

When one looks at this higher, "macro" level of segregation, a different picture emerges. While segregation within metropolitan neighborhoods has declined, segregation between cities and suburbs, and
between one suburb and another, has been increasing as affluent whites
move to all-white neighborhoods and gated communities. "The suburbs
are fragmenting," Lichter explains. He's particularly interested in new
suburban fringe counties, like Naperville, thirty miles west of Chicago.
"It was a rural farming community forty years ago," Lichter says. "Now
it's one of the richest communities of its size in the country, and it's
almost all lily-white."

Research by Lichter's Cornell colleague Kendra Bischoff and Stanford's Sean Reardon shows that since 1970, the percentage of Americans living in middle-income or mixed communities has dropped from
about sixty to forty. Meanwhile, the share of people living in uniformly
poor or affluent communities has more than doubled. As Lichter sees it,

this splintering based on economics negatively affects American society. "For some of these suburban neighborhoods that were actually part of the city, they are trying to pull themselves out," he explains. "It's the opposite of annexation—they're trying to disengage from the larger community because they're wealthier or whiter because they want to make choices rather than have choices made for them."

What's driving this sudden interest in self-governance? "A big motivation is schools," Lichter says. "People want to go somewhere safe with good schools." Lichter means white people. "Whites are hunkering down in white neighborhoods," he says. The problem is that, unlike Michael Petrilli and his family, most don't even realize they're doing it.

When Annette Lareau interviewed parents in three suburban school districts about how they'd chosen their neighborhood, she presumed she'd find that they had operated just like Petrilli. Lareau, who's at the University of Pennsylvania, made her mark studying parenting styles. Her key finding was that upper-middle-class parents employed a hyper-engaged style of parenting, which she called "concerted cultivation." It only made sense that they would employ the same process when it came to the supremely consequential decision of where to live. Lareau was surprised by what she found.

Many parents shrugged when asked how they ended up where they did. They spoke about connections they had to the area—their college roommate lived there and said it was a good area. Even among those who said they'd moved for "good schools," almost none did any meaningful research. It was their social networks that mattered. When the sociologists Maria Krysan and Kyle Crowder interviewed Chicago residents about their searches for housing, they found the same thing that Lareau had. Parents trusted their networks and sought to live with "people like them."

No one questioned white parents who moved to white suburbs. These seemed like obvious, responsible choices. It was the middle-class parents who sent their children to diverse schools that faced the most intense questioning. "They are seen as compromising their children's life chances, and are questioned by families, co-workers, and even neighbors," Lareau said. Seeking diversity was the difficult choice. Reproducing segregation was considered normal.

To Lareau, this dynamic is what makes the problem so disquieting. Parents are simply reproducing their social networks. They're moving within their "micro-climate," as Lareau calls it. It's not the sort of problem that lends itself to easy solutions because it's not the sort of behavior that feels problematic. Parents are simply moving to places that feel comfortable and safe. In this sense, it's almost identical to the dynamic behind college admissions—seemingly benign individual behavior with pernicious social effects. Nevertheless, the culprit is clear: White people. Lichter says, "I think we ignore what whites are doing way too often."

Rebecca Sibilia doesn't. Growing up in Bridgewater, New Jersey—a white, upper-middle-class bedroom community serving the Raritan Valley pharmaceutical and telecommunications industries—didn't predispose Sibilia to becoming a reformer. Her father, a cop, leaned right. When she started at Clemson University, Sibilia chose political science as a major, attended meetings with the college Republicans, and even landed a prestigious placement in the office of Senator Strom Thurmond, then a spry ninety-five. She seemed headed for life as a lobbyist. It's easy to imagine that she'd have been a star. Sibilia is smart and engaging, with a magnetic personality that commands a room.

Things changed when Sibilia was twenty and her mother died. For a while, she drifted. She followed a boyfriend to Washington, DC, and took a job at the Office of Budget and Planning, which oversaw DC schools, then under federal control. She rose through the ranks and ultimately landed in the mayor's office as an advisor on education policy. In the budget office, schools had been abstractions. Under Tony Williams, they became real. In 2005, she joined the mayor on a school visit, and her entire worldview shifted.

"The first time I walked into a school in DC was my aha moment," Sibilia told me. It wasn't just any school. H.D. Woodson High was one of the most famously dilapidated school buildings in the United States, a crumbling monolith built in the Brutalist style—from béton brut, the

French term for "raw concrete." Think Khrushchyovka—those Eastern bloc apartments (named for Nikita Khrushchev) that you might have seen on the HBO series *Chernobyl*—only somewhat less glamorous. The students crammed into the emergency stairwells, walking up as many as nine flights, because the escalators had been condemned. In the hallways they dodged falling tiles. The swim team practiced on tables—like "starving dogs in a meat factory," as their coach recalled—because sewage had seeped into the pool.

"It was in such disrepair," Sibilia said, "that I could not believe—one, that we were sending children there. Two, that they were going. Three, that they felt at any point in their schooling career that the government cared about them." Sibilia obsessed about the message kids were receiving about their place in American democracy. "This is the first time that people in our society engage with the government in a meaningful way," she said. "If you're a kid who goes to a school where three-quarters of the bathrooms don't work, there's no privacy from toilet to toilet, the smell of sewage is evident, mold is growing on the walls, and the pool is just cracked concrete, I can't imagine what that does to a young child's psyche. But I can extrapolate what that does in terms of their trust and distrust of government."

In 2011, Sibilia joined StudentsFirst, a nonprofit run by Michelle Rhee, the notorious, former superintendent of DC schools. StudentsFirst supported charter schools, which Sibilia saw as a way to disrupt the system, and tepidly endorsed vouchers in the interest of stimulating competition. But StudentsFirst was perceived, fairly or not, as partisan. Sibilia came to see this as a limitation, and she began to conceive of a different pathway. Early in 2014, she landed a grant from the Buck Foundation to study equity in Connecticut, which had no school funding formula, and then a second grant from the Broad Foundation to do similar work in Georgia. The mandate of her new organization—EdBuild—was to show what a more equitable system might look like. The question was how to do it.

They stumbled on the answer almost by accident when a member of EdBuild's small staff, Sara Hodges, started playing with census data. A geographer by training, Hodges had a background in environmental

mapping. As with Dan Lichter, her life experience led her to visualize the data in different chunks than tracts. Hodges separated it—
disaggregated it as they say in the biz—by school district, looking
specifically at how poverty rates had changed between 2006 and 2013.
On the map she drew, you can see poverty spreading across the nation,
school district by school district, like a virus.

Hodges is quiet, and she put her map away, but EdBuild's chief of
staff tweeted it to Emma Brown, a reporter at the *Washington Post*,
who wrote a piece about Hodges's work and the new organization. The
response was overwhelming. Within a week, EdBuild had raised half a
million dollars—a total that ultimately grew to $9 million—to graphi-
cally portray how funding disparities shaped student opportunity.
"The map brought people into the conversation who weren't into data,"
Sibilia said.

EdBuild's first major report, released in 2016, is called *Fault Lines:
America's Most Segregating School District Borders*. It began when
Hodges drew a simple line for Sibilia—between Camden, New Jersey,
and neighboring Haddon. Camden had a median household income
of $26,000, a poverty rate of 36 percent, and was 99 percent non-white.
Haddon had a median income of $86,000, a poverty rate of 6 percent,
and was 83 percent white.

And this border was hardly the most extreme. Rochester, New York,
and adjacent Penfield look, on paper, like different countries. Rochester
has a poverty rate of 47 percent. In Penfield, it's merely five. In Detroit,
45 percent of the students live in poverty and 98 percent are non-white.
Across the border, in Grosse Pointe, just 6 percent of students live in
poverty, yet Grosse Pointe raises nearly three times as much in local
revenue per pupil as Detroit. In total, EdBuild identified 671 districts
that had at least twenty-point lower poverty rates than their neighbors.
(Hodges's map also revealed extreme race disparities—as between
Birmingham, in which 1 percent of students are white, and adjacent
Mountain Brook City, where 96 percent are. EdBuild would cover the
race issue in a later report.)

When EdBuild published *Fault Lines*, Sibilia had a second aha
moment of sorts. "The only reason that could uphold such a system,"

she said, "is that they are purposefully creating winners and losers."
To translate, Sibilia means white people. To create the widest possible
escalator for their own kids, they were freezing out everyone else. One
way they did this was by literally seceding.

EdBuild's second report was—impossible as this is to imagine—even
more maddening than the first. In it, they identified 128 communities
that had attempted secession from their school district since the turn
of the millennium. Seventy-three succeeded. The goal was always the
same: to hoard resources within the new district's lines. In the south-
east corner of East Baton Rouge, Louisiana, residents of the tony St.
George neighborhood, where homes sell for over $1 million, sought an
amendment to the state constitution so that they could incorporate as
a new municipality and create their own school district. (They won a
referendum on the amendment, but, as I'm writing this, legal action is
pending.) EdBuild titled this report *Fractured*. Though they've never
met, Sibilia had identified the same concept as Lichter meant when he
talked about "fragmenting."

As they've mapped inequities across the American education land-
scape, the most head-scratching (or head-banging) phenomenon
EdBuild has identified is the "island school district"—a district surrounded entirely by a single other school district, of which 180 exist
in the U.S. They're the school district equivalent of gated communities. Perhaps the most shocking example was Piedmont, California, the
"city of millionaires," in which the average household income exceeds
$300,000 and the poverty rate is 2 percent. It's surrounded entirely by
Oakland, where the poverty rate is 24 percent. In California, property taxes are capped by the state constitution, theoretically meaning
wealthy districts shouldn't be able to outspend poorer ones by much.
Piedmont evaded this by creating a "parcel tax"—a flat fee that went
directly to the district and wasn't subject to the cap. They spent about
50 percent more per student than their circumscribed neighbor.

EdBuild exposed these massive funding disparities in *Dismissed*,
their final major report. In the most extreme example, tiny, overwhelmingly white Storey County, Nevada, generated $18,000 per pupil, about
twice as much as their massive neighbor, Washoe County, home to

Reno. It's a typical story. In districts where more than 75 percent of the students are white, enrollment averages around 1,500 students. In districts where more than 70 percent of the students are non-white, enrollment averages more than 10,000 students.

EdBuild identified 969 borders across which a 10 percent gap in funding existed. In total, white school districts received $23 billion more in funding than non-white districts, despite enrolling approximately the same number of students. Of course, this often excludes unofficial spending through PTAs and booster clubs, which can dramatically expand the officially reported gap. On Manhattan's Upper West Side, for example, several PTAs raise more than $1 million per year to support the schools. In Hillsborough, California, the parent foundation raises about $3.5 million per year—about one-fifth of the school budget.

What's the motivation? When Gardendale, Alabama, sought to create its own school district, the mayor told the press that local school governance was about "keeping our tax dollars here with our kids, rather than sharing them with kids all over Jefferson County." Why did they care about gerrymandering their own district? Why would the parents of Piedmont create a new kind of tax? It's impossible to know what's in their hearts, of course, but Sibilia offers an educated guess. "Because we have a competitive higher ed system," Sibilia says, "every dollar more that your local school district gets is just that one extra step that your kids get compared to the kids next door." In other words, it's college that drives the obsession of affluent, white parents with good schools.

Thing is, the concept of a "good" school doesn't exist in a vacuum. The word is used imprecisely, even recklessly, like "love." Sometimes "good" is used to mean "white." Sometimes it's used to mean "well-funded." Rarely is it used to talk about a school's philosophical approach to pedagogy or the value that it adds. Almost never is it connected to empirical evidence.

We've known since 1966—from data—that where you go to school matters a great deal. In the spring of that year, James Coleman, a Johns Hopkins sociologist, holed himself up in a DC motel room with a single change of clothes and reams of survey data. The U.S. Department of Health, Education, and Welfare, which commissioned Coleman's survey pursuant to the Civil Rights Act of 1964, expected him to find that southern schools were discriminating against poor Blacks. Indeed, Coleman became the first sociologist to document what would come to be known as the Black achievement gap—African American students were several grade levels behind their white peers. But Coleman's central finding said much more about class than race. The biggest factors that determined a student's success were their family's background and socioeconomic diversity in the classroom. Kids did better when their classmates came from wealthy, educated families. It's part of why Stanford's Prudence Carter and University of Colorado's Kevin Welner, among others, have reconceptualized the gap as one of opportunity rather than achievement.

Coleman's findings have been replicated countless times—including by Lichter, Bischoff and Reardon, and Stanford's Caroline Hoxby, among many others. UCLA's Gary Orfield and Susan Eaton of Brandeis call it "one of the most consistent findings in research on education." A student's success is determined at least as much by the networks to which they are exposed as the "quality" of the schools they attend. In fact, Coleman found, to the feds' surprise, that a school's physical amenities mattered almost not at all.

Often, when people talk about "good schools," they're referring to the physical structure or to programs that are the equivalent of fancy window dressing—a course in multivariable calculus, a fencing program, a model United Nations team that travels to The Hague. None of these have greater intrinsic value than other formative life experiences. Almost all of my students—and precious few elite college students—have been working since high school, often nearly full time. I would argue that learning to balance work and study is much more directly related to cultivating grit and optimism and the "softer" traits that Angela Duckworth's research shows matter more than raw intelligence.

The data on the significance of networks is so overwhelming that talking about the "quality" of schools without discussing their socioeconomic diversity is meaningless. Of course, it's then fair to ask whether elite colleges are adding any value beyond creating networks of rich students who can then draw upon alumni networks over the course of their lives. It's a good question—one that Chetty and Friedman are trying to answer. What we know for sure is that elite colleges are driving the system.

Annette Lareau teaches us that even affluent white people, otherwise predisposed to helicopter parenting, aren't engaging in extensive research about the efficacy of schools or what they should teach. Rather, they're riding with the current. And that massive, terrifyingly forceful current is elite colleges. The imprimatur of a degree from one of these institutions can carry a young person to extreme affluence and act as a bulwark against downward mobility. What suburban communities value in their schools, therefore—what's considered "good" in a school—is what elite colleges establish as priorities.

For at least the past half-century, this has meant excellence in sports, well-roundedness, connections to the institution, and academic peacocking, measured principally by performance on the ACT or SAT. Each of these factors is tied directly to wealth. Testing, the subject to which we next turn, is, depending on your charitability, either the greatest example of unintended consequences in American history or the biggest scam.

5

Cracking the Code

God shed his grace upon Harvard for its 1946 commencement. To commemorate the first graduation since the end of World War II—and the second anniversary of D-Day—Harvard conferred honorary degrees upon the chiefs of the four divisions of the military, including Army chief of staff General Dwight D. Eisenhower. Slanting through the red oaks, honey locusts, and resilient elms of Harvard Yard, sunshine bathed the coterie of military leaders in light.

A sense of relief pervaded this first peacetime assembly, but one needn't have looked hard to find somber notes. Of the 1,500 freshmen who'd started four years earlier, only thirty-two graduated on time. A total of 649 Harvard men had lost their lives in the war. Many Gold Star parents were in attendance. Almost everyone wore a uniform.

The speeches hinted at the battles both behind and ahead. Frank Graham, the president of University of North Carolina, lamented the pace at which the power of machines was outrunning the power of people. Modern men, Graham said, were "biological organisms in possession of dynamic scientific mechanisms without the necessary social devices for intelligent and human control." Universities were part of the problem, he said. They were "narrowly scientific" and "reluctantly social-minded."

Harvard's president, James Conant, nodded in agreement. A chemist by training, Conant had played an integral role in the war. He'd been FDR's liaison to the Los Alamos National Lab in New Mexico, and it had been his idea to drop the first atomic weapons on cities that were military industrial centers where the workers lived nearby—like Hiroshima and Nagasaki. Conant understood as well as anyone there how close the United States had come to losing the arms race.

More importantly, the threats hadn't ended with the defeat of the Axis. Conant believed the Soviet's contributions to the war effort had proved the appeal of what he called "the Russian experiment." As an ideology, communism posed a dire threat, and the Russians would have atomic weapons soon enough. If Truman decided to go ahead with developing the hydrogen bomb, that would escalate the stakes exponentially.

A new war had already begun.

And Harvard wasn't ready.

If you had a time machine to go back to Cambridge on June 6, 1946, little about Harvard would be recognizable. The campus would feel familiar to those who know it today, but the nature of the institution, and its place in American society, would seem vastly different.

For starters, it was easy to get in. An applicant just had to pass a series of subject-based exams, which they could take as many times as they liked. One of the subjects was Latin, which made getting in impossible for public school graduates, but among wealthy, prep school types, admissions were wonderfully egalitarian. The Ivies liked paying customers.

In addition to being overwhelmingly wealthy, the students were overwhelmingly local. Harvard drew most of its students from private schools in New York and New England. The standard life course for Boston Brahmins—as Oliver Wendell Holmes Sr. dubbed the city's WASP elite—was prep school, Fair Harvard, Wall Street bank. Okay, maybe that last bit looks familiar. The point is that 1946 Harvard was much more finishing school than rigorous institution. The students lived in lavish apartments, often with servants. They weren't very smart or inclined to study. Those who did were looked down upon as "grinds." The college admitted a handful of scholarship students, but the scholarships didn't include room and board, so the recipients were largely local and universally regarded as second-class citizens. It was de rigueur for faculty at the Ivies to complain about their students, but the truth was they weren't such great shakes either. The German university system trained hard-core academics to teach its undergraduates. Harvard simply drew its professors from the Boston area.

There's much about America you wouldn't have recognized either. Less than half of Americans owned a home, and less than a fifth lived in a suburb. Abraham Levitt wouldn't start building his first community until the following year. Class inequality existed, of course, but to a significantly lesser degree than it does today. In 1945, the top 1 percent controlled about 15 percent of pretax income, and the top one-tenth of that 1 percent controlled about 5 percent. These numbers seem quaint in retrospect. Today, the wealthy control about twice the share they did then.

Still, Conant saw great peril in American inequality. This belief was no doubt informed by his background. Conant was, literally, a kid from the other side of the tracks—a townie from Dorchester whose father had started a photography business and then made a small fortune as a real estate speculator. Even as an undergraduate, Conant was critical of Harvard's caste system, which he believed deprived America of the best talent.

Now, at the end of the war, the challenge of class mobility seemed existential. Conant was greatly influenced in his thinking by Frederick Jackson Turner, the eminent Harvard historian. Turner believed that open land in the West had fueled the equality and democracy that the French political scientist Alexis de Tocqueville had identified as colonial America's defining features. He also believed that the closing of the frontier had predisposed immigrants to socialism, by crowding them into industrialized cities. If America were to prevent communism from prevailing, it would need to provide meaningful opportunity to its millions of returning veterans. This would mean creating a fluid society— one closer to Thomas Jefferson's ideal of a natural aristocracy of talent. But when Conant floated the ideas of a 100 percent estate tax and abolishing private education, his proposals landed with a thud. This would be a daunting challenge.

Nevertheless, Conant saw great opportunity in the G.I. Bill's extension of education benefits to millions of returning veterans. This was

again, no doubt, because of his background. Conant believed in the power of science to identify and cultivate talent. In 1933, when he became
president of Harvard at the age of forty, Conant created the Harvard
National Scholarship program—the first step in achieving his vision of
replacing the anti-democratic elite with smart, public-minded people
drawn from all sectors of society. The program targeted Midwestern
students, to be chosen solely based on academic promise. The question
was how. Conant believed that those subject-based tests—the "college
boards" as they were called—were biased toward the prep schools that
had organized them. They'd be of no use in identifying promising Midwesterners. Conant assigned the task of creating a system to identify the
right candidates to one of his assistant deans, Henry Chauncey.

In Chauncey, the Brooklyn-born son of an Episcopalian minister,
Conant found a true devotee of testing. The *New Yorker's* Nicholas
Lemann, author of the definitive history of the SAT, attributes this to
a Puritanical attraction to improving the human condition through
order. Whatever the reason, Chauncey never met a test he didn't like.
Chauncy saw standardized exams as a way to advance "progress," however vaguely defined.

Chauncey was particularly smitten with the work of Carl Campbell
Brigham, a eugenicist operating out of Princeton. It'd be hard to get
tenure in that field today, but Brigham rode it a long way. In his big
book, *A Study of American Intelligence*, Brigham used data from Army
IQ tests that had been administered during World War I to argue that
intelligence testing was an important means of eliminating "defective
strains in the present population." You can guess who those were. Spoiler: it wasn't the Nordics.

The College Board was so impressed with his work that it hired
Brigham to develop an intelligence test to use in college admissions.
That was the SAT. In June 1926, they administered it for the first time to
approximately eight thousand high school students. Harvard's choice
came down to the SAT or a series of achievement tests that had been
developed in connection with a study of progressive education reforms
sponsored by the Carnegie Foundation. Conant rejected the achieve-

ment tests because they favored rich kids. Don't think about this too long or your head will explode. Suffice it to say that both options were shaping up to be outrageously biased.

Even with Harvard's endorsement, the SAT remained, until the 1940s, almost exclusively an instrument for identifying scholarship candidates to Ivy League schools. When the United States entered World War II, fewer than twenty thousand students a year sat for the exam. But testing demonstrated its value during the war. Under the auspices of the College Board, Chauncey supervised the V-12 and A-12 tests, programs by which the Army and Navy identified recruits with the potential to perform advanced technical jobs. These were widely regarded as successes.

With the advent of the G.I. Bill, and the American elite's perception of testing as virtuous, Conant and Chauncey had an opening to achieve their larger vision. They chartered a new national organization—the Educational Testing Service (ETS)—to control all the leading tests. By at least one metric, it was a resounding success. By 2020, the number of students who took the SAT had grown more than a thousand-fold—to 2.2 million.

In 1985, *Rolling Stone* magazine ran a college special riddled with irony. The cover featured *Miami Vice*'s Don Johnson and Phillip Michael Thomas, neither of whom finished college, and included an article about an upstart SAT prep company, which denied the test's validity. Accompanying the article was a mischievous cartoon featuring the Scarecrow from *The Wizard of Oz*. The mangy guttersnipe never speaks in it, but it's easy enough to infer the premise: The Scarecrow has acquired a brain but has bombed his college boards. To this end, he's seeking the help of a pair of tutors who, according to the transom window, possess "Ph.D.'s in S.A.T."

The chap presenting the duo's plan for beating the test—"without hardly ever thinking"—has a shock of curly brown hair, piercing blue eyes, and sports a green blazer that smacks of the Ivy League. "You won't be any smarter, mind you," he says, "but you will get a higher test score." As he hands over a summary of their system, he adds a cautionary note. "Remember: A mind is a terrible thing to waste. Use it sparingly!"

The pitchman is John Katzman.

If you lived in the East Coast tri-state area during the 1980s or 1990s and aspired to get into a top college—or knew someone who did—it's almost inevitable that you've heard of Katzman and his story. After graduating from Old Nassau in 1981 with a degree in electrical engineering and computer science, Katzman went to work as a coder at Manufacturers Hanover on Wall Street. He hated it from the beginning. A few weeks in, Katzman thought back to the two bits of life advice given to him by his father, who ran an electric vaporizer company that he'd inherited from his own father. The first was not to get married until he turned thirty. The second was that it was more fun to work for yourself.

Katzman quit Manny Hanny and started an SAT-tutoring school. This didn't come entirely out of the blue. While in college, he'd done some tutoring for a company run by a Wharton grad named Bob Scheller. The money was good—twenty dollars an hour—a lot better than his first job at Wawa. And Katzman was a natural—he'd gotten a 1500 on the SAT without taking a course himself. "I was made for the SAT," Katzman told me. "It measures a certain kind of thinking, and it happens that's how I think. I didn't prepare for it, except that everything I did was preparation for it."

He ran his new course out of his apartment on the Upper West Side. The first session had nineteen students. The second had forty-three. Soon each had hundreds—all without advertising. The results spoke for themselves. His students were seeing improvements of hundreds of points. Plus, Katzman's course had a catchy name. He called it Princeton Review.

Katzman looked at the SAT as a systems engineer would. He used computers to analyze student performance. Did they fade over the course of an exam? Were there patterns to the mistakes they made? Did they jump at early choices? What types of answers distracted them? The same approach informed how he taught. Katzman told his students that the SAT was a game. "I told them that they're not competing with each other, they're competing with ETS." With a smile, Katzman would add, "And the mindset is: Let's blow these assholes away."

The essence of Princeton Review was—and is—the Joe Bloggs method. The SAT's main objective was to create variance—to separate the wheat from the chaff. To do that, ETS needed to lay traps for average test-takers. Princeton Review taught its students to avoid these traps by learning how the average test-taker thinks. They called this person Joe Bloggs. Princeton Review's essential conceit was to teach its students how to avoid Joe Bloggs's mistakes. The results were stunning—average gains of 150 points on the verbal section and 90 points on math—across the board for all kinds of students. "There was no group I couldn't help," Katzman said.

Whatever the merits of the Joe Bloggs method, embracing it put Katzman directly in competition with Stanley Kaplan, the son of a Brooklyn plumber who ran a successful tutoring business out of a second-story office on Kings Highway and Sixteenth Street. Unlike Katzman, Kaplan admired the SAT and sought ETS's approval. "Kaplan thought this was a test of English and math, instead of seeing this as an object with a pretty idiosyncratic language and construction," Katzman said. By contrast, Katzman told his kids that he wasn't a teacher. "This isn't school," he'd say. "I'm not going to teach you English. I'm not going to teach you math. I'm going to teach you the SAT." The conflict between these approaches devolved into a fight to the death.

Kaplan never had a chance. Katzman was both a test-taking and marketing genius. He registered the domain name, www.kaplan.com, and taunted his competitor by having visitors criticize Kaplan's course on the website. He hired a young cartoonist named Matt Groening to pen a series of hilarious cartoons promoting Princeton Review. He took out ads on city buses and subways that said, "Friends don't let friends take Kaplan." Princeton Review ate away at Kaplan's market share until it became the dominant player. The point of the ads was crystal clear: the SAT was a game you could win and Kaplan was for losers.

It'd be difficult to imagine a more heretical message. ETS had always maintained that the SAT was an aptitude test and, hence, not susceptible to coaching. Katzman blew that notion out of the water. But that wasn't his goal. "I didn't mean it as a political manifesto," Katzman told me. "I had no animus." Katzman wasn't an insurrectionist by nature. He'd played lacrosse in college and even appeared in a *Playgirl* spread featuring men of the Ivy League. But it was hard to love ETS.

"It was calling itself an aptitude test," Katzman said, "but none of this was about intelligence. The way I could make you comfortable and get a good performance was to change the mindset to us versus them—and they're idiots." It didn't sit right with Katzman that ETS was repeating the mistakes that kids fell into—the very patterns that were the essence of the Joe Bloggs method. "It's telling you that you're an idiot," Katzman said.

Still, Katzman believed that ETS had good intentions—or at least didn't have malicious intent—until he could believe it no longer. "When I really got political," Katzman said, "was when I saw that they had no interest in learning the truth." One of many amazing things about Katzman is that he operated his business transparently. He was public about Princeton Review's secret sauce—the Joe Bloggs method and all. He even paired with the author of the *Rolling Stone* article, David Owen—himself a Harvard grad—and turned his method into a best-selling book, *Cracking the SAT*. For $9.95, anyone could learn the nasty secret that ETS was trying to trick people, and that those tricks particularly bad effects on people who couldn't afford a course.

ETS didn't budge.

Katzman invited ETS to examine his records and study his results. "I'd say, 'You're lying about who the test helps and hurts.'" ETS ignored him. In 1984, Owen wrote College Board president George Hanford and offered for him and Katzman to give a coaching demonstration at the Board's annual meeting. Hanford declined. Owen began a quixotic quest to get ETS to respond to what Princeton Review had learned. He and Katzman got nothing—until 1985, when ETS responded by suing Princeton Review for copying questions, which they guarded assiduously, lest anyone have a sense of what was on the test that would determine their fates before they took it. "The point of the suit wasn't copyright infringement," Katzman said. "It was to put us out of business."

Ultimately, Katzman couldn't deny the truth. He sat for an interview with *Frontline* and let what had been on his mind for years spill out. "The SAT is a scam," Katzman said. "It has been around for fifty years. It has never measured anything, and it continues to measure nothing. And the whole game is that everybody who does well on it is so delighted by their good fortune that they don't want to attack it. The SAT is a bad test. It is biased. It measures nothing."

Lest there be any ambiguity in Katzman's position, he summarized it succinctly for the PBS audience. "The SAT," Katzman concluded, "is just bullshit."

The proposition that the SAT is bullshit—let's call it Katzman's Theorem—has been proved repeatedly and conclusively. To be clear, Katzman means that it's bullshit in two particular senses. The first is that it doesn't measure very much. The second is that whatever the SAT does measure is either associated with wealth or simply can be bought.

Neither of these facts would have come as a complete surprise to Conant and Chauncey. By the time they created ETS, Brigham, the eugenicist-cum-IQ tester, had renounced his own work. In the 1930s, Brigham openly rejected the idea that IQ tests and the SAT measured any innate capacities. They measured something—schooling, family background, familiarity with English. But, Brigham wrote, "the 'native intelligence' hypothesis is dead." (In modern times, Charles Murray is against the SAT. When the eugenicists are united in opposition to a test, that should really tell you something.)

In 1948, shortly after ETS got off the ground, a pair of prominent educators argued in *Scientific Monthly* that testing fraudulently cloaked wealthy kids with the appearance of scientifically validated superiority. Conant himself had suspected that the SAT might be an achievement test masquerading as an aptitude test. But let's give him the benefit of the doubt. Conant could reasonably have believed that the benefits of mass testing might outweigh the costs.

Today, that position would be impossible to maintain. Over the ensuing decades, ETS devoted its energies to destroying John Katzman, Stanley Kaplan, and anyone else who dared to suggest that the SAT could be beaten. In 1978, when their own researcher, Lewis Pike, convincingly showed that the test was coachable and recommended that ETS repudiate their prior denials, ETS responded by firing Pike. When *American Lawyer* editor Steven Brill, Ralph Nader, and a pair of researchers at Harvard Medical School published independent works questioning the validity of the SAT and the integrity of ETS, the organization responded by publishing a pamphlet in which it deemed criticism of standardized tests as "an attack on truth itself."

After years of hemorrhaging market share to the ACT, which was widely perceived as more democratic and aligned to what high school students actually learned, ETS finally had no choice but to admit to reality. In 2012, as part of an effort to rebrand itself, it released data showing that among students who took the test in the prior year, those who came from families making more than $200,000 annually scored an average of 1156, while those who came from families with annual incomes less than $20,000 averaged just 870. This led Harvard Law School professor Lani Guinier to call it simply a wealth test.

It's tough to know precisely how much tutoring—what Ohio State's Claudia Buchmann calls "shadow education"—is adding to the equation. What we know for sure is that rich kids are far more likely to take a prep course or hire a tutor. Of course, they've also enjoyed a lifetime of advantage—they're more likely to have college-educated parents, which is also highly associated with success on the SAT, and they receive many more enrichment opportunities. Furthermore, kids who take courses might be signaling that they're more motivated than those who don't. Still, after controlling for all these factors, the most careful studies have found that prep courses are worth an average of twenty to thirty points, and private tutors closer to forty. Remember, that's after ETS changed the SAT to make it less coachable and less like an intelligence test.

Maybe, you say, none of this matters. The kids who do well on the SAT would get into elite colleges anyway based on their grades. For some people, that's true. About two-thirds of high school students get SAT scores that line up with their high school grades. The other third either overperform or underperform their high school average. When the College Board looked at the data, it found that overperforming students were twice as likely to have parents who earned more than $100,000 per year than those who underperformed. The students in the underperforming group were twice as likely to be female or Black. They were three times as likely to be Hispanic, come from a family that earned less than $30,000 a year, or to have parents who hadn't gone to college.

James Conant wanted a system to identify poor students who might otherwise slip through the cracks. The SAT does some of this. What it does far more often is open the door for affluent students who, through prep courses and tutoring, get a score that gets them into schools to which they otherwise couldn't get in based on their grades—in other words, the very opposite of what Conant intended.

It's easy enough to understand the behavior of ETS and its parent organization, the College Board. They're nonprofits, but let's just say they ain't the Little Sisters of the Poor. The College Board is headquartered at a tower on Vesey Street that it shares with Merrill Lynch. It generates revenue of over $1 billion per year. The CEO, David Coleman, made about $1.8 million in 2018. ETS has a lavish campus at Princeton, complete with swimming pool and jogging trails. The College Board and ETS are simply protecting their brand.

The more difficult and important question is why colleges place such high value on factors that are utterly lacking in predictive value and highly correlated with wealth. Nearly all schools speak the language of concern with equity and inclusion. "We know that the best predictor of college performance is high-school performance—not the SAT," George Washington University president Thomas LeBlanc told the *Washington Post* in a 2018 interview, three years after the school went test-optional. "We see the world more broadly," he boasted. In the wake of COVID-19 and the Varsity Blues scandal—in which the college counselor William "Rick" Singer corruptly influenced admissions of more than 750 rich kids by, among other things, helping them cheat on the SAT and ACT— many more schools have become test-optional. It's a way they pay lip service to the concern with standardized testing bias.

The unspoken premise is that, given time, test-optional policies will promote diversity. They won't. We don't need to speculate about what the data will show when it finally comes in. Bowdoin proudly boasts of being the first American college to eliminate standardized testing requirements—that was in 1969. So we've had more than fifty years to study the question of how much socioeconomic diversity a test-optional admissions system produces. The answer? Not much. Bowdoin students have a median family income of $177,600—that's the twenty-second highest in the country. Of their students, 2.6 percent come from the bottom income quintile, 69.2 percent from the top quintile, and 15.4 percent from the top 1 percent. Their mobility rate is 1 percent—ranking them 1,584th, just behind North Central State College in Ohio and slightly ahead of Lakeshore Technical College in Sheboygan. Going test-optional hasn't done much for race diversity either. Just 7.7 percent of Bowdoin students are Black.

The problem is that a test-optional system still allows for rich applicants to submit test scores. "Test-optional" isn't the same as "no testing" or "mandatory testing." One of the simplest, most commonsensical proposals to narrow the income gap, advanced by University of Michigan professor Susan Dynarski, is to require all high school students to take the SAT or ACT. That wouldn't eliminate the inequities of the test, but at least would help students who miss a deadline or can't afford the exam and haven't gone through the hoops to get a fee waiver. This currently happens in only a dozen states. Everywhere else the advantage is to the rich.

So many of the practices that are marketed as touchy-feely exacerbate the very mechanisms that make standardized tests inequitable in the first place. Consider super-scoring. This is the practice of counting only a student's highest scores on individual sections of the exam. Take the example of a student who took the SAT five times, each time scoring 1300. On one occasion that 1300 consisted of a 700 in verbal and 600 in math, and on another occasion consisted of a 700 in math and a 600 in verbal. Their super-score would be a 1400, even though they never cracked 1300. Those 100 points are about the difference between the average SAT scores at Williams and Skidmore.

Whom does super-scoring help? Obviously, the more times you

take the exam, the greater the likelihood of getting a super-score that exceeds your actual average. And who takes the exam most often? Take a guess. When the Harvard Kennedy School's Josh Goodman and his collaborators looked at ten million SAT-takers between 2006 and 2014, they found that low-income students were twenty-one percentage points less likely to retake the exam, even though retaking the exam was worth about ninety points on the super-score and increased their chance of enrolling at a four-year college by thirty points. This effect was so strong that it explained about a quarter of the college enrollment gap between low- and high-income students.

And Goodman's study doesn't even address the phenomenon of students who take the exam more than twice. The College Board offers fee waivers but limits the number of times you can take the exam to two. When I lived in Manhasset, it was routine for high school students to take the college entrance exams seven or eight times. One basketball player I coached registered for every administration of both the SAT and ACT during his junior year.

Ah, the ACT. It once held great promise. Its creator, the psychologist E. F. Lindquist, who also created the Iowa Tests of Basic Skills, had a democratic, populist view of education. Lindquist believed that academic achievement in high school mattered most, and so his test aligned much more closely with what public school students studied. The aim was to identify the students best prepared to succeed at public universities. But, as it has evolved, performance on the ACT is also highly correlated with income. Between 2012 and 2016, test-takers from families with incomes over $80,000 scored an average of 23.6 on the exam. Students from families that made less than $80,000 scored an average of 19.5. That converts to a difference of about twenty percentiles. The ACT has always allowed super-scoring, and they've only leaned into the practice over time. In 2020, they began allowing students to retake individual sections instead of having to sit for the entire exam. While their fee waiver policy is slightly better than the College Board's (they allow three rather than two), it's hard to imagine that if Goodman replicated his study on ACT-takers the results would be any different.

What makes this state of affairs incomprehensible is that there's a readily available substitute that works better than standardized test scores. Since at least the 1980s, when James Crouse and Dale Trusheim published *The Case Against the SAT*, it's been an open secret that the test added almost nothing to the quality of admissions decisions beyond an applicant's high school record. The only entity that has ever denied this is ETS, despite their own internal research showing that SAT scores alone explained at most 15 percent of the variation in freshman grades. As an experiment, DePaul University asked admitted students who were admitted without submitting test scores to send them anyway for research purposes. Their freshman GPAs were the same as those of applicants who submitted their scores.

The data is so overwhelming that it's hard to resist cynicism. Indeed, Katzman says that the SAT's and ACT's correlation with wealth is precisely why colleges rely upon them. The whole point is to give colleges a justification to let in who they want to let in. Tests like the SAT convert the natural advantages of birth and wealth into a neutral score, which has a veneer of scientific validity that makes it feel fair, or at least not grossly unfair.

Katzman offers this simple key to understanding the mystery of college admissions. "All of the mechanisms," he says, "are to justify admitting rich kids."

When I started working on this book, I proposed to find out what happens when we give the white glove treatment to a smart, less privileged young person. The fair lady of this *Pygmalion* story is Brianne Ortiz. As I'm writing this, she's a senior at John Jay. Teachers aren't supposed to play favorites among their students, so I'll simply say that Brianne is one of my favorite people I've ever met. One time, during a weekly game night that I held during the pandemic, Brianne's classmates voted her Most Likely to Succeed, Most Likely to Sacrifice Themselves for Someone Else, and Best Dancer. This made perfect sense to me. Brianne has boundless optimism. She and I joke that her worst day is better than my best day.

Brianne has very little in the way of material things. What she does have is great parents. Her dad works as an electrician. Her mom started working at a White Castle after graduating from high school in Hill-crest, Queens. A few weeks later, she became the manager. It's not surprising. Sometimes during Zoom sessions, I hear Yesenia Ortiz in the background. She has an effervescent personality, and it's clear that she's the tree from which Brianne's apple fell. After leaving the fast-food industry, Yesenia tried almost every type of job imaginable. She's worked as a bartender, in hotels, cleaned homes, and even worked for a while as an exterminator, which wasn't a bad gig, but she gave it up after Brianne ingested some rat poisoning as an infant. Today, she sells solar panels.

The Ortizes lived in Kissimmee, Florida until they lost their home in the subprime mortgage crisis. After that, they lived "room-to-room" with family and friends for a while. Finally, they returned to New York and moved in with Brianne's dad's parents in a two-bedroom apart-ment in Bushwick until they got back on their feet and got their own place.

Brianne attended the High School for Law Enforcement and Public Safety in Jamaica, Queens, a charter school that aims to prepare stu-dents to be lawyers, which is what Brianne hopes to do. Though neither of Brianne's parents went to college, they set high expectations for their daughter. "I wasn't allowed to have bad grades," she told me. They did something right. Despite skipping her junior year, Brianne was valedic-torian of her class. In addition, she was class president, captain of the volleyball team, editor of the yearbook, and held a leadership position in basically every club at the school.

Brianne's unique in a million ways, but her college preparation is typical of kids from lower socioeconomic backgrounds. For starters, she only took one AP course—in English language and composition. Her high school only offered two others—U.S. history and environ-mental science—and the way they structured the requirements, it was impossible to graduate having taken more than two. That's typical. Schools where more than three-quarters of the students qualify for free or reduced lunch—a standard measure of a school's wealth—offer an average of four AP classes. By contrast, schools where less than a quarter of the students qualify for reduced lunch offer an average of twelve. About half of these schools offer more than sixteen AP courses. Approximately 10 percent offer twenty-six or more. (The College Board only offers thirty-six.)

Brianne only took the SAT twice—because that was the limit on fee waivers. She received only the most modest training for the exam from an organization called Sponsors for Education Opportunities, one among an array of nonprofits that tries to close the opportunity gap for underserved and underrepresented communities. The preparation consisted of a pair of three-hour sessions on Saturdays during which "they explained the basics of the exam." No private tutoring for Brianne. That's also quite typical. I interviewed approximately fifty John Jay students for this book. None took the SAT or ACT more than twice. Only one took a prep course—a mom-and-pop-type operation geared toward Asian students. It was no Princeton Review.

Despite taking the exam cold, Brianne managed a 1310, which put her around the ninetieth percentile. That score in combination with her grades and background would have given her a shot at some elite colleges, but no one coached her on how to play the admissions game. "I never had a this-is-what-we're going-to-do-with-your-career conversation with my guidance counselor," she says. Brianne applied to about ten colleges—half of what most suburban kids would. The only reach she got into was the Macaulay Honors College.

Macaulay's tough to get into—the average SAT score for the class of 2020 was over 1410—but it's a pretty good deal for those who make it. The program covers full tuition, a laptop, a cultural passport, and gives students access to an opportunity fund for travel and experiential learning. Students in the program get a dual degree—one from their home college and a second from Macaulay. Since its founding in 2001, it's been consistently ranked among the top honors programs in the country.

It seems fair to say that Brianne has made the most of the opportunity. She has a 3.8 GPA and runs about as many clubs as she did in high school. When she landed in my honors ethics class at the start of her sophomore year, I saw her potential immediately. She told me that I was the first college professor to tell her that she was smart, which made me even more determined to see her make good. In Brianne's case, I've set the bar quite high. Apologies to AOC, but I've publicly predicted that she'll be the first Latina senator from New York. First, though, we needed to get her into law school. That means excelling on the Law School Admission Test—the LSAT—which tests many of the same skills as the SAT.

I asked John Katzman whether he might know a tutor willing to help Brianne. Katzman is currently the CEO of Noodle Pros, a studio he founded as an umbrella for several education-related companies. It's the second business he's started since selling Princeton Review. First, he began 2U, which helped universities develop online degree programs. Then he left and started a new company to compete with them. Katzman's one of a kind.

Katzman introduced me to Lisa Liberati, who normally charges about three hundred dollars an hour but quickly agreed to tutor Brianne pro bono. "It's nice to do one for the other team," she said. Liberati's from the other team herself. A proud graduate of Forest Ridge Convent of the Sacred Heart in Renton, Washington, she remembers being pulled out of parochial school when her dad lost his job at Honeywell and put back after he had a good day at Longacres racetrack. She's about as cynical as you could imagine regarding the tests she coaches people for. "The SAT most reliably predicts parental income," she says. "As long as schools need to fill their budgets, they need a way to pretend it's a meritocracy and still figure out who can pay."

Liberati's also way cooler than any tutor you've ever met. She majored in theatre at Dartmouth, and, after a brief stint as a stockbroker, worked a variety of Hollywood jobs. These included gigs as a film distributor for the company that marketed *Stop Making Sense,* as a project developer for Frank Mancuso Jr.—who produced *Species* and several of the *Friday the 13th* sequels, and as an assistant to magicians Penn and Teller. In the late nineties, she caught the bridge bug and wanted a job that would allow her to balance playing professionally. She'd worked for Princeton Review in college, and tutoring fit the bill. For the record, Liberati got a 1500 on the SAT, despite only taking the exam once and not taking a course.

Liberati and Brianne let me eavesdrop on several of their sessions. I didn't take Princeton Review either, but some of Liberati's advice might be familiar to those of you who did. Liberati spent a lot of time talking with Brianne about how to approach the exam strategically. "One of the skills the LSAT is testing is time management," she told Brianne. "On every section there are ways that the test is there to mess with students who need to do things in order." It's a key insight. All the questions count the same on the LSAT, as they do on the SAT, so there's no advantage to spending extra time on a hard question than an easy one. On the reading comprehension section, a related trap is reading to understand. Liberati advocated "working" a passage as opposed to reading it. She encouraged Brianne to read the *New York Times* science section to get used to the sorts of passages she'd encounter, and she talked very specifically about collecting data on her own performance so she could decide which types of questions to prioritize. "Be a scientist," Liberati said. "Observe yourself."

But what really distinguished Liberati, from my perspective, was the emotional support that she offered. Brianne also regarded it as the most important part of their sessions. It was clear that they clicked almost immediately, and Liberati often reminded Brianne that the test was a game and not a referendum on who she was.

It's hard to argue with the results. Brianne took the LSAT for the first time in the summer of 2020, as part of an enrichment program run by John Jay. She took it for the second time in the summer of 2021, after working with Liberati. Her score went up by seven points. That may not sound like much, but scores on the LSAT range between 120 and 180 and are clustered in the middle. She'd moved up twenty-six percentiles. In practical terms, it meant that Brianne had gone from a marginal candidate for law school to a near-certain admit to a top-tier school.

In six months.

Katzman thinks that he might have thought about the SAT and ACT more than anyone else alive. They built his house, as he likes to say. Even still, he's been calling to eliminate the tests for decades. The exams, he argues, give elite colleges a justification to let in who they want to let in.

But he doesn't think that's their biggest problem. He's even more concerned with how these tests dictate what schools teach.

"A single curriculum is ludicrous," Katzman says. "The test is the dog when it should be the tail. Schools are teaching to the test and constructing their curricula accordingly." Katzman advocates a marketplace approach to testing where students can choose among a big basket of exams that operate with transparency; that aren't necessarily multiple choice, which was the best technology in the 1920s, and that don't appear to make finer distinctions than they really can or should. "What's most important," he says, "is what's going to be relevant and interesting to you."

Katzman acknowledges that some teachers would teach to these tests but that, he says, is precisely what they should do so long as the tests sync with how teachers would normally approach the material. The SAT and ACT are best taught by super-smart, specialized tutors like Liberati who understand the idiosyncrasies of the test. "We want college to be an engine for social mobility," Katzman says. "When tests begin to jibe with school curricula, underwriting test prep for disadvantaged kids would simply mean properly funding K-12 education."

Katzman's larger point—let's call it Katzman's Second Theorem—is that the types of tests valued by the college admissions process shape communities. Given this, it would be desirable to shape them in virtuous ways. The current system does the opposite.

Consider the example of special accommodations for test taking. When the *Wall Street Journal* analyzed data from nine thousand public schools, it found that students from affluent districts qualified for so-called "504 designations" (after Section 504 of the U.S. Rehabilitation Act of 1973, which prohibited discrimination based on disability) at about triple the rate as in poor districts. At Scarsdale High School—recognized as the richest town on the East Coast for the second year in a row by Bloomberg—more than 20 percent of the students qualify for extra time. That's because getting certified can cost more than ten thousand dollars. People get what they pay for. Psychologists are supposed to act as gatekeepers, but the superintendent of Newton North, where about a third of students get extra time, says that everyone who gets an evaluation leaves with a recommendation for special accommodations. According to the Massachusetts Department of Justice, Rick Singer routinely encouraged his clients to get certified for extra time.

This seems trivial until you remember Liberati's admonition that part of how the SAT and LSAT achieve variance is by setting traps for people who can't manage their time. The ACT reports that about a sixth of test-takers don't manage to finish on time. But neither the College Board nor the organization that runs the ACT (called, creatively, the ACT) informs colleges who receives extra time on the exam. Requests for special accommodations on the SAT tripled between 2010 and 2018. The College Board approves 94 percent of these requests.

The pattern is unmistakable. People move to the suburbs to brandish the kinds of academic credentials that elite colleges choose to value, even though they have no connection to college performance potential. They move in search of higher SAT scores, access to AP exams, and schools with other rich kids—even as they lament the de facto segregation of American schools. The districts respond by offering more and more AP courses, by tracking students so that rich children can avoid the taint of the few middle- and low-income children who find their way into affluent suburban schools, and by inflating grades. Between 1998 and 2016, the average GPA in suburban schools rose from 3.25 to 3.36. In city schools, it barely moved. Grade inflation is most extreme at the wealthiest high schools. Affluent, suburban school districts do all of this because they understand the tacit pact underlying American education. Elite colleges will value credentials that are only available to the rich. Suburbs, in turn, will produce these disparate opportunities for families, like the Petrillis, that move there.

Nowhere is this more evident than in how they teach children to play.

6

Green Fences—The Games Kids Play

Staring out the window of the Acela, Simon Cataldo was on the verge of despair. He'd joined Teach for America as a true believer in the value of connecting people across race and class lines. At Concord-Carlisle High School, just north of Walden Pond, Cataldo had seen firsthand the benefits of programs like METCO, a voluntary desegregation initiative that had been operating in the Boston area since 1966. When Teach for America asked Cataldo where he wanted to be placed, he told them that it was Harlem or bust.

After his assignment came through, Cataldo rented an apartment on 125th Street and Lenox Avenue, near the Apollo Theatre, and spent the summer enthusiastically preparing to teach chemistry. At a staff development workshop four days before the start of the semester, Greg Hodge, the iconic tough-love principal of Frederick Douglas Academy, called Cataldo forward and introduced him to the faculty as the new special ed math teacher.

Cataldo scrambled to learn the curriculum, but it had been a struggle. "The first day was a fucking disaster," he recalled. The kids had wildly disparate skill levels. Occasionally the class devolved into violence. Senior teachers observed him from the back of the room, but they offered more sympathy than constructive ideas. In late September, a seventeen-year-old named John, who came to school every fourth day or so, looked at Cataldo and said, "They must have given up because they sent us you."

"He was so right," Cataldo said, reflecting. "It was an incredibly astute comment about society."

To make himself a better teacher, Cataldo worked day and night, so constantly that he planned on skipping Thanksgiving. When he decided at the last minute to spend the holiday with his family in Massachusetts, only first-class tickets were available. As New York receded from view, Cataldo ended up chatting with a finance-type from Brown Brothers Harriman, the oldest private bank in the country. It's easy to imagine Cataldo making a positive impression. He's clean cut, athletic, oozes integrity. When they arrived in Boston, the man handed him a business card and invited Cataldo to stay in touch.

The invitation led to some serious soul-searching. Cataldo spent his holiday reflecting on his choice to teach and whether he—or anyone for that matter—could make it work. He said to himself, "I need to do something drastic to change this or I need to quit." But Cataldo's great-grandfather had been head of the dockworkers' union in Boston—quitting wasn't in his blood. He resolved to make it work. On his way back to New York, Cataldo decided upon an extremely unconventional strategy to accomplish his goal—he would teach his students lacrosse.

Eleven kids showed up for the first day of practice—more kids than they had sticks, none of which had proper stringing. Their "field" was a handball court, a block away from the school, near the Harlem River Drive. Lacrosse balls are extremely bouncy, so teaching the game on pavement is essentially impossible. Many of the kids got bloody hands and noses. None of it mattered. "They became obsessed right away," Cataldo recalled.

More and more kids began to show. By December, he had a full team. In the new year, Cataldo looked to find a game for his squad. Every coach told him the same thing. "I really respect what you're doing, but no." Finally, in April, the coach of the JV team at Mount Saint Michael Academy, a Catholic high school in the Bronx, agreed to play Cataldo's motley crew. One parent came to the game—the mother of Cataldo's best player, who got concussed almost as soon as the game started.

(He'd later become captain of the Haverford team.) Frederick Douglas lost seven to five. Again, none of it mattered. "We were so happy about it," Cataldo said.

Lacrosse changed everything. The students respected Cataldo. He, in turn, gave them responsibility and independence. "I turned my classroom into a space where they always had a choice," Cataldo said. "They self-selected into the work that they were intellectually and emotionally prepared for." At the end of the year, the students got the highest math scores that had ever been recorded by special ed students at the school.

When he finished his tour with Teach for America, Cataldo spent an extra year at Frederick Douglas Academy coaching lacrosse and organizing a nonprofit to continue his work. Today, Harlem Lacrosse and Leadership has programs on twenty sites in five cities, serving about 1,300 students each year, less than 10 percent of whom are white. It is far and away the largest provider of opportunity in lacrosse to young men and women of color.

Cataldo adamantly states that the main objective of his organization is to help kids, not simply to promote diversity in the sport. "We're not a grow-the-game organization," he says. "We're a grow-the-child organization." Nevertheless, almost single-handedly, Cataldo and his program have boosted diversity in college lacrosse. If you count the numbers, it's possible to draw a straight line between the increased participation of athletes of color and the HLL graduates who have gone on to play in college. In 2012, the year after the program began, of the 5,169 American college lacrosse players, 115 players—60 women and 55 men—were Black. That's 2.2 percent.

By 2019, that had grown to 211 out of 6,971 players—or 3 percent.

"Stickball" was developed by the Algonquian tribes of the St. Lawrence Valley in the seventeenth century to toughen up young warriors. As the game spread to other tribes across eastern North America and the Great Lakes, it took on other functions. Some indigenous peoples played it at festivals, occasionally with gambling involved. For others it had religious significance. Occasionally it was used as a way of settling intertribal disputes.

From historical accounts, the game sounds like vaguely organized chaos—and a lot of fun. As many as one hundred thousand players participated in a single contest. The rules—if one can call them that— were simple. No one could touch the ball with their hands and nothing was out of bounds. A ball was tossed into the air, signaling the start of the game. The players then tried to advance it toward their goal— generally a large rock or tree, or, in the Southeastern version, a pole, often adorned by the figure of a sacred animal. Because of the enormous size of the teams, these scrums moved slowly. It didn't help that passing was regarded as a trick and dodging an opponent as an act of cowardice. Not surprisingly, the games often lasted until sunset.

Native tribes identified the game by the techniques employed in their version, as in dehuntshigwa'es—"men hit a rounded object"—the Onondaga name, or by its function, as in tewaarathon—"little brother of war"—the Iroquois designation. In 1637, a French Jesuit missionary named Jean de Brébeuf watched the Huron tribe play a game and called it *la crosse,* which translates to "the stick." This came from the French name for field hockey—le jeu de la crosse or "the game of the stick." De Brébeuf wasn't very original, but he was white and so the name stuck.

Lacrosse remained the domain of the Indigenous Americans until some English-speaking Canadians noticed the Mohawks playing the game and took it up themselves. In 1860, a Canadian dentist named George Beers, who'd organized a lacrosse club in Montreal, codified the rules—reducing the number of players by several thousand to twelve— and ushered in the "modern era." In universal sports lingo, "modern" means played by white people.

Today, lacrosse is just about the whitest sport in America. Overall, 84 percent of college men's lacrosse players are white. Merely 4 percent are Black. The representation among head coaches is even worse. Of the 366 head coaches in the U.S., just thirteen are Black. Ninety-five percent are white. In the women's game, the statistics are about the same. When one looks at Division III schools, which are defined by their decision not to award athletic scholarships, the picture is bleaker still. Among the 235 Division III men's lacrosse programs, 87 percent of the players and 96 percent of the coaches are white.

Among the myths of college in America—and there are many—one of the biggest is that college sports increase the diversity of the student body. People believe this because, by and large, the only college sports they watch on television are men's basketball and football. Indeed, basketball and football are quite diverse. Only 46 percent of college football players are white. (Eighty-five percent of the coaches are, but that's another story.) In basketball, just 39 percent of the players are white (and 79 percent of the coaches). But these statistics mask a larger athletic system that is deeply and profoundly white. Two dynamics drive these disparities.

The first is that sports at Division III schools are significantly less diverse than at Division I schools. While whites are in the minority in college football, at the DIII level they're a significant majority. As Figure 1 shows, overall, 16 percent of college athletes are Black. At the DIII level, only 10 percent are. These numbers have a significant impact on diversity because these schools are so small.

It's helpful to think of college admissions in terms of buckets—a bucket for the children of alumni, a bucket for budding mathematicians, and a bucket for the number of students from poor and working-class families the college chooses to admit. Each, in a sense, runs a separate

FIGURE 1. REPRESENTATION IN COLLEGE ATHLETICS

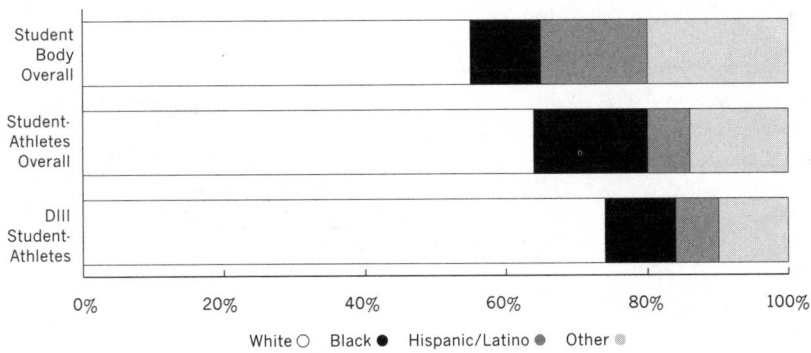

admissions contest. At Division III schools, the biggest bucket is filled
with athletes—all participating in white-dominated sports. At Williams
College in Massachusetts, 35 percent of the students participate in intercollegiate sports. At Trinity College, outside Hartford, Connecticut,
40 percent do.

The second dynamic is that every sport other than Division I basketball and football is dominated by white athletes. As Figure 2 shows,
hockey is 75 percent white, while baseball is 80 percent white. The disparities are even stronger at Division III schools. For example, DIII
college baseball is 85 percent white. Many sports such as golf, skiing,
and women's water polo have hardly any Black participation. Of the
approximately six thousand college field hockey players in 2020, a total
of 119 were Black and 157 identified as Hispanic or Latino. In women's
ice hockey, the numbers are even worse. Among the 2,585 women who
played college ice hockey in 2020, 35 identified as Asian, 25 identified as
Hispanic or Latino, and 10 identified as Black. Whatever opportunity
college sports writ large may offer isn't going to people of color.

Moreover, the trend is going in the wrong direction. Take Harvard as

FIGURE 2. REPRESENTATION IN SELECTED SPORTS

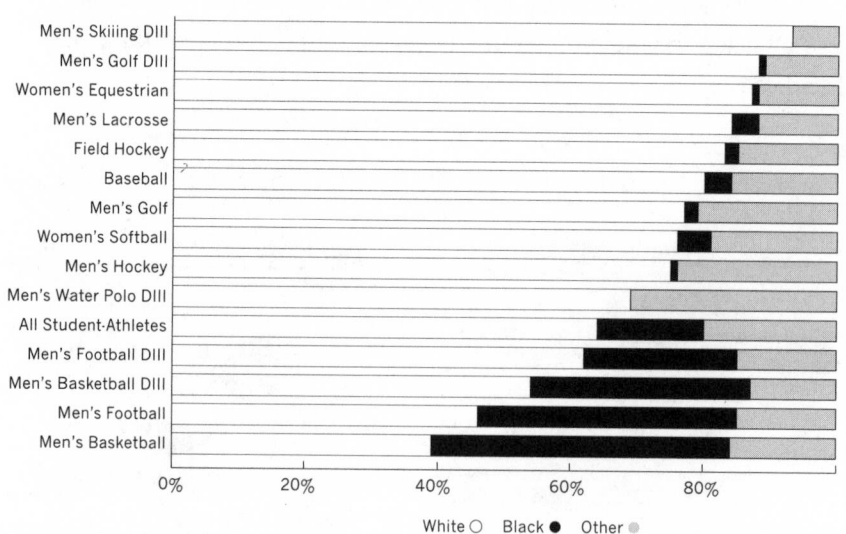

an example. Since 1980, it's added men's and women's teams in water polo and volleyball, and women's teams in golf and rugby. These are all among the whitest college sports. During the 2019 season, a total of fourteen Black water polo players competed at the intercollegiate level—ten women and four men.

It's tempting to understand these statistics and trends as simple racism. In their effect, they're highly racist. But I've never met a college coach who wouldn't take a player who'd help them win. In truth, the race disparities are the surface manifestation of a deeper, far more pernicious inequality that's embedded into the very structure of American society. Entire communities are organized to produce lacrosse players, fencers, and rowers—precisely because elite colleges choose to value them. It'd be so much easier to combat the inequities in college sports if they were the product of overt racism. This is, rather, a secret system, known primarily by the affluent, and which they alone possess the resources to navigate.

To help us understand how it works, we're going to need the help of someone who's seen the system from the inside.

Kirsten Hextrum is tall. She's also brilliant and charming, but you'll probably notice the tall thing first. The crew coach at UC Berkeley did. When he met her at an athletics department event, to which Hextrum had tagged along with her father, the coach encouraged her to come out for the team. Her dad, who'd been a star football player at Berkeley, explained that she'd only rowed for a week at a camp in middle school and hadn't liked it very much. It didn't matter. As Hextrum remembered it, "He saw two hugely tall parents with a hugely tall daughter, and said, 'Have her show up at practice.'"

Hextrum had always had a bit of a chip on her shoulder about sports. She'd swam and played soccer as a kid and joined the basketball and volleyball teams in high school. "But I was never as good as I thought I should have been," she said, "And I didn't feel a lot of joy." Crew seemed different. It was all-consuming. The team practiced six days a week, twice a day—first at 5:00 a.m. and then again in the afternoon. "It wasn't fun fitness," Hextrum said. "The goal was to break down your muscles. If you weren't in pain, it wasn't working." But she liked it. "Sports started to become an affirming community," she told me.

After a few months, Hextrum made the freshman boat. In the spring they won the Pac-10 team championship. Success spiraled. During her sophomore and junior years, the team won the NCAA championships. She sat in the seven seat, which had a special connection to the eight seat in the stern and required lots of intelligence to time the stroke. This she had in abundance. "I was never the strongest or the fittest," Hextrum said, "but I was also never going to slow the boat down."

After graduation, she did a stint as an event planner and then gravitated back to Berkeley, where she took a low-paid internship in the athletic director's office and a side job tutoring. She didn't love working in the athletic department, but she found working with college athletes fulfilling. Soon Hextrum was promoted to a full-time academic support role. Her charges were ten Black football players, all with the highest academic need. Many of them couldn't deal with a college-level reading load, but Berkeley, unlike other big-time sports programs, didn't have an easy academic pathway for athletes. They'd been admitted to fail.

Meanwhile, Hextrum said, "they were put through a dehumanizing experience." She'd thought crew was the most a body could endure, but the football coaches expected just as much physically, while imposing their own rigorous curriculum—playbooks and meetings and film sessions. The players had the narrowest window for academics—eight to ten o'clock at night, when they were understandably exhausted. Few had support networks to draw upon. Several had family members who'd been murdered. Most had financial need. All had encountered racism and anti-athlete sentiment on the campus.

"I had bought into the meritocracy to this point," Hextrum recalled. "Now I started to see the cracks in the system." For her master's degree, she examined academic outcomes for athletes at Berkeley and found that Black football players had the lowest graduation rates. She published her results and made some waves. Her advisor, Murray Sperber, told Hextrum she should get a PhD. Sperber, who'd gained notoriety as a critic of Indiana University for coddling its legendary—and legendarily abusive—basketball coach Bobby Knight, told Hextrum she had a knack for stirring the pot. Hextrum knew exactly what she wanted to take on next.

"I wanted to test the NCAA's basic premise," she told me. "It says that combining elite academics and elite athletics produces a better experience both for the individual and the institution." Like elite colleges, the NCAA also consciously cultivates an image of itself as an avenue of upward mobility. "I just wasn't seeing this as a reality," she said.

Hextrum didn't just mean that it didn't work for poor students of color. She didn't think it worked for anyone. Personally, she'd found it almost impossible to balance the demands of crew with academics. So, she set out to test the NCAA's narrative by speaking to the athletes who were most primed to succeed. Naturally she gravitated to rowers. As a point of comparison, she also interviewed track-and-field athletes. These conversations led to Hextrum's aha moment. "I started to see these amazing similarities," she said. They all came from similar schools and backgrounds. Their experiences were the same as the rowers. "It got me thinking, 'Whoa, what does this mean?'" Her study changed from an examination of how universities fail athletes of color to how affluent communities advantage white athletes.

Hextrum's book, *Special Admission: How College Sports Recruitment Favors White Suburban Athletes*, is about as damning an indictment of higher education and the American Dream as you'll ever read. Operation Varsity Blues was redundant, she argues. Successfully recruited athletes "did not directly pay for admission but instead indirectly purchased access over their lifetime." How? By living in suburbs.

When Hextrum crunched the data, she found that college athletes were even more likely than college students to have come from wealthy communities. Less than 3 percent of track athletes came from communities where family incomes averaged less than $50,000 annually. Rowers came from even more affluent communities. Overwhelmingly, they were white suburbs.

Hextrum found that affluent suburbs conferred advantages on athletes in a variety of ways. Most importantly, they gave them space in which to play. Coaches say that one commonality of top athletes is that they play a lot of sports as kids. For that to happen, there need to be fields, playgrounds, and gyms. One rower Hextrum interviewed described her community as having twenty-seven pools and two lakes surrounding a recreation center. "It's literally as suburbia as you can get," she told Hextrum.

It also helps for the community to offer the sport that you're aiming to play in college. Hextrum is the rare example of someone who picked one up in college and excelled. As a parent, if you're only interested in maximizing the chance that your child will play a college sport, you should hook them into fencing, gymnastics, beach volleyball, or rowing. Consider this point of reference, as presented in Table 8: For every one hundred high school basketball players, there's about one college roster spot available. By contrast, there are about 54 roster spots for every 100 high school male rowers, and 264 for every 100 female rowers. You read that correctly—there are more seats for women in college crew than high school rowers to fill them. Only .06 percent of public high schools have a rowing team. Another point of reference: 84 percent of girls from low-income urban schools report having no physical education classes in eleventh or twelfth grade.

Having access to a team doesn't mean that everyone gets to participate. Many sports require kids to pay to play. Rowing clubs routinely charge $5,000 or more per year. (A shell—a long, narrow boat designed specifically for racing—can cost as much as $65,000.) Even the more egalitarian sports can be expensive. In baseball and basketball, private youth leagues have largely replaced low-cost community organizations. Even track programs can cost over $1,000 per year. This neither includes the cost of the equipment nor the time that's required—an average of about seventeen hours per week, Hextrum found. That isn't in the cards if you have to work or care for a family member. Many athletes need to take a gap year after graduation to physically mature—that's expensive, too.

Still, none of this is quite so maddening as the club system, which has come to dominate lacrosse and many specialized sports. These clubs

TABLE 8. HIGH SCHOOL TEAMS AND ROSTER SPOTS FOR SELECTED SPORTS

SPORT	RATIO OF COLLEGE TO HS TEAMS		RATIO OF COLLEGE TO HS ROSTER SPOTS	
	MEN	WOMEN	MEN	WOMEN
Baseball	1.8%	0.0%	2.2%	0.0%
Football	1.8%	0.0%	2.8%	0.0%
Basketball	1.9%	1.9%	1.0%	1.2%
Rugby	2.1%	3.2%	59.4%	19.3%
Lacrosse	2.4%	4.1%	3.0%	3.8%
Gymnastics	14.7%	3.9%	18.7%	5.9%
Fencing	17.4%	21.9%	16.2%	20.2%
Beach Volleyball	0.0%	42.5%	0.0%	53.9%
Equestrian	0.0%	82.6%	0.0%	126.5%
Rowing	39.7%	118.9%	54.7%	263.9%

run practices and games year-round. The cost of membership and travel to tournaments can easily run more than $10,000 per year. Dom Starsia, the winningest lacrosse coach in NCAA history, told me that the club system is the single biggest change that he's seen during his near-half century in the sport. Clubs arose because competition for lacrosse players is an unraveling market, a concept that we'll consider in more depth in the context of early admissions. In simple terms, it means that coaches are recruiting earlier and earlier. Before the turn of the century, Starsia basically recruited only high school juniors and seniors. Now coaches sometimes recruit players in middle school. Because these players are too young to play on their varsity teams, they need another way to be noticed. Hence clubs.

"All of a sudden," Starsia says, "it went from high school coaches who were beholden to athletic directors and high school rules to club coaches who were beholden to making a profit. They could literally charge whatever they wanted." Without access to a club, a young player has no

chance of getting noticed. I'd say "almost no chance" if NCAA regulations didn't preclude camps from subsidizing poor players' attendance,
as they do. "Lacrosse had been a suburban sport to begin with," Starsia
said. "The changes made the economics of playing lacrosse even more
harsh."

To Hextrum, even more outrageous than the ways that suburbs and
club teams restrict access to sports is that all of this occurs in secret. You
won't find a webpage explaining that the way to get into Johns Hopkins
is to play for a club that acts as a feeder. There's no portal through which
to submit your tapes. Most high school athletes will never even speak
with a college coach. Hextrum found that the affluent kids in her study
had learned how to catch a coach's eye by proactively contacting them,
sending portfolios, and constructing narratives of teamwork. In other
words, they'd learned how to network—that's the crux of the advantage
their communities confer. "Sports are an endemic part of white, suburban parenting," Hextrum says.

Indeed, Manhasset, where I lived for nine years, is organized around
lacrosse. The annual game with its archrival, Garden City (one of the
whitest districts in America), is the highlight of the year. The star players are known in the community. The varsity team has three coaches.
Amazingly, in the middle of the pandemic, when the district cut $1 mil-
lion from its budget because of fears over shortfalls, they authorized an
additional $15,000 to spend on a goalie coach.

Hextrum, drawing upon the French sociologist Pierre Bourdieu, sees
these expenditures as acts of violence. I'm married to a sociologist, and
I've spent the past year interviewing them, so I'm as keen as anyone to
avoid any high theory, but there's no avoiding Bourdieu, who has influenced almost every academic that you'll meet in this book. In Bourdieu's terms, sports are serving as "legitimating" institutions. They take
a form of capital that doesn't have direct economic value—like SAT
scores or lacrosse prowess (there's no money in professional lacrosse,
after all) and turn it into something that does, like a degree from Johns
Hopkins. The violence is in telling everyone who doesn't have access
to SAT tutors or lacrosse clubs that degrees are earned and that the
system is just, denying the reality that it's arbitrary and elitist. Most

of the time we don't feel the violence, but it's constantly at work, like when elite employers value the hard work that's required to play college sports, as Lauren Rivera found they do, and diminish the hard work that's required to pay one's way through college.

"Our attention is drawn to the shuffling cards, and we miss the game that was rigged from the start," Hextrum says. "Parents can purchase admission for athletes. It just occurs over a lifespan."

But, you say, athletics make colleges lots of money, which they use to create opportunity for poorer students. Another myth. It's an easy one to fall for—there are some eye-popping numbers out there. University of Texas football grossed about $156 million in 2019. But football and basketball are the only money-making programs, and only for a handful of Division I schools. Every other program loses money. And sports are expensive to run. UT Austin spent about $175 million to generate $215 million in overall revenue, including $15 million on coaches' salaries. Head coach Steve Sarkisian makes about $6 million per year, and that's not even the ceiling. Alabama coach Nick Saban makes over $9 million a year.

Merely twenty-five athletic departments turned a profit in 2019. All of those were in either the Southeastern Conference (SEC), Atlantic Coast Conference (ACC), Big Ten, Pac-12, or Big 12—the so-called "autonomy" conferences, referring to a 2014 NCAA decision that gave them freedom to make their own rules regarding scholarships, recruitment, and staffing. Among these schools, the median profit was $7.9 million. The other forty "autonomy" schools lost an average of $15.9 million. Every Division II and Division III athletic program lost money. At DIII schools, these losses represented about 5 percent of the schools' operating costs. What makes this even more incomprehensible is that schools are hemorrhaging money on sports even though they get their principal labor for free. Most athletes, many of whom could play professionally but for explicit restrictions by the professional leagues, never make a dime. (A 2021 Supreme Court decision found that the NCAA could not restrict colleges from compensating athletes for academic-related expenses.)

At least they're the beneficiaries of scholarship aid, you might say. Again, not true. Very little of the money is going to athletes of color. In total, DI schools awarded $2.66 billion in athletic scholarships in 2019, an increase of $1.6 billion since the NCAA began collecting data in 2003. Eighty-six percent of the athletes play nonrevenue—read white-dominated—sports. Overall, in DI, 60.4 percent of scholarship recipients are white. Among women, 67 percent of scholarship athletes are white.

The truth is nearly the opposite of the myth. Athletics cost colleges lots of money, and much of the expense is the opportunity that they create for affluent white students. Still, that's not the extent of how sports corrupt colleges. Many create special, less rigorous academic pathways for athletes—like at North Carolina, where athletes took over 1,800 sham classes between 1999 and 2011. All make massive compromises in their admissions processes. Among Harvard applicants with average academic qualifications, athletes are admitted at about one thousand times the rate of non-athletes.

So why do colleges retain sports? We'll talk later about some of the deep psychological and institutional dynamics that are at work. Let's just say for now that every college academic and administrator with whom I spoke noted how problematic they are. One conversation stands out in my mind. Charley Ellis was a Yale trustee from 1997 to 2008. He's exactly the sort of person you'd want to run your board. He made his fortune by advocating passive investing—that is, by investing in an index, like one that tracks the Dow Jones, rather than speculating or day-trading. He's incredibly nice, and our conversation was pleasant, but not overly critical of elite colleges—until we turned to discussing sports.

"I think sports are just wonderful and athletes are terrific," Ellis said, "But I think we've got a serious distortion in admissions, particularly with the big sports." Until 1970 or so, Ellis said, Yale teams were filled "with the right kids to have at Yale" who happened to be good athletes. "But," he continued, "over the last thirty to forty years, there's been an enormous shift toward 'get the athletes and then be sure to talk to the coaches and the faculty to be sure the grades aren't all that bad.'"

"It's a travesty," Ellis concluded. "And the worst of it is, the kids all know it."

Near the end of the first of our many Zoom conversations, during the winter of our collective discontent, Cataldo expressed ambivalence to me about sharing his story. He'd seen firsthand the almost insurmountable obstacles confronting impoverished children of color. Maybe, he worried, the success of Harlem Lacrosse would signal that the problem of access in high school and college sports had been solved. Maybe, he said, it would simply prove the American Dream. It's a reasonable concern. After all, elite colleges seize upon narratives like the Liz Murray story to create the illusion that they're engines of upward mobility. Maybe they'd do the same with the students who'd benefitted from his program.

I argued—with some trepidation—that the Harlem Lacrosse saga proved something different. Cataldo isn't the sort of person you want to get into an argument with. After serving as managing editor of the *Virginia Law Review*, he held a prestigious clerkship on the First Circuit Court of Appeals and then became a trial lawyer at the Department of Justice. Today, he's a partner in the Boston office of former U.S. senator John Ashcroft's law firm and a candidate for Massachusetts State Senate—at the age of thirty-four. My point was that Harlem Lacrosse had benefitted from his unique leadership and skill set. His program had changed the course of hundreds of student lives and had done more than any other to bring the sport to poor students of color. Yet it had barely moved the dial at the college level.

Maybe, as John Friedman suggests, the lesson of lacrosse is something different entirely. "The institution is not falling apart because we have lacrosse players on campus," he says, noting that athletes as a group are less academically prepared. "The question," Friedman continues, "is whether you could do that same thing focusing on economic diversity. Not totally changing what you're doing—just bringing in a few more people. You already give legs up to people who are legacies, people who are athletes. What would happen if you gave that same advantage to kids from low-income families?"

You'd change the game, that's for sure. What would these sports look like without the incentive of an advantage of college admissions? Probably Quidditch or ultimate frisbee or rugby before it became a varsity team—club sports played on open fields by students for the love of the game, as they are played, exclusively, at every European university. Imagine club volleyball at Harvard. It's easy enough to do since that's how it was played until 1980.

If elite colleges stopped recruiting athletes altogether would the games really suffer? It depends on what you value in sports. College sports began as spectacle. Ivy League and DIII colleges have implicitly conceded that, even today, winning isn't the most important goal. They reject athletic scholarships, thereby existing in a weird, in-between state in which they don't field the best possible teams but also confer an undue advantage onto affluent, white athletes.

Cataldo kept talking to me. For him, it's about building community and teaching leadership and responsibility. When he played in high school, his mother found the game aesthetically pleasing, but he didn't share her view. "I never found lacrosse especially beautiful," Cataldo told me. "But I found beauty in what my students did in the game."

7

The Well-Rounded Man

When he was eight years old, Michael Wang decided he wanted to go to Harvard. "I don't know if it's the Asian stereotype," he told me, "but I saw it as an avenue to social mobility." Though he probably didn't think of it in these terms when he was eight, Michael means the type of top-end mobility that we discussed in Chapter 3. Specifically, he wanted to be a neurosurgeon. Because he was that sort of kid, he read several peer-reviewed articles about cloning and checked the authors' credentials. When he saw that many of the researchers had gone to Harvard, he knew that was the college for him.

From that point forward, Michael's parents made it their life's work to help their only child achieve his goal. Michael's dad—who goes by Jeff—had a sense of what it would take. He'd come to the United States from Shanghai in the 1980s, as part of the wave of Chinese students who emigrated to the West when Deng Xiaoping implemented the Four Modernizations following Mao Zedong's death. Jeff got a PhD in physics from the University of Wisconsin–Madison, worked in banking for a while, and then transitioned to tutoring math and science. Today he runs a Mathnasium franchise in Union City, California, where Michael grew up. Many of his students went on to top colleges, and Jeff emulated what he saw. Ann Lareau would call it concerted cultivation. Amy Chua might say that he became a Tiger Dad.

In fifth grade, Jeff persuaded the school district to let Michael take algebra. Each day, Jeff picked his son up at his elementary school and drove him to the middle school for his advanced math class. In seventh grade, he picked Michael up at the middle school and drove him to James Logan High School to take Algebra II. By his sophomore year, Michael had finished BC Calculus. He ended up taking fifteen AP courses. Michael's 4.67 GPA made him salutatorian of his class. He got a perfect 36 on the ACT and a 2230 out of 2400 on the SAT. Each score placed him squarely in the ninety-ninth percentile. He also played piano, debated at a high level, and founded a math club. In the fall of 2012, Michael sent off his college applications—about twenty-five in all—with optimism and the satisfaction of knowing he'd done everything within his power to increase his chances of getting into a top college.

To say he was disappointed by the replies would be a vast understatement. By any ordinary standard, Michael did quite well, and he's soberer about the experience in retrospect, but at the time he felt devastated. Yale said no. Princeton said no. Stanford said no. Harvard put him on the waitlist. Then it said no. Columbia did the same thing. He wasn't consoled by Berkeley's offer of a free ride or by Penn and Georgetown's offers of half scholarships. "I was definitely disappointed receiving that many rejections," Michael told me. "I thought to myself, 'what more can I do at this point?'" He decided to go to Williams, which offered to cover 90 percent of his tuition.

If Michael Wang's story ended here, it'd be typical of high achievers in the modern era, in which acceptance rates hover around 5 percent. At this point, though, Michael did something decidedly atypical: he wrote the colleges asking why he'd been rejected and suggested that he'd been the victim of discrimination. Ten years later, he still has their replies. Yale's dean of admissions wrote that the college believed that its policies "do not disadvantage Asian American students relative to majority white students in a holistic admissions review, and also that we are in compliance with all relevant legal requirements."

Not surprisingly, Yale's letter didn't make Michael feel much better. He obsessed about the matter during his freshman year. Over summer vacation, he read U.S. Supreme Court decisions on affirmative action and *The Chosen*, Berkeley sociologist Jerome Karabel's definitive history of college admissions at Harvard, Yale, and Princeton. All this further convinced Michael that the system was rigged against him, and that Asians were the new Jews of college admissions—undesirables whose numbers needed to be restricted lest they overrun the schools. Finally, in 2014, Michael filed a complaint with the Department of Education's Office for Civil Rights. "As recipients of federal funding," he wrote, "these private universities cannot discriminate on the basis of race, sex, gender, sexual orientation, age, disability, etc. Yet, they all resort to race-conscious admissions practices that violate existing federal laws and infringe upon my rights guaranteed by the Constitution." The universities, he said, were guilty of race-norming. Though Michael asked for his admissions decisions to be reconsidered without reference to race, he understood there was almost no chance of this happening. "My concern was helping out high school friends who were juniors," he says. "These policies affect a lot of people."

Investigators from three different offices of the Department of Education reached out to Michael. A lawyer in the Boston office told him that they'd been investigating Harvard since the 1990s, but as Michael puts it, they didn't have a smoking gun. He did what he could to advance the cause. In July, he wrote an op-ed in the *Mercury News* against SCA-5, a bill that would have reinstated affirmative action in California, which had been illegal since 1996. SCA-5 went down, but it soon became clear that Michael's civil complaint wasn't going to get anywhere.

All was not lost. Michael had caught the eye of Ed Blum. Blum is the only person I've ever heard of who's described in Wikipedia as a "litigant." He was the architect of *Shelby County v. Holder*, the 2013 Supreme Court decision that eviscerated the Voting Rights Act of 1965, and *Fisher v. University of Texas*, a 2016 decision that, but for Antonin Scalia's untimely death, would have gutted affirmative action. Blum called Michael at Williams, said that he was gathering potential plaintiffs for a lawsuit against Harvard, and asked whether Michael would be willing to serve as their spokesperson.

Michael said yes.

Students for Fair Admissions v. Harvard is the most significant challenge to affirmative action in a generation. Through discovery—the pretrial production of documents and deposition testimony—it also opened the first significant window into Harvard's admissions process. We'll discuss the legal issues the case raises in a bit. For now, let's peek at how Harvard makes its Mangalitsa sausage.*

Finding the right metaphor is challenging. Think federalism with a constitution that protects the rights of rich whites. Applications are divided into geographic dockets based on high school location. Each is initially reviewed by an admissions officer who rates the applicant based on academics; extracurriculars; athletics; personal qualities—including integrity, helpfulness, courage, kindness, empathy, self-confidence, maturity, and grit; and school support—meaning, basically, the strength of the applicant's recommendations. The first reader also gives a summary rating. Alumni interviewers separately score applicants on the same categories. The scores range from one to six, with one being the highest and plusses better than minuses. Very few people are given worse than a four. It's the admissions version of grade inflation.

Throughout the process, officers are allowed to give "tips" to applicants for "distinguishing excellences." These include capacity for leadership, creative ability, and geography. They also include economics, race, and ethnicity. This speaks directly to a 1978 Supreme Court decision, *University of California v. Bakke*, which held that quotas are unconstitutional, but that race could be considered as a "plus" factor. Harvard, like most elite colleges, also gives explicit preference to recruited athletes and the children of faculty, donors, and alumni. The latter are known as "legacies."

SFFA's claim against Harvard is simple: The Asian plaintiffs say the subjective admissions factors are stacked against them. The plaintiffs presented most of their statistical case through Peter Arcidiacono, an econometrician based at Duke. Arcidiacono testified that if Harvard relied solely on academics, Asian Americans would constitute more than half of its admitted classes, as opposed to the 20 percent who currently make it in. Race might be a plus factor for others, but for Asians it's a big minus.

---

* The world's most expensive sausage. I looked it up.

If you're skeptical about Arcidiacono's claim, consider this evidence from New York City. By state law, the sole criterion for admission to the city's eight specialized high schools is performance on the Specialized High School Admissions Test, or SHSAT. These eight schools include Brooklyn Tech—where my dad was principal, Bronx High School of Science—where my wife went, and Stuyvesant—which has the highest cutoff. In 2020, Asians filled 524 of the 766 available slots at Stuyvesant—that's 68 percent. It's fair to question, as many have, whether the SHSAT, like the SAT, is simply another instrument correlated with wealth, or whether any single factor should decide someone's fate, but it's undeniably strong evidence that Arcidiacono's claim has significant merit.

What held Asian American applicants back, Arcidiacono found, was their personal ratings. A lower share of them received a rating of one or two from an admissions officer than from any other racial or ethnic group. An investigation by the Department of Justice during the 1990s found a similar pattern. Asian applicants were presumed to be oriented solely toward math and science. They were routinely described as bland, flat, or unexciting, as in, "He's quiet and, of course, wants to be a doctor." Of all the factors Arcidiacono identified, nothing was quite so damning as to be labeled "standard strong." In a sample of 10 percent of the applicants to the class of 2018, 255 students were labeled as lacking the special sauce that made someone a Harvard man or woman. Of these, 114 were Asian American.

None got in.

Several months after SFFA filed its complaint, a company named Ivy Coach made fun of Michael Wang on its blog. Ivy Coach is one of the many private consulting firms that guides parents through the process of getting their kids into elite colleges and boarding schools. After CNBC reported that Ivy Coach charged over $100,000 for its services, the company boasted on its blog that the news station had "grossly underreported" their fees. When the *New York Post* reported that they charged a Vietnamese mother $1.5 million, Ivy Coach didn't deny it. Rather, they said on their blog that "they make absolutely no apologies" for what they charge. More than 20 percent of incoming Harvard freshmen who come from families making more than $250,000 a year report using a private admissions counselor like Ivy Coach.

Ivy Coach said that Michael made a fundamental error in how he marketed himself. In emphasizing his piano ability and debating skills, he'd presented himself as well-rounded "when that is the precise opposite of what schools like Yale, Princeton, and Stanford seek." If only Michael had been reading Ivy Coach's blog, he'd have known to be "extraordinary at one thing" as opposed to "ordinary at lots of things." Ivy Coach explained, "Ordinary's boring. Extraordinary's anything but boring. Highly selective colleges don't want boring. They want extraordinary. Understood? We hope so."

In Michael's defense, Harvard's own data contradicted Ivy Coach's advice. Harvard presented its statistical case through David Card, an economics professor at Berkeley. Card argued that strength across multiple dimensions mattered enormously. He found that only 12 percent of admitted students were "one-dimensional stars," meaning that they got a rating of one in one dimension, but fewer than three ratings of two or better. By contrast, 46 percent of admitted students were multidimensionally excellent, meaning they got three or more ratings of two or better. Another 31 percent were "multi-dimensionally solid." In the context of the lawsuit, Card's argument was that Asian applicants tended to be one-dimensional academic stars while whites tended to have better nonacademic ratings and were generally more multidimensionally excellent or solid. So Michael could be forgiven for not understanding whether investing another few thousand hours into his piano practice, to further cultivate his distinguishing excellence, risked branding himself as a one-dimensional star.

We may not know what a distinguishing excellence is, but we certainly know what it's not. It's not working at Taco Bell. Taco Bell did not come up once in Professor Card's report. In fact, jobs only came up twice in Card's report—each time to say that Arcidiacono hadn't considered them, but never to say how much weight Harvard attached to them. That's because Harvard doesn't attach any weight to them. The college might give a tip to a socioeconomically disadvantaged student, but that's in spite of their disadvantage not because of it. No one views working a near-full-time job—as almost all my CUNY students do—as a virtue.

SFFA's case is complicated by a simple truth: it's probably not Harvard's direct aim to disadvantage Asian applicants. Harvard's admissions office is reasonably diverse, and during the trial several of the officers adamantly denied any animus or conscious prejudice. When one Asian admissions officer was asked her reaction to the allegations, she said, "It's not what I know our office to be. It's not who I am. I would never be part of a process that would discriminate against anyone, let alone people that looked like me, like my family, like my friends, like my daughter."

U.S. District Court Judge Allison Burroughs credited this testimony, and she was probably right to do so, though it's easy to be skeptical. James Conant himself had suggested using letters of recommendation and interviews to assess "aptitude and character" as a way of addressing the so-called "Jewish problem." The notion of the Yale man—of "sound physique" and "grace of body"—evolved to combat what was known in New Haven as the "Hebrew invasion." So too, Princeton's commitment to educating "leaders" not "bookworms." Nevertheless, elite colleges have made undeniable strides in improving the race diversity of their classes—even if, almost certainly, it's also true that Asians have been disadvantaged by some of the policies that have promoted these gains.

The case is far less complicated when we consider the evidence in the context of socioeconomic status. *Every* experience valued by elite colleges is directly correlated with wealth. The experiences that allow a young man or woman to "distinguish" themselves are not uniformly available—not by a long shot. About 90 percent of kids from the highest-SES quartile participate in school-based extracurriculars. For kids from the lowest income quartile, the rate is twenty-five points lower. Thirty percent of kids from poor families participate in neither sports nor club activities. (Overall, the rate of nonparticipation is 10 percent.) A poor kid is about half as likely as a non-poor kid to participate in both sports and clubs.

Relying upon survey data from the National Center for Education

Statistics, a team including Robert Putnam, whose book *Our Kids: The American Dream in Crisis* lays out a damning indictment of America's exploding opportunity gap, found that affluent high schools offer about twice as many team sports as schools in high-poverty neighborhoods. They're also far less likely to require students to pay to play, as many poorer high schools do—even in California where the practice has been ruled unconstitutional. (They evade the legal requirement by calling the fees "donations.")

When the sociologists Elizabeth Stearns and Elizabeth Glennie used high school yearbooks to explore extracurricular opportunities in North Carolina, they found a similar pattern. Affluent schools offered both more activities and had higher participation rates. This continuing disparity creates a vicious cycle because the experiences that allow one to distinguish themselves in the college application process also help keep kids in school. Poorer kids, already at higher risk of dropping out, have less opportunity to have the kind of experience that makes a young person love school and feel loved by it.

As damning as all of this is, the picture is even bleaker when we probe deeper into the depth and quality of extracurricular experiences. Putnam's team found that a high school senior from a rich family is about twice as likely to have served as a sports team captain as one from a poorer family. They also found significant gaps in private music, dance, and art lessons. Participating in a high-quality Model United Nations program seems like the sort of experience that could change a young person's life, and maybe even help them get into college. Of the top-twenty-five ranked Model U.N. programs, ten are housed in private schools. Of the remaining fifteen—listed in Table 9—only one has a Black student population over 10 percent.

In 2018, Elizabeth Heaton, a college consultant who worked as an admissions officer at University of Pennsylvania, published a piece in the *Huffington Post* that asked, "What Kind of Hook Do I Need to Get Accepted to an Ivy League College?" It's all about distinguishing excellences, she argued. Being an Eagle Scout isn't a distinguishing excellence, Heaton explained, because 50,000 kids achieve that rank

TABLE 9. BLACK REPRESENTATION AT TOP-25 NORTH AMERICAN PUBLIC SCHOOL MODEL U.N. PROGRAMS

School	%
Huntington Beach High School (CA)	0.9%
Adlai E. Stevenson High School (IL)	1.5%
Glenbrook South High School (IL)	1.5%
Langley High School (VA)	1.7%
Thomas Jefferson H.S. for Science & Tech (VA)	2.1%
Bergen County Academies (NJ)	2.4%
McLean High School (VA)	3.1%
Gulf Coast High School (FL)	4.4%
West Windsor Plainsboro H.S. South (NJ)	5.0%
Cerritos High School (CA)	5.1%
Mira Costa High School (CA)	5.4%
Wootton High School (MD)	6.0%
J.P. Stevens High School (NJ)	7.0%
West Windsor Plainsboro H.S. North (NJ)	8.5%
The Beacon School (NY)	17.0%

every year. Valedictorians are a dime a dozen. So too are class presidents. Creating a nonprofit that solicits a thousand dollars and serves five hundred meals isn't a distinguishing excellence either. "But it can become one," she wrote, "if you are raising $100,000 and serving 500,000 meals." Her other examples included a debate champion, a "future global leader fluent in eight languages," a gold award at the USA Biology Olympiad, and heading up the regional volunteer corps for a U.S. Senate campaign.

It's impossible to imagine a child of even ordinary means having any of these experiences. All are available only to the wealthiest of the wealthy. Who else has the access to get—and can afford to take—an unpaid internship on a high-profile political race? What child of ordinary means can win a science Olympiad? For a hefty fee, Heaton's organization—Bright Horizons College Coach—will help you build a science profile that'll be an adequate distinguishing excellence. Their "Research Mentorship Program" will match you "with a researcher from a top institution, such as Harvard, Princeton, Oxford, and MIT." The goal is to develop a college-level research project that's "a meaningful addition" to the college application. It also includes ten mentoring sessions and help getting the work published or presented at a conference. Be forewarned, though: this program is only available to people in the Premier and Elite plans.

Since college admissions officers may not be familiar with reverse-transcriptase inhibitors or machine-learning algorithms, distinguishing research needs to be translated into accessible language. Ideally, this language should include a narrative of personal growth that syncs with the sort of diversity that Harvard and its brethren value. Not to worry. Ivy Coach, Bright Horizons, and all the private college counselors will be more than happy to "edit" your college essay. Maddeningly, but unsurprisingly, a team of researchers at Stanford found that the quality of an applicant's college essay has an even stronger correlation to reported household income than his or her SAT score. Surely professional editing is exacerbating this disparity. Yet, no elite college has a policy against this sort of assistance, even though, as John Katzman has proposed, it'd be easy to imagine requiring the essay to be written while sitting for one of the standardized exams.

Still, that's not the worst of it. Elite colleges exacerbate hoarding by attaching value to "distinguishing excellences." The message to parents is that they need to expose their children to elite extracurricular experiences to get them into elite colleges. This shapes the communities in which they live. Yet, paradoxically, almost everyone in the academy embraces the research (and often their own teaching experience) showing that the best predictors of well-being and achievement are characteristics like resilience, not academic or extracurricular brilliance.

Extracurriculars aren't a reflection of a person's inner wealth or value—they're a reflection of their opportunity. Working at Taco Bell while going to high school isn't something to be looked down upon. Rather, it's a marker of resilience and a predictor of success—if only the young person can overcome the prejudice against their experience and get themselves into the right college.

At my son's high school graduation, the guidance director told the parents that their kids' graduation was proof that "anyone can succeed." She explained, "It's just a matter of hard work." Richard Rothstein calls the belief that children born into low-income families can escape that status through hard work and education "a fantasy that we share." It's a fantasy in part because elite colleges don't value hard work—or at least not hard work as it's understood and available to ordinary people. Instead, they value distinguishing excellences, available only to the wealthy, and act as if weighing these experiences is the only conceivable mechanism by which to select capable students.

It isn't.

After graduating from Brandeis, Debbie Bial worked briefly as a paralegal, then took a job at CityKids, a foundation that uses art to help at-risk children find their voices. While there, she met a young man nicknamed Stein—short for Einstein—who'd given up a scholarship at a major university. When Bial asked why he'd dropped out, Stein said, "I could have done it if I had had my posse with me."

Stein's comment inspired Bial to start the Posse Foundation. It sends scholarship students in groups of ten—posses—to participating colleges so that they can support one another. The approach has been extraordinarily successful. Posse currently recruits students from ten cities and has sixty-three partner colleges. Since its creation in 1989, Posse has selected more than ten thousand scholars who have received a cumulative $1.6 billion in scholarships. In 2007, Bial won an award from the MacArthur Foundation.

Posse's amazing, but Bial didn't get a $500,000 genius grant just for sending kids to college in groups. She won it for how she picked the kids. Even in the late 1980s, Bial understood that the SAT systematically disadvantaged poor students, especially those who are Black or brown. She understood, too, long before Angela Duckworth, that people with the highest grades weren't the ones who went on to succeed. If Bial wanted to cultivate a new generation of disadvantaged students who would go on to become leaders in their colleges and communities, she would need a different way to pick people.

So Bial developed a test that measured initiative and persistence through group activities. The Bial-Dale College Adaptability Index is sometimes called the "Lego Test" because of a ten-minute segment that asks groups of students to reproduce a robot made of Lego blocks. The students are allowed to examine the structure individually but are prohibited from taking notes. Success requires cooperation and teamwork. In another part of the three-hour exam, rather than mirroring the traditional college interview, students are asked to lead a group discussion on a random topic. Observers note not who has the biggest vocabulary, but rather who collaborates well and who shows resilience.

How well does it work? Even though Posse is choosing among the most underserved students, who are at the greatest risk of dropping out, more than 90 percent graduate. It's difficult to imagine more definitive proof of something we all know in our hearts: The college interview is a scam. Unstructured interviews are notoriously bad at predicting job performance. What they do, rather, is reproduce social inequalities. People like people like them. So, the college interview becomes an exploration of shared experience, even though many of those experiences are unavailable to poor applicants of color and an alternative system exists that's better at predicting success.

Most tragically, the status quo represents a lost opportunity. Remember Katzman's Second Theorem: what colleges value shapes what communities teach and value. That's why Katzman imagines a world in which the SAT is used as an incentive to teach students material that would be meaningful and valuable to them. Imagine, in a similar vein, if we told communities that the skills elite colleges valued were cooperation, hard work, and listening. To be sure, the rich will learn to manipulate any system to sustain their class position. But think about what it would do for the perception of working-class people to signal that holding a real job signified something of honor and predicted success instead of treating it as a disadvantage. Consider, too, what communities would look like if instead of creating incentives to hoard extracurricular opportunities and hire $100,000 consultants, colleges instead encouraged young people to be the best team players they could be. It would hardly be a panacea, but as my grandmother liked to say, "It vouldn't hoit."

8

Affirmative Action for Rich Whites

Fun fact: When I was a senior in high school, I won one of James Conant's scholarships for middle-class Midwesterners. I'd never heard of Conant, and I was no Midwesterner, but I was most definitely middle class. My parents raised me in an apartment building in the Madison subsection of Sheepshead Bay, not far from Marine Park. When they moved there in 1970, the rent was $200 a month. At the time, my dad worked as a math teacher at Midwood High School, making about $5,000 a year. The rent represented about half his take-home pay.

Shortly after I turned twelve, my family moved to East Meadow, a nondescript hamlet of about 40,000 people smack dab in the middle of Long Island's Nassau County. The main drag—Hempstead Turnpike—featured a Roy Rogers, a McDonald's, a bowling pro shop, and a pool hall. It was about as white and middle class as you could imagine. There—and this is the most important detail of this story—my parents bought a house: a three-bedroom, one-bathroom split-level with a creaky, wooden basketball hoop and a leaky in-ground pool in which several unfortunate squirrels met their demise. For their dream home, my mom and dad paid $61,000.

When I got into Harvard in 1985, tuition ran $10,200. Including room and board—but not including books or tickets on the Eastern Airlines Shuttle, which cost forty bucks—the tab for my freshman year would come in a little bit over $16,000. That's a bargain by today's standards, but to my parents it was a fortune. At the time, my dad had just become the principal of Brooklyn Tech, for which he earned an annual salary of approximately $60,000. After taxes and paying his mortgage and bills, full Harvard tuition would leave him with—well, nothing.

Unfortunately, the Harvard National Scholarship offered no money. It may seem odd to you that a scholarship program neither served the people it was originally intended to serve nor offered any financial aid to students, but after twenty years of sitting in faculty meetings, it makes perfect sense to me. My dad appealed. Harvard said it would help him out if he really got into trouble. The message was clear: my parents were going to have to pay. And they didn't have the money.

Still, they never hesitated. "We had made the decision that you would go to the school you wanted to go to," my dad told me. He took out a home equity line of credit for $40,000, and, when that ran out during my senior year, he refinanced our house. He used credit cards to pay for my books and didn't take a vacation for twenty years, but he and my mom got their kid through Harvard.

I asked my dad what he would have done if they hadn't bought a house. "Oh, that's an interesting question," he said. "If I didn't have a house, it would have been hard."

My student Denisse Batista's story didn't turn out quite the same way as mine.

It took a village to raise Denisse. As with so many of my students, the responsibility for raising her fell onto the shoulders of her mother, a Peruvian immigrant who works as a medical receptionist. To make ends meet, Denisse, her mom, and her two half-sisters moved into a house in Ozone Park, Queens, with Denisse's aunts, uncles, cousins, and grandparents, with whom she shared a room. At one point, twenty people lived in the house.

Studying was a challenge in such a crowded home, and Denisse worked long hours at her uncle's restaurant, but, against the odds, Denisse thrived academically. At Forest Hills High School, a beautiful but overcrowded behemoth, Denisse maintained a weighted average of 103. Without taking any sort of prep course, she scored 1180 (out of 1600) on her SATs, placing her in the top quartile. Forest Hills only had two guidance counselors per grade—each thus serving approximately four hundred kids, but Denisse got some useful advice. Her counselor told her about HEOP—the Higher Education Opportunity Program—a Rockefeller-era initiative that helps disadvantaged students apply to and attend a long list of partner institutions in New York State. Denisse's college application list looked surprisingly common. She applied to eighteen schools—all with fee waivers. The list included many safeties, including several CUNY colleges, a few private colleges that seemed within her grasp, like Syracuse, and a couple of reaches. In May 2020, she sat alone in her room, held her breath, and opened a very important envelope. She'd gotten into Barnard.

"I felt a little bubble of happiness," Denisse told me. "I really didn't think I was going to get in."

Here's where Denisse's story diverges from mine. Denisse opened her acceptance letters by herself because she expected that going to an Ivy would cause controversy within her family. Her instincts were correct. One of her aunts was especially worried about the family going into debt to support Denisse's education. There was no reason to believe that this would happen. The package from Barnard and HEOP covered full tuition and room and board. But Denisse's aunt didn't buy it. She called Barnard and, after persistent questioning, extracted an admission that the pandemic might cause a small cut in funding. Denisse could be on the hook for $1,000 per year.

"Are you gonna feel good putting your family in debt?" her aunt asked her, time and again.

Finally, Denisse capitulated. "I really can't put my family through this," she thought to herself. She retracted her acceptance to Barnard and matriculated at John Jay. It's impossible to know precisely how much a degree is worth in any individual person's case, but on average, giving up a nearly-free Ivy League degree costs a person in Denisse's situation about $1 million in future earnings. With such a gross difference, the forensics squad is going to demand an investigation. The obvious suspect in this tragedy is differences in education, but that can't explain what happened here. Denisse's aunt went to CUNY, as both of my parents did.

The difference was our house.

* * *

For his dissertation at Columbia University, the sociologist Dalton Conley proposed to answer an unorthodox question. Many sociologists had documented that Blacks and whites had grossly different outcomes in terms of education, work, and family structure. The conventional explanation was that these disparities were the product of differences in income or, simply, racism. But Conley suspected something else was at work. Instead of race, he wondered whether the differences were really driven by class, something sociologists considered, as he put it, a dirty word.

It's a question Conley was seemingly born to answer. Conley spent his entire childhood as an outsider both in terms of race and class—first, with his sister, as the only white kids in a federal housing project on the Lower East Side. Then, as one of the poorest kids at the Greenwich Village elementary school into which his mother, a novelist, managed to get him transferred. Conley's memoir of his extraordinary childhood, *Honky*, is riveting.

To answer his novel question, Conley examined data from the Panel Study of Income Dynamics (PSID). Originally designed to assess President Lyndon Johnson's War on Poverty, the PSID has been operating since 1968. It's the world's longest-running longitudinal study of families. It's also the most comprehensive. The survey tracks 25,000 people in almost 10,000 families using a multitude of economic, social, and health factors including employment, marriage, and education.

The survey's thoroughness allowed Conley to address a problem that vexes social scientists: Sometimes a correlation might be attributable to a variable that's not included in a study. Suppose, for example, a researcher examined the relationship between vegetarianism and heart disease. She might conclude that eating a plant-based diet prevented heart attacks. But vegetarianism is associated with other behaviors that prevent heart attacks such as exercise, low weight, and avoiding smoking. It's possible that including these other variables—or more fully specifying the model, as they say in the stats biz—would lead the researcher to conclude that vegetarianism by itself didn't mean very much.

Conley found that in a more fully specified model, which the PSID enabled him to build, income didn't matter very much at all in predicting educational outcomes. In fact, parental household income had no impact whatsoever on whether a child finished college. Income, like vegetarianism in our example, was acting as a proxy for something else. That something else was wealth. More specifically, it was home ownership. Conley found that the single best predictor of whether a child finished college was the equity that their parents had in their primary residence.

If we characterize income inequality in the United States as "extreme," we're going to struggle to find a phrase to describe American wealth inequality. Mind-bogglingly, stupefyingly, super-gargantuan comes to mind. The median white family income in the U.S. is approximately $60,000. The median Black family income is about $37,000. That's a ratio of about 1.6-to-one. The median white household has wealth of approximately $134,000. For Black families it's about $11,000. That's a ratio of about twelve-to-one. The disparity is about twice as great as when Conley began his research in the mid-1990s. Today, the top 1 percent holds fifteen times more wealth than the bottom 50 percent combined.

Intergenerational wealth mobility is even lower than intergenerational income mobility. Forty-one percent of children born into the lowest wealth quintile remain there. Again, it's worse for Black Americans. Fewer than one quarter born into the lowest wealth quintile make it to the middle quintile or higher.

The why of this is no secret. In his tour-de-force history of government-imposed residential segregation in America, *The Color of Law: A Forgotten History of How Our Government Segregated America*, Richard Rothstein details how racist government housing policies, redlining, zoning, and legally segregated projects made suburban homeownership available to white families but not to Black ones. Not all the difference in white and Black family wealth is attributable to these racist policies, Rothstein writes, "but a good portion certainly is."

As Rothstein explains it, suburban homeownership exploded the wealth gap through several interrelated mechanisms. First, the mortgage interest tax deduction, which made owning cheaper than renting, effectively served as a subsidy to suburban homeowners. Second, while renters accumulated no equity, suburban homes appreciated significantly. Parents can bequeath assets to their children, which partially explains why wealth inequality is even more persistent than income inequality. Most importantly, homeowners can draw upon their equity to fund exceptional spending, like college tuition. "White families," Rothstein writes, "are more often able to borrow from their home equity, if necessary, to weather medical emergencies, send their children to college, retire without becoming dependent on those children, aid family members experiencing hard times, or endure brief periods of joblessness without fear of losing a home or going hungry."

Homeownership (and the history of it) gives whites—especially affluent ones—greater access to the narratives that elite colleges choose to value, like athleticism and well-roundedness. And if, or more aptly *when*, their children are admitted, these white homeowning families are better able to pay for their children to attend those elite colleges—even if, as in my own case, there's no trust fund set aside or a family yacht sitting at the dock.

Since we've spent so much time discussing standardized tests, I'd like to offer an SAT-style analogy: standardized test scores are to income as "legacy" status is to wealth. Legacy, you'll remember, means having a family member who's an alumnus of the college to which you're applying. Given that the advantages of wealth—like access to well-funded suburban schools and private tutoring—help build the income advantages that affluent college applicants possess—like higher standardized test scores, more APs, and "stronger" extracurriculars—you might think that legacy status would be considered a negative or, at least, not afforded very much weight. In fact, elite colleges give legacy candidates a significant advantage, and the practice is firmly embedded in their culture.

Legacy evolved in the early twentieth century as part of a two-prong strategy for dealing with the Jewish problem. The first was to define character in such a way as to disadvantage Jewish applicants. The second, in case the first wasn't adequate, was to simply give explicit preference to the children of alumni, who were overwhelmingly not Jewish. Today, elite colleges defend legacy as necessary for fundraising. The practice has been condemned by the *New York Times*, *Harvard Crimson*, and the *Boston Globe*.

The tips offered to legacies are substantial. First, they represent, returning to our earlier analogy, a huge bucket. Legacies are often grouped together in the acronym ALDC with children of donors (the "D"), which is explicitly a wealth advantage; children of faculty members (the "C"), another advantage of birth; and recruited athletes ("A"), who also benefit greatly from wealth advantages, as we've discussed. Combined, ALDCs represent 30 percent of each Harvard class. Approximately half of ALDCs are legacies. About 43 percent of white students at Harvard are an ALDC.

In terms of admission rates, being an ALDC improves your chances by an order of magnitude. According to the data produced in SFFA's lawsuit, approximately 33.6 percent of legacy applicants (and 86 percent of recruited athletes) are admitted. Harvard's overall admissions rate is approximately 4.6 percent—and remember that includes the ALDCs. A team of researchers at Princeton found that being a legacy was worth about 160 extra points on the SAT—nearly as much as being African American or Hispanic—even though legacies tend to do slightly worse in college, academically, than non-legacies. *The Atlantic's* Joe Pinsker likened it to having a superpower.

Not all superpowers are created equal. Being a legacy is good. Being related to a major donor or a faculty member is like being The One Above All—the mysterious, omnipotent uberhero of the Marvel universe. Some candidates make it onto the "dean's interest list" or the "director's interest list," referring to the dean and director of admissions. (These applicants receive a separate rating, based on the institutional "interest" in the candidate's admission.) For people on either of these lists, the admission rate is about 42.2 percent. It's even higher for candidates who are related to a faculty or staff member. Approximately 46.7 percent of these candidates are admitted.

These rates are largely consistent across elite colleges. It's difficult to say anything conclusive because schools guard the data closely and most haven't been forced to lay their statistics bare in litigation discovery, as Harvard has. Moreover, different schools define legacy differently. Nevertheless, it's widely accepted that elite colleges generally reserve between 10 and 25 percent of their seats for legacy applicants. Notre Dame and Baylor have notoriously high rates of legacy admissions. Approximately 21 percent of Notre Dame students are legacies. About a third of Baylor's students are.

The University of Virginia is a particularly egregious offender. UVA is no paragon of diversity. In Chetty and Friedman's study, UVA ranked 2,015th out of 2,137 colleges in terms of overall mobility. Only 6.2 percent of their students are Black. The college, which was largely built with slave labor, didn't even admit Black students until 1958. Nevertheless, UVA has a special office—the Admission Liaison Program—dedicated to helping legacy candidates navigate the admissions process. The program's website boasts that the college admits nearly 47 percent of legacy applicants. They even have a special scholarship for legacies. Preference is given to Life Members of the Alumni Association.

Legacy preference often includes concierge care. While less than 3 percent of applicants to Harvard get a staff interview, more than 20 percent of ALDCs get one. Approximately 79 percent of ALDC applicants who get a staff interview are ultimately admitted. I had a series of conversations with the director of development at an Ivy-Plus college who asked to remain anonymous. Most of our conversations were about the efforts that their college had made to expand opportunities for first-generation students. They said the fundraising office didn't get involved with admissions, but that they'd call a donor whose child had applied to personally inform them of the admissions decision.

It's the precise opposite of a progressive admissions policy. Likely you've seen a chart showing how the learning outcomes of rich and poor kids diverge beginning almost at birth. Instead of attempting to compress that disparity, elite colleges explode it exponentially by rewarding the accumulated inequality with a degree of enormous, independent value. This thereby creates a further incentive to hoard the very opportunities that created the disparities in the first place.

* * *

It's tough not to be cynical about whether Ed Blum cares about Asian Americans. Michael Wang is. It's tough, too, not to feel conflicted about race-based affirmative action. SFFA's argument is effectively that Asians as a group were academically stronger than white applicants and, hence, more would have been admitted under a race-blind admissions process. But college admissions is a zero-sum game, and Harvard's argument is that focusing strictly on academic markers would reduce overall racial diversity.

On this count, Harvard is almost certainly right. At Stuyvesant High School, the downside of the robust numbers of Asian students who are admitted through the SHSAT are paltry numbers for other students of color. For the same class to which 524 Asian kids won slots, only twenty Hispanic and ten Black people made the grade—that's a combined 3.9 percent. These numbers are a large part of why single-factor admissions are so controversial in New York City schools.

These statistics are also why Michael Wang describes himself as a supporter of affirmative action. What he's against is affirmative action where the lion's share of the preference goes to rich whites. In other words, precisely what elite colleges do. Elite colleges use the advantage that they give to a few students of color to mask the reality of a process that amounts to, in its totality, affirmative action for rich, white applicants.

This fact should have lost the lawsuit for Harvard.

Here's everything you need to know about the constitutionality of affirmative action in one paragraph: Under the Civil Rights Act of 1964, the Equal Protection Clause applies to any university that accepts federal funds. Only a handful of mostly right-leaning, religious colleges that you've probably never heard of don't accept this money. Harvard does. The Equal Protection Clause prevents discrimination on the basis of race. A race-conscious admissions program, like Harvard's, must withstand "strict scrutiny"—meaning that it must be "narrowly tailored" to serve a "compelling interest." A program cannot be narrowly tailored if the college could achieve its goal in a race-neutral way. In other words, race can only be considered as a last resort. Race-conscious policies must also be limited in time. In a 2003 decision that nearly ended racial preferences, Justice Sandra Day O'Connor said that the Court expected that affirmative action would no longer be necessary in twenty-five years.

Pretty much everyone except for Ed Blum acknowledges diversity as a compelling interest in college admissions. The rub is in the question of whether there's a race-neutral way to achieve it. With the threat of litigation looming, Harvard convened a committee to examine race-neutral alternatives to its admissions practices. The committee's work never got off the ground. After SFFA filed its lawsuit, it disbanded. Harvard then convened a second committee to explore whether it could achieve its diversity goals through race-neutral means. The committee summarily determined that it could not.

SFFA disagreed. At trial, it presented the expert testimony of Richard Kahlenberg, a fellow at the Century Foundation, a left-leaning think tank founded by Edward Filene, of department store fame. Kahlenberg, who's a graduate of Harvard College and Harvard Law School, has spent most of his professional life advocating for equity in primary and secondary education, greater socioeconomic diversity in colleges, and generally acting as a commonsensical, data-driven voice for reform. Characteristically, Kahlenberg offered a sensible proposal: Harvard could end ALDC preferences. He also testified that Harvard could increase the weight it gives to socioeconomic disadvantage, which correlates closely with race, and its commitment to geographic diversity—an idea championed by the ethicist Danielle Allen, who holds—wait for it—the James Bryant Conant university professorship at Harvard.

Kahlenberg's logic is almost impossible to refute. Harvard's own analysis said that the difference in admission rates between whites and Asians could be explained almost entirely by the preference afforded to ALDCs. The difference between SFFA's expert and Harvard's turned on whether they included ALDCs in their model. Arcidiacono left them out. Card included them. Card said, in effect, that Harvard didn't prefer white people over Asians—it was just that the institution needed

lacrosse players and faculty kids, who just happened to be disproportionately white.

Card owned the pivotal moment in the case. He testified that eliminating both race and ALDC tips would cause Black and Hispanic enrollment to drop. But why would Harvard have to do both? Why couldn't it
simply end ALDC preferences? Wouldn't that be the narrowly tailored,
race-neutral way to achieve its goal of improving diversity? Isn't that
what the Equal Protection Clause required?

The trial judge, Allison Burroughs, a graduate of Middlebury and
Penn Law School, said no. "Eliminating tips for ALDC applicants would
have the effect of opening spots in Harvard's class that could then be
filled through an admissions policy more favorable to non-white students," she wrote, "but Harvard would be far less competitive in Ivy
League intercollegiate sports, which would adversely impact Harvard
and the student experience." The First Circuit Court of Appeals agreed.
Athletes, it said, have demonstrated "discipline, resilience, and teamwork." As if working kids who help support their family haven't.

Burroughs added that eliminating tips for the children of faculty and
staff "would adversely affect Harvard's ability to attract top-quality
faculty and staff," buying Harvard's argument without any supporting evidence. The dean's and director's lists, she wrote, were "far too
small for the cessation of any such practice to contribute meaningfully
to campus diversity." In other words, only a few people buy their way
in, so don't worry about it.

Finally, again following Harvard's lead, Burroughs wrote that eliminating legacy would come at "considerable cost" and prevent the college
from achieving "desired benefits from relationships with its alumni and
other individuals who have made significant contributions to Harvard."
To be clear, "benefits" means money. Harvard's committee concluded,
after seven meetings, that ending legacy would "jeopardize the generous financial support," that made Harvard, which has an endowment of
nearly $52 billion, "a leading institution of higher learning."

In effect, Harvard and its lawyers defended an admissions program
that amounts on balance to affirmative action for rich, white applicants.
It did this by framing any change as an existential threat to the small

amount of race-based affirmative action that it does—little of which benefits poor applicants of color—and by convincing a federal judge that wealth preferences are essential to the survival of the university.

They're not.

We don't have to speculate what would happen to its endowment if Harvard ended legacy preferences. The answer is nothing. When a team led by the economist Chad Coffman examined alumni giving at the top one hundred American universities, as ranked by *U.S. News & World Report*, they found no relationship between giving behavior and whether the school afforded preference to legacies. Pretty much the only thing that mattered was the wealth of the alumni. At trial, Harvard offered no evidence to support its claim that ending legacy would jeopardize its financial position. That's because none exists. No study has ever shown a significant relationship between legacy preference and alumni giving.

Over the past twenty years, several colleges, including Texas A&M and the University of Georgia, have abolished legacy preferences. None have reported a significant change in alumni giving. Since taking office in 2009, Johns Hopkins president Ronald Daniels, a Canadian, has gradually eliminated legacy tips. He said that the preference struck him as unnecessary given that most "children of alumni come from affluent families and have other social and educational advantages." Johns Hopkins has the eighteenth largest endowment among American universities and recently attracted a $1.8 billion gift to support financial aid from Michael Bloomberg, who made ending legacy preference a plank of his presidential campaign.

MIT has never practiced legacy. Chris Peterson, a straight-talking, civil libertarian from Reading, Massachusetts, who's been an admissions officer at MIT for a dozen years, told me that it's "isomorphic with a broader MIT cultural attachment to evaluating and rewarding people on the basis of their substantive achievement." The "Institute" awards no Latin honors, has no honors college, gives no merit aid, and grants no honorary degrees. "That's part of the same cultural substrate," he explained.

Peterson says that the MIT admissions office has a "laser-like focus" on academic excellence, measured in the context of the applicant's opportunity. "We try to ask ourselves the following question in admissions: What has this student done relative to what we might think they could have done with the resources they had available to them." MIT is the only Ivy-Plus college that doesn't accept the Common App. Peterson says the different essay structure throws applicants "out of their standard narrative." One of last year's prompts asked applicants to write about something they did simply for the pleasure of it. "We don't put any weight on how elegant you are," Peterson said, pointing out that MIT runs a January charm school, at which they teach a wide range of social skills including dating etiquette, dinner table manners, and when you can ask about salary during an interview.

Harvard and its brethren would have you believe that a healthy dose of nepotism, cronyism, and corruption are essential to the survival of the modern university. On their telling, MIT's commitment to demonstrated achievement, as Peterson puts it—carefully avoiding the construct of "merit"—would lead alumni to feel less loyalty to their alma mater. That's a myth, Peterson says. "The family aspect of MIT isn't gone," he explains. "It just takes a different form."

Peterson's official title is director of special projects for MIT's admissions office. For many years, he ran "talented outreach," meaning he oversaw the recruitment of kids who excelled at international math and science competitions, like my classmate who scored a fifteen on the AIME. As part of his job, he talked to lots of parents who'd graduated from MIT and now had their own children applying. "When I talk to parents who went to MIT, often they love MIT and want their kid to go to MIT, but even more they like the idea that MIT isn't going to give their kid special treatment," Peterson says. "It flatters the parent to say, 'This is the place I went to—the place that cared about your substance and your rigor. The place that cared about what you could do and not your fame and fortune.' I see lack of legacy preference as an expression of that bedrock, cultural foundation." Peterson attended MIT for graduate school and says that he would never want the benefit of legacy preference for his own children.

The prevailing fundraising model also presumes a finite universe of potential donors, all motivated to give solely by the indirect benefit that their children receive. Another myth. Peterson says that MIT's steadfast refusal to reward connections expands possibilities. "On balance, we grow our family," he says, "because we make kin with new people." MIT students, Peterson explains, are overwhelmingly new Americans—meaning immigrants or the children of immigrants. "We have a student population that is culturally aligned with the idea of, 'you are going to come here to strive and work hard to catapult yourself into a different ecosystem in a way that isn't true at other institutions.'"

Their graduates are exceedingly generous to MIT's ideals. Its endowment of $27.5 billion ranks sixth largest among American universities, far larger than dozens of elite colleges that give preference to legacies and donors. Generous too are the alumni of Berea College in Kentucky—which charges no tuition, and admits mostly students from Appalachia and exclusively students from families whose income is in the bottom 40 percent of U.S. households—and Cooper Union in New York, which was tuition free until 2014 and plans to reinstate full-tuition scholarships in 2028. They have endowments of $1.25 billion and $826 million, respectively. Berea's is bigger than Middlebury's, Oberlin's, and Hamilton's. Cooper Union's ranks ahead of Drexel, Haverford, and Trinity.

MIT's development office wouldn't have things any other way. "I have never heard our resource development team say that they thought we should change how we admitted students because it would help them with their fundraising," Peterson said. I asked him what his office would do differently if it had an additional $20 billion endowment. "Nothing," he replied. "We do not in any way admit kids based on their ability to pay for MIT."

Theoretically, MIT should be doing much worse than its competitors in terms of upward mobility. They won't let you in unless you've taken calculus, and less than half of low-income schools offer calculus. Yet MIT's mean family income is $242,000. That sounds like a lot, but ranks it 109th, behind progressive colleges like Vassar, Brandeis, and The New School, and behind all the Ivy-Plus colleges. These are led by

Princeton, where Chetty and Friedman determined the average parent family income to be $519,000 per year, and Brown, where it's $543,000. MIT produces far and away the most upward mobility of the Ivy-Plus schools—nearly twice as much as Harvard, and two-and-a-half times as much as Princeton—all without rewarding children for the wealth of their parents.

The signature movie of elite colleges shouldn't be *Homeless to Harvard*. It should be *Scarsdale to Stanford*. It should be the story of a young man who, after a lifetime of advantage—of tutors and coaches and summer camps—had slightly lower SAT scores than his classmates but got into his dream school anyway because he was good at an esoteric sport that no one can play as a career, or because his mom or dad taught at or went to the school, or who simply bought his way in. For every Liz Murray, there are a hundred Alistair Sinclairs. As they walk through the ivy-covered iron gates of elite schools, their grand welcome marks the beginning of a carefully curated identity as the very best and brightest among us. And then the trouble really starts.

PART III

How Elite Colleges Distort Student Lives

9

Doing Good

Krystle Salvati's hero is her mom. Though she'd never gone to college, Lisa Salvati managed to carve out a successful career in marketing at Random House. Then, as with so many of my students' parents, she got laid off—a victim of the publishing giant's merger with Penguin. Krystle was in middle school at the time. Her older sister had just started high school. Their father, who struggled with alcoholism, offered no support. The entire responsibility for holding the family together fell on Lisa. She did whatever it took. Lisa borrowed against her 401(k), moved in with her mother (the other heroine of Krystle's life story), and started over, taking a job as a secretary in a dentist's office.

Despite the financial and personal upheaval, Lisa made sure that her daughters focused on their education. Krystle aced the entrance exam to Catholic high schools and landed a full scholarship to Christ the King in Middle Village, Queens. There she proved herself an academic superstar, ending high school with a 103 weighted average, good enough to be salutatorian of her graduating class. Krystle couldn't afford a prep course, but after two tries—one for each fee waiver—she scored an 1890 (out of 2400) on the SAT, which placed her just around the ninetieth percentile. Fordham offered her a partial scholarship, but Krystle decided to go to CUNY's Macaulay Honors College.

As a kid, Krystle had one of the Barbie career sets, and for a time thought she wanted to be a veterinarian. At John Jay, Krystle found her purpose. She enjoyed debate and gained further clarity from internships at the Bronx Family Court and Legal Aid. By the time she landed in my death penalty course in her junior year, she'd decided that she wanted to be a lawyer—specifically one who helped vulnerable children.

We aimed high for law school. At my urging, Krystle took a prep course for the LSAT. With the benefit of that experience, she nailed the exam—landing in the ninety-fifth percentile. We went through thirteen drafts of her personal statement, carefully explaining the hardship that she'd overcome and how it had shaped the course she wanted her career to take. We paid particular attention to a program at the University of Pennsylvania that offered a full scholarship to students who'd commit to spending their careers working in the public interest. One essay prompt asked if Facebook or LinkedIn profiles had personal mission statements, what yours would say. "I advocate for others the way I'd want others to advocate for me," Krystle wrote. "I aim to use the law to protect those who cannot protect themselves."

In the spring of her senior year, Krystle learned that she'd been admitted to Penn as a Toll Public Interest Scholar. Her mom cried. Her grandmother cried. I cried. As I'm writing this, Krystle is finishing her 1L exams and getting ready for her summer internship. While her colleagues will be earning $4,000 a week and courted over extravagant lunches as summer associates at Debevoise & Plimpton and Skadden Arps, Krystle will be spending her summer at the federal public defender's office in Montgomery, Alabama. The pay won't be nearly as good.

She'll be making nothing.

Krystle's commitment to public service is typical of the kids I teach. About 60 percent of John Jay graduates with a job work at either a nonprofit or in the public sector. That's slightly higher than the CUNY average, but not by much. Nearly half of all CUNY grads work in public service. If you're in New York and meet a teacher or a cop on the beat, ask them where they went to school. More likely than not, they went to CUNY.

Career outcomes are similar at the other colleges that produce significant upward mobility. At Cal State LA, for example, the three most common career choices among alumni are education (25 percent), health care (11 percent), and social services (11 percent). At tuition-free Berea College, the top jobs are teaching, education administration, and nursing. Many of these colleges make promoting the public good an explicit part of their mission. At John Jay, the goal of advancing social justice is emblazoned on almost every wall.

Harvard is another story. Of the 61 percent of the class of 2020 that entered the workforce after graduation, the overwhelming majority went into either finance (23 percent), consulting (22 percent), or the technology sector (18 percent). Over 70 percent of Harvard seniors apply to investment banks or consulting firms. Once upon a time, the Ivies produced doctors and lawyers. Not anymore. Only 4 percent of 2020 Harvard grads went into the health industry and another 3 percent into law. Merely 4 percent said they'd be working in public service or at a nonprofit.

These numbers are more or less consistent across elite colleges. About 1 percent of Duke graduates identify themselves as entering public service. At Dartmouth and Brown, the rates are 4 and 5 percent, respectively. The picture is slightly better at Yale. Nine percent of Yale grads say they'll enter public service—but only 4.7 percent of students who were involved in Greek life. No elite college comes anywhere close to producing public servants at the rate of CUNY and Cal State. And public education is almost never a career choice for elite college grads. Of Harvard, Stanford, and Yale graduates, 2, 3, and 4 percent, respectively, enter education. The lion's share of these join Teach for America, which requires only a two-year commitment. The overall picture could hardly be clearer. The CUNYs and Cal States of America produce our nation's teachers and public servants. The Ivy-Plus colleges produce investment bankers, management consultants, and Silicon Valley entrepreneurs.

Elite colleges offer a familiar reply to this data. Their response to the damning statistics on socioeconomic diversity is that they're merely reproducing the underlying disparities in American wealth and educational opportunity. It's the same with jobs. When I presented this evidence to a professor friend of mine who's the public interest director at a top-five law school, they said that the outcomes principally reflected the underlying social attitudes of the super-wealthy kids that the law

FIGURE 3. TOP CAREER CHOICES FOR HARVARD AND JOHN JAY GRADS

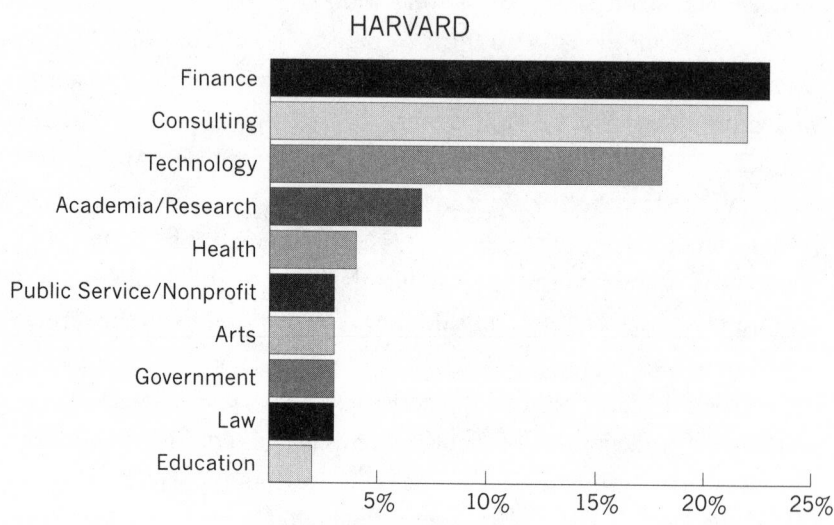

HARVARD

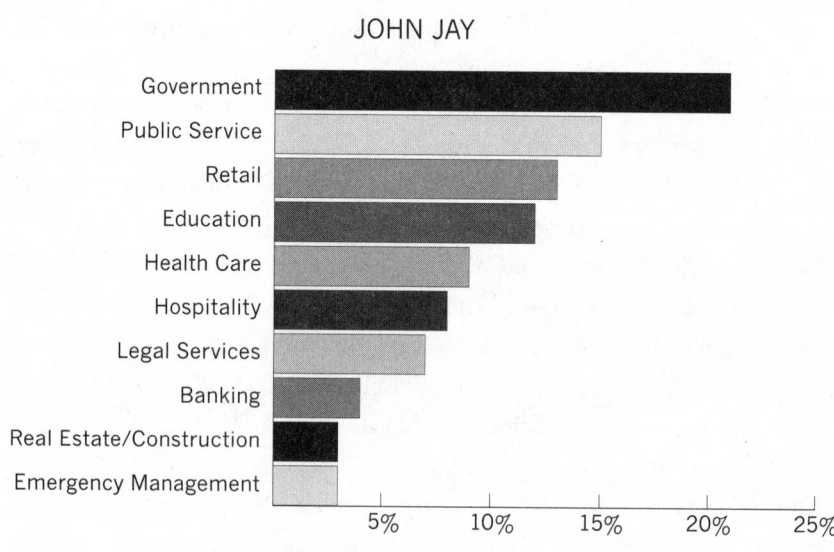

JOHN JAY

school admits. Harvard couldn't be held responsible for changing people. Kids will be kids, they said in effect, and kids these days want to go to Goldman Sachs and McKinsey.

The truth could hardly be more different.

When the young sociologist Amy Binder read her class report, shortly before her ten-year Stanford reunion, her first thought was that a lot of her classmates "were doing a lot of boring shit." Her second thought was that they were squandering the opportunity they'd been given. "They had the privilege of going to this great school and now they were in sales, or banking, or something like that," she said. Binder was especially bothered by the gender dynamics she observed. "A lot of the women said things like, 'my first five years I was in management consulting and then I met Gary, and then we had a child, and then I realized the most rewarding thing I could do is be a stay-at-home mom.'" Binder said to herself, "Screw this. This isn't supposed to be what you're doing with your education." She became skeptical about Stanford's entire enterprise. "I started to have this sense of, 'was this a finishing school or just a status thing,'" she told me.

Binder, who's today the nation's most careful observer of how colleges socialize students, was raised to do what she does. After her father died when she was four, her mother took a job as the office manager for Donald Fraser, a progressive Minnesota congressman who formulated much of Jimmy Carter's human rights agenda and later served four terms as mayor of Minneapolis. Binder's mother brought her to work meetings and out with friends and generally lavished her in unconditional love. "She was a model of how to live an engaged life," Binder says.

In tenth grade, Binder applied on her own to the Blake School, a preparatory academy that counts Al Franken, Tom Davis, and Poppy Harlow among its notable alumni. Impressed by her grades and chutzpah, Blake let her in. Binder calls applying to Blake the smartest decision of her life, but as much for the challenges it presented as the opportunities. Binder was "blown away" academically but struggled to fit in. "I was a budding sociologist even back then," she says. "There were Pillsburys [of baking fame] and Daytons [of Dayton's department store—later Target] and lots of nouveau riche. Meanwhile, I was reading Dostoyevsky's *Notes from Underground*."

Binder went to Wellesley for a year, which she found fascinating in some ways, but it felt a bit like high school to her, and she didn't love the single-sex environment. Before her sophomore year, she transferred to Stanford. "I had no qualms with it at that point," Binder says. "It wasn't overrun by the whole tech industry." After graduation, she worked for a dance troupe in San Francisco, living a Bohemian lifestyle, until she decided that dancers were narcissistic. Binder then followed a boyfriend to Chicago, where he was pursuing a PhD in marketing, got to know Northwestern and somewhat reflexively decided to get a doctorate in sociology.

She began her career studying representations of race, but after taking a class on the sociology of education—and encountering Bourdieu—Binder began to think about the ways that schools shaped the opportunities and identities of the students that attended them. Following her college reunion, she wondered more specifically whether her Stanford classmates' career choices were inevitable. Binder was really asking the most basic chicken-and-egg question about institutions and identity: Were elite colleges shaped by the students they admitted or were the colleges shaping their students more than they cared to admit?

As a professor, first at USC and later at UC San Diego, where she teaches today, Binder has spent the lion's share of her career interviewing students—mostly at elite colleges—about how they form their ideologies, identities, and aspirations. She's found that elite college graduates might end up wanting to be investment bankers and consultants, but they don't start out that way. Out of sixty Harvard and Stanford students that Binder interviewed for one of her studies, only two knew anything about these careers when they started college. One was the daughter of a Wall Street banker. Most new students had only the vaguest plans about their professional lives, like a Harvard alum named Kevin who told Binder he planned to "study philosophy and go to law school and have a nice life." Generally speaking, freshmen were motivated and idealistic but directionless.

Investment banks and consulting firms exploit this naiveté. Once upon a time, relatively few Ivy Leaguers went to Wall Street. Back in the 1970s and '80s, most high achievers aspired to become doctors or lawyers. But banks and management consulting firms saw that having a lot of kids from Harvard and Yale on staff was good for their brands. Starting in the 1980s, the Goldman Sachses and McKinseys of the world implemented a strategy that targeted elite undergraduates. The colleges were only too happy to help.

At the heart of the strategy is what Lauren Rivera calls "the baller lifestyle." Recruiters host receptions at the fanciest hotels, dinners at the best restaurants, and fly interviewees to big cities where they stay in top hotels. Those who make it through the winnowing process and receive a summer internship are lavished with extravagant meals, golf outings, and access to the hottest clubs. For the wealthiest students, the courtship recapitulates many of the experiences and mechanisms that carried them to elite colleges in the first place. For the rest, it's a seduction into the upper-class lifestyle. The aim, Rivera says, is to convince impressionable students that the baller lifestyle is what they want and deserve.

As Binder sees it, elite colleges' first sin is one of omission: They don't provide students a visible alternative to working on Wall Street. "Students come in naïve, and then they see juniors and seniors getting dressed up and taking over the campus each fall," Binder says. "It'd be great if the university supplied models for other careers." Many students told Binder that they applied for finance jobs out of inertia. They simply didn't know what else to do.

The failure to present alternatives becomes far more culpable when one considers the types of students involved. After all, these aren't ordinary kids. These are the highest of high achievers who have spent a lifetime competing and excelling in educational contests. Finance and consulting firms exploit this competitive instinct. They set up the recruiting process so that landing a job on Wall Street becomes the next game to win—preying upon the high achiever's fear of being left out. "At Harvard," one student told Binder, "you always want to seize every opportunity you can."

It's no coincidence that Teach for America, the one public service initiative that's made a dent among Ivy Leaguers, was founded by a Princeton grad. The competitions on each campus for the coveted slots in the program tie into the same desire for prestige that Wall Street firms play upon. Outside of this context, though, careers in education are worse than afterthoughts. A white, upper-class Stanford student named Izzy was one of many students Binder interviewed who dropped her plans to become a teacher after college. "I'd be a nothing," she told Binder. "You can't just be a teacher after graduating from Stanford." Rivera, too, found that budding teachers and artists began to doubt whether those careers were good enough for them. Whatever their initial aspirations, they came to believe that elite students deserved the most elite jobs. They feared being left out of the action or, even worse, having their options closed. "It's a bizarre status game," Binder told me. "The students wind up in a frenzied competition with each other over jobs that they had previously never heard of or thought of as dull and lacking much social purpose. Colleges play a role in not providing a counter."

The bigger sin, however, is one of commission. Colleges have long offered career services to help students plan for life after graduation. Many of these offices have operated synergistically with the finance and consulting sectors. Binder and her colleague, Daniel Davis, have documented the rise of formal partnerships between universities and corporate firms that explicitly commodify students.

The first so-called "corporate partnership program"—or CPP—was established at Stanford in 2003. Loosely modeled on the "industry affiliate programs"—under which tech firms pay for access to faculty research—CPPs go by different names at different schools, but the idea is the same: CPPs function as an on-campus headhunting agency. For an annual fee, they allow a company to outsource most of its hiring work to the career services office.

These partnerships fundamentally change the nature of these offices. Traditionally, career services offices were organized to empower students to conduct their own job searches. CPPs, by contrast, try to deliver students to their corporate partners. In fact, they're not referred to as students, but rather as "talent," who are either "specialties"—students with specific technical expertise, or "non-specialties." Schools aspire to attain "core" status so that firms will hire both their non-specialty and specialty talent. There's little ambiguity about who holds the power in these relationships. "We are not trying to make Microsoft a core company to us," one career services staffer told Binder and Davis. "We are trying to become a core university to them."

Binder and Davis found that more than half of the schools in the invitation-only Association of American Universities have formal CPPs. Many of those that don't offer other arrangements like "platinum membership," whereby prospective employers get the choicest tables at career fairs, curated email lists, and assistance setting up personal interviews. In addition to the practical assistance they offer, these relationships send a clear message about what colleges value. Bastian, a Harvard senior, told Binder, "I guess a good job means consulting or finance because, well, look, that's what the Office of Career Services has."

More than helping students realize their dreams, elite colleges are teaching them what to dream about. The students, in large part, are blank slates. By exploiting their impressionability and high-achieverism, colleges teach rich kids to want to be bankers, thereby reproducing the power dynamics that fuel educational inequality in the first place. Simultaneously, the schools act like they're powerless to do anything else.

They're not.

Clayton Spencer didn't lightly take the job as president of Bates. When the college reached out to her, she was Harvard's vice president for institutional policy. For most of her fifteen years in Cambridge, she'd felt like a kid in a candy shop. "Yo-Yo Ma actually knew my name," she told me, with a glowing smile. Moreover, when she was offered the job, Bates was still reeling from the 2007 financial crisis. But Spencer felt pulled. She'd felt an attachment to Maine since spending summer vacations with her children on Sutton Island in a house owned by Harvard, and she'd always felt romantic about liberal arts colleges. A faculty brat, Spencer had literally grown up on the campuses of Mary Baldwin and Davidson, where her father had been president, and at Williams, where she did her undergrad work.

It was easy, too, for Spencer to love Bates. It felt familiar. The cozy, idyllic campus of Victorian halls and garnet gates in Lewiston, an old mill town about forty miles north and inland of Portland, was home to about 1,800 students—almost exactly as many as at Davidson. But Bates was different in ways that mattered. Founded by abolitionists, the college admitted Black students before the Emancipation Proclamation, had been co-ed from the beginning, and has never had fraternities or sororities. It counted Ed Muskie, Bobby Kennedy, and the sportscaster Bryant Gumbel among its alumni. Tony Soprano drove his daughter Meadow to visit Bates, confidently leaving her in the Quad to chat with undergrads on a beautiful spring day while he took a break to garrote Febby Petrulio.

Before assuming the presidency, Spencer spent several months thinking about how she wanted to move the institution. "How do we make this a thing of value instead of a precious, luxury good for a certain privileged set?" she wondered. To help answer her question, she met with students, faculty, and parents. Jobs were on people's minds. "Coming off the recession, the dominant meme was a liberal arts graduate living in the basement of his parents' house and working as a barista," Spencer said, noting the irony that many students were again living in their parents' basements because of coronavirus. The poor job outcomes weren't entirely coincidental. "Historically, the better the college, the worse the career services," Spencer said. "It was like, 'why would you sully the liberal arts with getting a job?'"

This didn't sit well with Spencer. If you speak with her for even a few minutes, you'll feel the sincerity of Spencer's commitment to the liberal arts mission of "educating the whole person in community." Educating the whole person included helping them find a job in which they'd find meaning. "I think of work as a very deep thing," she told me. "What you do needs to align with who you are."

The equity considerations didn't sit right with Spencer either. Rich kids didn't need career services in the same way that lower-SES students did. "Middle- and upper-class kids can get internships anyway," Spencer said. Mostly, though, Spencer worried that many students were getting pushed into academic tracks and careers that didn't make them happy. "A lot of first-gen and international students were under intense parental pressure to major in economics for instrumental reasons," Spencer told me. "That's fine if it speaks to you, but if it doesn't, you can't do well or have your creativity unlocked."

So, Spencer defined her presidency around work. In her inaugural address, wearing the cap that her father had worn throughout his academic career, Spencer quoted Steve Jobs ("your time is limited, so don't waste it living someone else's life"), said the line between theory and practice was breaking down, and talked about Bates's "obligation as a liberal arts college to prepare our students for a life of purposeful work."

Two years later, in 2014, Bates opened its Center for Purposeful Work. Among other things, the center encouraged faculty members to connect their courses to discussions of meaning and careers, created practitioner-in-residence positions, and built a life architecture course to help students think about their direction. Spencer didn't specifically worry about promoting public service. "I'm an optimist," she told me. "If you set a goal of helping young people tap into who they are, you'll tap into a lot of idealism." In this instance, Spencer's optimism was well founded. The leading career choices among Bates graduates are education and health care, which attract 17 and 13 percent of the class, respectively. At Harvard, the rates of entry into these professions are 2 and 4 percent.

A program like the Center for Purposeful Work is hardly a panacea, but it at least suggests that it's possible to stimulate a conversation about how to live a meaningful life and to shape career choices in the process. Many of the students Binder interviewed offered commonsensical reforms. A student named Opal said, "I just think Stanford could do a much better job at cultivating the idea that it's okay not to go into consulting and finance, and to also encourage a more level playing field for smaller nonprofits." Another said, "If you're McKinsey, you should have to sponsor two or three of the smaller nonprofit organizations at career fairs or something that creates almost like a progressive taxation system on companies with more resources."

I asked Binder whether any elite college had asked her to help them raise their participation in public service careers by even 10 percent.

"No," she answered.

Their failure to do so suggests that these explicit and tacit partner-ships between elite colleges and the corporate world may not be a hold-your-nose byproduct of the system, but rather the whole point. When it comes to the stories these schools teach students to tell about themselves—the subject we turn to next—there's no such ambiguity.

10

The Best and the Brightest—
Building the Meritocracy Myth

The day after April Fools, 2014, a Princeton freshman named Tal Fortgang published a piece in the school's conservative magazine, the *Princeton Tory*, titled "Checking My Privilege: Character as the Basis of Privilege." A few weeks later, *Time* republished it under the title "Why I'll Never Apologize for My White Male Privilege." One might think the magazine was trying to be provocative.

Long story short, Fortgang didn't like being told to check his privilege. "The phrase, handed down by my moral superiors, descends recklessly, like an Obama-sanctioned drone, and aims laser-like at my pinkish-peach complexion, my maleness, and the nerve I displayed in offering an opinion rooted in a personal Weltanschauung," he wrote. Fortgang condemned his Princeton classmates for having diminished everything he'd accomplished as the product not of his hard work, but rather of "some invisible patron saint of white maleness." He'd taken his classmates' challenge, investigated his family history, and determined that it was the opposite of entitled. His grandfather had fled Poland and done hard labor at a Siberian displaced persons' camp. His grandmother had been marched through the freezing cold to Bergen-Belsen, where she'd have died had the Allies not liberated the concentration camp in time. "I have checked my privilege," Fortgang concluded. "And I apologize for nothing."

While Fortgang's essay was superficially about his own experience, and his frustration with a kind of rhetorical exchange that's familiar to anyone who's spent time in a college classroom recently, he connected it to a broader ideological framework. This was Princeton, after all. On Fortgang's telling, the challenge to him was more broadly a challenge to the American Dream, the Constitution, and even to our collective sanity. "Check your privilege," he argued, "and realize that nothing you have accomplished is real." It's easy enough to imagine him holding a copy of *Atlas Shrugged* in one hand and a gin and tonic in the other as he rails against the looters in a late-night, dorm room bullshit session. Fortgang refused to brand his accusers as racist, but he couldn't forgive them for their greatest sin. "I condemn them," he wrote, "for casting the equal protection clause, indeed the very idea of a meritocracy, as a myth."

Unsurprisingly, Fortgang's piece triggered strong responses. Katie McDonough, who's currently an editor at the *New Republic*, offered a typical one in *Salon*. "It's likely," McDonough wrote, "that Fortgang will have the opportunity at Princeton to learn about the racial wealth gap, the legacy of redlining, the unemployment rate among college educated men of color versus their white counterparts, the convergence of racism and sexism that leaves women of color disproportionately impacted by domestic violence, the gender pay gap experienced by black women, the deadly violence faced by black children and the myriad other manifestations of racism in the United States. Basically, all of the things that he will never have to experience as an extraordinarily privileged white man."

Maybe Fortgang deserves McDonough's rage, but his views didn't come out of nowhere. The real villains are the institutions that indoctrinated him with that ideology. Allow me to present a prime suspect: Just seven months earlier, at Princeton's opening exercises, Fortgang and his classmates got a clear sense of what the institution valued. Princeton honored seven students in the University Chapel that windy September afternoon—including four for the George B. Wood Legacy Sophomore and Junior Prizes. As the dean of the college presented the winners, she announced where each had gone to high school. Five had attended prep schools—Groton, Archmere Academy in Delaware, San Francisco

University High School, Dalton, and Bolles. One had attended Chaparral High School in Scottsdale, where 2 percent of the students are Black. The last attended Horace Greeley in Chappaqua, where less than 1 percent of the students are Black and the average family income exceeds $200,000 per year. All the students were white.

President Christopher L. Eisgruber, the son of an academic and himself a graduate of Princeton, Oxford (on a Rhodes), and University of Chicago Law School, praised the 1,286 entering freshmen as an "extraordinarily accomplished" group. "All of you have been blessed with exceptional talents," he said, "and your time on this campus is itself a great gift. When, four years from now, you graduate from Princeton, you will find it easier than most people to be successful at whatever career you pursue."

No one said anything that day about the importance of public service or the students' good fortune in being born into wealthy families. No one was summoned to the pulpit for holding down a full-time job while going to college or for getting good grades while studying in their bathroom. No, they were instead honored for their prodigious talents and accomplishments. The message could hardly have been clearer: You deserve this.

That's pretty much how it always is at events like these. "This class is one of the most talented we have ever assembled," said Stanford president John Hennessy, shortly after taking the college's reins in 2000. "Academically, your credentials are stellar." In case any of the freshmen entering a school where the mean family income is around $472,000 a year worried that they didn't merit their position, he offered the sort of hail-fellow-well-met joke that's just the thing to put a wealthy, angst-ridden teenager's mind at ease. "Our admission office is one of the best in the country," Hennessy said, "and we don't make mistakes!"

Over the past five years or so, a cottage industry has emerged of intellectuals publishing books decrying the advent of the concept of meritocracy. None of these authors advance the nihilistic straw man that Fortgang constructs and rebuts in his essay. They don't say that no accomplishment is deserved. None say either, à la McDonough, that it's impossible for a white male to have suffered adversity. What they have in common is that all the authors believe, for different reasons, that meritocracy is bad. Each is also a professor at an elite college.

If you've read even one of these books, you'll probably remember that a self-taught sociologist named Michael Young coined the term "meritocracy" in a 1958 book as a sarcastic critique of Great Britain's post-war Education Act. This legislation (slightly) expanded opportunity for working-class children by admitting select eleven-year-olds to free public grammar schools, oriented toward white-collar jobs, based on an IQ-style exam called the "eleven-plus."

The Rise of the Meritocracy is an odd book. Young drafted it in the form of a PhD thesis written from the perspective of a sociologist in 2030. A publisher urged him to turn it into a work of fiction, then, after reading the resulting novel, urged him to turn it back. One detects shades of Aldous Huxley in the finished product, if only Huxley had styled *Brave New World* as Bernard Marx's dissertation. In Young's counter-history, the landed gentry are displaced by a superiorly educated (but similarly inbred) new elite of the super-intelligent, who are debatably more deserving of their status, but inarguably more arrogant because they believe in the myth of their own superiority. "The upper classes," wrote the sociologist of the future (coincidentally named Michael Young), "are no longer weakened by self-doubt and criticism." The book seems prescient in many respects, including Young's prediction of the rise of the test-prep industry.

Regardless of whether you've read any of these books, you probably have the sense, too, that the term "meritocracy" is being and has been used in different ways. Sometimes it's employed prescriptively—and often persuasively—as a rallying cry against an unfair status quo. Civil service exams, which the U.S. government implemented after President James Garfield's assassination in 1881, may have their problems, but they're way better than the spoils system they replaced. James Conant's advocacy of the SAT was similarly progressive in context. Testing has major problems, but it's surely superior to taking everyone from boarding schools or letting people buy their way in.

The trouble starts when the term is used descriptively, as in "college admissions are meritocratic." Almost inevitably, when used in this sense, it's to rationalize an inequitable status quo. Often, it's liberals making these excuses. For meritocracy is a seductive temptress. It's particularly alluring to the successful, says Harvard's Michael Sandel, author of *The Tyranny of Merit: What's Become of the Common Good*, because it affirms their freedom and soothes whatever ambivalence they may have about whether they deserve their position.

Meritocratic belief makes elites smug. That's annoying. The bigger problem is what it leads them to believe about others. After all, meritocracy is a double-edged sword. If one believes that they deserve their place at Harvard or the yacht club then, as Sandel says, "it means that those who are left behind deserve their fate as well." The winners are tempted to look down upon the losers with disdain. Indeed, social psychologists have found that college-educated elites look down on "less-educated" people more than the poor. Ironically, these less-educated people internalize the judgments of the elite and blame themselves for their situations.

America's obsession with elite credentials only worsens this dynamic. At one point, thirteen of President Obama's twenty-one cabinet members had gone to Harvard or Yale. More than two-thirds went to Ivy League schools. As we know from Lauren Rivera, the window offices of Goldman Sachs, McKinsey, and Skadden Arps are filled almost exclusively by these types. The clear signal is that only an elite degree matters. This is impossible to reconcile with the liberal mantra that going to college solves everything. It also ignores the barriers to getting any college degree, let alone an elite one. The message of meritocrats is that ordinary people, who often lack a voice and power, deserve their status.

From here, Sandel and Yale's Daniel Markovits, author of *The Meritocracy Trap*, draw a straight line to Donald Trump. Meritocracy's implicit framing of disadvantage as a failure of skill and effort leads to a sort of politics of humiliation. Unemployment is seen as a reflection of personal failure rather than a societal or economic design flaw. More than twice as many Americans as Europeans—approximately 70 percent—believe that poor people can escape poverty on their own.

This opens the door to populism and nativism. When whites who can't get ahead are told that they're deficient, Markovits says they develop "a deep and pervasive mistrust of expertise and institutions." When they simultaneously hear the liberal cries for affirmative action, which suspends meritocratic principles, Markovits argues that they have literally no choice but to devolve into identity politics. It's only in this context that one can understand Trump's professed love of "the poorly educated."

It has become standard fare for Republican politicians to exploit this anti-elite resentment. Ironically, many of them, including Senators Ted Cruz and Josh Hawley, graduated from elite schools, and nearly all want their kids to attend them. Nevertheless, among Republican voters, faith in the academy is eroding. In 2012, 53 percent of Republicans said colleges and universities had a positive impact on the country. Seven years later, that figure had dropped to 33 percent. (By contrast, 67 percent of Democrats say colleges have a positive effect versus just 18 percent who say their impact is negative.) It's no coincidence that Donald Trump's key base is white men without college educations—among whom he held a 48 percent advantage in 2016 and a 42-point edge in his loss to Joe Biden.

Sandel argues that belief in meritocracy erodes the national moral fabric. "The more we think of ourselves as self-made and self-sufficient, the harder it is to learn gratitude and humility," he writes. "And without these sentiments, it is hard to care for the common good." Harvard Law School's Lani Guinier says that meritocracy has similarly degraded colleges and universities. Belief in meritocracy changes the very nature of education. It places emphasis on who wins the admissions beauty pageant over what is learned. It treats intelligence as static, instead of something that can be nurtured. Universities, she argues, should be measured not by test scores, but by how their students contribute to society—a shift from "testocratic" to "democratic" merit. "What's urgent for this world," Guinier writes, "is a student's capacity to collaborate and to think creatively."

At a psychological level, social scientists have shown that belief in meritocracy makes people act more selfishly and less self-critically. At an organizational and sociological level, meritocratic cultures are more prone to discrimination. In an MIT experiment, participants playing the role of managers awarded more money to men over equally qualified women when the fake company was described as embracing meritocratic values and practices like performance-based raises. Richard Rothstein describes a similar dynamic in affluent suburbs. "The false sense of superiority that segregation fosters in whites contributes to their rejection of policies to integrate American society," he writes. On top of everything else, the crushing demands meritocracy places on both successful white-collar workers and students makes even the winners miserable. Ask anyone who works at Goldman Sachs. The pay is great, but the hours suck, and the wheel never stops turning.

Michael Sandel reports that more and more of his students believe, like Fortgang, that their success is earned. "Among the students I teach," he writes, "this meritocratic faith has intensified." This is ironic since Sandel devotes a significant part of Justice, his famous course, to the teachings of the eminent American philosopher John Rawls, who believed that ethical questions should be analyzed from the standpoint of a hypothetical "original position" in which people don't know their race, gender, class, or position in society. From behind this "veil of ignorance," it's clear that no one would ever choose a college admissions system in which legacy status, wealth, or athletic prowess were excessively rewarded since they're the result of what amounts to a natural lottery. Yet, the students in Justice think they deserve to be there.

Sandel is hardly alone in his observation. Tufts professor Natasha Warikoo spent three years interviewing Harvard, Brown, and Oxford students about their views on race and merit. She found that Harvard and Brown students have a firmly held, implicit belief that they deserve their position. "They express strong faith in the way that their college selects students. They obviously have gotten in and they believe in that system pretty strongly," Warikoo said. Ironically, elite U.S. students had greater faith in meritocratic admissions than their European counterparts, even though admissions to Oxford are based solely on academic criteria. That's because Ivy League schools propagate an ideal of diversity, which Warikoo calls "collective merit." This framework conveniently rationalizes both affirmative action and ALDC preferences. "Students will say things like 'we all bring something different, so what makes me meritorious might be different than what makes you meritorious,'" Warikoo told me. "I might have a lower SAT score than you, but I'm an athlete—that's my contribution. And they buy into that."

Other sociologists have observed similar dynamics at elite boarding schools. After embedding himself for a year as a teacher at St. Paul's in New Hampshire, Shamus Khan reported that the wealthy white students believed it was their hard work that had gotten them in. Ruben Gaztambide-Fernandez found the same thing after two years of ethnographic research at the "Weston School," which sounds suspiciously like Phillips Exeter Academy. The white Westonians believed they'd gotten in because of their initiative and well-roundedness, not their family's wealth or connections.

At CUNY, I see almost none of this. I've never seen or heard anyone boast that their college status is deserved or look down upon someone who dropped out or didn't make it past high school. This is almost certainly due at least in part to the differences in parenting styles that Annette Lareau talks about. When wealthy parents concertedly cultivate their children, they're doing it with an eye on the types of opportunities that will preserve their child's class position. To be sure, concerted cultivation of the would-be elite teenager involves substantial rigors— AP exams, SAT tutors, leadership in clubs. This gauntlet of stress, as Sandel calls it, makes successes feel earned and predisposes concertedly cultivated kids to succumbing to the temptation of meritocratic belief.

I've never met a John Jay student whose mother or father engaged in concerted cultivation. In fact, other than at graduation, I've never met a parent at all. In twenty years, I've had two students complain about their grade. By contrast, almost all the people I interviewed for this book—most of whom teach at elite colleges—reported to me that they were frequently challenged on grades by parents and students alike.

Compounding matters, meritocracy is a very sticky belief. It's deeply embedded in American culture through Horatio Alger-type novels, folktales like *The Little Engine That Could*, and marketing slogans with near-gospel status such as "Just Do It." Researchers have found that meritocratic beliefs can be easily enhanced in experiments, suggesting it's a narrative that people are predisposed to believe. Once someone has formed a belief in meritocracy, it's tough to budge. For example, the psychologist Allison Ledgerwood found that people were more likely to judge a scientific study positively when it confirmed the idea that hard work leads to success and were disinclined to believe a study contradicting that premise. It's thus hardly surprising that, despite the overwhelming evidence to the contrary, Americans believe—by a 71-to-21 margin—that hard work and determination influence economic mobility more than external conditions like the economic circumstances in which someone grew up. Ledgerwood found that biased assimilation is so strong that after reading a passage saying that the system rewards luck, subjects worked harder at an arbitrary task, presumably to disprove the premise.

In the most stunning version of this, Amy Binder found that Harvard and Stanford students come to believe that they and their institutions are superior to their peers. For example, they regard the University of Pennsylvania as too vocational. A Harvard alumnus named Nathan told Binder that Penn students were only interested in education as a "means to an end," while he valued "learning for learning's sake." Nathan ended up in finance. They dismiss MIT and Cal Tech as overly "technical," the University of Chicago—"the place where fun goes to die"—for not offering a social experience that could benefit them, and Duke for being too fun. Schools outside the *U.S. News & World Report* Top Ten were branded by these Harvard and Stanford students as safeties and backups. In short, they became hierarchical in the extreme.

To fight the human tendency to see one's place in the world as deserved, elite colleges would have to try to keep meritocratic beliefs from forming in the first place, and, after they arose, combat them vigilantly. They do almost precisely the opposite.

You won't find the word "merit" in Clayton Spencer's inaugural address or in any of the ten commencement speeches she's given since. Part of it's because the concept is difficult to defend, she says, "once you're not so naïve about what standardized tests are measuring—vocabulary, analogies—things that are so culture bound." Spencer thinks the concept of merit has been interpreted too narrowly and overlooks potential and creativity. "I think to use the word is deeply ignorant," she says, "and you'll never find me using it."

But Spencer's the exception to the rule. Far more typical is the welcome that Drew Faust offered at her final Harvard commencement as president in 2018. "Heartfelt congratulations to you, our graduates, and to your families," she said, "for the hard work and many accomplishments that have brought you to this day." Stanford's president Marc Tessier-Lavigne must have hired the same speechwriter the following year. "To the class of 2019," he said, "I want to express how proud we are of all that you have accomplished during your time at Stanford, and of all the hard work that brought you to this stadium this morning."

For sure, these speeches, and the hundreds like it that are offered each spring, say many noble things about the ethical obligations of the university and its graduates. Few, however, question the contradictions of the institutions themselves. Yale president Peter Salovey delivered a rousing commencement address in 2019, titled "What Are You For?" It was really about what Salovey was for. "I am for the American Dream in all its rich promise," he proclaimed that day, "the idea that opportunities are shared widely and that access to education is within reach for the many, not the few." Conspicuously absent from Salovey's speech is any mention of the fact that the average Yale student's family income exceeds half a million dollars and that more students come from families in the top 1 percent than the bottom 60 percent.

When Arizona State's Jenifer Partch and Richard Kinnier examined the content of commencement speeches, they found a fair amount of consistency. The most popular theme was a call to "give back" or "serve humanity." Almost as many speakers urged graduates to act ethically. Just over half encouraged them to improve themselves by seeking challenges and expanding their horizons. Being humble and grateful appears nowhere on their list.

In this context, the synergy between suburbs and elite colleges is palpable. High school graduation speeches inevitably begin, like Faust and Tessier-Lavigne, from a premise of taking "pride" in "accomplishment" and "hard work." Few, if any, acknowledge the luck that makes the accomplishment and hard work possible.

These omissions become all the more culpable when one understands how easy it is for belief in merit to become anchored and how difficult it is to dislodge once it does. The notion that hard work makes privilege deserved—the essence of meritocracy—is the precise dynamic that makes winners comfortable with hoarding.

The graduates of Harvard and Yale are not the best and the brightest or the hardest working. They are, more precisely, some of the best, brightest, and hardest working among the rich and the richest. An honest speech would balance recognition of their hard work with a healthy dose of humility and recognition that they were the winners in a game where the table had been tilted in their favor from the start.

But that would be incompatible with the brand.

11

The Doubly Disadvantaged

Joyce Suslovic is, for want of a better word, a teacher. More accurately, she's the sort of professional for whom education is a passion and a cause, who fundamentally changes the lives of the students she touches, and who you're lucky if you get one of in your lifetime. At Henninger High School in Syracuse, where white students are in the minority, she's a legend. Known to her students as "Miss S" or "Miss Sus" (or "J-Sus," as she identifies herself in a decent rap that she laid down for the class of 2020), Joyce routinely stays until nine at night, works weekends, teaches outside during fire drills, feeds hungry kids, takes them on field trips, lobbies the school board, mobilizes her students to lobby the school board, and writes college recommendations for apparently everyone. On top of everything else, Joyce somehow found time to be a single mom.

To raise her own kids, Joyce bought a modest home in a nearby suburban school district. Jamesville-Dewitt is known for its high school, which Barack Obama called the "best in the world," and for its diversity. Indeed, Joyce's daughter, Brianna, recalls attending consecutive birthday parties in a trailer and a mansion. Brianna Suslovic, whose father is Black and who identifies herself as Black, flourished at the high school. She penned multiple opinion pieces in the *Post-Standard* on various social justice issues for which she won a series of awards. She also played the bassoon in the Syracuse Symphony Youth Orchestra, won a playwriting festival, and received a gold medal in a national

Spanish competition. During her senior year, she applied to eight colleges, including one Ivy—Harvard—because she had an uncle who lived in Cambridge, which she found fun to visit. When she got in, she knew almost nothing about Harvard. "I didn't have any understanding of what it would mean to be there," she told me.

When Brianna met her roommates on the first day of school, it seemed as if they'd all come from different worlds. One had gone to Andover. Another was a lacrosse recruit. Only the third, a child of Taiwanese immigrants, was "normal like me," as Brianna puts it. She coped by keeping out of her room as much as she could, spending most of her time with a pair of friends she met in a Facebook group who, like her, identified as queer and "janky"—meaning vocal people on a shoestring budget.

Money occupied a central place in Brianna and her friends' thoughts. "We were frantic about how we'd get cash," she told me. "So much of what we experienced was about being broke." Joyce, who'd taken out a second mortgage to pay for Brianna's bassoon and her brother's cello, was paying as much as she could. Brianna made up the difference by working. She volunteered for psychology studies, scanned archival Persian documents for a professor, and spoke with prospective students on behalf of the undergraduate minority recruitment program. This was one of many respects in which she and her friends felt different from their classmates. "We were constantly scraping to make a few extra bucks," she said, "while all of these people were out at parties talking about things we didn't care about."

Initially, when Brianna thought about why she didn't fit in at Harvard, she interpreted her disaffection principally through the lenses of sexual orientation and race. In November of her first year, the *Crimson* printed an op-ed arguing against affirmative action. "How would you feel if you were assured before going into surgery that your surgeon was the beneficiary of affirmative action in medical school?" asked the author. "I do not see why higher academic institutions should lower their standards for admission." Brianna knew that affirmative action benefited white women more than any marginalized group, and the author had identified herself as a legacy. But the promotion of the idea that affirmative action for disadvantaged populations was a mistake, and the implication that all students of color were the beneficiaries of affirmative action, only furthered her sense of isolation.

During her sophomore year, a pair of experiences shifted Brianna's perspective. At Harvard, sophomores move from a dorm in Harvard Yard to one of twelve "houses" where they spend the remainder of their undergraduate career. Shortly after joining Winthrop House, Brianna overheard a woman in the dining hall ask, "Doesn't everyone have an au pair?" Brianna thereafter posted the following snarky comment on Facebook—without identifying the speaker:

> Overheard in Winthrop Dining Hall: "I had a British au pair when I was little."
> #umcanyounot
> Yes, this is me judging (perhaps unfairly) but SERIOUSLY THAT IS SO BOUGIE I CAN'T EVEN

Now your reaction to this little nugget almost certainly depends on your own class status. If you were raised middle class, like me, you probably chuckled. It's a solid hashtag and the word "bougie" is pretty much always funny. I found it quite funny. I could also relate. When I was a young lawyer, I had a similar experience. At a birthday party, I was chatting amiably with my friend's sister—who worked as an investment banker at Goldman Sachs and was married to a consultant at Morgan Stanley—when she bemoaned that the couple's third nanny had just quit. I spit out my beer and asked incredulously, "Three nannies?"

"You obviously don't have children," she replied.

It was true. I didn't. But I have three now and we've somehow managed without three nannies. Maybe my friend's sister meant that I obviously wasn't an investment banker. Regardless, I think Brianna's post is amusing and, indeed, it got its fair share of LOLs. But if you were raised with money, you probably think Brianna missed some important context. Perhaps you're even offended.

Many of her classmates were.

"Wealth happens. It's O.K.," replied one.

"Actually, au pairs aren't expensive," replied another.

Other comments were harsher. "Your experience is totally cool, but so is everybody else's. How about trying to stop judging and regulating what's 'okay' for people to relate as their own experiences. Being heard is different from shutting people up." That one got the most likes. Of course, they didn't know that au pairs were entirely out of Brianna's frame of reference. J-Sus, being who she was, had carted her daughter along to basketball games, plays, and college fairs.

Brianna felt compelled to issue an apology later that day. "This was just my initial gut reaction to something out of the realm of my class experience," she wrote. "Au pairs are something I obviously don't know much about and I'm willing to apologize for my emotional reaction. Sorry!" In the end, the weight of Harvard public opinion had forced Brianna into apologizing for "wealth shaming." But it wasn't wealth shaming. She hadn't identified anyone. It was wealth naming. Admitting the reality of their advantage was more than Brianna's classmates could handle.

Around the same time, Brianna met, through the Black Students Association, a young researcher who offered her twenty dollars to let him interview her about her experience at Harvard. He had an office in a corner of Mather House, an uninviting, homely building built in the Brutalist style. It looks like it was made from a Girder and Panel set, for anyone old enough to remember those. The researcher had made the office as cozy as possible, which is to say not all that cozy. Brianna spent her two hours with him sitting in an upholstered chair looking out on the Mather House courtyard.

The interviewer was an imposing man, standing a full six-foot-five, but he had a gentle demeanor—she'd later learn that he was a knitter and a foodie. Almost immediately, she felt comfortable with him. He seemed genuinely interested in where she was coming from. "I got a sense that he wanted to be a resource to the people he was interviewing," Brianna said. "He was warm, and he was clearly invested in people of color." Given that Joyce was white, Brianna had worried that she might not be the best person for the interview, but she soon saw that the researcher's interest went beyond race. Many of the questions were about things that no one ever asked about, like meals, travel, and money.

As she reflected on the interview, the way she thought about the au pair exchange began to change. "I had always seen things more in race terms," she told me, "but the incident felt like a real-life example of the questions he had asked." Increasingly, she felt that being a woman of color couldn't by itself explain the sense of dissatisfaction that she felt with Harvard. Today, it's only part of the story she tells. "When I was there, I understood a lot of the alienation to be about race," Suslovic said, "but I now see it as about class." Being an outsider in multiple ways intersected to make her experience, and others like her, uniquely challenging.

Suslovic's interviewer was Anthony Abraham Jack, then a doctoral student in sociology and today the nation's leading scholar on how race and class inequities on college campuses intersect to create unique barriers to academic success. Jack, like Suslovic, was raised by a single mother, who supported him and his two siblings by working as a security guard at the local middle school. Jack describes himself as a "Head Start kid," and his hometown of Coconut Grove, Florida, as "a neighborhood that time forgot," but he was a good student and his mom kept him on track.

At Coral Gables Senior High—where 84 percent of the students identify as Hispanic—Jack took up football and became an excellent offensive tackle. During his junior year, he blew out his shoulder. As Jack tells it, his coach loved athlete-students but disliked student-athletes. When he learned that Jack needed to have surgery, he kicked Jack off the team. Jack responded by securing a scholarship to spend his senior year at Gulliver Prep, an elite private school about five miles southwest on Route 1. In Jack's view, that year changed the course of his life.

At Gulliver Prep, Jack excelled enough academically and athletically that the coach recommended him to his counterpart at Amherst, which was both the best school he got into and which offered him the most financial aid. Landing at Amherst felt like a shock to Jack's system. Until his senior year, he'd never encountered rich people. He'd only heard of them from his grandmother, who would tell him stories of the doctors and lawyers whose houses she cleaned. But *everyone* at Amherst seemed rich. Even the students of color appeared to have parents who were investment bankers and consultants. On his first day on campus, Jack asked himself, "Where are the other poor Black kids?"

In time, Jack found some. Most of them struggled. Jack, however, survived—even thrived. He came to believe that the year he'd spent at Gulliver was what made the difference. It enabled him to adapt to Amherst better than his classmates who'd never encountered wealth. Jack made understanding that distinction his life's work. As a doctoral student in sociology, he explored the experiences of low-income students at a college he called "Renowned," which is obviously Harvard. His two years of fieldwork—including interviews with more than one hundred students in his Mather House office—became his PhD dissertation, supervised by the renowned sociologist William Julius Wilson, and a widely acclaimed 2019 book, *The Privileged Poor: How Elite Colleges Are Failing Disadvantaged Students.*

"Privileged Poor" is the name Jack gives to students, like him, who'd grown up in poverty but had managed through admission to a prep school to secure an early introduction to the world of privilege. The Privileged Poor face some challenges but not nearly so many as their counterparts who enter college directly from under-resourced, over-crowded, and de facto segregated poor local schools. Jack calls these students "Doubly Disadvantaged."

The Doubly Disadvantaged struggle mightily. The language they used with Jack to describe the arc of their academic careers closely resembles the narratives of hope that CUNY students offered to Christina Ciocca Eller. "We come here, we're so alive and full of hope," said Jose, a talkative senior from a poor, mostly Latino neighborhood in Los Angeles. But four years at Harvard had beaten him down. "The place puts you in a depression," Jose told Jack. He called the environment "toxic."

Isolation is one of the dynamics that contributes to the toxicity Jose describes. "You feel like you don't fit in," Jose said. "You feel like you're alone, like there's no one that can relate." This narrative, and the many like it that students shared with Jack, call to mind the student who told

Debbie Bial that he could have made it through college if only he'd had his posse. The number of poor students at elite colleges is below a critical mass that would allow them to connect with one another and offer mutual support. Elise, a white junior whose family had been evicted many times and later disowned her because they looked upon going away to college as akin to desertion, told Jack, "When I need help, I don't have anyone to turn to. I don't have a support network. I'm on my own."

Exclusion is another toxic dynamic. Money creates massive, sometimes humiliating, disparities of opportunity. One student after another told Jack about being left out of excursions to shop or dine out for "cheap" lobster. Some were offered money for the best room in a dorm suite. Many were—and are—forced to perform janitorial services as part of their work study or for extra money. "Hiring poor students to clean the toilets in rich students' dorm rooms is not a way to break down class boundaries," writes Jack.

These differences of opportunity create a universe of insiders and outsiders. They also pervert values. Many of the students Jack interviewed regarded this as the more serious consequence. William, a poor, white Midwesterner, explained how Harvard encouraged poor students to join the elite and pursue selfish careers. "The biggest challenge is the pressure to become one of them," he said, using language that evokes Amy Binder's research. "They just expect the goal of all this is to have money and be part of the upper class," William told Jack. "Forty percent of people don't come into Renowned thinking of consulting. People are transformed. It is just expected that one social class is inherently better than the other, more desirable."

Jack calls elite college admissions a "bundle of confusing contradictions." The schools admit some poor students of color but simultaneously maintain policies that stigmatize them and prevent them from succeeding. Some of these policies, like dorm crew and closing dining halls during breaks, are explicit. The most daunting challenges, however, remain unspoken. Unless you're in math or science, success in college depends largely on whether you're able to forge relationships with faculty members, who can write recommendations and serve as conduits to research opportunities, graduate programs, and coveted internships. Jack calls this the "hidden curriculum." It tests whether you can decipher and navigate the social world of an elite institution.

Acing the hidden curriculum requires students to reach out to professors. But this expectation is unspoken, and, unless you've lived in this universe before, not understood. Only about a third of the Doubly Disadvantaged reported having positive relationships with faculty members. A significant contributing factor is that they don't visit professors in their offices. Jack says that Gulliver Prep had mandatory office hours, and so he became habituated to interacting with advisers and teachers in a way that made him more at ease when he landed at Amherst.

The Doubly Disadvantaged don't have that experience to draw upon. To them, faculty and administrators are "authority figures who should be treated with deference and left unburdened by their questions and needs." They talked about being grateful to professors rather than demanding. Shaniqua, a doubly disadvantaged Black woman who'd spent parts of her childhood living in shelters, told Jack, "When you're poor and you're homeless, you get used to taking what is given."

At first blush, the fix to this problem may sound easy: Encourage doubly disadvantaged students to go to office hours. But when one understands the motivation behind their reluctance to do so, the problem is revealed as infinitely more daunting. Poor students of color don't go to office hours because they don't think that's how academia is supposed to work. Talking to professors would be an imposition or, worse still, kissing up. As they see it, the teacher-student relationship should operate within the boundaries of the coursework.

They believe, in other words, in meritocracy—both as a prescriptive and descriptive matter. "The Doubly Disadvantaged express strong faith in the idea of meritocracy," Jack writes, "believing that focusing on 'the work' is enough for success." Maybe the work should be enough for success. But the mistaken belief that it's enough—a belief that elite colleges foster with their narratives of hard work and desert and the image that the students they admit are the best and the brightest—could hardly be more destructive. "They actually stand to lose the most for believing so," Jack says.

Tressie McMillan Cottom—the magnificent writer, sociologist, and public intellectual—echoes Jack's sentiment. "Nobody believes in mobility more than Black people," Cottom told podcaster Ezra Klein. "Nobody believes in the promise of this country more than Black people, and nobody has less reason to believe it than we do, and I think holding those two ideas at the same time is probably why our health outcomes are as poor as they are."

My sense from dinner table conversations with well-intentioned white people is that they perceive the dynamic Jack describes—what he calls structural exclusion—as a bit trivial. Not unimportant. Not unworthy of redress. But not the type of phenomenon that can explain massive disparities. From where I sit—as a former student and current professor—it's almost the whole ballgame.

Of course, I didn't experience Harvard as a person of color, and my family wasn't poor, but we definitely weren't rich. I would say I oozed middle class. I'd been to a few Broadway shows on field trips with my father's high school because my mother loved theatre, but that was about the extent of my exposure to higher pleasures, as John Stuart Mill would say. My family still thought of eating out at a Chinese restaurant as fancy. None of us had ever left the country. Corduroy pants were the staple of my wardrobe. (Okay, delete "were.") My sport was bowling. I'm going to go out on a limb here and say I'm the only student in Harvard's history who had a poster of Mark Roth hanging in his dorm room.

At the time, I didn't think about the world in terms of class. More or less everyone I'd ever known had lived in an apartment building or a split-level home that cost between $65,000 and $85,000. I'd read about wealthy people—principally in *The Great Gatsby*, but even though the West Egg was less than fifteen miles away from my own home in the Valley of Ashes, they seemed like abstractions. I thought of the rich the same way I think of aliens—something that probably exists in the universe but that I wasn't likely to meet in my lifetime. Presumably, the reciprocal was true of my future classmates. They'd probably read about working-class people in *The Outsiders* and regarded them as a novelty, like a violet M&M.

What happens when rich and poor mix? If you learned anything from S. E. Hinton, it should be that no Soc wants to be a Greaser. When I arrived at Harvard, I felt excluded in little ways. My clothes didn't look quite right. I couldn't afford to go out to eat with people or I stressed about the money when I did. Shockingly, no one cared about my bowling prowess. I felt excluded and alone. This was unpleasant but survivable.

Other differences mattered far more, in ways that I didn't appreciate at the time. Many of my rich classmates who'd attended private school—the Doubly Advantaged—had cozy relationships with faculty members. They spoke directly to professors, which I thought of as brownnosing, and called them by their first name, which I thought of as rude. Like Jack's interviewees, I believed the academic relationship should operate within the context of the classroom. Harvard, like many other elite colleges, does nothing to contradict this belief. Courses often have several hundred students, and most grades are given by a graduate student section leader. It's easy to never interact with a professor. I did my undergraduate thesis with Nathan Glazer, a renowned sociologist of education, CUNY graduate, and, like me, a New York Jew. We spoke twice during the year he served as my mentor—once in person for thirty minutes, the other on the phone for ten. I thought we understood each other quite well. The significant downside of this approach was that—though I revered teachers—I left college having formed precisely zero relationships with professors.

Now that I sit on the other side of the table, I want to shake my younger self by the collar. Most people get into teaching because they want to help students. Maybe that's less true at elite colleges or true in a different way—often it's graduate students that elite faculty prefer to focus their attention on. But it's certainly true where I teach, and so far as I can tell, at pretty much all public colleges. At a human level, professors crave that contact far more than formal classroom interaction. And it's what the students need. At John Jay, none of our students are Doubly Advantaged. They need to be connected with internships, strategize how to prepare for law school, and advised what to wear for an interview. But the barrier Jack describes is there. For the most part, the students don't come. When they do, the relationships are often overly formal. I try to get the students I teach to call me by first name because it's an important first step to demystifying the elite. But it's challenging for them, as it was for me. They believe it should be, and is, all about the work. This false belief that the world operates as a meritocracy is a massive obstacle to success. When you're also navigating the world as a person of color, this obstacle can be close to insurmountable.

We don't know precisely how many students are Doubly Disadvantaged. Harvard, like many elite colleges, carefully guards demographic data regarding its students of color. In Jack's study, more than half of the Black students came from upper-income families. Of the lower-income students, about half satisfied his definition of Privileged Poor—meaning they'd gone to a private high school. Only about a quarter of the Black students in his sample were Doubly Disadvantaged. The profile of the Latinx students with whom Jack spoke was somewhat different. None came from wealthy families. Approximately one-third were Privileged Poor. Overall, less than half of the students of color Jack interviewed were Doubly Disadvantaged.

It's entirely possible that Jack's sample isn't representative. As a qualitative researcher, his interest is more in the richness of narrative than statistical precision. He also employs snowball sampling—meaning he interviews people referred by other participants. So, his selection process isn't random. I would argue that this makes it likely that Jack's study oversampled poor students. This intuition is supported by former Princeton president William Bowen and former Harvard president Derek Bok's study of affirmative action at elite colleges, which found, like Jack, that a majority of Black students came from high-income families. But it's true that we don't know exactly how many students of color are Doubly Disadvantaged. We can, however, draw some inferences from what we do know.

We know, first, that socioeconomic diversity at elite colleges is really bad. As a reminder, merely 3 percent of Harvard students come from the lowest income quintile. That means that out of the roughly 1,700 freshmen who are admitted each year, approximately fifty are poor. If we assume, generously, that a quarter of these students are Black, that would mean about twelve per cohort. Kiki, a Princeton student who Paul Tough profiled in *The Years That Matter Most*, said that she'd met this very number of low-income Black students in her class. Even if one fudges the math, we're talking tiny numbers.

Those numbers are likely to be tinier still because we know—second—that race diversity at elite colleges is also quite bad. Overall, the Black population at elite colleges hasn't increased significantly since the 1970s. In fact, the rate of Black admissions has been so steady that Shaun Harper, the executive director of the Race and Equity Center at the University of Southern California, has accused Ivy League colleges of collusion. "It just seems to me that there has been some determination about how many Black students are worthy of admission to these institutions," Harper said. "It's just too similar."

Harvard's race numbers have improved recently. In the class of 2024, about 47 percent of students are white, 24 percent Asian American (tracking Harvard's language), 15 percent African American (again, tracking their terminology), and 13 percent Hispanic or Latino. In a ranking of the top one hundred universities by diversity, Harvard comes in twenty-second.* But Harvard is an outlier in this regard. Black representation at other Ivy-Plus colleges has historically hit a ceiling of around 8 percent. At Dartmouth, Cornell, Brown, University of Pennsylvania, and Duke, the percentage of Black students are 4.9, 5.3, 6.5, 6.7, and 6.9, respectively. It's the consistency of these statistics, and their upper limit, which fuels Harper's suspicion.

---

* The ranking is based on the Herfindahl–Hirschman Index (HHI), which measures diversity in a variety of settings such as competition in a business market or biodiversity in an ecosystem. Mathematically, it's the sum of the squares of the market shares. So, in a market where two firms each controlled half the market, the HHI would be $0.5^2 + 0.5^2 = 0.5$. An HHI above 0.25 is generally regarded as indicating high concentration. By this definition, basically every college and university ranked among the top one hundred is highly concentrated. Astute observers will note that a lack of white students could negatively affect diversity. Only one school—California State University, Los Angeles—suffered in the ranking because of a lack of white students. Some of the higher-ranking schools have significant Asian representation. For example, at MIT, which ranks third, a plurality of the students, 42 percent, are Asian. Thirty-nine percent are white, 14 percent are Hispanic or Latino, and 11 percent are Black or African American.

Generally speaking, elite colleges are overwhelmingly white. For example, at Wake Forest, which comes in ninety-first in the diversity ranking, 67 percent of the students are white. Blacks account for 7.8 percent of the student body, Hispanics 4.6 percent, and Asians merely 3 percent. Overall, liberal arts colleges are even less diverse. Middlebury, which ranks fortieth, looks pretty typical. There, 62 percent of the students are white, 4 percent are Black, 10 percent are Hispanic or Latinx, and 7 percent are Asian.

Another reason to be pessimistic about the representation of the Doubly Disadvantaged is that we know—third and finally—that elite colleges have treated boosting diversity as a game. When reporters write about socioeconomic diversity on colleges campuses, the metric they usually cite is percentage of Pell Grant recipients. Named for Rhode Island senator Claiborne Pell and passed as part of the Higher Education Act of 1965, the Pell Grant program was intended to expand opportunity for low-income college students. But eligibility is based on many criteria. Some families making over $80,000 per year qualify, and some families making under $30,000 don't. Many more middle-income families became eligible after a significant expansion of the program under President Barack Obama.

In 2019, Caroline Hoxby and Sarah Turner examined the data at two (unnamed) colleges that had received significant national attention for expanding their socioeconomic diversity. They found that these colleges were effectively cherry-picking the Pell Grant recipients they admitted. The majority of Pell Grant recipients came from families with incomes just below the federal cutoff. In fact, Hoxby and Turner found that the schools admitted precious few low-income students. Any doubt that the schools were consciously gaming the system was eliminated by the fact that they admitted almost no students with incomes slightly above the federal cutoff. Applicants just below the Pell line were ten times more likely to be admitted as students just above the line. None of this would be possible if admissions were need-blind, as elite colleges claim they are. The opposite is closer to the truth. Schools are exquisitely need-conscious. They want both the richest of the rich and the richest of the poor. It's no stretch to infer from this that they're letting in precious few doubly disadvantaged students.

So, what kinds of students of color are elite colleges letting in? When it comes to Black students, it's largely mixed-race children and the children of recent immigrants from the Caribbean and Africa. Lani Guinier and Henry Louis Gates first noted this pattern at a reunion of Black Harvard alumni in 2003. Only about a third of Black students, they said, came from families in which all four grandparents had been born in the United States. Their informal observation was subsequently confirmed by the sociologist Douglas Massey. While nationally about 10 percent of Black Americans are first- or second-generation immigrants, at Ivy League colleges the figure exceeds 40 percent. Why did the colleges take so many immigrants and so few descendants of enslaved Americans? Drawing on Massey's research, Paul Tough suggests that it's likely because the children of immigrants have higher SAT scores, are more likely to have attended private schools, and are more likely to have parents with advanced degrees. In other words, they're the wealthiest students of color.

How do white students explain the dearth of poor students of color in their communities? What types of stories do they tell about their few doubly disadvantaged classmates? And what stories do they tell about themselves and the community to which they belong? Natasha Warikoo identified three.

About 10 percent of the white students Warikoo interviewed blamed the culture of poverty for the low representation of economically disadvantaged students and their perceived poor performance. These students said, effectively, that when poor students of color were left behind it was because of collective cultural deficits, such as the lack of a strong work ethic or nuclear families. Some sociologists refer to this simply as cultural racism.

About half of the white students invoked a frame of color-blindness. These students said, essentially, that they didn't notice race. For some, the essence of this claim was descriptive—that thanks to desegregation and the expansion of opportunity, America has evolved into a post-racial society, in which race has little social meaning. Others felt that prescriptively, whatever the reality, race should not matter. A few conservative Black students shared this belief.

Most commonly, white students used a diversity frame. This means different things to different people but, broadly speaking, the view celebrates multiculturalism. Students embracing this frame say that they're enriched by being exposed to different cultures and that classroom discussions are enhanced by different perspectives. About 85 percent of white students employed this sort of language. It'd be hard for them not to. Harvard repeats "diversity" like a mantra. Not coincidentally, diversity is the single rationale that the Supreme Court has acknowledged as a justification for affirmative action.

What Warikoo did not find is white students who viewed race through a lens of power. Of the forty-six white Harvard and Brown students Warikoo interviewed, only four talked about structural inequality. None of the Asian American students she spoke with did. The other students of color certainly saw the inherent tension between a college's commitment to diversity and its reproduction, through admissions and access to the elite, of the very conditions that produce social inequality. Imani, a Black undergraduate at Brown University, told Warikoo, "If you have a place that is about being elite and where we're committed to building the new upper crust of society, you can't truly be committed to diversity. It's a fundamental contradiction to me."

Almost everyone—white and Black students alike—sees the value in diversity. At the same time, the diversity mantra has a downside that's almost never discussed. On the diversity view, every person contributes to the university in their own way. Lacrosse players, legacies, and the children of faculty members are not symbols of a problem. Their numbers are not statistics that reveal the ways in which colleges reproduce social inequality. Rather, their whiteness and affluence are contributions to the life of the college and its academic discourse. Diversity sanitizes these advantages of birth and opportunity as cultural and intellectual contributions.

When push comes to shove, Warikoo found that white students support diversity only so long as they perceive a benefit to themselves. She calls this the "diversity bargain," the title of her 2016 book. "Underrepresented minority students can be admitted with lower SAT scores or GPAs," Warikoo writes, "as long as those students then contribute to the educational experiences of their peers by not getting rewards 'over' white peers and by integrating so that the collective merit can enrich everyone's education." No elite college talks about compensatory affirmative action. Maybe it's because it could be deemed unconstitutional. More likely it's because it doesn't serve their institutional interests.

The intersecting narratives of diversity and merit reveal elite colleges at their worst. Students of color are not admitted to compensate for past injustices—though many elite colleges benefitted from slavery—or to redress structural inequality—though the colleges cause much of it. They are admitted instead, they are told, because they enrich the community. In other words, because they deserve to be there. It's a seduction. Perhaps one that can only be understood from within. Warikoo, who was raised in rural Pennsylvania by Indian immigrants, says it was only after she arrived at Brown and began to struggle that she "came to understand how meritocracy does a once over on you."

The problem isn't the diversity narrative itself. All students do have something unique to contribute. The problem is that it's the *only* narrative. Without an offsetting institutional narrative reminding people of the arbitrariness of success, and without transparency in showing how college admissions perpetuates social inequality, admitting a handful of poor students of color is tokenism, which collectively benefits rich whites, and the mantra of diversity acts only to reinforce rich students' belief in their own merit.

The solution is simple: Elite colleges need to talk less about why poor students of color aren't there, and more about why rich, white students are.

12

Learning to Party

Hannah Williams is really good at games. She's good at games of strategy, psychology, and knowledge. At our virtual game nights during the pandemic, she won pretty much everything—Codenames, Pictionary, poker, trivia, Among Us. As they say in Boston, she's like wicked smart.

Her mom is, too. She has two law degrees—one from the University of Puerto Rico, where she grew up, and a second from Touro Law School. She met Hannah's father while visiting her sister, who was an undergraduate at Penn State. They married, had Hannah and her younger brother, then divorced a few years later. Hannah's father paid the minimum in child support, often was late, and stopped contributing entirely when he moved to Abu Dhabi, in part to evade his obligations. Hannah's family became severely poor. Her mom did what needed to be done. She filed for bankruptcy to save their home, took a civil service exam that qualified her for a job as a probation officer, and managed to keep her family together. As with so many of my students, Hannah's mother is her hero.

Hannah's story is familiar in other respects. Though she had a 99.5 weighted average in high school, no one encouraged her to take an SAT course. She took the exam once—cold—and got a 1350. No one at her high school advised her about getting into college either. What little she knew, she gleaned from YouTube videos. Hannah told me that, entering the process, her main goal was to save money and not go into debt. As a bright student of color who'd overcome serious economic disadvantage, she possibly could have gotten herself into an Ivy League school and would have gotten significant financial aid, but she didn't apply to any. Hannah submitted a total of seven applications, with St. John's the highest ranked school among them. It's a classic example of undershooting. She ended up in the Macaulay Program at John Jay, where she has a 3.97 GPA as a computer science major.

But I don't want to talk about how Hannah got to college.

I want to talk about how Hannah spends her weekends.

Growing up in Port Jefferson, a former shipbuilding community on Long Island's north shore, Hannah played soccer and softball and practiced karate. She describes herself as having been a bit of a tomboy. Port Jefferson is small and so overwhelmingly white that Hannah's family constitutes about 3 percent of the Black population. Hannah says that she didn't encounter much racism. She had friendships in many different groups and socialized with all sorts of people in various kinds of settings. None of these interactions, however, involved alcohol. Drinking was a big part of the culture for what Hannah called the "popular group." She wanted no part of that. "My thing was having fun with people without having to drink," she told me. Hannah didn't even go to a party until March of her senior year.

In college, Hannah says that she's loosened up a tiny bit. She'll host parties, by which she means gatherings of a handful of her friends. They'll often order food, but she and her friends are always careful to think about the cost before they do. "We're very blunt with each other," Hannah says. "We're like, 'I'm broke. I can't afford that right now.'" When money is tight, they'll all pitch in and order from a less expensive restaurant. Often, they take the subway to pick up the food so they can avoid delivery charges.

Sometimes drinking is involved, but it's inevitably in moderation, and certainly nothing like frat parties—there are no kegs, no blasting music. You may wonder how teenagers possibly can have a fulfilling college experience without shotguns, funnels, and flowing rivers of warm Budweiser. What do she and her classmates do for entertainment instead? They do what Hannah is best at—they play games.

*   *   *

Hannah's story isn't idiosyncratic. To the contrary, it's entirely typical of working-class students' college experience. Of the fifty or so students I interviewed for this book, and the hundreds more with whom I spoke informally, none reported spending a significant amount of time partying. For some this was a function of opportunity, or lack thereof. They worked evenings or weekends and didn't have time to drink. Others felt that the stakes of succeeding in college were too high and didn't want to squander the opportunity they'd been given. Many simply didn't have the money.

Nor are these accounts particular to CUNY. They've been confirmed by one researcher after another at all kinds of colleges. The nation's leading expert on financial aid, Temple University professor Sara Goldrick-Rab (with whom we'll visit in a little while), finds that low-income students spend very little of their money on alcohol. In her definitive study of three thousand financial aid students in Wisconsin, Goldrick-Rab found that the majority spent no money on alcohol. Only 56 percent reported drinking, a rate significantly below the national average. In interviews with Goldrick-Rab, the students indicated that drinking was simply too expensive. The sociologists Elizabeth Armstrong and Laura Hamilton found the same thing in their ethnography of students at an unnamed Midwestern university.

One racist stereotype that's sometimes invoked to explain why poor students of color struggle in college—what Natasha Warikoo called the culture of poverty frame—is that they waste their money partying and drinking. In fact, the opposite is true. If any group is guilty of wasting its time and money partying and drinking, it's the rich, white students.

For their study, Armstrong and Hamilton did something many adults would envy—they went back to college. In the fall of 2004, fifty-three young women arriving at one of the freshman dorms at "Midwest University," which is almost certainly Indiana, would have encountered a sign on one of the doors reading, "This room is occupied by sociology researchers studying college student social life." (It feels like the sign was meant to include the word, "caution," but it didn't.)

Armstrong and Hamilton spent several nights a week living in the dorm, got involved in the minutiae of the students' lives, and interviewed them dozens of times. The project arose from Armstrong's curiosity about her students, who seemed to be using class to take a break from college. "They were doing crossword puzzles and taking naps," Armstrong recalled. She wondered how they could be so anti-intellectual, but she also understood the reality of their lives. "I knew enough that the social stuff—the rush and the drinking was hard work," she told me.

Originally, Armstrong and Hamilton, who was her graduate student at the time, set out to explore the sexuality of these students. By the end of the year, their conception of the study had changed. One wrote to the other, "I don't know how this project has become so much about class." But it had. Class shaped everything they saw. It shaped the social interactions on the floor, defined who was an insider and who was an outsider, and almost perfectly predicted who succeeded and failed. Armstrong and Hamilton tracked the women they met for five years. Few of the less-privileged women in their study achieved significant upward mobility. Few from privileged backgrounds failed to reproduce their parents' success.

This finding was ironic because while the less-privileged students studied intensely and worked to support themselves, the wealthier students gravitated to less demanding majors such as fashion, interior design, and apparel merchandising. Indiana—ahem, Midwest—has five majors—sport management, recreational sport management, outdoor recreation and resource management, park and recreation management, and tourism management—that draw Jesuitical distinctions in the study of how to have fun while also torturing the meaning of the word "management."

Freed from the burden of rigorous academics, the rich women in Armstrong and Hamilton's study spent an inordinate amount of time focusing on the campus social scene. Many went out four times or more a week. All seemed to be obsessed with who was hooking up with whom. Armstrong and Hamilton call this the "party pathway."

For students on the party pathway, socialization isn't incidental to the college experience. It is the college experience. The sociologist Jenny

Stuber says that affluent students see meeting people and expansion of social networks as the most important part of college. Armstrong and Hamilton argued that Midwest had evolved to satisfy that expectation. "The social and academic infrastructure of the university," they wrote, "seemed tailor-made for a particular type of affluent, socially-oriented student." Emphasize affluent. Even the finest class distinctions made a difference. Some of the worst and most poignant outcomes came for a class of women Armstrong and Hamilton called "wannabes," who aspired to the elite but lacked the financial resources to compete with the socialites.

Not to worry, though—the rich students thrived. Through partying and hooking up, they learned a mode of socialization that they could rely upon throughout their lives. That mode of socialization meant interacting with people who looked almost exactly like themselves. College is often touted as a melting pot, but that's more myth than reality. Indiana allowed students to segregate themselves in a way that made the campus a true microcosm of society. The rich kids stayed to one side of the floor, and referred to the other, where the research team happened to have its office, as "the dark side." This de facto segregation became permanent the following year when the rich women entered Greek life, as they nearly all did. By contrast, none of the working-class women Armstrong and Hamilton studied ended up joining a sorority.

Not surprisingly, none of the sorority women held a term-time job. When they worked over the summers, it was almost inevitably through parental connections. Almost as an aside, Armstrong and Hamilton tell how Hannah—not to be confused with my student, Hannah Williams—landed an internship at a top media studio in New York. Midwest Hannah's father was the chief financial officer of a Fortune 500 company. He called in a favor from a friend of a friend, who owned a major sports team. Like so many of the mechanisms we've discussed, this feels innocuous in its operation. Someone is helping a friend's kid. The helper's subjective experience would be that they were performing an act of kindness, just as fraternity and sorority members show loyalty to their brothers and sisters.

It's easy to forget who is left out and how powerful these forces of exclusion can be. Nearly half of the women on the floor Armstrong and Hamilton studied ended up experiencing significant isolation, which they defined as having one or no people on the floor that they could claim as a friend. Almost all these women came from less-privileged families. None graduated within five years.

Even Armstrong felt affected by these social forces. She's brilliant and youthful, with an impish sense of humor, but Armstrong regressed after interacting with a student they named Whitney, who carried a Dooney & Bourke purse. (Full disclosure: I don't know what this is.) "I always feel like the biggest loser around her," Armstrong wrote in her field notes. "In general, I feel totally over being intimidated by the popular girls that I never was, but she is something else." Armstrong was a tenure-track professor at the time.

These forces are hardly idiosyncratic to Midwestern. Greek life is an integral part of the social fabric at Brown, Chicago, Columbia, Cornell, Dartmouth, Duke, and Penn. At Yale, the pecking order is defined by its secret societies. At Princeton, it's set by its ancient eating clubs. Harvard's social hierarchy is dominated by its all-male final clubs, which the college briefly banned, only to reverse itself following alumni pressure. (Harvard cited an unrelated Supreme Court case on gay and transgender workplace rights as evidence that its policy couldn't withstand a legal challenge, even though Bowdoin students have long been prohibited from joining fraternities, sororities, and other selective social organizations.)

Brianna Suslovic is one among many Harvard graduates who have written about how final clubs contributed to their feeling of being marginalized. Her op-ed in the *Harvard Crimson* sparked a massive backlash. Club members asked Suslovic why she didn't believe in their value. As with the women Armstrong and Hamilton studied, they thought only about the benefits to themselves. "Club members told me about their incredibly positive and affirming experiences in getting to know fellow club members and developing the sorts of long-lasting, deep social bonds that one comes to college to develop," Suslovic said. "They cited the value of accessing networks that they didn't ever think they would be able to access." No one mentioned the costs imposed on the people left behind.

The protection of exclusionary institutions like fraternities and final clubs makes it impossible for elite colleges to claim they aim to produce an egalitarian experience. Perhaps the marginalization that these institutions cause isn't intended or desired, but the fact that this massive cost is tolerated makes it impossible to resist the conclusion that the marginalization is of secondary importance to a larger set of goals: to teach elite students how to socialize, make connections, and, most importantly, do lots and lots of drinking.

In this regard, it's easy to draw a straight line between suburbs, top colleges, and elite careers. The most stunning conversation I had during my time living in Manhasset was with an administrator at the high school. As we sat together watching a baseball game, the administrator explained to me that underage drinking was rampant and parents in our town routinely drank with their children. I believed the first fact but not the second. How could parents rationalize this, I asked.

"They want their kids to learn how to use alcohol responsibly," the official replied.

My skepticism notwithstanding, the phenomenon is common enough that many addiction agencies feel the need to comment upon it. Seaside Palm Beach, a luxury rehab facility in Florida, offers a typical message on its website: "Although many parents may view allowing their children and their friends to drink within the confines of their home as a safe and alternative method to discover the effects of alcohol, researchers and doctors throughout the country believe this isn't the most effective teaching method."

After our diamond-side conversation, I reconsidered my experience in college and the suburbs through the lens of alcohol. I was a foreigner at Harvard in many respects but perhaps none so much as in my distaste for drinking. This wasn't religious. I just didn't like it. But alcohol fueled everything—college parties, recruiting events, and later, when I became a lawyer, every summer associate function and firm party. It opened a rift between me and my first post-college roommate. In

Manhasset, my wife and I were aliens in many ways, but none quite so pronounced as our lack of interest in booze. On the rare occasions we'd have dinner with people, they'd get things rolling with a pair of gin and tonics, while we'd sip on sodas. To us, the scene seemed like a novelty, as if we were tiptoeing through the set of *Days of Wine and Roses*. But those gin and tonics are the fuel of suburban culture.

If rich, white kids are guilty of wasting their college years partying and drinking, it's because they learn to do so from their rich, white parents. Again, the culture of poverty frame is contradicted by the data. It's rich people who drink the most. In a 2015 study, 47 percent of people with an income over $75,000 reported drinking within the past day as opposed to 18 percent of people making less than $30,000. Forty-five percent of college graduates admitted drinking within the past day, as opposed to 28 percent of people with a high school education or less. Research by the Centers for Disease Control and Prevention shows that heavy episodic drinking—six drinks or more—is lowest among individuals with low incomes who did not graduate from college. The biggest drinkers are wealthy college graduates.

And they pass this behavior along to their children. A British study of 120,000 teenagers found that teenagers from affluent families had double the risk of being a regular drinker. Less than half the kids from the most deprived backgrounds reported having tried alcohol. The pattern is the same in the United States. Sometimes it's attributed to "affluenza," the malaise of wealthy youth, symptomized by a sense of restlessness and isolation that suburban life has no charms to soothe. Indeed, a Manhattan Institute study found that suburban kids were much more likely to have tried alcohol and drugs than their urban counterparts.

Why would wealthy parents want to teach their child to "use" alcohol? Why do colleges turn a blind eye to widespread campus drinking? One answer is that they're acclimating young people to a style of play that's stock-in-trade at elite firms.

We know from Lauren Rivera that investment banks and management consulting firms draw almost exclusively from top colleges. But how do they choose among the many undergraduates who are attracted to the baller lifestyle? Rivera found, time and again, that interviewers cared much more about play styles than they did job skills. They hoped to find "buddies," "formidable playmates," and colleagues who could "actually be your friend." Rivera said that hiring more closely resembled the choice of a romantic partner than the rational model that economists say drives the process.

Poor students of color suffer the most from this dynamic. They're often unaware how important it is to "pound the pavement," as Rivera puts it, because they believe it's the hard work that matters. In truth, the work matters very little. Hiring at elite firms isn't done by human resource types but rather by young professionals who, Rivera found, systematically discounted objective signals such as GPA and recommendation letters. They cared far more about participation in sports that they thought of as requiring extreme dedication such as field hockey, tennis, squash, crew, and lacrosse. They wanted evidence of sustained participation in what they deemed to be hard things, beginning in early childhood. They wanted people who'd worked "real" jobs as opposed to, as one subject told Rivera, "working at Starbucks or mowing lawns or whatever." What they wanted, in short, was people who looked like themselves.

The cruel irony is that these heuristic biases end up excluding many of the most capable applicants. In *Outliers*, Malcom Gladwell explains how overcoming disadvantage can be a significant advantage. Dyslexia may lead you to drop out of school, but if you make it through, you'll really be something. It's the same with growing up poor. Research shows that successful poor students tend to display unusual resilience, persistence in the face of adversity, and are more likely to make sacrifices for the good of the group. Yet few of the poor students of color who survive the brutal winnowing process of getting into an elite college parlay their degree into a high-status job at an elite firm.

Here one feels most palpably the symbolic violence of which Pierre Bourdieu spoke. Elite colleges convert advantages of wealth, like high SAT scores and extracurricular opportunities, into a tradable currency—a prestigious diploma. This degree takes the gap in outcomes between rich and poor, which have been diverging since birth, and explodes it exponentially.

To legitimize that "system"—or laundering scheme—elite colleges admit a handful of poor students of color. But the playing field onto which those lucky few graduates step isn't level—not by a long shot. In fact, they're not even playing the right game. While they balance working to support themselves and studying to keep their grades up, their more privileged counterparts are learning how to excel at the game that matters most, one that they've been playing for their entire lives. They're studying how to drink and party. They're shaping the bodies that elites favor. They're being taught that what matters is power, influence, and money rather than doing good. They're becoming comfortable with exclusion, with believing that they deserve to be on the inside while Hannah Williams and everyone else deserves to be on the outside. They're learning, as Berkeley's Zeus Leonardo puts it, "that the world belongs to them."

PART IV

Barriers to Change

13

How Liberals Become Conservative

During the peak of the pandemic, John Katzman and I had a standing phone date at 7:30 on Friday mornings. Katzman usually walked along the beach near his house in the Hamptons while we spoke. I'd sit in my office, try to visualize the beauty of Long Island's southeastern shore, and listen.

Katzman was among the first people I interviewed in depth. He's astonishingly knowledgeable about the American educational system, and our talks shaped some of the argument I've presented here. We didn't agree on everything, but our worldviews largely overlapped, and with respect to standardized testing, we found complete common ground. It's difficult to imagine someone who's been more critical of the SAT than he has been, or who has more vividly illustrated the advantage of wealth in college admissions—often to his own detriment.

As our conversations progressed, a question began to nag at me. Near the end of our last interview, I asked Katzman why he was so disparaging of the organizations that run the SAT and ACT but not the colleges that empower the exams they administer. After all, those scores only meant something because colleges said they did. Katzman paused for a long time before answering. In the background, I could hear the waves lapping against the beach.

"I don't know," he said, finally.

In this one regard, there are lots of John Katzmans.

Over the course of researching this book, I interviewed many of the

most outspoken critics of American higher education. Almost all are
professors. As a group, college faculty are about the most left-leaning
professionals in the United States. Samuel Abrams, a professor at Sarah Lawrence College, found that liberal college professors outnumber
conservative professors by about six to one. At New England colleges,
the ratio is twenty-eight to one. Another study of social science departments at forty top American universities found a ratio of twelve Democrats for every Republican. At Harvard, 73 percent of faculty members
reported voting for Hillary Clinton in the 2016 presidential election.
About as many (2 percent) voted for Jill Stein (class of 1973) as voted for
Donald Trump.*

My interviewees were a skewed subset. Almost all were sociologists,
who are about the most liberal members of the academy. In a 2018 survey of 479 sociology professors, 293 (61 percent) identified themselves
as liberal and 101 (21 percent) identified themselves as radical. By comparison, ten (2 percent) identified themselves as conservative. More
identified themselves as libertarian. And mine wasn't even a representative sample of sociologists. Almost everyone with whom I spoke has
dedicated at least part of their career to studying inequality in higher
education. Most are qualitative researchers, meaning they're skeptical
of simple orthodoxies and dedicated to a nuanced understanding of
systems. The one economist in my sample, John Friedman, worked as
President Obama's special assistant for economic policy. In short, these
were some of the most left-leaning of a left-leaning group.

At the end of each interview, I'd ask my subject what he or she thought
about the culpability of their own college. Each dismissed the question.
Several told me that we spent too much time talking about elite schools,
even though most focused their life's work on the study of elites. A
couple told me that their colleges were not guilty of the most egregious misbehaviors—like my friend who boasted that their law school

---

* The students they teach are at least as liberal as they are. Fifty-three percent of the
members of Harvard's class of 2020 said they were registered Democrats compared
to 6 percent who said they were Republicans. Seventy percent of the class identified
themselves as either "very liberal" or "liberal." Merely 8 percent identified themselves as "conservative" or "very conservative." Ninety-four percent of graduating
seniors reported having an unfavorable view of Donald Trump.

didn't sell preferred positions at career fairs. Almost everyone defended their school. One memorably told me that their college's president was a first-generation college student who'd significantly expanded their efforts to recruit first-gen kids. She didn't seem overly bothered when I showed her data that 25 percent of her college's early action admits were legacies. None of the sociologists seemed to have thought about whether their institution's modest promotion of upward mobility was outweighed by its significantly greater reproduction and expansion of upper-class status.

If you look carefully enough, you can spot signs that elite professors understand that elite college admissions practices are untenable. Stanford's Faculty Senate recently adopted a set of proposals ostensibly designed to reduce the influence of wealth in college admissions. But the measures are milquetoast: improve data collection by requiring applicants to list who read their application, study the effect of admissions on philanthropic support, and "initiate surveys to track the distribution of income and wealth levels for parents and undergraduates." Improving data collection and initiating surveys is hardly a rallying cry for urgent social change. Conspicuously absent from the Stanford Faculty Senate resolution was any language criticizing the social responsibility of an institution where the average family income of an entering freshman exceeds $470,000.

That's pretty much how it is across the board. Like Katzman, experts are happy to decry the unfairness of higher education as a system but unwilling to assign blame to any individual or group of institutions. Consider the books that have shaped the recent public dialogue. Robert Putnam's poignant *Our Kids*, Paul Tough's magnificent *The Years That Matter Most*, and Charles Clotfelter's meticulous *Unequal Colleges in the Age of Disparity* offer staggering portraits of the disparity of opportunity in America but spare the rod for the institutions that shape it. So, too, that cottage industry of damning books about the insidious harms of meritocracy offers only oblique institutional critiques, as if "meritocracy" is an independently existing Platonic ideal rather than a construct that elite colleges actively help to build and nurture.

One obvious explanation is that almost all these critics teach at elite colleges, as do most of the scholars whom I interviewed for this book. It's natural not to want to bite the hand that feeds you. But academics often take positions that put them in conflict with their employer. Faculty have played important roles in divestment from South Africa, climate change, and criminal justice reform. They aren't shrinking violets.

Something deeper is going on. If we're going to figure out how to make things better—the question to which we now turn—we're going to need to understand what that something is. Why do faculty speak so differently about things that happen in their house as opposed to everyone else's? Answering this might help us to begin to understand the paradoxical question that's ultimately at the heart of American higher education: How can a system run by liberals be so conservative?

Like anyone trying to work out a cognitive dissonance, we're going to need a psychologist.

After graduating from Queens University in Ontario, Leanne Son Hing wanted to take a year off before starting graduate school. She was concerned about environmental issues, and so she responded to a classified ad placed by Greenpeace. The organization ignored her first two calls, which they do to weed out people who aren't serious, but Son Hing persisted. After her third try, Greenpeace gave her an interview and hired her as a canvasser.

To me, the job sounds like a nightmare. I can't imagine any circumstances under which I'd enjoy going door-to-door, but these seem downright horrifying. Each canvasser had to fundraise enough money to pay for his or her own salary, which was minimum wage. If they didn't attract enough donations to one of the campaigns they promoted—such as deforestation, climate change, and reduction of plastics—they'd be let go. So there was lots of pressure—but no toilets. They'd either have to go at McDonald's or roll the dice and ask a prospect to use the bathroom. And it was cold. This was Canada, after all. Their union rules said that they had to work so long as the temperature exceeded twenty-five degrees below zero. But Son Hing is brilliant and personable (and used to the cold), and she quickly earned a promotion to organizer, meaning she got to decide which members of her team to send to which houses. She also did plenty of walking herself.

Pounding the pavement gives you a lot of time to reflect. A budding psychologist, Son Hing began thinking about the higher education paradox. She wasn't thinking about it in terms of perceptions of fairness of college admissions, but the underlying dynamic was the same. People didn't like being challenged.

One would think that someone canvassing for Greenpeace in Toronto would be warmly received. Canada has a long history of conservationism, Toronto is predominantly liberal, and when Son Hing was canvassing, in 1995, environmental issues were far less politicized than they are today. But Son Hing and her colleagues weren't received warmly at all. To the contrary, people were often hostile. Many yelled at them to get off their property. One homeowner hit Son Hing's colleague in the head with a can of soup. "The vitriol against Greenpeace," she told me, "was the most surprising part of the job."

Somehow, the magnitude of global warming's risk seemed to make fundraising harder, not easier. The problem was just too big. "The threat is so huge," Son Hing said, "that if you're not changing your life and advocating for all systems to change to address it, then it's like you're a complete idiot." Rather than think of themselves as stupid or insensitive, people resolved the dissonance by minimizing the problem or choosing not to think about it. "A lot of it is just not facing it," Son Hing explained. "Like with deforestation. They would say things like, 'People just have to have jobs.' Like that's really the counterargument."

Today, Son Hing, who's a professor at the University of Guelph in southwestern Ontario, would say that her fundraising prospects were engaging in "system justification." She's dedicated her career to understanding this process. Identified by NYU's John Jost and Harvard's Mahzarin Banaji around the same time Son Hing was walking the streets of Toronto, system justification is the idea that people tend to defend not only their individual actions but also the social, economic, and political systems to which they belong—even if these systems work to their detriment.

This is the opposite of what economists and political scientists argue. The leading rational-choice model holds that as income inequality increases, voters will support redistributive tax policies and vote accordingly. Son Hing's research shows that the opposite is true. The more inequality there is, the more favorably it's viewed.

For people in power, this is easy enough to understand. Indeed, the most uncomfortable conversation I had in the course of writing this book was with the former president of an elite university who told me that they didn't like the way their institution was portrayed in "books like these," even though I hadn't described my thesis. Son Hing wasn't surprised by this story. She says that the more embedded someone is in an unfair system, the stronger their motivation to defend that system. "For a college administrator, the university reflects their identity," she says. "The more people rise, the more their investment in it." This seems entirely intuitive.

The tendency of disadvantaged people to also defend the system seems entirely counterintuitive. Case in point: Donald Trump was elected with the resilient, persistent support of downscale whites, and yet the signature achievement of his presidency was the most regressive tax cut in American history. How can this be? Son Hing says it's because inequality activates many of the same psychological mechanisms that stifle outrage. Some of these mechanisms—or "heuristic biases"—may be familiar to readers of Daniel Kahneman's *Thinking, Fast and Slow*. For people at the top of the heap, the process loosely resembles confirmation bias, the human brain's tendency to interpret new evidence in a way that supports its preexisting assumptions. Confirmation bias protects people's self-esteem. If facts are uncomfortable, the brain simply tunes them out.

People on the lower rungs of the ladder are engaging in something like the "ostrich effect," the brain's tendency to avoid unpleasant information—as with people who live along the San Andreas Fault. They're also almost certainly falling prey to the "just-world hypothesis," a bias toward believing that the world operates fairly. When something bad happens to someone, we tend to search for explanations about why they deserved their fate. If someone is poor, for example, our instinct is to blame them—by saying they're lazy or unreliable—rather than situational factors. When rich people do this, it's ego-protective, in the same way as confirmation bias. But poor people's belief in a just world is strong too, as Tressie McMillan Cottom reminds us. One explanation is that children are socialized through religious and secular fables to believe that good is always rewarded and evil punished. Another is that the alternative is too difficult to bear. "It's hard to have no sense of control," Son Hing says, "and to believe that the odds are stacked against you."

These heuristic biases lead to a sort of blindness. Son Hing's research shows that, when it comes to thinking about the extent of inequality, the blindness can be extreme. "People don't form their impressions of inequality levels after poring over years of data," Son Hing says. Rather, they rely upon unreliable shortcuts. My friend bet that the fraction of Harvard students who came from families making less than $65,000 per year would be around four in ten. Even I thought it might be as high as one in four. We were both way off. In truth, it's around one in eight.

As inequality levels rise, people become more inaccurate in their estimates. This is the heart of the paradox. When the problem gets too big, they stick their heads in the sand and start working extra hard to make the facts seem more comfortable. It's the same as Son Hing's experience with Greenpeace. Stand outside a Wal-Mart in a Santa Claus costume and people will drop quarters in your Salvation Army can to help feed needy kids. Tell them about cataclysmic climate change and they start throwing soup cans.

Not only do they adjust their perception of the facts, when it comes to inequality, they also adjust what they think is fair. Specifically, the more inequality people believe there is, the more they think there ought to be. In experiments, when Son Hing and other psychologists expose subjects to data showing higher levels of income inequality, the level they judge as fair increases. In this case, real life offers the best data. As the wage gap between low and high occupational wage earners exploded in the United States between 1987 and 1999, people widened their judgment of what constituted an appropriate wage gap. This sets in motion a vicious cycle. The more inequality exists, the more likely people are to believe that society operates meritocratically. The more people perceive the world to operate meritocratically, the less likely they are to believe the full extent of inequality.

These mistaken descriptive beliefs about the extent of inequality—and how much inequality is just—prove to be quite sticky. That's because they're entwined with bedrock American ideologies: the free market system, the American Dream, and meritocracy. Harvard economist Benjamin Friedman—John's dad—traces these beliefs, and America's support of regressive tax structures and relatively ungenerous safety-net programs, to a turning away from a Calvinistic belief in predestination in favor of voluntarism. This is the notion, held by more than two-thirds of white evangelical Protestants in the United States, that most government services are best left to religious groups and charities.

The belief in meritocracy is deeply entrenched precisely because it acts as a rationale to justify the system. UC Davis's Allison Ledgerwood and her colleagues found that participants in a study worked harder at an anagram task when they were told that success depended on luck rather than effort—but only if they were also told that the study was an exploration of the relationship between effort and success in American society. Participants who were told that the study was about doing well at scrambled word tasks worked no harder. The desire to justify the system is what led them to attend to their task more diligently.

Given the human inclination to justify the system to which we belong, and the stickiness of meritocratic beliefs, colleges would have to work hard to make their students and faculty understand the extent of inequity in American higher education. They'd have to be transparent with the socioeconomic data of their students, explain how the admissions process recapitulates class advantages, and foster a critical conversation about their role as social actors. This they almost never do. Eighty percent of Stanford seniors think their university "has a positive impact on society."

Elite colleges simultaneously reproduce class inequality and belief in the justness of that inequality. This process begins with who they let in. Nothing makes rich people feel more secure in the fairness of the system than spending time around other rich people. Son Hing says that people are more apt to overestimate meritocracy and social mobility, and less likely to support redistribution, when they operate "within their narrow social context." It's hard to imagine narrower social contexts than those created on elite college campuses.

The process continues with how colleges operate. "Everything we do in academia is based on the assumption that merit can be assessed," Son Hing says, citing Michèle Lamont's *How Professors Think*, a remarkable behind-the-scenes look at the peer review process. Everything Lamont uncovered suggests that the assessment of merit is highly subjective. She worries about how such a system affects the participants. "What's really harmful is the competitiveness that it feeds, and the fact that it encourages a very unidimensional way of evaluating worth," Lamont told me. Yet virtually every evaluative mechanism in the academy—peer review of scholarly articles and grant applications, grading, and tenure evaluation—purport to be objective and are supremely hierarchical.

The process culminates with the types of careers elite colleges steer students into. One of Son Hing's key findings is that people with a higher social-dominance orientation tend to underestimate inequality and are more likely to endorse belief in meritocracy. Social-dominance orientation is a measure of people's support for hierarchy. In other words, it's how much they want their group to be better than others. Hierarchy-enhancing occupations, like investment banking and management consulting, tend to increase social-dominance orientation. So elite colleges let in people predisposed to denying inequality, surround them with similar people, teach them in a system that confirms their belief in merit, and, finally, steer them into careers that solidify their hierarchical orientation.

Son Hing says these effects could partially be counteracted by talking about higher education as a shared public good. Once again, elite colleges do almost precisely the opposite: They work tirelessly to cultivate loyalty to the college's unique brand. Mitchell Stevens is a professor at Stanford's Graduate School of Education and the author of *Creating a Class: College Admissions and the Education of Elites*, a memoir of a year and a half he spent working in the admissions office of an unnamed bucolic New England college, which I'm fairly certain is Hamilton. Stevens says that schools try to develop "clan-like" emotional connections with students and alumni. Part of the motivation is to solicit contributions. Another part, Stevens says, is "so that wherever in the world those people are, they give some special deference or recognition to others who hold that identity." In other words, so that a Harvard or Yale degree can produce the type of connections that allow it to guarantee reproduction of upper-class status.

Stevens is a fierce critic of American higher education. "Elites are coming to understand that the social contract is no longer viable," he told me. "The institutions that we've invested in and believed in as mechanisms of social mobility aren't working." Stevens sees the expansion of college following World War II as a spectacular example of unintended consequences. "No one imagined that project would come to divide America," he said. "No one imagined that a college degree would be a caste-like line in life prospects, but that's the world that has come to be, and that's the world that got us Donald Trump elected in 2016." But as elites lament the state of the world, Stevens points out that applications to selective institutions are way up. "The higher end is going for the reproduction insurance with more gusto," he says. "They're doubling down on upper-class insurance."

For the universities themselves, that insurance takes the form of an endowment, and they are literally doubling down. Harvard's endowment has grown since 2000 from $19.2 billion to $51.9 billion today. At this continued rate of growth, Harvard will have assets of over $1 trillion by 2120. It's hard to have a sense of numbers this big. Harvard's current endowment is larger than the annual gross domestic product of Libya, Jordan, and 107 other countries. It's larger than the annual budget of every American city except New York. One percent of the earnings—$519 million—would be approximately $150 million greater than the cost of offering free tuition to all its 6,755 undergraduates. The inequity is so massive it's almost impossible to comprehend. The twelve schools with the highest mobility rates—listed in Table 10A—have a combined endowment of $1.5 billion. This would rank them fifty-eighth—just behind Wesleyan University in Connecticut and Middlebury in Vermont. The dozen schools with the highest stability rates—listed in Table 10B—control over $227 billion.

TABLE 10A. ENDOWMENTS AT COLLEGES WITH HIGHEST MOBILITY RATES

1. CUNY—Baruch College	$295.7 million
2. CUNY—City College	$290 million
3. CUNY—Lehman College	$7.7 million
4. Cal State—Los Angeles	$46.2 million
5. CUNY—John Jay College	$7.3 million
6. Pace University	$193.8 million
7. SUNY—Stony Brook	$266 million
8. CUNY—City Tech	$12 million
9. Texas A&M International University	$83 million*
10. CUNY—Brooklyn College	$98 million
11. CUNY—Hunter College	$136 million
12. CUNY—Queens College	$85 million

*About half of this total comes from a 2020 grant of $40 million from MacKenzie Scott, philanthropist, author, and ex-wife of Amazon CEO Jeff Bezos.

TABLE 10B. ENDOWMENTS AT COLLEGES WITH HIGHEST STABILITY RATES

1. Princeton	$37.7 billion
2. Washington and Lee	$2.1 billion
3. Georgetown	$1.7 billion
4. Duke	$12.7 billion
5. University of Pennsylvania	$20.5 billion
6. Notre Dame	$18.1 billion
7. Villanova	$1.1 billion
8. Stanford	$37.8 billion
9. Holy Cross	$1.0 billion
10. Yale	$42.3 billion
11. Harvard	$51.9 billion
12. Colgate	$1.3 billion

Yet elite universities continue to fundraise. Michael Bloomberg just gave $1.8 billion to his alma mater, Johns Hopkins—to allow the college to become permanently "need-blind," offer no-loan financial aid packages, and increase the percentage of students receiving Pell Grants to twenty. That's great, but don't think about what else might be done with that money or you'll cry. Bloomberg's $1.8 billion would be more than enough money to run all of John Jay—where the vast majority of students receive Pell Grants—for ten years.

In 2016, Phil Knight gave $400 million to his alma mater, Stanford, to bring together between fifty and one hundred highly accomplished recent college graduates and let them think about the world's problems. Shortly thereafter, Malcolm Gladwell tweeted that Stanford should give half its endowment away to schools that needed the money. The following day, Gladwell, who's beaten the drum on this issue loudly and more effectively than just about anybody, got an email from John Hennessy, Stanford's then-president. Hennessy wanted to persuade Gladwell that he was wrong. Gladwell played excerpts from their conversation on his podcast, *Revisionist History*.

"How much is enough for an institution like Stanford?" Gladwell asked.

"How much is enough?" Hennessy replied. "Um, I think it, we, um . . . If our ambitions don't grow, then I think you do reach a point where you have enough money and I would hope that, um, our ambitions for what we want to do as an institution, both in our teaching and our research, uh, grow."

In other words, Gladwell says, "there really isn't such a thing at Stanford as enough money."

"Do you ever imagine," Gladwell went on to ask, "that a president of Stanford might go to a funder and say, at this point in our history, the best use of your money is to give to the UC system not to Stanford?"

"Well, that, uh, that would be a hard thing to do, obviously," Hennessy replied.

But that's what's needed for meaningful change to occur—candid acknowledgment of the inequities and some surrendering of advantage. Endowment fundraising is the most egregious example of what Richard Reeves of the Brookings Institution calls dream hoarding. Reeves asks the same question that's at the center of Chana Joffe-Walt's podcast *Nice White Parents*, in which white parents literally overwhelm a middle school in Cobble Hill, Brooklyn. It's also the same question that Kirsten Hextrum asks of every parent who sends their children to play on the lush, green fields of affluent suburbs. The question is: Will rich, white families accept even slightly less advantage for their children?

It's impossible to imagine any relinquishment occurring without a shared understanding of the problem. For this to happen, universities would have to work hard to combat the psychological mechanisms that keep people from perceiving inequality and justifying the system to which they belong. Instead, they exploit these mechanisms for financial gain by cultivating loyalty and shining a spotlight on the good that they do, but not the greater good that could be done. It's a textbook example of how, as Yale's Paul Bloom explains, empathy can lead us to make stupid, unethical decisions.

The spotlights that elite colleges shine upon their good works blind faculty and alumni to the systemic consequences of their actions taken as a whole and to the suffering of those less visible. We instinctually empathize with people who look like ourselves and whose stories resemble our own, but the moral claims of the powerless and voiceless are at least as compelling. Sure, the students helped by Bloomberg and Knight's bequests are worthy of help, but so too are the students at public colleges, where the money they gave would go so much further.

No one could stop Bill Gates from panhandling for his foundation or even for himself, and people are free to give, but dropping dollar bills into his bucket is hardly anybody's idea of charity. It's the same when Harvard, Yale, or Stanford come with hat in hand. No one can stop them—it's a free country after all—but this sort of giving isn't ethical by any standard. To the contrary, it's decidedly unethical. These solicitations, and the resulting donations, are the culminating acts of an illusion that often begins at birth, and to which almost all students, alumni, and faculty at these schools ultimately fall prey: a false belief that the system to which they belong does good.

14

Still Separate, Still Unequal

Shortly after ten o'clock on June 27, 2019, all of America felt the momentum in the Democratic presidential primary swing to Kamala Harris. Rachel Maddow and Chuck Todd had just come on for the second shift of questioning. Maddow began by asking Mayor Pete Buttigieg about a recent shooting in his hometown of South Bend, Indiana, and the underrepresentation of Blacks on the city's police force. Ten candidates had been crowded onto the stage that evening, and after Buttigieg finished his mea culpa, everyone scrambled to get in a word. John Hickenlooper boasted about his record as mayor of Denver. Eric Swalwell took a shot at Buttigieg for not firing the police chief. Marianne Williamson snuck in a pitch for reparations. Chuck Todd tried to move things along, but Harris shouted over him, "As the only Black person on this stage, I would like to speak on the issue of race."

Even on TV, you could feel the air go out of the room.

The California senator didn't have anything to say about Mayor Pete. Her comments were so unrelated to Maddow's question one might even think Harris had planned her statement in advance.

"I'm going to now direct this at Vice President Biden," Harris began. Then she turned over her right shoulder—stared past Bernie Sanders, who looked like he wanted to crawl into his podium—and said to Biden, "I do not believe you are a racist."

If Scranton Joe knew one thing after half a century in politics, it was that nothing positive ever comes after the words, "I don't believe you are a racist."

He was right.

"But I also believe," Harris continued, "and it's personal—it was hurtful to hear you talk about the reputations of two United States senators who built their reputations and careers on the segregation of race in this country." Harris was referring to John Stennis and James Eastland, a pair of segregationists from Mississippi, whom Biden had indirectly praised in comments lamenting the decline of civility in the Senate. "And it was not only that, but you also worked with them to oppose busing," Harris added. Then she delivered the zinger. "You know, there was a little girl in California who was part of the second class to integrate her public schools, and she was bused to school every day. And that little girl was me."

After the applause subsided, Biden stumbled through a response. He said he had not praised racists, number one. Number two, he'd be happy to litigate the campaign on the candidates' civil rights records. Then he added a second number two and reminded everyone that he'd served with Barack Obama, who'd dealt with civil rights issues in a "major, major way."

Harris wouldn't let him off the hook. "But, Vice President Biden, do you agree today—do you agree today that you were wrong to oppose busing in America then?"

"I did not oppose busing in America," Biden replied, about as angrily as he gets in public. "What I opposed is busing ordered by the Department of Education."

Biden's own zinger received no applause. In the first Quinnipiac poll after the debate, Harris surged into second place. Biden's lead over Harris shrunk from eighteen points to two, and his campaign teetered on the edge of collapse until James Clyburn came to his rescue on the eve of the South Carolina primary.

If elite colleges are guilty of cementing, reproducing, and exacerbating inequality in America, as I've argued, America's grossly unequal K-12 education system is their primary enabler. Though superficially about busing, Harris and Biden's exchange is really about the issue at the heart of this book—it's about the meaning and promise of *Brown v. Board of Education* and whether rich and poor should be entitled to similar educational opportunities. To decode their give-and-take, we first need to understand a little bit about the history of busing and one of the worst Supreme Court decisions in American history.

People forget that busing wasn't always a bad word. Oliver Brown sued for the right of his daughter to attend her *neighborhood* school in Topeka. Linda Brown was forced to walk across railroad tracks and take a bus to an all-Black grade school that was miles away, despite there being a school just four blocks from her home. School districts in Kansas, and many other states, routinely transported Black children long distances over county and district lines to preserve single-race schools. Southern whites quite liked busing when it served the interests of segregation.

Despite the unanimity of the Supreme Court's decision, not much changed after *Brown*. Eastland and Stennis—the senators Joe Biden praised for their civility—joined seventeen of their colleagues and eighty-two representatives in signing the Southern Manifesto. This document accused the Supreme Court of abusing its power and pledged to obstruct *Brown*'s implementation. In Virginia, Prince Edward County closed its public schools for five years rather than comply with the decision. By 1964—ten years after the Court decided *Brown*—98 percent of southern Black children attended all-Black schools.

Things only began to shift after the release of the Coleman Report in 1966. The Department of Health, Education, and Welfare began negotiating—and then imposing—busing agreements with cities. This is presumably what Biden meant to say that he opposed. The Supreme Court began to expect more from states, too. In 1968, the Court rejected a Virginia school district's so-called "freedom of choice" plan. Under this plan, all the white families exercised their freedom and chose to attend the district's historically white school. The Court said that removing the language of segregation wasn't enough. School districts had to take proactive steps to integrate their schools. Three years later, the Court upheld a court-ordered busing plan in the Charlotte-Mecklenburg school district, where the majority of Black students previously had attended all-Black schools.

Busing worked. This is often forgotten, too. By 1972, nearly half of all southern Black schoolchildren were attending predominantly white schools. Black high school graduation rates surged. The standardized test gap shrunk. Even the performance of white students improved. Though hardly a panacea, busing transformed the South from the nation's most segregated region to its most integrated, which it remains today.

It was the North that resisted *Brown* most strenuously. This was in part an unintended consequence of Lee Atwater's "Southern Strategy," which had proven key to Richard Nixon's electoral success. To build support among voters, Republicans appealed directly to racism. One of the ways they accomplished this was by developing a coded vocabulary. This new language also empowered racism among northern whites. No one wanted to be "pro-segregation," but it was perfectly acceptable to be "anti-busing." And Northerners were intensely anti-busing. As J. Anthony Lukas recounts in *Common Ground*, white Bostonians rioted and pelted Black students with rocks rather than comply with federal judge Arthur Garrity's cross-city busing order.

Still, this conflict paled in comparison to what happened when deseg-regation plans threatened suburbs. Desegregating Charlotte—where 29 percent of the students were Black—and Boston—where 32 percent were—was daunting enough. How was the Department of Education or the courts supposed to desegregate a city like Detroit, where 64 percent of the city's 290,000 students were Black? There was simply no way to do it without involving the surrounding communities.

Here's where the rubber met the road. When the NAACP Legal Defense Fund sued, it showed a direct relationship between discrimina-tory housing practices, such as redlining, and educational segregation. Stephen Roth, the federal district court judge who heard the case, was skeptical at first, but he soon realized that busing within Detroit would be futile. Roth implemented a desegregation plan that included both Detroit and its 98 percent white suburbs.

The reaction made Boston's seem quaint. Bumper stickers on cars throughout the Detroit area called Roth a child molester and said his name was a four-letter word. In Wyandotte, a suburb about ten miles south of the city, protestors hung the judge in effigy. After he received numerous death threats, the police and federal marshals were called in to protect Roth and his family. In Congress, Michigan senator Robert Griffin introduced a constitutional amendment that would have banned busing.

The case reached the Supreme Court in 1974. The chief justice, Warren Burger, assigned the opinion to himself. Discussing *Milliken v. Bradley* over lunch with his law clerks, the chief expounded on the state of race in the nation. Burger explained that, just recently, he'd told his fellow trustee at the Smithsonian Institution that unemployed Blacks could be trained as gardeners to tend to the Capitol Mall because they had such a wonderful sense of color. When the conversation turned to housing discrimination, Burger explained that, unlike Blacks, Jews could get mortgages because they were more successful and trustworthy.

The Detroit desegregation plan never had a chance. In upholding Judge Roth's decision, the Sixth Circuit Court of Appeals had said that if school district boundaries were absolute barriers to a desegregation plan, the courts "would be opening a way to nullify *Brown*." Warren Burger didn't care. His opinion chastised the district court for treating district boundaries as "no more than arbitrary lines on a map drawn for political convenience"—though that's precisely what they are. He said that the plaintiffs had failed to show evidence that the white suburbs had purposefully discriminated against students of color. Most importantly, Burger vigorously defended the importance of local control over the operation of schools. "No single tradition," he wrote, "is more deeply rooted." Thurgood Marshall grieved. He said it was as if the Court perceived a "public mood that we have gone far enough in enforcing the Constitution's guarantees of equal justice."*

---

* Joe Biden perceived the same mood. Facing protests over a court-ordered desegregation plan for Wilmington, Biden joined with Senator Jesse Helms in supporting a failed amendment that would have prevented the Department of Health, Education, and Welfare from collecting data about the race of students and teachers. Biden then proposed his own successful amendment to a $36 billion education bill, which prevented federal funds from being used to assign teachers or students to schools on the basis of race. "I have become convinced that busing is a bankrupt concept," Biden said.

The consequence of the decision was predictable and predicted. There were too few white students in Detroit to achieve meaningful desegregation, and *Milliken* created an incentive for further white flight. Burger's decision virtually invited families to avoid desegregation by moving to the suburbs. Today, Detroit schools are 3 percent white. But the Supreme Court's decree had more far-reaching implications: Thereafter, American cities would belong to poor, minority students, while the suburbs would be the province of affluent whites.

If there's a villain in this story—other than Harvard, Yale, and Stanford—it's local control. When Warren Burger wrote, "the notion that school district lines may be casually ignored or treated as a mere administrative convenience is contrary to the history of public education in our country," it was literally true. The history of public education in America has been effectively governed by the doctrine of separate but equal. *Milliken* is the modern equivalent of *Plessy v. Ferguson*. It simply isn't possible to create meaningful equality of opportunity if political boundaries are treated as metaphorical walls. Harvard Law School professor Martha Minow says that *Milliken* "marked the beginning of the end of serious efforts to desegregate America's public schools." The case immortalized de facto desegregation by cementing local control into the fabric of American society.

Nearly fifty years later, *Milliken* continues to cause incalculable damage. Its effects are most profound in the most liberal regions of the country. In EdBuild's *Fault Lines* report, the overwhelming majority of the nation's most segregated borders are in the Northeast. The most segregated border in the country is between Detroit and Grosse Pointe. When *Milliken* was filed in 1970, Detroit's poverty rate of 15 percent was five times its suburban neighbor's. Today, almost half of Detroit residents live in poverty, nearly ten times as many as in Grosse Pointe.

Poverty spreads through cities like an infectious disease. NYU's Patrick Sharkey found that 66 percent of Black children live in a poor neighborhood, which he defines as one in which 20 percent of the families have incomes below the poverty line. The comparable statistic for white children is 6 percent. More than two-thirds of African American children who were raised in the poorest neighborhoods continue to live there as adults. That's because kids who grow up in impoverished communities have few role models, suffer stress from being exposed to violence, have fewer summer opportunities, eat worse food, have less access to doctors, have trouble finding a place to study, and experience high rates of breathing disorders. A high concentration of children with so many disadvantages in a school makes it difficult to give anyone special attention.

Yet, disadvantage could hardly be more concentrated. In New York, students in the five boroughs constitute about two-thirds of the state's total Black, Asian, and Latino populations but only 10 percent of the white students. New York City schools are about the most segregated in the nation. Nineteen of the city's thirty-two school districts have less than 10 percent white students. A report by UCLA's Civil Rights Project classified 73 percent of the city's charter schools as "apartheid schools," meaning they have less than 1 percent white enrollment.

Jonathan Kozol, the writer and education reformer, says that, nationally, schools are as segregated as they ever were. To research *The Shame of the Nation*, his account of American apartheid, Kozol visited sixty public schools in eleven states. "In all the inner-city schools I visit, I simply never see white children," Kozol said. "If you took a photo of the typical classroom that I visited in the South Bronx, it would be indistinguishable from a photograph of a class in Mississippi in 1925 or 1930." Richard Rothstein reports that in 1970, the typical Black student attended a school where 32 percent of the students were white. By 2010, this exposure had declined to 29 percent. "High average achievement," Rothstein writes, "is almost impossible to achieve in a low-income, segregated school, embedded in a segregated neighborhood." Kirsten Hextrum says, simply, "Today, the U.S. educational system is more segregated than before *Brown*."

These dramatic inequities are only possible because of local control. With more than 15,000 school boards, education in the United States is more decentralized than in any other advanced nation. Warren Burger was right. Local control is deeply ingrained in the American psyche.

What makes fixing inequality in America so uniquely daunting is the peculiar, intractable coalescence of opinion behind it.

In 2020, shortly after the start of the pandemic, I ran for school board. Manhasset had been slow to respond after schools shut down. Three months in, the district was only offering one hour of online instruction, four days a week. My platform had two main planks: First, I said that people would lose confidence in public schools if they failed to teach. Second, I said that poor students of color would be left behind.

I was hardly surprised when I lost. Manhasset is an overwhelmingly Republican town, and my Facebook cover photo is of my family with Elizabeth Warren. I was surprised, though, by how much resistance I met from liberals when I discussed equity and inclusion or noted the absence of a single teacher of color at my daughter's elementary school. Privately, I often harkened back to a conversation I had with someone on the school board shortly after we moved to town. She asked me what I would do if I were on the board. I answered that I'd want to start a voluntary desegregation program like METCO in Boston, where we made the ample resources of our district available to some students from poorer neighboring communities.

My new friend turned white. (Whiter.) "They'd lynch you," she told me.

That reaction isn't idiosyncratic to Manhasset. One of the few issues on which affluent Americans agree is their shared desire to protect their communities from infiltration by the poor. "Liberals are just like the right when it comes to housing and education," Dan Lichter says. Let's call it Lichter's Law. "Whenever these issues come up," he says, "they get all bent out of shape about moving low-income housing into their neighborhood." Lichter told me that his faculty colleagues often sound like Tea Party-types. "Many send their kids to private schools and don't want to pay taxes," he says. "I've spoken with some very progressive sociologists who are worried about low-income people moving into the community." EdBuild's Rebecca Sibilia notes the same phenomenon. "People who are otherwise proud liberals, start to turn against their own political ideals when it comes to how much money their schools will receive."

Lichter says that conversations about inequality focus too much on the actions of the have-nots and too little on the actions of the haves. "This stuff is always driven by how whites are thinking about these issues," he told me. In 2018, Annette Lareau and her colleagues published a remarkable piece about a wealthy district named "Kingsley," where 85 percent of the residents are white and the average home costs about half a million dollars. When the school board tried to redistrict its two high schools, the word "backlash" doesn't do justice to what ensued. The parents overwhelmed the board with emails, data, and spreadsheets, drawing upon their collective professional expertise and networks to impose their will in a way that would be inconceivable for poor parents of color. None of the white parents' arguments had anything to do with academic quality at the high schools. One argued, paradoxically, that scientific data showed that bus rides of less than an hour did not affect student performance and that walking to school is an essential part of an education.

With language echoing Richard Reeves, Lareau calls this "opportunity hoarding." In more formal terms, Natasha Warikoo would say that whites are willing to embrace the diversity script, but not the power inequality script. Whatever one calls it, Lareau says it's "the dark side of parent involvement." It's the instinct to hoard that motivates PTAs in affluent communities to raise more and more money for their well-funded schools. In Dallas's opulent Highland Park community, the PTA raises more than $1.4 million and $2 million for its elementary and high schools every year. The fifty richest PTAs raise approximately $43 million per year—roughly 10 percent of the total raised by PTAs nationally—without ever thinking about the schools left behind.

It's all the legacy of *Milliken*. The incentive to exert power for the benefit of one's own children is simply too overwhelming to resist. "If you wanted to have people behave in the most selfish way possible, this is how you'd do it," says Cardozo Law School professor Michelle Adams, who's an expert on *Milliken*. "You have to ask people to be incredibly magnanimous not to engage in segregated behaviors because all of the structures are set up to drive them in that direction."

*   *   *

In *Milliken*, Michigan's main defense was that there'd been no government action and, hence, no basis for the courts to find a constitutional violation. Sure, Detroit was all Black and the surrounding suburbs were all white, but that wasn't the product of official race discrimination. It's just that houses in Grosse Pointe were expensive. That wasn't really anyone's fault. It certainly wasn't Michigan's. Elite colleges offer a similar defense. They're not the cause of inequality, they say. They're merely reflecting America's underlying inequities. Whatever else, they can't be blamed for opportunity hoarding by suburban whites.

This wasn't true when Michigan said it, and it isn't true now when Harvard does.

There was state action in *Milliken*—lots of it. The NAACP Legal Defense Fund went to pains to show that housing discrimination in greater Detroit wasn't merely "de facto," but rather "de jure"—the product of official, state-sanctioned efforts to "contain" Blacks. Whatever plausible deniability there might have been at the time has been shredded by Richard Rothstein. It's difficult to imagine an argument that has been refuted more conclusively than the idea that the federal and state governments were blameless for segregation. In the 1950s and '60s, residential segregation was enforced through an array of quasi-legal mechanisms such as redlining, racial covenants, and restrictive zoning supplemented by the threat of violence and actual violence to which the police turned a blind eye. Today the means are less brutal, but the government's fingerprints are no less visible.

Suburban communities are literally shaped by the mechanisms of exclusion. When we lived in Manhasset, we had a cesspool. More than 90 percent of Nassau County was connected to sewers, but the five villages of Manhasset incorporated largely so they could retain the right to live over their household waste. Why? Sewers make apartment buildings possible, and apartment buildings bring all kinds of undesirable diversity. Aside from a single small government-subsidized development, the only way into Manhasset is to buy a home. As I'm writing this, 102 homes are for sale there. The least expensive is asking $999,999. Single-family exclusive zoning, which many suburban communities adopted after the Supreme Court struck down racially explicit zoning, is modern redlining. Rothstein says, "Moving from an urban apartment to a suburban home is incomparably more difficult than registering to vote."

Elite colleges are implicated every bit as much as state and federal actors in shaping the physical boundaries that limit opportunity. Their behavior ranges from willful blindness to unapologetic, overt racism. In 1935, Cambridge, where Harvard and MIT are located, demolished an integrated tenement neighborhood to build Newtowne Court, a whites-only apartment building. Later, local and federal agencies built a segregated project nearby. Between 1933 and 1947, the University of Chicago spent $100,000 to enforce racially restrictive covenants and evict African American families who tried to settle in the adjacent neighborhood. President Robert Maynard Hutchins said the university "must endeavor to stabilize its neighborhood as an area in which its students and faculty will be content to live."

MIT historian Craig Steven Wilder calls the nation's early colleges "the third pillar of a civilization based on bondage," alongside church and state. Many elite colleges were founded and supported by slaveholders. Maryland Jesuits sold 272 slaves in part to pay Georgetown's debts. Dartmouth's first president, Eleazar Wheelock, brought eight slaves to campus. Columbia University announced the swearing-in of its first trustees in a newspaper notice paid for by an advertisement for a slave auction. The professors at these schools fabricated the pseudoscience of race as an "intellectual" basis to support slavery and violence.

Lest you think higher education's crimes against humanity are ancient history, consider the curious case of Ozan Jaquette and Karina Salazar. Jaquette describes himself as having been a lackluster student at Newton North High School outside Boston, where 5 percent of the students are Black and 61 percent are white. He got Bs, avoided tough classes, and performed mediocrely on the SAT. Nevertheless, Jaquette received stacks of college brochures. By contrast, Salazar graduated third in her class at Tucson's Sunnyside High School, where approximately 93 percent of the students are Hispanic and 2 percent are white. Salazar had a GPA over 4.0, took every AP course her school offered, and aced the SAT. She received neither glossy college brochures nor visits from fancy colleges—only from military recruiters and the local community college.

Salazar, who's today a professor at the University of Arizona, and Jaquette, who's at UCLA, decided to take a deep dive into where colleges invest their recruiting time. After "webscraping" the admissions websites of more than one hundred top colleges and universities, they found a clear pattern. In deciding what high schools to visit and which college fairs to attend, recruiters focused on affluent communities and private high schools while largely overlooking poor communities of color. Twelve of the fifteen public research universities in Salazar and Jaquette's study visited more out-of-state high schools than in-state. When they did, the focus was on affluent, predominantly white schools.

Milliken v. Bradley cemented residential segregation into the DNA of American society, and consequently did the same for school segregation. No one could reasonably deny that counteracting its effects would be the most daunting of challenges. But, despite their claims and glossy brochures bragging of diversity, that's not what elite colleges do. They hoard themselves, in the form of massive endowments. And whom does this money benefit? If you remember one statistic from this book, remember this one. About half of Americans describe themselves as living in the suburbs. Among the Harvard class of 2024, the rate is 63.3 percent. Elite colleges don't combat residential segregation. They reward it.

15

How Michael Lewis Ruined Baseball

Michael Lewis didn't set out to ruin baseball. Quite the contrary, Lewis loves the game. He played in high school and views his coach as a transformative figure in his life. Lewis simply set out to tell a good story. Superficially, it's about how Billy Beane, the general manager of the Oakland Athletics, the lowest of low-budget teams, consistently outperformed the sport's behemoths, like the Yankees and Dodgers. More deeply, Lewis's bestseller, *Moneyball: The Art of Winning an Unfair Game*, is about how orthodoxies stifle innovation.

Beane was a disciple of Bill James, the founder of "sabermetrics." Named for the Society for American Baseball Research, sabermetrics is the empirical study of the sport. Beane succeeded by quantifying things that others hadn't noticed and using that information to exploit market inefficiencies. Most famously, this attracted Beane to Scott Hatteberg, a slow-footed catcher with nerve damage in his throwing elbow whose main virtue was an uncanny knack for drawing walks. Other general managers laughed when Beane signed Hatteberg for next to nothing. They stopped after Hatteberg helped propel the 2002 A's to a twenty-game winning streak and their division title.

At first, people dismissed Beane's success as a fluke. This was especially true of the old-school baseball types. They circled the wagons against the empirical approach, which devalued the observational, impressionistic evidence that was their stock in trade. Hall-of-Famer Joe Morgan dismissed Beane, Lewis, and pretty much anyone who expressed even modest sympathy for Lewis's book or the ideas contained therein. Morgan famously said that the Moneyball approach couldn't win in the playoffs, which is like saying Warren Buffet could never make his second hundred billion. Today, every baseball team emulates Beane's approach.

Moneyball is widely read in the business world as a compelling, accessible example of the bandwagon effect—the heuristic bias in favor of adopting the same behavior as everyone else. Baseball teams' persistence in relying upon their scouts and visual evidence is a stunning illustration of herd mentality, if also an ironic one. Today, teams in all sports are falling over themselves to rationalize their behavior. But Lewis's book did something else that's less talked about: It changed the way the game is played.

To understand how, you need to know a little inside baseball. The Moneyball approach places great value on "true outcomes." A true outcome is something that doesn't depend on luck and can't be defended. For example, line drives can be caught, but 450-foot fly balls will be home runs no matter what. Under Moneyball, homers became commodities of greater value. (In 2019, Mike Trout, who averages 35 home runs per season, received a $426 million contract, the largest in baseball history.) Understandably, hitters began training to hit balls with higher launch angles. Batters who excelled at putting the ball in play became a thing of the past.

As hitters evolved, pitchers adapted by throwing more rising fastballs, which tend to generate swings and misses, especially to batters with uppercuts. A strikeout is also a true outcome. Infielders can boot groundballs, but not much can go wrong with a strikeout. The problem is that inducing strikeouts requires more pitches than pitching to contact does. Moneyball also teaches that relief pitchers are less effective, so batters became more selective, hoping to force the opposition into their bullpen earlier. It worked. Starting pitchers began to last fewer innings. Today, teams use an average of one more pitcher per game than they did before *Moneyball* was published.

Play changed too. Teams stopped bunting and stealing bases or trying any of the exciting, risky plays that might give the defense a free out.

Shifts further drove down batting averages. The game began to look like a contest between who could hit the most home runs on offense and who could strike out the most batters on defense. The game is so widely recognized as more boring that Major League Baseball executives publicly worry about the risk of baseball becoming a niche sport. The single biggest problem is the pace of play. In 2003, the year Lewis published his book, the average baseball game took a little over two and a half hours. In 2020, it took three hours and sixteen minutes.

And it was all because of *Moneyball.* Closely observing the game had changed the game.

In the early 1980s, while pursuing a master's degree in sociology at Arizona State, Wendy Espeland landed a job as a field worker studying the social impact of a proposed dam at the confluence of the Verde and Salt rivers in Central Arizona. The most expensive project ever proposed by the Bureau of Reclamation (as in "reclaim the West"), the Orme Dam would have allowed the agency to control the flow of four rivers, brought water to the Sonoran Desert, and helped protect Phoenix from floods. One small problem: it also would have inundated the Fort McDowell Reservation, thereby forcing the Yavapai tribe of Native Americans off their ancestral home. Espeland's job was to talk to the Yavapai.

What most struck Espeland was that no one involved was speaking the same language. The Bureau was divided into two camps. A group of older engineers who viewed success in terms of how many dams got built, and a cohort of younger employees who were ideologically committed to "rational choice." The latter group viewed pretty much everything as a cost-benefit calculation. After elaborate deliberation, the Bureau made the Yavapai an offer for their land they seemingly couldn't refuse—$40 million, or approximately $100,000 for each of the 400 residents. The Yavapai said no. Their "participation" with the land, as they thought of it, was essential to how they understood themselves. It was, in another word, sacred.

Later, as Espeland reflected on the experience, she kept thinking about the young rationalists' instinct to put a value on everything. The sociologist Karl Marx had given the name "commensuration" to the process of converting intangible characteristics into a common metric. Marx thought a lot about what it meant to transform someone's distinctive labor—like a carpenter's chair or an artist's painting—into a common unit of exchange, such as gold. When the Bureau tried to convert the value of the Yavapai's land into dollars, they were effectively doing the same thing as when sabermetricians reduced the value of players to a single statistic known as "wins above replacement." But commensuration was antithetical to the Native Americans. Today, there's a casino near where the Orme Dam would have been. Commensuration, and the inability to find a common denominator, had literally shaped the land.

The dam experience whet Espeland's appetite to study commensuration further. In the late 1990s, she heard from colleagues that law schools were going crazy about the *U.S. News & World Report* rankings. Perhaps no act of commensuration is quite so audacious as reducing an education experience to a numerical order. Together with Michael Sauder, a precocious graduate student who's today a professor at the University of Iowa, Espeland undertook to understand how the rankings were affecting law schools. She and Sauder interviewed more than two hundred law school administrators and faculty and visited seven focus schools, where they interviewed pretty much everyone.

Almost everyone Espeland and Sauder spoke with loathed the *U.S. News* rankings. They'd changed who law schools admitted. "Accountability measures have a tendency to transform the phenomena they are meant only to reflect," Espeland says. It all started with LSAT scores. Even though the test only loosely predicts law school performance, about 90 percent of a school's ranking was based on the average LSAT scores of its students. Because of this, law schools became obsessed with applicants' performance on the test. To attract students with higher scores, they diverted money that they'd used for need-based financial aid to begin offering "merit" scholarships. This negatively affected diversity, which *U.S. News* didn't consider at all. It especially affected socioeconomic diversity since LSAT scores correlate so directly with wealth.

The rankings even changed the schools themselves. Law schools became homogeneous. Schools that once had distinctive missions, such as commitment to public service, were forced to play the LSAT game. The rankings pitted one law school against another, creating a universe in which education was perceived a zero-sum game. This encouraged corruption, as people tried to game the system. It also changed power dynamics within schools, shifting influence to an emerging cadre of "enrollment managers," who were driven by data rather than pedagogy. They were the Moneyballers of education.

It was only natural to imagine that the forces at work on law schools would be having a similar effect on colleges and universities. Test scores increasingly drove the rankings there, too, and every institution in higher ed seemed to be obsessed with its standing. To satisfy their curiosity, Espeland and Sauder interviewed enough people at colleges to have a point of comparison. The dynamics were indeed the same. *U.S. News* rankings had changed college—and not for the better.

When the Canadian real estate and media magnate Mort Zuckerman bought *U.S. News & World Report* in 1984, the magazine had fallen far behind its rivals, *Time* and *Newsweek*, in a shrinking market that would soon collapse.* To help revive its fortunes, Zuckerman poached *Newsweek*'s Washington bureau chief, Mel Elfin, a graduate of Brooklyn Tech and Syracuse University, who had a reputation as a brilliant but high-strung boss.

Before Elfin took over, *U.S. News* had toed the waters of the rankings game. The magazine had been running a ranking of "Who Runs America" since 1974. In 1983, they'd produced their first rating of American colleges, based almost entirely on a reputational survey. Elfin had the idea of publishing a guidebook of college rankings. He thought it essential that they have an air of scientific validity and charged Robert Morse, a twenty-eight-year-old graduate of the University of Cincinnati from the magazine's economics unit, with creating a model based

---

* In 2010, the *Washington Post* sold *Newsweek* for one dollar. Ten years later, the magazines with the largest circulation were *AARP: The Magazine*, the *AARP Bulletin*, and *Costco Connection. Time* was thirteenth. Its circulation of 2.3 million was approximately one-tenth of *AARP: The Magazine*.

on quantitative data. Morse's initial formula placed significant weight upon selectivity, test scores, and endowment per student, conveying a sense of precision that pretty much everyone in academia deplored, but Elfin loved.

Today *U.S. News* is America's Rancor-in-Chief—sorry, Ranker-in-Chief. In addition to producing lists of every type of academic institution imaginable, it also ranks hospitals, diets, stocks, mutual funds, states, countries, cars, places to live, real estate agents, vacation destinations, cruise ships, hotels, law firms, dentists, doctors, nursing homes, and Medicare plans, among many, many other things. It's like *Consumer Reports*, without all the toasters. Also like *Consumer Reports*, it's basically their entire business model.

One could fill a book with the problems with the *U.S. News* rankings—Espeland and Sauder did. We'll focus on four. The first is that ranking systems create a bottom where there didn't use to be one. For example, back in the day, you might have sent your son or daughter without reservation to the extraordinary Reed College in Portland, Oregon. Reed requires all freshmen to take a multidisciplinary humanities course covering everything from the Bible to the Harlem Renaissance, emphasizes narrative evaluations rather than grades, has no fraternities or sororities, only club sports, an honor code, and a nuclear reactor run by undergraduates. Its alumni include Barbara Ehrenreich, Wikipedia co-founder Larry Sanger, and Steve Jobs. Today, you'd be sending your kid to the sixty-third ranked liberal arts college.

"We don't need to turn everything into a zero-sum game," Sauder told me. "There shouldn't be competition among lighthouses." *U.S. News* doesn't rate lighthouses. I checked, just to be sure. But it sure does rate colleges, and in so doing causes incalculable harm. The phony precision exacerbates the fear of falling—of sliding down the metaphorical mall escalator. No wealthy parents want their kid to do the sixty-third ranked anything. More damagingly, *U.S. News* created a zero-game where there wasn't one before. Billy Beane rated players, but his work, and Michael Lewis's description of it, didn't change the number of winners and losers in baseball. Bob Morse, on the other hand, created a new universe of losers—and I don't just mean the lowest-ranking schools.

The biggest losers in Morse's commensurated universe, as we'll discuss in a moment, are poor kids.

The second problem with the rankings is that some things are impossible to quantify. What if Reed views its essential mission as producing independent thinkers, like Jobs, and do-gooders, like Ehrenreich? *U.S. News* has no ranking for promoting social justice. Often, they're comparing grossly dissimilar things. This is the essential problem with commensuration. What does Bob Jones University, a conservative Christian college in Greenville, have to do with the Citadel, a military college in Charleston, other than being in South Carolina? Nothing apparent, but *U.S. News* rates them in the same category—Regional Universities South, whatever that means. (Harvard is in a region, too.) It's tempting to go with an apples-to-oranges metaphor here, but at least they're both fruits. This is more like including NASA nutritional paste in the same category as sashimi.

A third issue is that rankings depend entirely on the factors that are chosen and even small changes in the criteria can produce big changes in the order. Consider cities. *U.S. News* ranks them, of course. Here are their top five:

1st   Boulder, Colorado
2nd   Denver, Colorado
3rd   Austin, Texas
4th   Colorado Springs, Colorado
5th   Fort Collins, Colorado

Their methodology allocates 21.6 percent of the weight to the job market (evaluated by unemployment rate and average salary), 23.4 percent to a "value index," (essentially the ratio of housing costs to average incomes), and 25.7 percent to quality of life (defined as crime rates and quality of education as measured by—you guessed it—the *U.S. News* high school rankings). Let's not linger on the preposterousness of the phony precision. (Why not 21.7 percent to the job market?) These are factors that someone might reasonably consider, and, though the list is Colorado heavy, these seem like fine places to live.

But look what happens when the criteria are changed even slightly. Niche.com, a competitor of *U.S. News*, formerly known as College Prowler, produces its own list of best cities. They afford a bit less weight to cost of living (12.5 percent) and housing (10 percent), a bit more to the quality of public schools (10 percent), and add some factors *U.S. News* omits, including percentage of residents with a college degree (afforded 12.5 percent of the weight) and, at long last, diversity (7.5 percent). This also seems like a reasonable list, and while there are some differences in the criteria, they're seemingly outweighed by the similarities. One would expect only modest reshuffling of the resulting list. It's still the United States, after all.

Here's what Niche came up with:

1st   Woodlands, Texas
2nd   Arlington, Virginia
3rd   Naperville, Illinois
4th   Overland Park, Kansas
5th   Cambridge, Massachusetts

Not a single city in common. You'd have to go down to fifteenth on Niche's list before you'd find a city—San Francisco—that's in the *U.S. News* top ten (it's tenth). Everything turns on the factors that are chosen, which leads to the fourth—and most significant—concern: every factor that *U.S. News* relies upon favors wealthy colleges that admit wealthy students.

Shortly after she became president of Vassar in 2006, Catharine Bond Hill committed the institution to becoming radically more diverse. Hill, who's known as "Cappy," came to Vassar from Williams, where she'd been the provost. In 1999, after Princeton announced that it would implement "need-blind" financial aid, Cappy asked the economist C. Gordon Winston to help her figure out whether Williams should match the pledge. Winston said they didn't have the data to figure out how much it would cost. So, they collected it. Hill and Winston found that Williams didn't have many low-income kids and was asking the families of those they did to pay more than half their income. When Cappy got her own ship to command, she resolved to reshape it in her vision.

During Cappy's ten years in office, Vassar more than doubled the number of low-income students it admitted. The school's financial aid budget grew by about as much. The percentage of students of color increased from 20 to 33 percent. The number of first-generation students grew from near zero to about 100 per class. (Vassar admits approximately 660 students each year.) In 2015, shortly before Cappy retired, the Jack Kent Cooke Foundation awarded Vassar its inaugural $1 million prize for Equity in Educational Excellence. Around the same time, Malcolm Gladwell asked Cappy how she'd done it. "You make tradeoffs," Cappy answered.

Gladwell's interview with Cappy became the subject of an episode of his *Revisionist History* podcast called "Food Fight," in which Gladwell compared Vassar's decision to concentrate on socioeconomic diversity with Bowdoin's commitment to producing a world-class dining experience. Bowdoin howled at Gladwell's characterization of them. Among other things, the college said it only hosted two lobster bakes a year.

Though he touched a nerve, Gladwell's premise is entirely fair. On its website, the college itself proclaims in bold type: **"Food at Bowdoin is a big deal."** The Polar Bears boast that all their meals are made from scratch by a staff of "talented culinary professionals." Their head baker—every college needs one—has a YouTube video on how to make a Bowdoin log—vanilla ice cream in pulverized chocolate wafers that'll give you a quick start on the freshman fifteen. They also have an in-house meat shop and an organic garden.

Obviously Gladwell is drawing a metaphor. It's fair, too. Vassar and Bowdoin are quite different institutions. At Vassar, the median family income is $132,800. Less than 1 percent of students come from the top 0.1 percent, 9.3 percent come from the top 1 percent, and 5.4 percent come from the bottom quintile. At Bowdoin, the median family income is $177,600, 2.4 percent come from the top 0.1 percent (nearly triple Vassar's rate), 20 percent from the top 1 percent (more than double), and just 3.8 percent from the bottom quintile. About 23 percent of Vassar students receive Pell Grants, nearly 50 percent more than at

Bowdoin. But we have bigger fish to fry than Bowdoin. For now, I'd like to use this data as a vehicle for talking about rankings.

In 2006, when Cappy took over, *U.S. News* ranked Vassar thirteenth among liberal arts colleges. When she left ten years later, it was in an eight-way tie for twelfth. Cappy literally remade the institution and its ranking effectively fell. Over the same period, Bowdoin's comprehensive fee rose dramatically, as well as its operating expenses per enrolled student. In other words, they invested more in food. *U.S. News* approved. Bowdoin's ranking *rose* from sixth to fourth.

If it's overstated to say that every factor in the *U.S. News* rankings is tied to wealth, it's not by much. At the very least, they wouldn't reward the sort of investments that Cappy made in Vassar. The rankings criteria change a bit from year to year, but mostly in the weighting. Let's consider the most recent criteria—listed in Table 11 below—in connection with Cappy's efforts to improve socioeconomic diversity and Bowdoin's efforts to improve its food.

The biggest ticket item, graduation and retention rates, is tied directly to wealth. The Education Longitudinal Study—run by the Department of Education's National Center for Education Statistics—tracked a representative sample of 15,000 students from high school through their

TABLE 11. *U.S. NEWS & WORLD REPORT* 2021 RANKING CRITERIA

Graduation and Retention Rates	22%
Undergraduate Academic Reputation	20%
Faculty Resources	20%
Financial Resources Per Student	10%
Graduation Rate Performance	8%
Student Selectivity	7%
Graduate Indebtedness	5%
Social Mobility	5%
Alumni Giving Rate	3%

early twenties. Fourteen percent of students from the lowest-income quartile graduated from college, as compared to 60 percent from the highest-income quartile. It may be tempting to attribute this to differences in academic preparation, but the disparity persisted even among students who scored in the top quartile in math. Forty-one percent of the academically strongest students from low-SES backgrounds graduated from college, as opposed to 74 percent from high-SES backgrounds. By letting in more poor students, Cappy hurt Vassar on this metric.

U.S. News assesses "reputation" with a survey that includes more than six hundred questions and asks college leaders to rank more than two hundred peer institutions into five tiers of quality. This is hardly an objective process. How would you rate Princeton's undergraduate business program? College presidents rated it quite highly. Problem is, Princeton doesn't have an undergraduate business program. The peer leaders fell victim to the "halo effect," the tendency of people to be influenced by their previous judgments and their positive impressions of a brand. Cappy almost surely did nothing to enhance Vassar's reputation, at least in the way U.S. News measures it. If that had been her aim, she'd have followed the lead of Northeastern president Richard Freeland, who made it his singular mission to crack the Top 100. His strategy included relentlessly contacting the roughly 750 people who had a say in Northeastern's peer assessment. Today, Northeastern is ranked forty-ninth.

Cappy egregiously dropped the ball when it comes to the financial resources criterion. "Faculty resources" means class size, compensation, and percentage of faculty with a terminal degree in their field. Pretty much everyone who teaches at a wealthy college has a PhD, and class sizes at Vassar were already quite small. To game this criterion, Cappy should have invested in faculty salaries. The average Vassar professor makes about $112,000 a year. It's about the same at Bowdoin, even though the cost of living in Maine is lower than New York. It's nothing compared to the average Harvard professor, who makes about twice as much. It's also utterly irrelevant to the student experience. Elite colleges aren't hiring star faculty because of their skill in the classroom. Many see undergraduates only in large lecture classes and often consider teaching a nuisance. No worries from a rankings standpoint. Bob Morse and his team make no effort to measure the quality of education.

Bowdoin's investment in food paid the biggest dividends in the student resources category. Here, *U.S. News* measures average spending per student on instruction, research, public service, academic support, student services, and institutional support. It rewards spending money on the students a school lets in rather than spending money to let in needy students. This bias taints other criteria in the *U.S. News* rankings. For example, a college's best strategy for doing well on the graduate indebtedness metric is to let in lots of wealthy students since they accumulate less debt. The graduation rate performance metric similarly rewards spending on admitted students as opposed to admitting needy students.

The same dynamic affects the social mobility calculation, which *U.S. News* included for the first time in 2019. But this isn't Chetty and Friedman's notion of social mobility. *U.S. News* defines it as the graduation rates of Pell Grant recipients and Pell Grant "performance"—a comparison of Pell Grant recipient graduation rates with the graduation rates of wealthier students. Very little consideration is given to how many Pell Grant students a school actually admits.[*]

Finally, Cappy was really off the mark when it came to student selectivity. This used to be measured by acceptance rate, which colleges tried to game by encouraging students to apply who were unlikely to get in. Bowdoin (with an 8.9 percent acceptance rate) trounces Vassar (24 percent) on this metric. Significant weight continues to be allocated to SAT and ACT scores. Given these incentives, and the fact that a one-rank improvement can lead to a 1 percent increase in applications, it's unsurprising that most colleges responded as law schools did—by diverting

---

[*] Specifically, *U.S. News* multiples the performance ratio by the percentage of students who receive Pell Grants, up to 50 percent. Cappy would thus have earned a tiny benefit for increasing Vassar's Pell Grant percentage to 22 percent. Schools like John Jay that significantly exceed the 50 percent threshold are effectively penalized.

financial aid from needy students to wealthier students with higher SAT scores. Much more on this in a moment.

The gist is that by significantly increasing the socioeconomic diversity of Vassar's student body, Cappy engaged in almost the opposite of the behavior *U.S. News* encourages. In their totality, the *U.S. News* rankings reward schools that pay their faculty a king's ransom, admit mostly wealthy students who are overwhelmingly likely to succeed, and lavish them with resources.*

Almost everyone in higher ed has a bad word to say about *U.S. News*. "It's one of the real black marks on the history of higher education that an entire industry that's supposedly populated by the best minds in the country—theoretical physicists, writers, critics—is bamboozled by a third-rate news magazine," Bard president Leon Botstein says. "They do almost a parody of real research. I joke that the next thing they'll do is rank churches. You know, 'Where does God appear most frequently? How big are the pews?'" Cappy faults them most for diverting money from needy students. "Any dollar spent on need-based financial aid receives little credit in the *U.S. News* rankings," she said. Katzman told me simply, "*U.S. News* is a negative force. It promotes the wrong narrative to parents and students." The question is: how does something so universally deplored persist?

Over the years, there have been modest efforts to buck the system. In 1995, Reed became the first school to announce that it wouldn't participate in the rankings. Reed wanted to avoid the homogenizing pressure of rankings, which its leadership saw as antithetical to their institutional ethos that education should be its own reward. Steve Koblik, the president at the time, asked *U.S. News* to simply omit his college from the rankings. The editors responded by assigning Reed the lowest possible value for each missing variable. Reed dropped from the second quartile to the bottom.

In 2005, Sarah Lawrence College stopped accepting SAT scores. The

---

* I detail my extensive efforts to interview Morse, who still oversees the rankings, in a lengthy endnote. If you've seen *Roger and Me*, you can skip it.

school didn't engage in the ruse of making them optional. It stopped taking them altogether, relying instead on high school grades and extensive writing samples. Since they didn't accept the SAT, they stopped providing SAT information to *U.S. News*. The magazine responded by making up a number. Specifically, they assigned Sarah Lawrence an SAT score one standard deviation below the average score of its peer group (or about 200 points). In other words, they harshly penalized Sarah Lawrence for marching out of lockstep and trying to improve the socioeconomic diversity of its student body. "Like unilateral disarmament," wrote President Michele Tolela Myers, "unilateral withdrawal from the *U.S. News* ranking system is dangerous."

In 2007, Lloyd Thacker, a former admissions officer at USC and the alter ego of an idealistic, one-man nonprofit known as the Education Conservancy, called on colleges and universities to stop completing the *U.S. News* reputational survey and to refrain from using rankings in promotional materials. At its annual meeting, a consortium of liberal arts colleges known as the Annapolis Group debated the letter. About sixty schools said they'd abide by Thacker's proposal. Robert Morse responded by denouncing the letter and inviting college counselors to complete the survey. The insurgency died in its infancy.

Conspicuously absent from this movement has been any leadership from the Ivy-Plus colleges. Defying the rankings is dangerous, but not fatal. Reed College ultimately prospered after leaving the system. Applications rose, as did their average SAT scores. Here's a ranking we can all get behind: Reed ranks fourth in the U.S. for the percentage of its students who go on to earn a PhD. If anyone would be in a position to survive the short-term hit of *U.S. News*'s wrath, elite colleges would. Yet nary a word.

"I understand why Mort Zuckerman and a third-rate news magazine, who looked into the crystal ball and discovered they were going out of business, hit on a life-saving formula," Bard's Botstein told me. "I don't fault them. They're smart charlatans. They're P.T. Barnum. I understand why such a scam would be created by a news magazine." Botstein can barely contain his venom as he gets going. "What I did not expect was that the leadership—the beneficiaries—would embrace it. For Harvard,

Yale, and Princeton to go along with this mediocre, ridiculous, undisci-
plined, undifferentiated, and harmful notion? They essentially became
whores."

Underlying Botstein's colorful metaphor is the reality that in this
context, as in so many others, elite colleges have shown no inclination
to disturb a system that benefits them. It's no coincidence that these
schools are at the top of the *U.S. News* rankings. Mel Elfin saw it as
essential that the magazine's order jibe with people's preconceptions.
"When you're picking the most valuable player in baseball and a utility
player hitting .220 comes up as the MVP, it's not right," Elfin said at
the time.

Botstein says that elite colleges could have nipped the rankings deba-
cle in the bud. "This could have been stopped by Harvard, Princeton,
Yale, Penn, and Chicago getting together and saying, 'we're not participating in this,'" he said. "'We condemn it and want nothing to do
with it.' They could have gone on a campaign to destroy its credibility."
Botstein shakes his head. "Instead," he continued, "they did the opposite." Today, it's almost impossible to imagine the status quo changing
without the leadership of Harvard, Yale, and Stanford. If Reed could
survive, surely they could too, but there's never been so much as a peep
on this from the elites. Christina Ciocca Eller says the explanation for
their silence is the obvious one.

"It's nice to be king," she says. "There's nothing not nice about
being king."

16

You Say You Want a Revolution

Growing up in Milwaukee in the 1960s, Nick Zeppos read anything he could get his hands on—encyclopedias, novels, biographies. As a nine-year-old, he talked his mother into plunking down $9.99 for an almanac called *Facts & Figures* that he'd been eyeing in Gimbel's department store and then read it cover to cover. Hope Zeppos had trained as an actress, and so her son also liked to read plays. Nick loved *A Man for All Seasons*, about Sir Thomas More, and *Inherit the Wind*, about the Scopes "Monkey Trial." Learning about Clarence Darrow made him want to be a lawyer.

Nothing in Nick's life should have suggested this as a possibility. The Zepposes lived in Bay View, a segregated, blue-collar neighborhood just south of the Kinnickinnic that had once been home to a steel-rolling mill. Nick's father, Stavros, had never gone to college. Hope ran PR for an architectural firm. Nick went to the public high school, just three blocks away from his childhood home on Logan Avenue. Its most famous graduate was New York Yankees shortstop Tony Kubek.

A determined and precocious student, Nick finished at the top of his class. He'd have been an obvious candidate for James Conant's National Scholarship for middle-class midwesterners, but Nick never considered applying to Harvard or any of the Ivies. "Nobody from Milwaukee went to elite eastern colleges unless they were affluent or a legacy," he told me. Instead, he enrolled at the University of Wisconsin to which he was, and is, enormously grateful. "I had a world-class university seventy-five miles away," he said. "It was two hundred fifty dollars per year, and I got a scholarship."

At the flagship campus in Madison, Nick started as a math major, switched to history, and stayed on at U of W for his JD. After graduation, he took his law degree to Washington, DC, where he worked briefly for the storied law firm Wilmer Cutler Pickering before moving to the Department of Justice. At the age of twenty-three, Nick argued a case in front of federal appellate court judge Antonin Scalia. Eight years later, in 1986, he went on the "meat market," as they call it, and landed a teaching job at Vanderbilt. He's been there ever since.

It's easy to see that Nick would be a great teacher. He's brilliant, funny, and genuinely interested in people. It's also easy to see how he'd succeed as an administrator. Professors are iconoclastic and idiosyncratic by nature, but Nick was the reasonable person everyone could talk to. After earning tenure as a professor, Nick naturally gravitated to law school administration. A few years later, he became Vanderbilt's associate provost for academic affairs. Overseeing admissions and financial aid for the entire university gave him a new perspective. "I started to get interested in the bigger picture of what a research institution is about," Nick told me. In 2001, Vanderbilt's chancellor, Gordon Gee, asked Nick to take over as provost. When Gee retired six years later, Nick succeeded him.

In the course of writing this book, I spent more than a dozen hours with Nick. At the end of our time together, my first thought was that he'd fit right in with my bowling team. You probably have enough of a sense of me at this point to know that's about the highest compliment I can pay someone. My second thought was that he was the subject of a social experiment run in plain sight. What if a working-class kid had been given a crack at running an elite college? No need to speculate as to the results of this trial. Vanderbilt had handed the keys to this straight-shooting, free spirit from Milwaukee, with his tortoise shell glasses and flying mop of curly black hair.

Nick's fingerprints are all over Vanderbilt. Zeppos College, opened in 2020, is the newest addition to a residential college system that he helped to build. The Zeppos Scholars—$8 million for students committed to public service—is but one of several programs of its kind that Nick created. Under his leadership, Vanderbilt formed one of the first partnerships with the Posse Foundation, which continues today. The university's endowment more than doubled during Nick's tenure— from $2.9 billion to $6.4 billion. He's proudest of the $400 million he raised for Opportunity Vanderbilt, his initiative to meet all undergraduates' financial need without loans. The inspiration for this was his conversations with students who considered withdrawing from college because they didn't want to saddle their families with debt. "Every one of those kids was someone that could have been me," Nick says.

In many respects, Nick reshaped Vanderbilt with his vision. When he took over in 2007, about 18 percent of Vanderbilt undergraduates were students of color. The reputation was of a strong regional college, comprised mostly of affluent southern kids. "We talked as if our competitors were Duke and the Ivies, but we weren't close in undergraduate admissions," Nick said. "We weren't as diverse on anything—race, class, religion. Vandy didn't have a Hillel." He joked, "We had fewer Jews than Notre Dame." At a retreat, Nick told the board of trustees, "There's a phenotype of a great university." By the time Nick retired, Vanderbilt had it. The share of minority students grew substantially during his tenure. In one diversity ranking, Vanderbilt came in tenth out of 3,514 schools. Nick would be the first to say things are hardly perfect, but they're light-years ahead of where they were when he landed.

In some other respects, though, Vanderbilt looks more or less the same as it always has, which is a lot like other elite colleges. If you sort the Chetty-Friedman data by mean family income, Vanderbilt comes in third—behind Middlebury and Brown—at $535,431. Twenty-two percent of students come from the top 1 percent. More come from the top 0.1 percent than from the bottom income quintile. Nick gets salty at this. He says, fairly, that the Chetty and Friedman data, which runs through approximately 2013, didn't allow enough time for the effects of the changes he implemented to be revealed. But even if Nick made a huge dent in the problem, Vanderbilt still looks a lot more like Harvard and Yale than CUNY or Berea.

Sports at Vanderbilt look familiar, too. The Commodores only field sixteen varsity teams, far fewer than Harvard's forty-two. But this is the big-time. The SEC. Derek Mason, the last football coach Nick hired, earned about $2.6 million per year, significantly more than Nick did. This is ironic since Nick is outspokenly critical of college sports. "The whole narrative is that sports raise money," Nick told me. "They don't raise money except maybe for athletics." Nick fought against the expansion of teams at Vanderbilt. "Tell me the socioeconomic implications of squash and sailing as sports," he says. Regarding the Varsity Blues scandal, Nick says that "anyone who knows anything about admissions knows that these spots are loosely supervised." This tortures him because he sees every seat in a freshman class as potentially transformative.

Why doesn't more radical change happen? Nick points a finger at organizational interest groups, like alumni of particular teams. "This turns democracy on its head," he says. Nick recalled that when his predecessor got rid of men's soccer because the school had shifted out of balance on Title IX, the backlash was fierce. Nick told Gee, "If you got rid of the English department, you'd get less blowback from the board." The larger lesson is that any university leader has a finite amount of political capital to expend.

"When you're president," Nick says, "you've got a limited number of bullets to shoot."

People often forget that college presidents have bosses too. The members of these governing boards go by different names—trustees, regents, overseers—but the idea is the same. Most higher education institutions are corporations. Board members are the caretakers of these legal entities. They're also paradigmatic examples of what C. Wright Mills called "the power elite."

It'd be unforgiveable to go through a book-long discussion of elite colleges as social actors without mentioning the motorcycle-riding, anarchic Columbia University sociologist and his seminal, heretical analysis of who runs America. I first encountered *The Power Elite* on my mother's bookshelf. I dared not touch out of fear that it contained *Necronomicon*-like power. Even in the age of QAnon, the title still sounds sinister. But Mills wasn't advancing a conspiracy theory.

In fact, he said elites often were unaware of their own status. He simply observed that the military, financial, and political systems were dominated by Ivy League alumni. More specifically, they were dominated by Ivy Leaguers who'd also been admitted into upper-echelon fraternities such as the Fly Club or the Skull and Bones Society. ("Harvard or Yale or Princeton is not enough," Mills wrote.) These elites, Mills said, shared a world view. They believed, for example, in the free enterprise system, private property, and the concentration of wealth.

This dynamic is key to unlocking the puzzle of why American universities are so conservative. College presidents are overwhelmingly former faculty members who reflect the values and political leanings of the academy. Trustees are a different story. If you conjured an image of what a group of revolutionaries might look like—young, diverse, anti-establishmentarian—university boards are almost the exact opposite.

Whatever limited progress has been made in diversity among college students has not been mirrored in college boards. According to the Association of Governing Boards of Universities and Colleges (AGB), whites hold about three-quarters of board seats at public institutions and approximately 88 percent at private colleges. This rate includes minority-serving colleges, which have higher minority participation on their boards. At many white-majority colleges, the rates are dismal. At USC, for example, only 5 percent of the trustees are Black. At UNC-Chapel Hill, the board that wavered on granting tenure to 1619 Project founder Nikole Hannah-Jones—leading her to accept a competing offer from Howard—included ten white men and one white woman among its thirteen members.

Women are consistently underrepresented. AGB's data shows that women hold less than 30 percent of board seats. Women of color on college boards are downright rare. When Randy Dumaling, an undergraduate at Fordham, explored the background of his college's current and past trustees, he found that eighty-six of the ninety-two were white. Only one was a woman of color. It goes without saying that almost no one is poor.

Given the data regarding boards, UC Riverside professor Raquell Rall says, "It isn't far-fetched to assume that race is not a top-of-mind issue when they make decisions on behalf of their colleges and universities." The same goes for socioeconomic diversity. Boards, she adds, "are not familiar with using an equity lens to do their work." The data bears out Rall's intuition. As a group, trustees aren't exactly down with The Squad. In a Gallup survey commissioned by AGB, 72 percent of respondents identified themselves as either conservative or moderate. When asked their biggest concern for the future of higher education, merely 4 percent of trustees cited "equal access to higher education among different demographic groups," slightly fewer than selected "other."

The prospects for change are bleak. Revolution is a young person's game, but university trustees on balance are old and have served a long time. According to AGB, more than 71 percent of trustees are over the age of sixty. Thirty-nine percent are older than seventy. About a third report having served ten years or more. This is because the boards of public institutions are generally appointed by governors. At private universities, they're self-perpetuating. For example, at Harvard, members of the principal governing body, the Harvard Corporation, are selected by—you guessed it—the Harvard Corporation.

Harvard's board exemplifies the national trends. Nine of its thirteen members are white, including the university's current president, Larry Bacow. Two are heirs to family fortunes. The majority attended prep school. Two, including Bacow, attended Andover. Four are publicly billionaires. (Out of approximately six hundred in the United States.) Eight of the trustees work in finance or business. Two are lawyers, including a current member of the California Supreme Court. Two are educators—the current president of Amherst and the immediate past president of Princeton. No one is a do-gooder, even by the broadest definition. Certainly no one has spent their life teaching or working with poor children. The Harvard Corporation looks less like the leadership of a nonprofit aimed at advancing the public good than it does the management committee at JPMorgan Chase or Goldman Sachs.

The analogy to a commercial or investment bank seems especially apt in the context of how universities manage their endowments. Harvard's endowment—$51.9 billion as of February 2022—significantly exceeds the cash reserves of most major banks. If Harvard were a for-profit business, its cash reserves would rank sixth among American companies—slightly behind Meta and GE but ahead of General Motors, Coca-Cola, and Ford. If it were a nation, its reserves would rank forty-first, just ahead of Kuwait, Australia, and Qatar. It's about as large as the endowment of the Bill and Melinda Gates Foundation, the largest nonprofit in the country, and nearly triple the size of the Open Society and Ford Foundations, which rank second and third.

Endowment wealth is almost as concentrated in America as personal wealth—12 percent of colleges and universities control 75 percent of endowment assets. Collectively, the $313 billion owned by the universities with the ten largest endowments (listed below in Table 12, based on 2022 data) exceeds the foreign exchange reserves of all but twelve nations, just behind Brazil, but ahead of Germany and the United States.

As one might expect, Harvard's board of corporate-finance types manages the endowment conservatively. In 2019, Harvard distributed approximately $1.9 billion from its endowment. That sounds like a lot of money, but Harvard earned a 6.5 percent return on its endowment that year—roughly $2.5 billion—and that doesn't include new contributions. After the payout, Harvard's endowment grew by $1.7 billion. In 2021, the endowment earned 33.6 percent and ultimately

TABLE 12. LARGEST ENDOWMENTS

Harvard	$51.9 billion
University of Texas System	$42.9 billion
Yale	$42.3 billion
Stanford	$37.8 billion
Princeton	$37.7 billion
MIT	$27.5 billion
University of Pennsylvania	$20.5 billion
Notre Dame	$18.1 billion
Texas A&M	$18.0 billion
University of Michigan	$17.0 billion

grew by $11.3 billion, even as the pandemic raged. Since its founding in 1974, the management company that oversees Harvard's endowment has averaged an 11 percent annual return, growing the fund by more than forty-fold.

The story is pretty much the same at each of the elite colleges. Yale has averaged 9.9 percent returns over the past twenty years. Stanford's management company has averaged 11.3 percent since its inception in 1991. Princeton reports 11.6 percent annual gains over the past decade. This data can't be completely trusted. Each school reports its returns over whatever period makes its results look the most impressive. Reading their annual statements, one gets a vibe of good old-fashioned Ivy League competitiveness among these management companies. Whatever the precise truth, it seems fair to say that the returns are largely consistent from one elite college to another and that all are doing quite well.

Elite colleges are also consistent in how much of their endowment they spend. Harvard spends roughly 5 percent of its endowment value each year. Stanford targets an annual 5.5 percent payout. Yale draws down 5.25 percent of a rolling average of its endowment's value over the past several years. This spending rule, which many universities and nonprofits emulate, was conceived by Yale's Nobel Prize-winning economist James Tobin, who promoted a notion of intergenerational fairness. "The Trustees of endowed institutions are the guardians of the future against the claims of the present," Tobin wrote. "Their task is to preserve equity among generations." When this passage is quoted, as it often is, it's generally left unsaid that elite colleges promote massive inequity across generations. Tobin's argument, essentially, is that the endowment needs to be preserved to make sure that elite colleges are equally well situated to preserve the class status of rich people in the future as they are today.

The concentration of endowment draws around 5 percent is no coincidence. The federal government requires every nonprofit to spend 5 percent of its investment assets every year to avoid paying taxes. Colleges and universities are exempt from this requirement, but one has the clear sense that they're distributing near the 5 percent minimum to avoid scrutiny. Among private colleges, the average payout is 4.4 percent.

The policy behind the "payout requirement," as it's known, is to force foundations to do good and to keep them from hoarding wealth. But hoard these colleges do. During the pandemic, college students and employees struggled to survive. Harvard College Students for Bernie Sanders launched a #40BillionForWhat campaign, urging the college to protect workers whose jobs were in jeopardy. Still, Harvard resisted drawing upon its endowment as a rainy-day fund. Every elite college did. Ted Cruz and Josh Hawley shamed Harvard into returning the nearly $9 million that it received under the Coronavirus Aid, Relief, and Economic Security Act. If Harvard and its brethren wouldn't draw down their endowments during the pandemic, it's impossible to imagine that they'll ever draw them down for anything. Rather than lasting forever, elite college endowments appear to be intended to grow forever.

Since the creation of the Harvard Management Company in 1974, the university's endowment has outpaced inflation by more than 700 percent. The results are similar at the other Ivy-Plus colleges. One again has the sense that these schools are competing to be the best endowed. As University of Pennsylvania's Peter Conti-Brown argues, "Universities use their endowments as a symbol of prestige and a point of competition between peer institutions."

Still, all of this might be tolerable if the lion's share of the endowment went to financial aid. It doesn't. Far more goes to private equity managers than to students. Law professor Victor Fleischer, former Democratic chief tax counsel for the U.S. Senate Finance Committee, points out that in 2014, Yale paid nearly half a billion dollars in management and performance fees, about triple what it spent on financial aid. Where does the money from the endowment go? Harvard dedicates the largest share of its endowment—approximately 30 percent—to "flexible" spending. The second largest share—24 percent—goes for professorships. Student support comes in third at 19 percent—about as much as goes to support research, libraries, and museums. The overwhelming majority, in other words, goes for things that preserve the *U.S. News* rankings.

*   *   *

My hunch is that elite colleges won't accept this book as an invitation to reassess their commitment to socioeconomic diversity. They'll say that they already do what I've called upon them to do. They'll say that it's not their responsibility to remedy American society's problems. Most of all, they'll say, "He doesn't understand endowments."

Harvard often makes such claims about its critics. "There is a common misconception that endowments, including Harvard's, can be accessed like bank accounts, used for anything at any time as long as funds are available," reads the university's 2019 financial report. "In reality, Harvard's flexibility in spending from the endowment is limited by the fact that it is designed to last forever." This is hard to square with the fact that Harvard designates the largest share of its endowment to a category it calls "flexible." Cappy says the schools shouldn't be let off the hook, despite their protestations. "I would put a lot of responsibility on the institutions for articulating and focusing resources on the things that are important," she says. "They just don't privilege access as among the top priorities."

Another elite college lamentation is that people don't understand the limits placed on gifts. Cappy rejects the thrust of this claim, too. "As an economist and having worked as a provost, money is pretty fungible," she told me. Sometimes bequests are specific—Cappy recalled a gift to buy cello music for Vassar's vast library—but she explained that it's easy to go to the state attorney general and ask that ancient gifts be reformed. "What really matters is the total amount coming in and the total amount going out." Cappy offers the example of a donor who wants to help the economics department. The party line is that money can't be spent on financial aid, but Cappy argues that it can be. "If we wanted to improve access, if we got money, regardless of whether it was specifically for access, it freed up the money to do what we wanted to do," Cappy said, adding, "There's a lot more flexibility than people like to talk about."

Cappy speculates that colleges promote the narrative about restrictions on endowments as a fundraising ploy. "I think they like to be able to say that we can't do this unless you give us the money." She says this approach never resonated with her. "Because then we say this isn't something we do with our own money. We only do it with your money." Vassar alumni were highly supportive of Cappy's financial aid initiative. She's not sure whether they'd have established this as a priority on their own, but they responded to her sense of its importance. "My experience with fundraising," Cappy said, "is that if the institution has a set of values that they care about, you could talk alumni into supporting those things." In other words, if Harvard and Yale said access was of paramount importance, it would become of paramount importance.

This is the larger, deeper lesson to be learned from Cappy's experience and leadership. Hers is a quaint, Burkean notion, that political leaders should exercise independent moral judgment rather than simply reflect the popular will. In *The Chosen*, Jerome Karabel advances the idea—let's call it Karabel's Theorem—that a university will retain an admissions policy only so long as it corresponds to its perceived institutional interests. Cappy asks, do elite colleges lack socioeconomic diversity because they have legacy, or do they have legacy because they don't want socioeconomic diversity? Her implication is that legacy continues to exist as a justification to admit lots of wealthy undergraduates, which elite colleges perceive to be in their institutional interest.

Ultimately, whether elite colleges want to embrace their unique ability and obligation to promote social mobility is a question of will. "It's not like I had endless amounts of money when I ended loans," Cappy told me, "I just said that I'm going to make it a priority and I'm going to do this and not that." Which is not to say it's simple. "I got so much blowback from a lot of quarters. These aren't easy things to do," she said. "You've got to make access and social mobility existential. I viewed it as existential."

It is existential. If Harvard increased its endowment draw by just 1 percent and dedicated that money to access, it would mean over $500 million a year—enough to fund tuition and expenses for almost seven thousand low-income students. That figure exceeds Harvard College's entire annual operating budget. Imagine a new or expanded Harvard campus dedicated to providing opportunity for low-income students. If the schools with the ten largest endowments acted similarly, they would collectively generate over \$3 billion per year. That would be enough money to cover full tuition for more than 50,000 students per year—half a million students over a decade. Elite colleges could save a generation of socioeconomically disadvantaged students without compromising any of their settled relationships with prep schools and alumni, simply by marginally diminishing the rate of endowment growth.

That point bears repeating: Their endowments would still grow.

So why don't they do it? Cappy is on Yale's board of trustees, for goodness sake. She's been saying these things for years. Today she runs Ithaka S+R, a nonprofit aimed at expanding education opportunities for students from diverse backgrounds and improving learning outcomes. Many of these board members live in the philanthropic world. They understand that missions evolve. In 1833, John Stuart Mill called out the irrationality of making "a dead man's intentions for a single day a rule for subsequent centuries." Yet, the fundamental mission of elite colleges remains class reproduction—generally referred to as "excellence"—rather than promoting opportunity.

It's easy to be cynical about this, or even to see a conspiracy at work. But C. Wright Mills is almost surely right to say that it's not sinister. University boards don't consciously think to themselves that they're reproducing class status. Rather, their conservative policies are the product of the types of people selected for these positions and the structural dynamics that leads these boards to reproduce themselves in perpetuity. These people are exceedingly well suited to manage money and ensure that the institutions they steward exist in perpetuity. But they're poorly suited to ask harder philosophical questions—like whether they should function in perpetuity if they serve principally as a tool of class reproduction rather than access and opportunity. And they're utterly unsuited to answer the ultimate question that Cappy asks: "Should we really exist if we don't embrace these things?"

PART V

Change

17

Making College Pay

After his parents separated when he was seven, Edmund Kennedy lived with his mother in South Euclid, a middle-class, inner-ring suburb on Cleveland's east side. His mom didn't have steady work and so his family got evicted many times. They often didn't have enough food or, as Ed puts it, "the things you need to be a happy human being." Shortly after he entered Charles F. Brush High School, where 81 percent of the students are Black, as Ed is, he went to work. His first job was with the school's AV squad. During his sophomore year, he started working at Mitchell's Homemade Ice Cream—a bougie, locally sourced, environmentally sustainable parlor serving exotic flavors including vegan salted caramel pecan and lavender honey scented with flowers from Mulberry Creek—on Cedar Road in Beachwood, where the overwhelmingly white, local school district spends about $5,000 more per student each year than South Euclid. It took Ed forty-five minutes to cover the two miles and the metaphorical chasm between his home and Mitchell's. In the summer, the heat could be oppressive. The pay wasn't great either. But when Ed was forced to quit in twelfth grade so he could take care of his brother, who had serious mental health issues, his family missed the money.

Neither caring for a sick sibling nor working three weeknights and both weekend days is conducive to studying, so Ed's grades suffered. During his senior year, he thought to himself, "No college for a Black man with a 1.8 GPA," and enlisted in the Marines. Ed served five and a half years, in Japan and the Philippines, until he fractured his tibia playing recreational basketball. Marines are required to be able to run, but after nearly two years of rehab, Ed couldn't meet the physical performance standard and was honorably discharged. He left the service with a bum leg, a modest VA disability payment that barely covered the cost of his car, and no idea what to do with the rest of his life.

Ed stayed in San Diego, where he'd been doing his rehab, and started working the graveyard shift for a security company, which he says is the only thing for which his military career had prepared him. On a whim, he registered for classes at Palomar Community College in nearby San Marcos. To his amazement, he loved it. He felt at home amidst the college's rich diversity. He was also really good at school. He took a heavy load of math and science courses and earned straight As.

After almost a year of courses, Ed had no idea where his education would go. The G.I. Bill covered his tuition. It also provided a reasonable housing allowance. But San Diego is the eighth most expensive city in the U.S., and one of the G.I. Bill's idiosyncrasies is that the stipend only remains in effect during the months you're taking classes. The program is predicated on the notion that you have a nest egg to draw upon and a stable home to return to for the holidays, neither of which Ed possessed. He had no clue how he'd get through the summer, let alone pay for his second year until he caught the first significant break of his life.

Looking through his junk mail one day, Ed by chance noticed a pamphlet from Stanford advertising a summer program for veterans who'd excelled at community college. Reflexively, Ed enrolled, and after the spring semester ended at Palomar, he hauled himself five hundred miles north. Palo Alto felt like a different universe. Ed had never been around rich people before. He felt uncomfortable. But he loved the academic experience. He got As in classes on international relations and law. His aspirations expanded. "I shifted to wanting to be a student," Ed told me.

He just didn't know how to do it. When the Stanford program ended, Ed still had no sense of where his life was headed. He'd given up his lease in San Diego, and he didn't have enough money for a down payment on a new place, so he headed east where his people were. After a few weeks in Cleveland, he landed a job working for a grassroots political consulting firm in Philadelphia. It had a fancy title—deputy campaign organizer—but the gig consisted of more or less the same thing as Leanne Son Hing's year working for Greenpeace. Ed hung out on corners soliciting donations to Doctors Without Borders and other do-gooder organizations. He hated it. To make matters worse, he was staying on the couch of a military friend's mother in Lancaster, which meant driving an hour and a half each way to work.

Ed was on the verge of despair when he received the second break of his life: A letter from Amherst inviting him to apply based on his good performance at the Stanford program. Ed applied and got in. He could scarcely believe his good fortune. After the acceptance letter arrived, he quit his job, packed his few belongings, and moved to Massachusetts. Ed had threaded the eye of a needle—he'd gotten himself into an elite liberal arts college without ever having taken the SAT.

That's when things got tough.

Shortly before he was set to start his first semester, in the spring of 2020, Amherst demanded his "family contribution"—$5,000—before they'd allow him to register for classes. Ed was old enough to be exempt from including his family on his FAFSA—the Free Application for Federal Student Aid—but his military earnings counted against him. (My student Hannah had a similar experience. In their financial aid calculation, Fordham included child support to which her mother was legally entitled but not actually receiving.) Ed explained that he was no longer in the Marines, but it was no use. The financial aid office said pay now, argue later. They wouldn't even waive his acceptance fee. Ed went to his father, who had a new family, and begged for the money.

Once classes started, he felt adrift. In Tony Jack's language, Ed was Doubly Disadvantaged. Jack's framework resonates with Ed. "People say there's a divide between athletes and non-athletes at Amherst," he explains. "I say the divide is between rich and poor. It's the starkest divide I've ever seen in my life. Far more classist than racial." At Stanford, his fellow veterans had provided a support network. At Amherst, he had no one. In time, Ed gravitated to other transfer students, who, he says, "were grounded in a better sense of reality." He got by.

Then, COVID struck. Ed's anxiety and self-consciousness about his financial security soared. "It was so obvious who was rich and who was poor," Ed told me. "The other students are saying, 'We're going to go to our house in LA or we're going to take our plane to Cabo until this blows over.' Meanwhile, the transfer students are trying to make sure everyone has someplace to sleep—we can ask our cousin in Boise who's got an extra basement or whatever." Ed shook his head. "It was very uncomfortable."

His more practical concern was how he'd survive. Like the G.I. Bill, Amherst's plan for navigating the pandemic was predicated on the notion that all its students had permanent domiciles and a stable support structure. Ed was brilliant, and he had his act together in almost every important respect, but, as he puts it, "I have homeless issues." Delete "issues." By the Department of Education's definition of the term, Ed became homeless during the pandemic. He lacked a fixed, regular, and adequate nighttime residence. He ultimately prevailed upon his father to let him sleep on the couch in the living room. Ed took his Zoom classes sitting outside on the balcony.

Despite everything, Ed is careful to say how grateful he is to Amherst. During our interviews, he paused many times to tell me how fortunate he considered himself, and how grateful he felt to be where he was. It's the first of several important lessons in Ed's story, and one of the most striking and memorable aspects of the interviews I conducted for this book. The needier the student, the more gratitude they express for a system that's stacked against them.

In 2008, a team of researchers led by the sociologist Sara Goldrick-Rab (whom we briefly met in the discussion of drinking and habitus) began speaking to lots of students on financial aid. That year, a husband and wife who'd graduated from the University of Wisconsin-Madison— where Goldrick-Rab was then a professor—created the Fund for Wisconsin Scholars with a gift of $175 million. The fund offered grants to 1,200 students—$900 a semester for two-year college students, $1,750 per semester for four-year students—for ten semesters, conditioned only on their making satisfactory academic progress. No applications were necessary. The fund selected students at random from among approximately three thousand eligible high school seniors, thereby creating a social experiment.

Goldrick-Rab and her team undertook a mammoth effort to understand the effect of the additional aid. After surveying all three thousand students and analyzing their academic records, they found that each additional $1,000 received increased the percentage of students who completed a bachelor's degree on time by an average of about four points. But that average masked a more complicated story. For most students, the extra money didn't help at all. For others, it had a profound effect. What the aid paid for made a huge difference. No one had really thought about that before.

Groundbreaking as this was, it wasn't Goldrick-Rab's most interesting finding. She and her team supplemented their quantitative data with in-depth interviews of fifty undergraduates. They usually started these sessions by asking one simple question: "How's college going?" Many of the interviewees responded with the sort of stories you'd expect to hear from young college students—about trying to meet friends, or keeping up with their courses, or finding the right balance in their life. But many also talked about struggling to find food. Some said they couldn't concentrate on their classes because of hunger.

To that point, no one had systematically studied hunger among American college students. Her curiosity piqued, Goldrick-Rab resolved to determine the extent of the problem. What she found shocked her. Nearly 40 percent of the four thousand community college students she surveyed were experiencing food insecurity, ranging from worrying about being able to afford food to skipping meals to not eating at all for days at a time. This couldn't be written off as an aberration. A separate study of low- and moderate-income students at Wisconsin colleges confirmed the result. More than 60 percent had experienced food insecurity within the past year.

Since those initial studies, Goldrick-Rab's findings have been replicated many times. Food insecurity among college students is rampant. Thirty-nine percent of CUNY students are food insecure. Across the University of California's ten campuses, the rate is 40 percent. At Western Oregon University, it's 59 percent. A large national study, conducted by the nonprofit organization Students Against Hunger, surveyed students at thirty-four colleges and universities. Nearly half of the respondents reported food insecurity within the previous month. Not surprisingly, the rates were highest among Black and first-generation students.

When Goldrick-Rab took a closer look at the students experiencing food insecurity, she found another disturbing trend. About 10 percent said they'd recently been homeless. This, too, is a persistent finding. For the past five years, Goldrick-Rab—who's now at Temple University—has been running a survey through her Hope Center's #RealCollege initiative. It has received 330,000 responses from students at more than four hundred colleges and universities. Forty-six percent of respondents report having experienced housing insecurity, and 17 percent say they've been homeless within the past year. Students Against Hunger reached similar findings. Sixty-four percent of the respondents to their survey had also experienced housing insecurity. Another 15 percent had experienced homelessness.

The problem isn't confined to students at public colleges. When students in Middlebury professor Molly Anderson's course on hunger and food security surveyed their classmates, they found that nearly 10 percent of Middlebury students either sometimes or often didn't have enough food to eat. A Cornell University survey found that 22 percent of students had skipped meals due to financial constraints. At Dartmouth, 76 percent of students on financial aid said they'd experienced food insecurity during interims.

Breaks from school are a particular problem. Tony Jack found that only one in five colleges—then not including Amherst—kept their dining halls open when school was out, causing significant food insecurity. "There's always famine during spring break," one student told Jack. At Amherst, Ed described a brutal competition. "Going into a break, they release this thing to the entire student body saying anyone who needs to stay on campus for whatever reason, here's your opportunity to 'Hunger Games' it out and explain why you're the most deserving to stay on campus." His invocation of Katniss Everdeen tracked language that other students used in their conversations with Jack. "I always thought this was bizarre," Ed added. "I have nowhere else to go. The other independent students and I would say, 'We live here.'"

The pandemic, the longest break from school in memory, exacerbated the problem. The Hope Center found that 11 percent of students at two-year colleges and nearly 15 percent at four-year schools shared Ed's experience of pandemic-related homelessness. Because socioeconomically disadvantaged students are rarely squeaky wheels, it feels as if stories like Ed's are aberrational. The truth is closer to the opposite. For poor students, even at the most elite colleges, food and housing insecurity are the norm.

Goldrick-Rab has spent most of her life thinking about opportunity. She attended Thomas Jefferson High School for Science and Technology in Alexandria, Virginia, where, mirroring a trend among highly competitive magnet schools, less than 5 percent of the students are Black or Latinx. She wanted more diversity in college, but her options were limited. Goldrick-Rab's parents had recently divorced, and she didn't have much of a fund to draw upon. Her guidance counselor recommended Northern Virginia Community College, even though Goldrick-Rab had a 1490 on her SAT. She landed at William & Mary, where she was repulsed by Greek life and lasted less than half a semester. Goldrick-Rab regrouped, transferred to George Washington, where her mom had a job, and supported herself by working thirty hours a week at Whitlow's on Wilson, a funky Arlington grill that now features a rooftop Tiki bar, where she served burgers and cocktails.

This work experience formed the tinder of Goldrick-Rab's career. The spark came several years later during her time as a graduate student at the University of Pennsylvania. While working on a study—about how federal welfare programs discouraged impoverished adults from attending college—Goldrick-Rab attended a presentation by a former Department of Education official at the American Association of Community Colleges' annual meeting. The official said that he'd noticed a trend in the data on college attendance. The students were moving around. Some were attending as many as five or six colleges. The speaker claimed they were having fun. This comment made the hair on the back of Goldrick-Rab's neck go up. "Something just said no," she told me. Goldrick-Rab reanalyzed the data and found that the students who were engaging in what she called "squirreling" were overwhelmingly low-income and first-generation students, not partiers. Since then, Goldrick-Rab has dedicated her career to understanding the experiences of disadvantaged students and how their opportunities are shaped and limited by government programs. More deeply, she's worked to refute the false narratives that are told about low-SES people—especially poor college students.

Goldrick-Rab is a force of nature who defies convention in many ways. She's the only academic I've ever met who identifies herself on her CV as a "scholar-activist." ("I don't like it when people are being trammeled," she told me.) And, unlike many academic works, her 2016 book, *Paying the Price*, is conversational, accessible, and readable. It tells the story of how six undergraduates, who begin college with what Christina Ciocca Eller termed "narratives of hope" and Goldrick-Rab calls "great expectations," are betrayed in their pursuit of the American Dream by excessive costs and an unworkable financial aid system. The stories are heartbreaking—like Chloe, a young woman who'd always loved horses and wanted to be a veterinarian but never had the chance to explore the career at her technical college. All she learned, Goldrick-Rab explains, was "whether she could manage five classes and two jobs."

The text of Goldrick-Rab's story is a massive disinvestment from public colleges both at the state and federal level, making college unaffordable for the poor even as the value of a degree has skyrocketed. Indeed, the purchasing power of Pell Grants has declined precipitously over the past half century. In 1974, grants covered nearly the full cost of attending a public four-year school and a little more than the average tuition at a public community college. Today, they cover about 22 and 31 percent of these costs, respectively. The net price of college as a share of family income for families in the bottom income quintile—meaning they make less than about $25,000 per year—has nearly doubled to 84 percent.

The subtext of the story is a massive, popular misunderstanding of what allows people to succeed in college. Here, Goldrick-Rab's observations jibe completely with my own. When people think about, and colleges calculate, the net cost of attending college, they inevitably exclude the opportunity cost of not working. But going to Princeton doesn't only cost $80,000 per year. It costs $80,000 plus the foregone income that one might have earned working full time. For an affluent family, this extra money is irrelevant. Few rich parents make their kids work at Wendy's. For poor families, a teenage child's extra income can mean the difference between survival and disaster. "If we truly accounted for the family financial contributions of these students," Goldrick-Rab says, "they would actually need to be paid to attend college to cover opportunity costs and help keep their families afloat."

The margins are thinner than people realize. Even the possibility of having to spend an additional $1,000 led Denisse's family to choose John Jay over Columbia. Ed's Amherst story almost ended before it began over $5,000. This is a reality that elite colleges either cannot or choose not to understand. Shortly after the publication of *Paying the Price*, some students invited Goldrick-Rab to speak at Amherst. The college had recently won a $1 million prize from the Jack Kent Cooke Foundation for sustainably increasing the number of high-achieving low-income community college transfer students—the very same initiative that benefitted Ed. During her visit, Goldrick-Rab had a roundtable discussion with several students who told her they were experiencing housing insecurity or were homeless.

One of Goldrick-Rab's deals is that she'll only visit your campus if she gets to meet with the head of financial aid. When she did this the following day, her head was still spinning with the gut-wrenching stories she'd just heard of young people moving from couch to couch or going hungry during breaks. "How many of your Pell Grant recipients graduate with debt?" Goldrick-Rab asked the director. Since Amherst claimed to meet full need, like many elite colleges, the answer should have been zero.

"About 25 percent," came the reply.

Goldrick-Rab gets emotional retelling what happened next. "So then you don't meet full need," she remembered saying.

"You can't stop them from taking those loans."

"Well," Goldrick-Rab said, "you'd stop them by meeting full need."

"We meet full need," the director insisted. "The things they take those loans for—" implying the expenses were frivolous.

"Can you give me an example?" Goldrick-Rab asked.

Without skipping a beat, the director told her about a first-generation student who'd recently taken a federal loan. "You'll never guess why," she said.

"Why?"

"She needed to borrow money for plane tickets so her family could watch her graduate from college." Goldrick-Rab recalled the derision in the director's voice as she added, "She took a federal loan for that."

"That's need," Goldrick-Rab explained before asking incredulously, "Why wouldn't you just give her the money?"

There was no reply.

In Goldrick-Rab's research on Wisconsin students, the X factor that made the difference was whether the extra money from the Scholars Fund went into students' pockets or whether it was used to relieve debt. When students used the extra money for school expenses or to work less, graduation and retention rates improved significantly. When the money was instead used to avoid taking out additional loans, it doesn't do any good at all. This again jibes with my own experience. Saddling poor kids with massive debt is unjust, but in terms of getting them through college, what matters much more is getting money into their pockets so they can live and study. The solution is simple: Make the expected contribution negative to reflect the reality of the opportunity cost of attending college for socioeconomically disadvantaged students. In other words, pay poor students to go to college.

Goldrick-Rab offers commonsensical ideas to improve outcomes for socioeconomically disadvantaged students: Make public college free. Create an affordable housing program for students. Let going to school satisfy the work requirement for all public benefit programs. Expand the successful national school lunch program to cover college-goers. Require all students to complete FAFSA and schools to publish mean-ingful data. "Right now, we're giving away money without any account-ability," Goldrick-Rab says.

Finally, Goldrick-Rab calls for the creation of a federal-state part-nership that guarantees adequate, equitable funding for public colleg-es and universities. The priority should be funding two years of free, post-high school public education. When Goldrick-Rab says prioritize, she really means it. She would cut off federal financial aid to private institutions—Title IV funds as they're known, in reference to the High-er Education Act of 1965—until community colleges, regional universi-ties, and minority-serving institutions are fully funded. Goldrick-Rab says, "I cannot stand the idea that CUNY students are getting screwed the way they are."

If the first piece of this puzzle is that poor students don't get as much financial aid as they need, the second, interlocking piece is that the wrong students are getting it. Many kids who jetted off to Cabo—while people like Ed searched for a couch on which to ride out the pandemic—are getting financial assistance. It's called "merit aid," and it's perhaps the greatest scandal in a grotesquely scandalous system.

According to the National Association of State Student Grant and Aid Programs, in 2017 only 46 percent of undergraduate aid was dis-tributed strictly based on need. More than $2 billion was allocated solely based on merit, and another $2.6 billion on the basis of merit and need. The trend is in the wrong direction. The percentage of merit-only aid increased between 2007 and 2017 from 14 to 22 percent. The long list of colleges that pay merit aid includes Duke, Trinity, Washington & Lee, Swarthmore, Wesleyan, University of Virginia, University of Chicago, Vanderbilt, Rice, Emory, Johns Hopkins, and Villanova. As Paul Tough reports, colleges now give more aid to kids from families earning over $100,000 per year than they do to kids from families with annual incomes under $20,000.

This dynamic is the product of an arms race that began in the mid-1970s when Boston College's then-dean of admissions, Jack Maguire, began thinking of college admissions in what we'd later think of as Moneyball terms, using data and market research to attract better students to BC's campus. One of his key innovations was merit aid. Giving money to students who didn't need it attracted wealthy kids and ultimately helped the bottom line. It was a new, powerful weapon.

The thing with a new, powerful weapon is that once someone has one, everyone wants one. This diminishes their collective value. Soon you're in a nuclear arms race. So it was with Maguire's brainchild. Colleges began spending more and more on merit aid while getting less and less bang for their buck. The situation evolved into a classic prisoner's dilemma. When Lloyd Thacker interviewed college presidents, he got a clear, consistent message: Everyone regarded merit aid as antithetical to the mission of higher education, but no one dared be the first to unilaterally disarm.

Cappy offers another seemingly simple solution to this problem: Let colleges agree to stop paying merit aid. Federal antitrust laws are an obstacle. Beginning in the 1950s, the Ivies and MIT began working together—the Department of Justice would say colluding—to give consistent financial aid packages to students who received multiple admissions offers. George H.W. Bush's Justice Department sued. The Ivies quickly settled, paradoxically contending that they'd never colluded while agreeing never to do it again. MIT, however, took the case to trial, arguing, among other things, that doling out financial aid wasn't commercial activity. Their appeal lasted long enough that the case carried over into the Clinton administration, which, worried that the Supreme Court might uphold the exemption, settled with MIT. The agreement allowed them to share data with other schools that committed to need-blind admissions. Senators Ted Kennedy and Howard Metzenbaum successfully pressed Congress into extending the terms of that settlement to all need-blind schools under an exemption due to expire in September 2022.

Another complication with Cappy's proposal is that collusion simultaneously produces two quite different effects: It shifts who gets financial aid while also driving down the total amount of money that colleges spend on financial aid. One of the main arguments the Ivies and MIT made in defense of collusion was that they had a fixed budget for financial aid. If that condition is true, then collusion might shift scarce resources from rich kids to needy ones.

Robert Litan, the attorney-economist who negotiated the settlement with MIT for the Justice Department, calls the idea that the Ivies only have a fixed pot of money for financial aid "obviously false." Their endowments, he says, "are mind-fuckingly large." Litan believes that in a fully competitive world, the Ivies would spend more on financial aid.* "Some schools would be more liberal than others," Litan told me, "but I guarantee you they'll end up spending more than 5 percent." Cappy thinks that ending the existing exemption would decrease the amount of aid available to poor kids.

It's impossible to know for sure whether Cappy or Litan's approach would do better for socioeconomically disadvantaged students, but one thing is clear: the status quo is the worst of all possible worlds. It's the colleges with the smallest endowments that could most plausibly claim that they have a fixed budget for financial aid (and hence can provide generous need-based assistance only if they're freed of the burden of paying merit aid). Yet the exemption belongs solely to elite colleges. It's just another respect in which the system makes the rich richer—largely at the expense of poor kids.

*   *   *

---

* The fact that economists think about competition over financial aid rather than tuition is yet another of the many oddities of the college universe. Ordinarily, producers compete by lowering their sticker prices. Tuition at American private colleges is remarkably consistent. Why didn't Jack Maguire and enrollment managers try to gain a competitive advantage by lowering BC's sticker price and thereby usher in a new world of tuition competition? One reason is that dropping tuition, say by $1,000, means that the college gets $1,000 less from all its students, regardless of whether they (or, rather, their families) were willing to pay it. Financial aid competition allows the college to extract more precisely what each student is willing and able to pay. Economists would call this extracting as much consumer surplus as possible. What's odd is that colleges leave tons of consumer surplus on the table. Elite college degrees are worth millions, and the average family income at most of these schools is over $500,000 per year. Many wealthy families would pay anything to get their kid into Harvard. If that's so, why isn't tuition, say, $1 million per year? From a poor or middle-class student's standpoint the outcome would be the same—the expected family contribution is the expected family contribution. What difference does it make whether a student whose family can only pay $10,000 per year gets $70,000 per year in financial aid or $990,000? I've never heard a convincing answer to this question. People generally laugh and say that's what it costs anyway—you just pay through donations rather than tuition. But most people don't donate $1 million per year. It seems like the status quo leaves a lot of money on the table that might be used to promote socioeconomic diversity.

After emphasizing the infrequency of their lobster bakes, in response to their skewering by Malcolm Gladwell, Bowdoin went on to emphasize their longstanding, unwavering, and unassailable "commitment to meeting the full financial need for all admitted students." Of course, this says nothing about how many needy students the school actually admits. It's a sleight of hand. Most stories elite colleges tell about financial aid are defined by these deflections.

Consider the term "need-blind." By law, colleges are allowed to collude if and only if they admit all students on a need-blind basis. But who determines need? And who determines blindness? I asked Litan, "Is it the colleges themselves?"

"Bingo," he replied.

We know that colleges don't meet all real need. "Need is a legal term that can be manipulated," Goldrick-Rab says, bluntly. "The no-loan promises are baloney." We also know that they're not really blind to the financial circumstances of their applicants. If they were, they wouldn't consider legacy status or how much money an applicant's parents had contributed or ask an applicant to state whether they could pay full tuition. But many elite colleges ask this very question, and reward affirmative answers in the admissions process. As Ron Lieber of the *New York Times* has reported, students who don't need financial aid are more likely to get in.

Some colleges admit to being "need-aware" or "need-sensitive." This list of schools includes American University, Bates, Boston University, Brandeis, Colgate, Colorado College, George Washington, Haverford, Macalester, Northeastern, Oberlin, Skidmore, Tufts, Wesleyan, and Washington University. The handful of schools that call themselves "need-blind" are being more coy. They don't really mean "blind." It's another deflection. What they really mean is that they won't deny an applicant solely because of financial need. When it comes to money, they're anything but blind. It's difficult but possible to imagine an application redacted of all evidence of financial advantage. "Need-blind" colleges haven't even tried. They want the signals. As Nick Lemann puts it, "The connection between family money and higher education was never truly severed."

The biggest deflection is that all the money elite colleges spend on financial aid hasn't much changed who goes to these schools. "One thing that has gone unremarked," John Friedman says, "is that the way most universities have tried to increase economic diversity is by expanding financial aid. That has not been successful in and of itself." That doesn't mean that expanding financial aid is bad. "It might be very helpful as a social thing for these mostly middle-class families who are getting this extra aid not to have such a financial burden for sending their kid to school," Friedman explains, "but the consequence of that is that it has made it quite a bit more expensive to expand the numbers."

What would change the numbers? We know from Goldrick-Rab's research that financial aid has the greatest impact when it can be used to reduce working hours or defray college costs as opposed to reducing debt. Grants like Michael Bloomberg's grab headlines, and upper-middle-class people buy newspapers (or read them online), but they aren't the pathway to creating greater socioeconomic diversity or producing better outcomes for the poor students that elite colleges do let in.

The fact that elite colleges nevertheless prioritize reducing the debt burden for upper-middle-class families makes it easy to question their intentions. "I despise Harvard," Goldrick-Rab says. "My kids know that if they say it in my presence, Mom's going to lose it." You can buy a t-shirt from Goldrick-Rab's Hope Center that says, "Shut up about Harvard." She explains that her colleagues forced her to delete two words from an earlier draft of the shirt's language. "Harvard is doing so much harm," Goldrick-Rab says. Regarding Penn, she adds, "I am so ashamed of my alma mater."

The difference between rhetoric and reality makes it almost impossible not to be cynical. "I think more than anything, Amherst wants to come off as if they're doing something good without acknowledging what they're really doing," Ed told me. He easily could have been speaking for the entire system. "They say they're all about letting in low-income students and doing all of these things for people of color, but they're not actually putting their money where their mouth is."

18

We Need You, Mr. Grassley

With a nod to Shakespeare, the American essayist Charles Dudley Warner said that politics make strange bedfellows. Perhaps none have ever been so strange as Iowa senator Chuck Grassley and Vermont representative Peter Welch. Raised on a farm in Butler County, Grassley spent most of his early adult life working in a sheet metal factory. He's pro-life, consistently earns an A rating from the National Rifle Association, and has opposed the Affordable Care Act since the start. Welch, from Springfield, Massachusetts, got his law degree at Berkeley and had a thirty-year career as an attorney before assuming Bernie Sanders's seat in the House. He has a 100 percent rating from Planned Parenthood, promotes green energy, and describes access to quality health care as a human right. But Grassley and Welch have one area of common ground: a shared concern with American universities' hoarding of wealth.

On September 8, 2008, Grassley and Welch convened a roundtable discussion on the use of endowment funds. The participants included the presidents of Berea, University of Vermont, University of Maryland, Princeton, and Amherst—schools at different ends of the spectrum of opportunity and diversity. Welch opened the proceedings by noting the enormity of disparity in the wealth of colleges and universities, offering the example of Harvard and its then-$35 billion endowment. Over the preceding year, it had grown more than the 188 schools with the lowest-performing endowments combined.

This growth, Welch explained, had been subsidized by the American citizen. Colleges and universities enjoyed—and enjoy—a double tax break: both individual contributions to endowments and earnings generated from their investments are tax exempt. If you give $1,000 to Harvard, that's deductible. If Harvard invests those thousand dollars, and makes its usual 11 percent return, the $110 it brings in every year is tax-exempt, too. With compounding, the exemption is worth even more over time.

Shortly before the conference, the Congressional Research Service estimated that the tax exemption cost the United States more than $10 billion in foregone revenue each year. (More recently, the sociologist Charlie Eaton placed the figure above $20 billion annually.) Welch argued that a benefit of such magnitude came with the expectation that colleges and universities would do good. After all, James Conant had argued that Americans had a duty to support the education of the new elite he hoped to cultivate because they would "later serve the taxpayer by serving the entire nation."

Senator Grassley, who'd been beating the drum on this issue for several years, had questions for the university leaders. Did they have long-term goals both to raise money and to spend it? Was subsidizing student aid included among these goals? Should endowment spending include loan forgiveness for graduate students who became teachers, social workers, and health care professionals in underserved communities? Finally, Grassley suggested that contributions to extraordinarily wealthy schools where the earnings on the endowment per student exceeded the cost of tuition plus room and board should no longer be tax deductible.

Approximately one hundred schools met Grassley's last criterion. This list included Amherst, which today has an endowment of about $1.9 million per student, and Princeton, which has an endowment of more than $4.4 million per student. To put these figures into context, given the schools' similar average annual endowment returns of 11.6 percent, and their reported operational costs, each college could let all its students attend for free and still have about $140,000 and $430,000 in earnings per student left over, respectively. Yet, neither

Amherst's president, Tony Marx, nor Princeton's president, Shirley Tilghman, found even the slightest merit in Grassley's proposal. Each opposed any limitation on how colleges used their endowments. Marx said he worried "that even slightly-less-well-endowed institutions might be hurt by a spending minimum during an economic downturn." Tilghman said any step limiting the freedom of universities to compete would be a "serious mistake."

Anyone searching the legislative history for a reasoned debate on the merits of the tax exemption for colleges and universities will be sorely disappointed. It's more like a case of athlete's foot—it's always been there, you're pretty sure where it came from, but you can never completely be certain. University of Illinois law professor John Colombo traces it to as far back as 1601, when an English law recognized the charitable nature of "schools of learning, free schools and scholars in universities."

In colonial America, educational institutions were spared from local taxes because of their ties to churches. Most colleges—including Harvard, Yale, Brown, Dartmouth, and William & Mary—were chartered with public land grants and the aim of training ministers. Today, almost every state has a law or constitutional provision exempting colleges and universities from state, property, and income taxes. When Congress implemented the first federal income tax, in 1894, it maintained the exemption for religious and educational institutions without any debate.

This quaint history seems appropriate to the modest origins of university endowments. In 1718, Cotton Mather approached Elihu Yale, a British-American merchant, to support the struggling Collegiate School, which had been chartered seventeen years earlier to train ministers. Until Mather's solicitation, the school's principal contribution had come from ten Congregationalist leaders—all Harvard grads—who'd donated their books to create the school's library. Mather got involved after his father, Increase, became disenchanted with Harvard, which he'd served as president but believed had grown too liberal. Increase Mather held out great hope for the Collegiate School. Eli Yale, who'd made a fortune as president of the East India Company and may or may not have been a slave trader, responded to Cotton's entreaty by donating 417 books, a portrait of King George I, and nine bales of goods, which the school sold for £800 pounds sterling—approximately $177,000.

For most of its history, Yale invested its modest holdings conservatively, chastened by an early toe-stubbing, when their leadership invested nearly the entire endowment in Eagle Bank, the creation of former university treasurer and cotton gin inventor Eli Whitney. It promptly went bankrupt, costing Yale over 90 percent of its $23,000 endowment and plunging New Haven into depression. After that, it was pretty much all belt and suspenders. Yale still had more than half its money in stocks, bonds, and cash in the mid-1980s when David Swensen, a veteran of Salomon Brothers and Lehman Brothers, took over the university's portfolio and changed the game. The so-called "Yale model," which Swensen pioneered with his former freshman mentee Dean Takahasi, emphasized diversification. Within twenty years, only 10 percent of Yale's endowment was invested in U.S. marketable securities. Their holdings included hedge funds, real estate, and even timber. Yale's competitors naturally followed suit. It may surprise you to know that Harvard's portfolio includes ten thousand acres of California vineyard.

Over time, elite college management companies began to look more and more like Wall Street firms, acting as if producing significant endowment returns and proving Gordon Gekko's mantra were part of their mission. Although it's not officially part of the Yale model, elite colleges also started to get quite aggressive about avoiding taxes. In 2015, Hofstra's Norman Silber and John Wei, then a Yale law student, surmised that many colleges and universities were using offshore havens and so-called "blocker corporations" to cheat Uncle Sam. Their suspicions were confirmed two years later when a data breach at the international law firm Appleby led to the leak of some 13.4 million electronic documents to a pair of German reporters.

The "Paradise Papers," as they came to be known, exposed many elite universities for parking cash in shadowy places like the Cayman Islands and British Virgin Islands. Columbia, Dartmouth, and Johns Hopkins were revealed to be partners in a Bermuda-based company creatively called H&F Investors Blocker, which produced sizeable tax-free returns on overseas investments. Many schools had interests in environmentally unfriendly ventures. Columbia and Duke, it came out, had invested millions in Brazilian iron mining. Northeastern had lots of money in oil and gas, even while it publicly decried climate change. Surely Cotton Mather, who took stealing linen as evidence of a young boy's possession by the devil, would not have approved.

In *The Color of Law*, Richard Rothstein calls out the IRS as an agent of de jure discrimination. "Universities, churches, and other nonprofit institutions cannot be considered state actors simply by dint of their tax exemptions," Rothstein writes, "but we have a right to expect the IRS to have been especially vigilant and to have withheld tax-exempt status when the promotion of segregation by nonprofit institutions was blatant, explicit, and influential."

The IRS, Rothstein explains, has always had a duty to deny preferential tax treatment to discriminatory organizations. "Regulations," he says, "authorize charitable deductions for organizations that 'eliminate prejudice and discrimination' and 'defend human and civil rights secured by law.'" Until 1970, the IRS routinely granted tax-exempt status to southern, whites-only private schools, which had proliferated following *Brown v. Board of Education*. But that year, following a change in its regulations, the IRS denied Bob Jones University's tax exemption because of its prohibition of interracial dating. In 1983, after more than a decade of litigation, the Supreme Court upheld the IRS decision. Writing for an 8-1 majority, Chief Justice Burger said that securing a tax exemption depended on meeting common law standards of charity and that the institution seeking tax-exempt status "must serve a public purpose and not be contrary to established public policy." In other words, colleges and universities merit preferential tax treatment if and only if they do good.

No doubt, at this point every elite college administrator is howling at the page or their Kindle screen, "We do good! We do good!" But some good won't cut it. The Supreme Court's standard requires us to examine the totality of what an institution does, not to cherry pick—with a sort of Hitler-loved-dogs logic—its few virtuous acts. After all, the IRS denied Bob Jones University's tax exemption despite the school's long-established scholarship program for needy Christian students.

This analysis will also require us to put the research function of colleges and universities to one side. Research is certainly a public good, but it's also a central part of the business model for elite colleges and universities. In 2020, Harvard attracted $918 million in grant funding, including $616 million from the federal government. Grants to Yale exceeded $821 million. Stanford's total topped $1.25 billion. (John Jay, by contrast, secured $29 million in funding, though it serves twice as many undergraduates as Harvard.) Generally, colleges keep about a third of research grants as what's known as "fringe"—their cut for providing the infrastructure and support to allow the work to occur. For elite schools, this money represents a significant portion of their operating budget. If anyone is acting charitably, it's the American taxpayer.

It's certainly not people who donate to colleges. Yale Law School professor Yair Listokin has argued that the IRS should stop treating alumni contributions as tax deductible. The goal of the exemption is to encourage charity, not to subsidize purchases of goods and services from nonprofits. That's why, for example, people who buy tickets to a charitable benefit can't deduct the cost of the meal they receive. It's a quid pro quo. Listokin argues that much of the $10 billion that alumni donate to colleges each year involves an implicit quid pro quo—preferential admissions consideration for their children as legacies or donors.

Ultimately, colleges and universities receive a triple tax benefit. Alumni contributions are tax exempt, as are the earnings they make off the investment of these donations, and they're generally immune from state and property taxes. Justifying such extraordinary treatment surely requires a greater institutional purpose than acting as a bulwark against downward mobility for rich people and promoting their access to super-elite jobs. It requires doing good. Doing good does not mean doing something that benefits the community—like opening a hospital—when the principal motivation is profit.

I can imagine three meaningful definitions of doing good in this context. The first would be steering college students into do-gooder careers. If Harvard and Yale encouraged a bunch of rich kids to become teachers and social workers that would be a public service. Instead, they exploit the competitiveness of Ivy League-types and steer them toward investment banking and management consulting. And while some professional schools offer loan forgiveness to graduates who go into public service, elite undergraduate programs do not.

The second version of doing good would be to admit a socioeconomically diverse cohort of students. Instead, elite colleges let in the most economically advantaged students—either through channels that explicitly preference their financial status, such as legacy and donor preference, or implicitly through the credentials they choose to value in the admissions process, like lacrosse acumen and high SAT scores.

Finally, colleges could do good by admitting students from historically disadvantaged populations. Yet less than a handful of elite colleges let in a representative share of minority students. A *New York Times* analysis of admissions at one hundred top colleges and universities found that while 15 percent of college-age Americans are Black, Black students constituted just 6 percent of freshmen at these schools. Hispanics represent 22 percent of the college-age population but only 13 percent of freshmen enrollment. For all their rhetoric and touting of diversity, elite colleges remain overwhelmingly white.

Berea College does good. CUNY does good. HBCUs do good.

Elite colleges don't do good. By and large, what they do harms the common weal.

Once upon a time, it might have been possible to attribute the decision to subsidize elite colleges and universities to ignorance. Even the professors and administrators at these institutions might have been unaware of their social impact. Today that argument doesn't hold water. "We've had some version of the Chetty data for twenty years," Cappy explains, "and I don't think that higher ed leaders are doing much." Her nonprofit, Ithaka S&R, recently published research showing that institutions with large endowments lowered net prices for students but didn't enroll a larger share of needy students. The *Boston Herald* called Harvard and other elite colleges nonprofits in name only. Astra Taylor, co-founder of the Debt Collective, which fights to cancel student loan obligations, says universities have become "billion-dollar hedge funds with schools attached." Wharton professor Peter Conti-Brown says that elite schools have come to view their endowments as having value that's independent of financial wealth. "An elite university's endowment," he writes, "represents a symbol of status and prestige, similar to the university's libraries, art museums, architecture, faculty, and the prominence of its alumni."

That's why it's almost impossible to imagine elite colleges and universities changing their behavior without some government intervention. "There're really no incentives for them to tackle it," Cappy told me. She also worries about the government bollixing things up, which is why she yearns for Harvard and Yale to do more voluntarily. "I wish the selective schools with the resources would realize that they have an obligation to help us as a society to address these issues, and not just talk about it, but do a hell of a lot more than they're doing." With an air of resignation, she adds, "But, again, the incentives aren't there." She shakes her head. "It's hard," Cappy says. "I wish I was more optimistic."

If there is hope, it must lie in the pols. "We are institutions that respond to incentives," Cappy concludes, "and if access to this federal money depended on us showing we were doing what the federal government was giving us money to do, behavior would change."

It's easy to imagine government intervention taking many different forms. The Trump administration imposed a 1.4 percent excise tax on universities with endowments greater than $250,000 per student and deposited that revenue in the General Fund. Simultaneously, Trump targeted Pell Grants for cuts, partially to subsidize NASA so that the U.S. "could return to Space in a BIG WAY!" (Emphasis original.) Between 2016 and 2020, Pell Grant expenditures dropped by about $1 billion, even as the cost of college rose. That's about the worst imaginable version of government intervention.

Cappy proposes, far more sensibly, that colleges be required to maintain a minimum percentage of Pell Grant recipients—say 15 percent, a paltry threshold that nearly two hundred colleges fail to meet. Senator Chris Coons has proposed that schools failing to meet this target be excluded from free public college programs or deemed ineligible to receive federal financial aid. Colleges exceeding the threshold could be rewarded with a credit against the excise tax. Cappy's proposal would create incentives, as opposed to the Trump plan, which is simply punitive.

Congressman Tom Reed, a Republican from an upstate New York district that includes Cornell, introduced legislation in 2018 requiring colleges with endowments over $1 billion to spend more than 25 percent of their annual endowment earnings on financial aid. It's easy to imagine earmarking the revenue from an excise tax for low-income students. The existing excise tax generates approximately $200 million per year. That's more than my college's entire operating budget—in other words, enough money to send twelve thousand kids to college for free in perpetuity. It staggers the mind to think what could be done if the tax exemption were repealed entirely. Here's one perspective: The $20 billion annual cost of the tax exemption for colleges and universities would be almost enough to double the Pell Grant budget.

Elite colleges have responded negatively to all such proposals. After Congressman Reed introduced his Reducing Excessive Debt and Unfair Costs of Education ("REDUCE") Act, the establishment attacked him as ignorant, as they will surely attack me. "He doesn't seem to understand the endowment is not one amorphous thing," said the director of Cornell's Higher Education Research Institute, perhaps thinking the American public didn't also understand that money is fungible. After Reed signaled that he'd be willing to negotiate over the 25 percent threshold, the director of government relations for the American Council of Education said, "I don't think we'd be interested in negotiating over the terms of the bill to make it less bad."

Elite colleges persisted in their position even after responses to a document request by Senator Orrin Hatch showed they had significant flexibility in the management of their endowment, just as Cappy said they did. Over $6 billion of Harvard's endowment had no restrictions whatsoever. At Washington University in St. Louis, more than a third of its then-$7 billion endowment was unencumbered. Brown had more than $1.5 billion that could be spent free and clear. As law professor Mae Quinn points out, elite colleges found money to hire expensive lobbyists and public relations gurus to fight the passage of the Trump excise tax. It's difficult to imagine more conclusive proof that endowment funds can be repurposed when it serves perceived institutional priorities.

It's also difficult to imagine anything more politically short-sighted than the position elite colleges have taken. News of the Grassley-Welch alliance should have sounded a claxon in Massachusetts and Wood-bridge Halls. Access isn't a Democratic or Republican position. The privilege of elites is a manifest injustice that cuts across party lines and evokes a visceral revulsion, into which Donald Trump skillfully tapped. On September 22, 2016, legendary basketball coach and occasional player-choker Bobby Knight introduced Trump to a group of MAGA-heads who'd gathered at Sun Center Studios in Chester, Pennsylvania. "I'll tell you one thing for damn sure," Knight said, wearing his trade-mark red sweater, "I know how to win and he's going to be the best win-ner we've had in a long time."

Trump emerged to the theme from *Rocky*, praised Knight's incred-ible winning record, and launched into a diatribe about elite colleges and universities, perhaps in response to Hillary Clinton's call for free in-state tuition for middle-class families. "Universities get massive tax breaks for massive endowments," Trump said to boos and cat-calls. "These huge multi-billion-dollar endowments are tax free," he explained. "But too many of these universities don't use the money to help with tuition and student debt. Instead, these universities use the money to pay their administrators or put donors' names on buildings or just store the money, keep it, and invest it." The chorus of boos loud-ened. "In fact, many universities spend more on private equity manag-ers than on tuition programs." Trump pledged to work with Congress to make sure "that if universities want access to all of these special fed-eral tax breaks and tax dollars, paid for by you, that they are going to make good-faith efforts to reduce the cost of college and student debt and to spend their endowments on their students, rather than other things that don't matter."

It's difficult not to nod your head in agreement, even if it also makes you want to scrub your head with Brillo. But if you thought Chuck Grassley and Peter Welch was an unlikely pairing, how about Donald Trump and Malcolm Gladwell? Stock up on steel wool, because on this point, they're in complete agreement.

"I've gotten increasingly incensed at the inequality in American higher ed," Gladwell told NPR's Scott Simon in 2015. "There's a handful of schools that just have too much money." Yale was doing fine, he said. "They're able to do great things with their money—you just have to walk through the Yale campus to see what money will buy you, which is a country club, right?" Endowments could do amazing things for underfunded schools. "It's one thing if a school has an endowment of $500 million that they are stretching a million different ways to meet the needs of its students, to say that as a society, we should allow them to escape taxes so they can spend their money on education. That logic does not hold when you've got $35 billion in the bank, as Harvard does," Gladwell said. "I think they have to stand up and say, at the very least, 'We do not deserve to have tax-exempt status for our endowments.'"

19

One Percent Solutions

In October of his senior year, Brendin Skakel's high school guidance counselor tapped his shoulder as he passed between classes at Newburgh Free Academy and said, "Hey, come with me." Together, they walked down the hallway and settled into her office in the guidance department. The walls were adorned with pencil sketches of the counselor, drawn by former students, and photographs of her family. Brendin nervously took it all in. He had a sense what this was about.

She wanted to talk about college.

The conversation should have happened earlier, but they'd both been busy. The counselor was the sole advisor to the nearly two hundred students in the P-Tech program, a partnership with IBM and SUNY Orange that prepares students for careers in science and technology. For his part, Brendin had been helping support his family. They'd been under stress since his father, a paramedic, had moved out three years earlier. Brendin taught code at the local rec center for eleven dollars an hour and babysat whenever he could. He'd had no time to prepare for the SAT, and certainly hadn't had the money to take a prep course, but there was cause for optimism.

In June, he'd taken the exam cold and got a 1450. He also had an unweighted GPA of 4.0 and would be salutatorian of his class. By the end of their half-hour conversation, Brendin and his counselor had decided upon a course of action. He would apply to four colleges: John Jay, St. John's, NYU, and Princeton.

If you're scratching your head at this point, you're not alone. It would have made sense for Brendin to have applied to more schools in the middle tier, like St. John's, to increase his chance at getting a generous merit aid package, and Princeton is a stretch even for salutatorians. Given Brendin's outstanding SAT score, top-notch academic record, and his strong background in math and coding, he'd have had a decent shot at a top computer science program, such as Carnegie Mellon or Rensselaer Polytechnic Institute. It also would have made sense to have applied to more than one safety school. Looking back, even Brendin can't discern any coherence in the strategy, other than wanting to be in the northeast. "Honestly, it was very arbitrary," Brendin told me.

In Monday-morning quarterbacking Brendin's search process, it's easy to forget that applying to college is expensive. "It was like sixty bucks for certain applications," Brendin said, "and I just didn't have it." Still, Brendin could have done one thing that would have dramatically improved his chances of getting into an elite college, and it wouldn't have cost him an extra penny. In second-guessing the advice he received, it's the mistake that stands out above all the others: If he was going to apply to Princeton, he should have applied early.

No one ever told him. "Honestly, it was very much the opposite," Brendin told me. "It was just kind of like don't worry about it—just apply in the next month or so. I remember being reassured in the opposite direction." Today, he sees this advice as the product of his high school environment. "My counselor worked in a school that was heavily minority and low-income," Brendin said. Indeed, less than 20 percent of P-Tech students are white and the average family income in Newburgh is just over $40,000. About a quarter of the residents live in poverty.

"The priority," Brendin said, "was getting people to go to college."

How much did this advice cost Brendin? It's impossible to say anything conclusive about what would have happened with any individual application, but we can make probabilistic statements about the relative chances of someone with Brendin's profile getting in early versus applying with the regular pool.

A total of 35,370 people, including Brendin, applied to be part of the Princeton class of 2022. Of these, 1,941 were admitted—meaning the overall admission rate was 5.5 percent. (Approximately 1,300—or 67 percent—of these successful applicants enrolled. In the biz, this is known as the yield.) Of 5,402 early applicants, 799 were admitted—a rate of 14.8 percent. It's therefore commonly reported that applying early approximately triples an applicant's chance of getting in, but that's a mistake. The overall admission rate includes all the early applicants. The actual admission rate for regular applicants is 3.8 percent (1,142 out of 29,968), meaning that not applying early reduced Brendin's chances of getting in by about 75 percent.

But that's not the whole picture. It might be useful here to return to our image of buckets. Early admissions is a big bucket. Almost everyone who applies early enrolls because Princeton follows a restrictive model that only allows an applicant to apply to one school early. Princeton thus fills almost 60 percent of its class early. And that's not the only special bucket. Recruited athletes take up about 20 percent of the seats. Legacies occupy approximately another 15 percent. Of course, a candidate could fill multiple buckets. Someone whose dad went to Princeton might also be a coveted squash player who applies early action. It's impossible to be exact about these numbers. Roughly speaking, as a non-legacy, non-athlete who applied regular admission, Brendin would have been competing for one of about two hundred seats. By this calculation, his odds would have been about 177-to-1 against. This still overstates his chances. Within this bucket, Brendin would have been competing against the few students of color to whom Princeton gives a leg up.

In sum, it would have been easier for a camel to go through the eye of a needle than for Brendin to have gotten into Princeton as a regular applicant. If he was going to shoot the moon, it's a no-brainer that he should have gone the early decision route. Lots of his college classmates faced similar circumstances. Yet, in the thousands of conversations I've had with John Jay students during my twenty-two-year career, and the dozens of formal interviews for this book that I conducted with students, many of whom had SAT scores in the 1400s and 1500s, I've never met anyone who applied to a private college early.

* * *

Until the end of World War II, you'll recall, the process of getting into an elite college was shockingly straightforward: Anyone who passed the entrance exam got in. Some schools gave their own exam. Others used an exam written by the College Entrance Examination Board—today known as the College Board. By focusing on subjects public schools didn't teach, such as Latin, the exams effectively excluded the overwhelming majority of high school students. This trifle aside, college admissions were egalitarian.

When things began to change, after the G.I. Bill flooded the market with millions of new prospective college students, admissions became more selective and the central challenge for colleges shifted from recruiting students to identifying the "best" among them. For every school other than Harvard and Yale, it also became a challenge to identify which successful applicants would actually matriculate. In the mid-1950s, colleges began to try to get a leg up on one another by sending admissions letters early. In 1954, Harvard, Princeton, and Yale introduced the "A-B-C" system, whereby applicants from feeder schools were given an early indication of whether they were likely to get in ("A"), uncertain ("B"), or likely to be rejected ("C"). This became the framework for early action.

For three decades, early admissions remained a modest part of how elite colleges filled their class. As late as 1983, Harvard admitted only 451 students early. Forty years later, the rate had nearly tripled to 1,223. An astonishing 62 percent of Harvard's class of 2025 got in early. What changed? For one thing, the *U.S. News & World Report* rankings. When Bob Morse and his gang published their first rankings in 1983, Stanford was number one. Neither Penn nor Columbia nor Brown ranked in the top ten. That wouldn't do. Yield counted, and so each of the relentlessly competitive Ivies set out to increase their rate. That meant more accurately interpreting the signal each applicant sent about whether they'd enroll if admitted.

Back in the day, applying to a school sent a strong signal. Each school had its own form. It was a huge hassle. I wrote my applications on an electric typewriter that my grandparents bought me for my twelfth birthday. It had an auto-correct ribbon, which was cutting-edge technology at the time, but if you made more than a couple of mistakes you had no choice but to start over. Cutting and pasting was entirely out of the question. Writing five different essays about which famous person I wanted to have dinner with may have been an ordeal for me, but it served an important purpose for the schools—it sent a very strong signal that I wanted to go.

That all changed with the Common Application, which came on the scene right around the same time as the *U.S. News* rankings. The nonprofit that runs the Common App—whose CEO makes $400,000 a year—touts it as an "engine for advancing access." It's not. If you take one lesson from this book, which I'll happily own as Mandery's Theorem, it should be this: any reform described as "student friendly" or "advancing access" will work to the advantage of rich kids.

Colleges love the Common App because it boosts application numbers, thereby increasing their "selectivity," which used to figure prominently in the *U.S. News* rankings. Students also like it because it makes applying easier. But the Common App dilutes the signal conveyed by an application. In 2005, just 17 percent of freshmen applied to more than six schools. In 2021, students applied to an *average* of 5.8 schools. For rich kids, the rate is much higher. IvyWise, an educational consultancy, recommends that students apply to between twelve and fifteen schools. The Common App sets a limit of twenty, which wealthy students routinely hit.

Since applications mean next to nothing, colleges are forced to look for other signals. Prominent among these are college visits. To the beleaguered, car-weary parent, the formulaic tours—dining hall, sample dorm room, obligatory question from a try-hard about whether you can double major—can seem pointless. Not from a college's standpoint. Students who visit a campus are about 60 percent more likely to enroll at that college than those who don't. Visits send a strong signal.

The problem is flying around the country visiting remote liberal arts colleges gets expensive. When a team led by Chris Avery of Harvard's Kennedy School of Government interviewed 350 students at Harvard, MIT, Princeton, and Yale, they found that 83 percent of freshmen from prominent private high schools visited the college they ended up attending. Among students who identified financial aid as a major concern, the rate was about half.

Avery found even stronger wealth effects associated with early admissions, which he likens to Martian Blackjack. The players don't know the rules of the game, and the colleges—the casinos in this metaphor—don't make them known. You won't, for example, find the data on Princeton admissions that I presented in connection with Brendin's application on their or any other college's website. You certainly won't find any accessible discussion about signals, of which applying early is the strongest. A repeat player could piece it together, but kids play Martian Blackjack just once. The only repeat players with an adequate incentive to learn the nuances of the system are professional college advisors. In a universe filled with nefarious characters, these are perhaps the most evil. Why elite colleges have created the conditions for their proliferation, and allowed them to operate unchecked, is one of the hardest questions these colleges have to answer.

"One way to tell that the market is dysfunctional is if you have to hire a guide," says Stanford economist Al Roth. "The college admissions process at one point was supposed to be something that high-school seniors could do for themselves." It was. Thirty years ago, fewer than one hundred people worked as full-time educational consultants. Today, Mark Sklarow, CEO of the Independent Educational Consultants Association, puts that number at greater than eight thousand. "We know anxiety is off the charts," Sklarow says. "Part of the reason anxiety is off the charts is the decision-making in colleges has become so opaque. We see that parents are willing to do just about anything."

Sklarow means affluent parents. Kids of ordinary means, like Brendin, can't afford professional college advisors. Kids of ordinary means also can't afford to matriculate at a college without knowing their financial aid package, as early decision requires them to do. It's universally accepted that the process benefits rich applicants, who are mostly white. The Century Foundation found that the early decision pool at elite schools had three times the proportion of white applicants as the regular decision pool. Avery and his colleagues found that applying early was worth the equivalent of about one hundred additional points on the SAT.

These effects have been widely known at least since 2003, when Avery published his book *The Early Admissions Game*. Today, any college administrator you speak with will quickly condemn early admissions, but things only seem to be getting worse. As with merit aid, it's a prisoner's dilemma. No one wants to blink first and run the risk they'll be left out on a limb. In 2001, Yale president Richard Levin said that early admissions discriminated against less affluent students, but Yale couldn't end them on their own lest they "be seriously disadvantaged relative to other schools."

A few years later, Harvard flirted with ending early admissions. In 2006, the university was led by Derek Bok, who'd served as president for twenty years and who'd stepped back into the role after Larry Summers resigned. Bok, a longtime critic of inequities in elite college admissions, announced that Harvard would stop letting students in early. Just five years later, the college reversed course, ironically citing diversity as the motivating force. Faculty dean Michael Smith said, "Many highly talented students, including some of the best-prepared low-income and underrepresented minority students, were choosing programs with an early-action option, and therefore were missing out on the opportunity to consider Harvard." Ten years after that reversal, Harvard's socioeconomic diversity numbers haven't budged.

If anyone can fix the college application process, it's Al Roth. Probably no one in America understands markets better. Over the course of his career, Roth has fixed the process by which medical students match with residency programs, eighth graders with New York City public high schools (of which he's a product), and Boston students with public schools. He also created a market for kidney exchange that's a national model. In 2012, Roth shared the Nobel Prize in Economics for his market design work.

In Roth's language, colleges admissions are a congested, unraveling market. "Congestion," he explains, "is what happens when you have a lot of people in the market and too many offers." The Common App is at the core of the problem. "It's gotten easier to apply to colleges," Roth says, "Now colleges get many more applicants. That changes the 'signal to noise' ratio."

"Unraveling" is Roth's term for what happens when market participants race one another to gain an advantage. In his book, *Who Gets What—And Why*, Roth offers the example of the Oklahoma Land Rush—more specifically the Cherokee Strip Land Rush of 1893—when thousands of people literally jumped a gun that signaled the start of a race to stake a claim to free land. Lacrosse recruitment is another example. Dom Starsia says that college coaches now make offers to recruits as early as eighth grade. "A lot of colleges are deeply unraveled in the sense that they take half of their entering classes early," Roth told me. "If it's binding early decision," he added, "it really causes high school students to have to face serious strategic decisions."

Most importantly, the market has not succeeded in producing socio-economically diverse classes. "Having good financial aid has not solved the problems of Harvard and Stanford," Roth said, echoing the sentiment of John Friedman, Cappy, and many others. "It's very hard," he added, "to go to Harvard or Stanford if no one in your high school has ever gone—if that's just not heard of."

What would make it better? Ending early admissions would be a start. "I'm not a fan of causing kids to have to decide early," Roth said. "Saying, you know, 'here's a silver bullet, where do you want to fire it,' is different from saying 'where do you want to go—what's your dream school.'" None of the markets Roth has designed, including the New York City and Boston public school markets, allow students or schools to choose one another before the application deadline. Ending early admissions would require granting colleges an antitrust exemption, something for which Cappy has long advocated. There's ample precedent for this. Congress granted the medical-residency match program an antitrust exemption in 2004. Even baseball has substantial immunity from antitrust laws.

Cappy has also proposed limiting the number of applications that students can submit. This would allow students to send stronger signals about the schools in which they have genuine interest. It would also reduce the ability of wealthy students to power through the process by submitting scads of applications while the Brendins of the world submit three or four. One appeal of this proposal is that it might not require an antitrust exemption since it could be implemented by the "nonprofit" that runs the Common App rather than explicit agreement among colleges.

Roth also supports making elite colleges bigger. Elite colleges haven't expanded in ages. In 1982, Harvard admitted 2,200 high school students. In 2020, they admitted 1,980. The size of Harvard's freshman class has remained at 1,600 students for more than forty years. (Their yield improved.) *Meritocracy Trap* author Dan Markovits says that class sizes should double. UC Berkeley professor David Kirp points to satellite campuses as another appealing option. NYU has campuses in Abu Dhabi and Shanghai. Imagine a Harvard campus in Detroit or Ethiopia. "Harvard, in particular, draws from a very international audience so they could do it easily," says Roth, noting that Stanford considered opening a Roosevelt Island campus when the Bloomberg administration solicited proposals for an applied science campus. This, he says, could have "easily been done without compromising at all on quality."

Roth's comments should be a clarion call to donors. Instead of investing in financial aid, much of which goes to wealthy kids, invest in infrastructure: Build new dorms, and demand that the additional capacity be used to increase socioeconomic diversity and serve historically disadvantaged populations. The beauty of this strategy is that it would allow colleges to offer more opportunity without disturbing their settled arrangements with prep schools. "That kind of approach," John Friedman says, "eases the pressure of saying 'who am I not going to let in for these new kids I'm letting in.'" Friedman recalled to me a conversation that he'd had with a group of college trustees. "I think everyone was on board with admitting more poor students," he said. "I'm not sure they were on board with admitting fewer rich students."

Zack Cooper, a health-care economist at Yale, related a story to *Freako-nomics* host Stephen Dubner about a lecture he'd delivered to a behemoth insurance company on the need for conducting randomized trials. The company was spending a fortune on lower-limb MRIs. Cooper had found that they could save $1 billion a year—about 1 percent of their spending—if they just had patients get the scan at the place closest to their home. After his speech, an executive complimented his speech, but said they wanted measures that would save them 15 percent, not 1 percent. "There isn't stuff that saves 15 percent," Cooper explained. "It's a series of half-percent or 1 percent steps."

Fixing college in America is a lot like fixing health care. One thing that's abundantly clear from speaking with experts is that there is no silver bullet. This may seem obvious, but it's a lesson that's been lost on even careful observers. In Students for Fair Admissions' lawsuit, Judge Burroughs rejected the idea that Harvard could improve diversity through race-neutral means with all-or-nothing logic. "Eliminating early action and tips for ALDCs, increasing outreach and community partnerships, offering more financial aid, or admitting more transfer students are all 'available' and 'workable' in some form and at varying costs," Burroughs wrote, "but they would likely have no meaningful impact on racial diversity." To the poor student of color who gets into Harvard instead of the rich, white legacy applicant, the impact would be quite meaningful indeed. The only way to make sense of Burroughs's sentence is that implementing these measures wouldn't fix the problem entirely and therefore should be rejected.*

If the standard is perfection, all is lost. But if the goal is to take lots of 1 percent steps, virtuous proposals abound. UNLV law professor David Orentlicher, who's also a Nevada state assemblyman, is a leading proponent of "top class rank" admissions policies. These take different forms in different places, but the gist of the idea is to base admission decisions

---

* In another head-scratching moment, Burroughs wrote, "Any minimal effect that these alternative admissions practices might have on racial diversity, if implemented individually or in combination, would be offset by the decline in African American and Hispanic students that would result if race-conscious admissions practices were eliminated." Her premise seems to be that ending preferences that benefit affluent whites requires also ending preferences that benefit historically disadvantaged groups.

largely or entirely on high school rank. The appeal is significant. High school grades are widely acknowledged as a better predictor of college performance than SAT scores, and they aren't tied to wealth. The system thus allows successful students from disadvantaged communities to have an equal chance of succeeding, instead of concentrating admissions in affluent school districts and private schools.

The evidence from institutions that have experimented with top class rank models is highly encouraging. In 1996, the Fifth Circuit Court of Appeals deemed the University of Texas's affirmative action program unconstitutional. The U.S. Supreme Court reversed the decision seven years later, but in the interim, to try to boost diversity, the Texas legislature implemented a policy under which 75 percent of the seats at UT are allocated based on high school class rank.

The plan transformed the institution. In 1996, half of UT Austin's entering class came from one of just fifty-nine schools—about 4 percent of the more than 1,500 high schools in the state. By 2006, half of its enrollment came from about twice as many schools. (Harvard has a similar concentration of wealth as pre-1996 Texas. One out of twenty members of Harvard's class of 2017 came from one of just seven high schools: Boston Latin, Phillips Academy in Andover, Stuyvesant High School, the Noble and Greenough School, Phillips Exeter Academy, the Trinity School in New York City, and Lexington High School.) UT's policy also increased the representation of students coming from high schools with larger populations of minority students and higher poverty rates. Nineteen percent of students admitted by high school rank came from families with incomes under $40,000—nearly triple the level for the quarter of students admitted under the traditional model.

Top class rank has the potential to disrupt the forces that fuel America's extreme geographical segregation. Today, everything points affluent, young parents in the direction of affluent, suburban school districts. Together with elite prep schools, these are the pathway to an elite college degree and the best insurance policy against downward mobility. Top class rank complicates the game. Under such a system, a parent might reason that their child would have a better chance at getting to the top of the class in a less affluent district and move accordingly. The evidence from Texas supports this. UC San Diego economist Julie Berry Cullen and her colleagues found that many Texas families interested in getting their children into the state flagship school operated strategically in choosing their high school. Under a top class rank model, Orentlicher explains, "The incentive for parents to congregate in a small number of high-performing school districts would drop substantially."

Despite this evidence, Harvard remains adamantly opposed to a top rank class model of admissions. This is ironic since Harvard's racist, anti-Semitic, and homophobic former president—A. Lawrence Lowell, for whom Lowell House is named—originated the idea in the early twentieth century as a means of attracting small-town Protestants. Under Lowell's system, any student from an approved school who finished in the top-seventh of his class (sexist pronoun intentional) would automatically be admitted to Harvard.*

A century later, Harvard's position has reversed. In SFFA's lawsuit, Richard Kahlenberg pointed to percentage plans as an effective means of increasing socioeconomic diversity. Harvard replied that this would overenroll its class. It's a stunning example of avoiding responsibility by focusing solely on 100 percent solutions. No one suggested that Harvard need determine its entire class by top class rank. The University of Texas doesn't. It's easy, too, to imagine conducting a lottery among applicants who qualify by class rank. But Judge Burroughs bought into the fiction that incremental change isn't worth pursuing.

An important 1 percent step would be for elite schools to partner with their local communities and secondary schools. Lani Guinier points to the example of Clark University's engagement with its surrounding city of Worcester, which included the creation of a public

---

* This list excluded schools from Long Island, eastern New York, and New Jersey, which had high concentrations of Jews. Practicing Ivy League-quality doublethink, Harvard denied that the principle discriminated against schools omitted from the list or implied that the excluded schools were of lower standing. "The specified group," admissions chairman Richard Gummere said in 1935, "has not been selected by Harvard for a special privilege."

college-preparatory academy with admission based on lottery, a second partnership with an underperforming local high school, and an ongoing offer of free tuition to qualified Worcester residents. Clark students often work as tutors at the partner high schools and, over time, have embraced a vision of the importance of service to the surrounding community.

These partnerships needn't be local. Bard's Early College high school program allows students to exit twelfth grade with an associate degree. Bard maintains campuses in some of the most underserved and segregated cities in the country, including Newark, Baltimore, Cleveland, and Washington, DC. Elite colleges routinely lament the deficiencies in these school systems, and blame them for their inability to attract a diverse student body. What if instead of passively criticizing schools in poor inner cities, elite colleges became involved in primary and secondary education? "These institutions," says Bard's Leon Botstein, "could make a real difference in American public schools."

Botstein's college offers a pathway to a bachelor's degree for incarcerated individuals in five New York State prisons. The Bard Prison Initiative enrolls nearly two hundred students each year. It has few analogs. Most prison education programs operate online or by correspondence. Elite colleges offer precious few programs, and those they do generally offer only college credit or an associate degree. One reason is that they're expensive—incarcerated individuals are barred from receiving federal financial aid. Mostly, Botstein says, elite colleges "don't want to devalue their brand."

The lowest-hanging fruit would be for elite colleges to create a pathway between community college and the Ivy League. Outstanding performance in junior college is about the most reliable predictor of success in a four-year college. Yet almost no one from community college makes it to the Ivy League. In 2018, about 5.5 million students enrolled in community colleges. That year, Princeton announced—with great self-congratulation—that it would reinstate its transfer admission programs. They thereafter offered admission to thirteen students. From nearby Mercer College, Princeton admitted two. Harvard admits about a dozen transfer students every year, with no particular focus on community colleges. Imagine if Princeton offered fifty transfer slots every year to outstanding CUNY students or if Harvard partnered with MassBay Community College?

Another 1 percent solution would be for elite colleges to share the burden of funding the public system. Natasha Warikoo asks, "Can you push the university to say to donors that 10 percent of whatever you give goes to Bunker Hill Community College or other places that are really engines of mobility?" Public colleges everywhere are in need. When Malcolm Gladwell asked John Hennessy whether Stanford had an ethical obligation to redirect new contributions to the state university system, the only defense Hennessy could have offered for keeping the money was if it lifted all boats—that is, if Stanford, Harvard, and Yale shared their abundance, and their abundant fundraising prowess, with public colleges. Instead, after some hemming and hawing, Hennessy told Gladwell that he could find use for another $10 billion.

In the sports arena, Kirsten Hextrum proposes that colleges reduce or end recruitment and use the money to expand participation. Like top class rank, eliminating sports as a pathway to college would change the incentives that drive segregation and hoarding. It would provide enormous opportunity. Cutting the lacrosse or field hockey team may seem like small potatoes. It's not. John Friedman offers a hypothetical to elite colleges. "Look," he says, "you already have lots of priorities in your admissions offices. You give priorities to people who are legacies and athletes. Suppose that you just took that same thing and gave it to lower-income families." Friedman pauses here to explain that he likes this exercise because it's already done. "It's something people understand," Friedman says. "The athletes come, and they underperform a little bit, but the institution doesn't fall apart. Can you do that same thing, just focused on economic diversity?"

So what would the numbers look like? Friedman says that the percentage of students who are Pell Grant eligible, which generally hovers around 17 percent at Ivy-Plus colleges—could double. "We're not talking about going from seventeen to nineteen," Friedman says. "We're talking about going from seventeen to thirty or thirty-five—really a major change in what that would look like just from this kind of marginal shift in the way the priorities work themselves out in the admissions process." Scale, Friedman says, is the friend of elite colleges—meaning little changes could make big differences. "It's not like you're going in one direction and need to go in the other direction," he says. "If you only went like ten degrees this way, you could admit people who your own admissions people think are great. We're not asking to totally change the academic focus of these institutions. It's just about a shift in priorities."

It's poetically just here to recall that James Conant, as chairman of the National Defense Research Committee, oversaw the Manhattan Project. The development of the atomic bomb received an AA-1 designation, meaning it got top priority in allocation of resources and personnel. Recall, too, Karabel's Theorem—admissions policies reflect institutional interests—and Cappy's Question: Do legacy and early admissions have the unintended effect of reducing socioeconomic diversity, or are they the rationalization for letting in the rich kids the colleges really want? Elite colleges could reduce the most pernicious influence of college counselors by requiring applicants to certify that they wrote their own essays or write them while sitting for an exam. Do they refrain from taking this obvious step because these counselors, most of whom served as admissions officers, help steer their wealthy clients to elite colleges?

What would the world look like if promoting socioeconomic diversity were designated an AA-1 priority? Quite different. The solutions would look different in different places, and no single reform would be sufficient. Ending legacy preferences or lacrosse recruitment wouldn't end inequity. Colleges face legitimate difficulties in getting low-income students to apply and enroll, and they alone cannot eliminate the underlying disparities in American public education. But if we have the collective will to make colleges significantly more powerful engines of opportunity than they currently are, the means are within our grasp.

20

Communities of Opportunity

On a sultry July day in the second summer of the pandemic, my family went to Peace Camp. The morning began with an icebreaker. We stood in a circle, passing a ball among ourselves. The object was to remember the order in which the ball traveled and the name of the person to whom you passed it. When we finished, the facilitator broke us into groups—a counselor or an older student with one or two of the younger campers. My younger daughter, Mattie, who was eleven at the time, mentored a pair of seven-year-old boys. One wrote to his parents. The other wrote to a Yeti named Tarzan. He described decorating tires and the games he'd played. He particularly liked the parachute.

After a snack of fruit and crackers, Mattie became a camper herself. She tie-dyed a blue and purple shirt, drew with chalk, and helped paint flower planters that would decorate an abandoned garage being repurposed into a community park. Between activities, a little girl showed Mattie how to feed cicada skins to the camp's baby chickens. Around one o'clock, we said our goodbyes. "The camp felt homemade," my daughter said. "I don't think I've ever had an experience where everybody knew each other. It felt like family."

In the afternoon, we got a tour of the surrounding community. The camp occupied a park at the head of a cul-de-sac where most of the campers and counselors lived in an eclectic mix of single-family homes and modest row houses from the 1920s. These were nourished by a running stream. My daughter and I lingered in the backyard of a man named Ulysses Archie, who maintained a working farm. Archie was a teacher before he suffered a traumatic injury on the job and is the founder of the Baltimore Gift Economy, whereby goods and services are given freely with no requirement of an exchange. The Department of Health had come that day to give Ulysses a hard time about Mr. Porkington, his gregarious, pot-bellied pig. Everyone liked Mr. Porkington and Archie's chickens, several of which worked the camp, except a real estate agent who was trying to sell a nearby house.

Kids wandered up and down the street. A few greeted us as Mr. Evan and Ms. Mattie. Everyone referred to each other semi-formally, in a display of mutual respect. Several young boys parked their bikes outside a home where the owner had left out ice pops and soda to help break the sweltering heat. All the doors were unlocked. One of the neighbors had built a granny flat in her backyard, which she made available to the community and stocked with an ample supply of games for kids of all ages. In the evenings, when the adults didn't have a meeting scheduled, the older kids gathered there to play Connect Four, Chinese checkers, and Stratego. The street doesn't feel like any place I've ever been in real life. It's somewhat evocative of Mayberry, North Carolina, in *The Andy Griffith Show* except the Black characters are plentiful and allowed to speak.

On our way home, I asked Mattie how she understood what we'd seen. "Everything was based on sticking together and helping each other out," she said. "Not just if your neighbor asked for a shovel, but if your neighbor asked you for a place to live for three days or 'will you watch my child for the next five hours?' That was the type of vibe I was getting. You could rely on everybody."

You won't find any fancy brochures advertising Peace Camp. It's free and open to anyone who knows about it. You won't find the community on any map either. Geographically, it's in Irvington, about a day's travel with laden cart from the port of Baltimore, a former country town that once served as a layover spot for weary travelers on the National Road. Today it's known as "Skulltown" because of its proliferation of burial grounds. The camp is on Collins Avenue, which dead ends into Maiden's Choice Run, the stream that sustains Archie's farm, and Loudon National Cemetery, an ancient graveyard that's the eternal resting place of Baltimore's most famous son, the essayist H. L. Mencken. There's no Welcome-to-Brooklyn-type sign announcing that you've entered someplace special, but you have all the same. There are no badges, either, but everyone knows who's in and who's out, just as certainly as everyone at Harvard knows who the legacies are, even if all the students wear the same Carhartt pants, Vineyard Vines pullover, and black Canada Goose puffer.

The community is the inspiration of Jill Wrigley, an attorney and social reformer who helped found an immigrant advocacy organization, built a hotline for workplace rights, and counseled labor unions until she died prematurely from lung cancer in 2016 at the age of fifty-two. The people who lived with Wrigley speak of her reverentially, in hushed tones, with equal measures of love and respect for her formidable intellect. After finishing first in her class at Pottstown High School in Pennsylvania, Wrigley graduated summa cum laude from Wellesley, did a Rotary scholarship in Sweden, and volunteered at a foster home in Guatemala. When she returned to the U.S., Wrigley earned a joint degree in law and political science from Columbia. Instead of parlaying her Ivy League JD into a small fortune, Wrigley dedicated her life to creating opportunity for others.

I say Wrigley inspired the community because "created" or "managed" would connote an inaccurate sense of hierarchy. There are no bylaws here—no chain of command or trustees or board of directors. No one can point to a formal charter with a mission statement describing what the Collins Avenue cul-de-sac is. Wrigley's husband, Michael Sarbanes, simply calls it "living in community." But, Sarbanes says, "we're intentionally flexible about what it means to be in community."

The son of a longtime former U.S. senator from Maryland, Sarbanes is another first-in-his-class type. He excelled at Gilman, an exclusive Baltimore prep school, played football at Princeton—where he won the top undergraduate prize—and studied history at Oxford on a Marshall. While later pursuing a law degree at NYU, a friend set him up on a blind date with Wrigley, thereby ending the slim chance of his living a conventional life.

Instead, Sarbanes dedicated his career to public service—first representing low-income community associations and, later, performing a variety of high-level government functions, including running the Maryland Office of Crime Control and Prevention. In 2007, he ran a credible campaign for city council president, at the end of which he was recruited to oversee community outreach for Baltimore City Public Schools. After seeing up close how underfunded the schools were, Sarbanes decided he wanted to be a teacher. With characteristic tenacity, he taught himself physics. Today Sarbanes teaches at a charter school about a mile from Collins Streamside, as the residents call their home.

In 1994, when Wrigley and Sarbanes were looking for a place to live, they did what any couple with four graduate degrees does: They carefully examined census data. But their priorities were different than the Petrillis and other prototypical white families. "When Jill and I looked for a place to live," Sarbanes said, "we wanted a neighborhood with racial and economic diversity." Irvington caught their eye. Skulltown was undergoing a major demographic shift. In 1970, it had been 90 percent white. As they conducted their real estate search, it was 75 percent Black. Five years after moving to Collins Avenue, they adopted two children from Ethiopia and would later adopt a third from East Baltimore.

From the start, Wrigley and Sarbanes threw themselves into the community. Irvington was, and is, a "food desert." McDonald's and bodegas abound, but fruits and vegetables are hard to find. A third of households don't have a car, so driving to Whole Foods isn't an option. After they settled, Wrigley made food security her cause. Her first thoughts were always local, and she began by simply providing healthy snacks to kids who knocked on her door, as many did. Over time, she developed a food education curriculum for Baltimore schools, advised the system about how to improve student nutrition, and helped transform an abandoned, overgrown lot into a thriving educational farm for children. Near the end of her life, Wrigley taught seminars on food systems at the University of Maryland.

For his part, Sarbanes coached basketball at the local rec center and built a court in their backyard, which he and Wrigley opened to the community. He also became vice-president of the neighborhood association. Both he and Wrigley offered their considerable expertise as lawyers on health care, criminal justice matters, and the schools to anyone who asked. They joined a nearby church, where many of the parishioners were hungry. Soon, people were coming in and out of their house constantly. One day, Wrigley told Sarbanes, "Doing this as a nuclear family is burning us out." Living among diverse neighbors wasn't enough. "This kind of commitment is best done as a community," she said. Sarbanes agreed. "My wife," he told me, "was more intelligent and more emotionally intelligent than me at all stages."

Wrigley began searching for other people who were interested in living in community. Soon, Jeffrey Ross, a legal aid attorney, and Suzanne Fontanesi, a nurse practitioner, bought the house across the street. Shortly thereafter, they were joined by Susan Goering, a friend who ran the Maryland chapter of the ACLU. As the community grew, they chipped in to buy one of the homes on the block, which they then leased to a family that otherwise wouldn't have qualified for a mortgage. The rent the family paid went into an account that allowed them to build equity in the house, which they could later draw upon—the precise opposite of the predatory lending practices that have devastated American families of color. They reclaimed a trashed lot at the top of the street, named it Peace Park, and engaged in a yearlong, youth-led collaborative design process. Wrigley secured grants to support their work. And in the summer, they ran a camp.

Sarbanes connects the community to different historical threads. He feels a connection to the settlement movement, most famously promoted by Jane Addams, the founder of Chicago's Hull House, which encouraged people to live together across race and class lines. He sees linkages, too, to the civil rights movements, when activists lived in the communities where they were trying to register voters, and especially to Freedom Schools, which arose after places like Prince Edward County closed their schools rather than integrate, and sought to cultivate young students of color as agents of change. He also draws a line to Dorothy

Day, the radical Catholic activist, and the principles of Christian community development.

Sarbanes is a student of history, a prodigy of the elite educational system upon which he has almost entirely turned his back. It's only natural that he thinks in these terms. To me, his explanations feel too intellectual. My own sense is that people gravitated to Wrigley's magnetic personality and determination to create a multiracial, economically, and religiously diverse community. If any academic concept describes Collins Streamside, it's Dutch geographer Louise Meijering's simple definition of an intentional community as "a self-identified group of individuals who challenge the norms of society."

That feels entirely authentic. Not much on Collins Avenue feels "normal"—not the free ice pops or the open doors or the abundance of civility. What feels most abnormal, though, is that in my interviews of parents in the community, no one ever mentioned college. It's the opposite of Manhasset, where hardly a conversation could go by without some discussion of the college application process. People on Collins Avenue want their kids to get a good education, but they have a broad understanding of what that means. They're not obsessed with where their children are going to go to school or accumulating credentials. No one leaves Peace Camp with a certificate. There's no student advisory board for which to run or community scholarship to compete for or any effort to translate the experience of living in Collins Streamside into the sort of objective measures of achievement that elite colleges understand and value. No one on Collins Avenue thinks much about Harvard and Yale. Which is appropriate because no one at Harvard and Yale thinks much about Collins Avenue.

The story we're told is that Harvard and Yale look the way they do because of America.

Elite colleges lack socioeconomic and, in many cases, racial diversity, the story goes, because inner-city high schools produce too few qualified students. No one propagates this narrative more than Harvard and Yale. Their faculty and leaders lament the inequities of public education, throwing up their arms in exasperation as if to say, "What else can we do?"

What if the story's reversed?

What if America looks the way it does because of Harvard and Yale? Imagine for a moment that elite colleges chose not to value the class-coded markers of achievement upon which their admissions processes currently rely so heavily. Imagine they afforded no preference to lacrosse players or Model U.N. champions or students who'd taken Princeton Review. Imagine they actively combatted some advantages of wealth, say, for example, by requiring that applicants write their own essays and not employ high-priced, private counselors. Imagine the admissions process was more egalitarian, perhaps relying at least in part on a lottery among students who'd finished at the top of their high school class. What would America look like then? Is it so far-fetched to imagine that more communities would organize around opportunity? Would this really be such a stretch?

According to Sarbanes, it's easy to envision such a world, but our collective imagination has been subdued into dormancy by a series of false narratives. These include the myths that legal segregation ended racism, that society must be organized so that affluent white parents can guarantee their own class standing to their children, and that elite colleges and universities have little power to spark change. Howard Thurman, a theologian who mentored Martin Luther King Jr., is another historical figure to whom Sarbanes draws a connection. Thurman warned that the end of legal segregation, though necessary, posed a hidden danger. "The walls that divide must be demolished," he wrote, but their destruction was such a monumental undertaking that "an ever-widening weariness is apt to sweep over the land." *Brown*, in other words, was the beginning, not the end. "When the walls are down," Thurman wrote, "it is then that the real work of building the healthy American society begins."

Sarbanes says the tragedy of the Thurman quote is that the ways of building the "healthy American society" are portrayed as being more difficult than they really are. "They are actually quite doable," he says, "but either are not visible and thus not considered at all or are framed as

the province of exceptional characters." I doubt you've ever met someone like Michael Sarbanes in your own life, but the truth is nothing he
and his neighbors do is so hard. The residents of Collins Streamside
don't suffer. They have running water, electricity, and precocious children. They laugh and play. If anything, they seemed far happier than
most suburban families that I know. They're just less susceptible to the
pressure most mortals feel, and which elite colleges exploit, to immu-
nize their children against the risk of downward mobility.

If we strain our imaginations further, it's possible to imagine a
world in which elite colleges actively work to combat inequality. One
in which they resolve to no longer prey upon fears over class anxiety,
and to become an active partner in promoting an equitable society—
to live up to the full measure of James Conant's vision of Harvard as
the engine of a fluid society rather than the agent for calcification of
the elite. What if they embraced 1 percent solutions? What if Harvard
forsook its unspoken agreements with prep schools and instead said
it was going to advantage high schools that reflected the diversity of
their surrounding community? What if elite colleges said they were no
longer going to solely prioritize individual achievement, and instead
would examine a community's collective commitment to promoting
access and opportunity?

The whole game would change. "You would change the incentive to
bring more kids across borders and change your borders," says Rebecca
Sibilia, who's thought as much about segregating borders as anyone
in the country. You would shift the focus from thinking about how to
build the best lacrosse program and offer the most AP courses to how
to poke holes in the walls that separate white suburbs from the rest of
society. "You could pressure your school board to accept out-of-district
kids because it would benefit everyone in the community," says John
Katzman, who has also proposed conditioning federal financial aid on
whether a college's diversity reflects the surrounding community.

Would such a world be perfect? Of course not. But we shouldn't
underestimate the power of 1 percent solutions. Bill Burnett, director of Stanford's design program, warns people against the dangers of
obsessing with perfection. "The unattainable best," Burnett says, "is the

enemy of all the available betters." A world of perfect educational equity would be unattainably best. A world in which elite colleges acted as engines of mobility would be undeniably and availably better and, in the aggregate, much more than a 1 percent solution. Elite colleges nevertheless refuse to embrace that reality.

"There are a lot of dimensions in which universities are vastly underperforming," Sarbanes told me, before wondering aloud, "What if students could imagine themselves in different settings? What could happen if the path to opportunity were really engaged?"

What exactly could happen, you might ask? Just how much could elite colleges really do?

It's so hard to have a sense of big numbers, but consider this: Of the one hundred largest nonprofits in the United States, twenty-five are a college or university, including sixteen of the top thirty-five. Combined, these schools control nearly half a trillion dollars in assets. That's about five times the estimated value of America's national parks and twice the value of the gold bullion reserves in Fort Knox.

Harvard appears twice on this list. The university is ranked third. Its management company is ranked eleventh. By itself, the management company is worth more than the Ford Foundation, the Open Society Foundations, and the Nature Conservancy combined. Harvard University's assets exceed those of the Gates Foundation by almost $10 billion. The poorest of the Ivies on this list—Dartmouth College, with assets over $9 billion—is worth more than the MacArthur Foundation and Bloomberg Philanthropies.

This fortune has been built with the massive support of the American citizen—with a tax break worth as much as $20 billion per year, a cumulative national investment of half a trillion dollars or more. What has the American taxpayer received in return? Not an engine of mobility. Rather, a Rolls-Royce engine of class stratification. Elite colleges provide opportunity to a tiny number of poor people. For the overwhelming majority, they take children who have been the beneficiary of a lifetime of privilege, convert that privilege into a degree of value, steer these students into careers in finance, cultivate disdain for those who work for the common good, systematically disadvantage the handful of poor students of color who manage to make it through their gates, and promote the myth that college admissions meritocratically rewards the best and the brightest rather than the rich and the richest, all while encouraging affluent, white suburbs to hoard wealth and opportunity even as visible, viable alternatives for organizing communities abound.

To whom much has been given, much will be required.

To date, nothing has been required of elite colleges.

The bill has come due.

POSTSCRIPT

A PLEA TO THE PRIVILEGED

On October 26, 1963, President John F. Kennedy made a quick trip to break ground on the new $3.5 million Robert Frost Library at Amherst College, where the poet had taught on and off for forty-six years. Frost had been an early supporter of Kennedy's presidential campaign and had delivered a poem, "The Gift Outright," at his inauguration. But their relationship had thawed after Frost returned from a cultural exchange to Russia and declared, in a sleep-deprived, jet-lagged stupor, that Khrushchev had called the United States too liberal to fight, making headlines in the *Washington Post*. Frost died before he and Kennedy could make peace. The air crackled with electricity as the president ascended the makeshift stage in Amherst's gym, which the students had filled to capacity.

But Kennedy had come to praise Frost, not to bury him, seemingly reminded that clear fall afternoon of the advice the poet had given him at the White House, shortly after taking office, to "be more Irish than Harvard." Kennedy started slowly, acknowledging Amherst alumni's record of military and public service. Then he said what he'd come to say: "Privilege is here, and with privilege goes responsibility." Although Amherst had been at the forefront of extending aid to needy and talented students, Kennedy said, "private colleges, taken as a whole, draw 50 percent of their students from the wealthiest 10 percent of our nation." Income inequality had become extreme, Kennedy explained. In 1958, the poorest quintile of American families earned just 4.5 percent of the total personal income, while the top fifth earned

44.5 percent. "There is inherited wealth in this country," JFK said, "and also inherited poverty."

Kennedy drew a direct connection between the data he'd shared and Robert Frost's life work. "The artist, however faithful to his personal vision of reality, becomes the last champion of the individual mind and sensibility against an intrusive society and an officious state," Kennedy said. The artist's obligation was to truth, to bear faithful witness to the world as they perceived it, no matter how unpopular their testimony might be. Poets did not rule the world, but they contributed as much as those who did. "The men who create power make an indispensable contribution to the nation's greatness," Kennedy proclaimed, "but the men who question power make a contribution just as indispensable, especially when that questioning is disinterested, for they determine whether we use power or power uses us."

The president then issued a challenge, which, more than half a century later, many of the students in attendance that day remember as a transformative moment in their lives. Kennedy said, "Unless the graduates of this college and other colleges like it who are given a running start in life—unless they are willing to put back into our society those talents, the broad sympathy, the understanding, the compassion—unless they are willing to put those qualities back into the service of the Great Republic, then obviously the presuppositions upon which our democracy are based are bound to be fallible."

Many people regarded it as the best speech of Kennedy's career.

It was also the last.

It's tempting to dwell on the data Kennedy cited. More than half a century later, the United States has made no progress in combatting structural poverty. Income inequality has grown more severe. The 4.5 percent controlled by the bottom income quintile when Kennedy gave his speech has shrunk to 3.1 percent, while the share owned by the top quintile has grown to 51.9 percent. Amherst hasn't made any progress either, a recent pledge to end legacy preference notwithstanding. Since Kennedy's speech, the share of Amherst students who come from families in the top 10 percent has grown to 58 percent. Seventeen percent come from families in the top 1 percent. The average Amherst student's family makes about $440,000 per year—that's about seven times the national average. The story is the same at more or less every elite college. Sixty years have passed since Kennedy called the academy to action, and things have gotten worse, not better. It's enough to make one cry.

But I want to focus instead on the audience to whom Kennedy chose to deliver his message. The President went out of his way to go to Amherst that day. He left the White House early in the morning for Andrews Air Force Base, flew to Westover Air Reserve Base in Chicopee, Massachusetts, near Springfield, then took a Marine helicopter twenty miles north, landing on practice fields downhill of the Amherst gym. Other than visits to his family compound in Cape Cod, JFK had traveled little since the premature death of his son, Patrick, in August. By two o'clock, he was on his way back to Washington. It must have seemed important to Kennedy to deliver his message to whom he did.

It does to me too.

Chances are if you're reading this book, you're an elite. I don't want to obsess about how a sociologist would define this word. I mean, simply, that you have a fancy degree yourself, or work with lots of people who do, or have children who either have one or hope to get one someday. If you're not an elite, you are most welcome here. I hope you share my outrage at a system that's stacked against you. But if you are an elite, listen: Without you, nothing will happen.

This truth is probably quite annoying. Elite colleges may be bad actors, but they're surely not the only bad actors. Affluent suburbs could have taken it upon themselves to open their doors to their neighbors. They could partner with cities and act as a safety valve to relieve segregation. They could create rather than hoard opportunity. They won't. History has proved this conclusively.

In the wake of the ghetto rebellions of the late 1960s, HUD secretary George Romney declared in 1970 that suburbs had tied a "white noose" around Black cities. He proposed a program called Open Communities, which would have denied federal funds to suburbs that failed to revise exclusionary zoning laws that prevented the construction of subsidized housing for low-income Black families. The reaction among the Republican base was so fierce that Nixon required Romney to repudiate his own plan and soon removed him from the Cabinet.

In 2015, the Obama administration made a trove of data on segregation and poverty available to local officials. Relying on a little-noticed provision of the Fair Housing Act, which required jurisdictions receiving federal funds to "affirmatively further" the law's purposes, they instructed communities to explain how they'd use the government's money to reduce disparities. Five years later, President Obama's successor repealed the law via a tweet addressed to "the Suburban Housewives of America." Evoking Nixon's Southern Strategy, Trump attempted to frame Obama's Affirmatively Furthering Fair Housing regulation—and all Democrats—as existential threats to personal safety, home values, and the suburban way of life. "Biden will destroy your neighborhood and your American Dream," he wrote. "I will preserve it, and make it even better!"

Richard Rothstein says that it's easy to come up with ways to redress America's history of residential segregation. The federal government could buy up properties in historically segregated communities, like Levittown, and sell them at reduced prices to help Black families recapture some of the equity out of which their parents and grandparents had been cheated by racism. It could offer direct subsidies to middle-class Black families to buy homes in racially exclusive suburbs. It could prohibit zoning bans on multifamily houses and deny the mortgage interest tax deduction to homeowners in suburbs that are not aggressively trying to attract their "fair share" of reduced-income housing. Alas, Rothstein writes, proposals like these are "both politically and judicially inconceivable today."

Remember the story of *Milliken v. Bradley* and Lichter's Law: When it comes to housing and education, liberals are just like conservatives. Without a substantial impetus, suburban whites will not sacrifice an ounce of local control. Change will not happen organically. If any is to happen, it will be driven by elites.

*   *   *

Robert Frost toiled in obscurity until he was almost forty years old. For nine years, he worked his grandfather's farm in Derry, New Hampshire, rising before dawn to write poems that no one would read for years. When the farm failed, he taught English at the local high school. "I have been," Frost wrote, "one acquainted with the night." Kennedy saw this as essential to the poet's gift. "Because he knew the midnight as well as the high noon," Kennedy said, "because he understood the ordeal as well as the triumph of the human spirit, he gave his age strength with which to overcome despair." Frost, Kennedy told the Amherst students, "brought an unsparing instinct for reality to bear on the platitudes and pieties of society. His sense of the human tragedy fortified him against self-deception and easy consolation." Kennedy concluded, "When power leads men towards arrogance, poetry reminds him of his limitations."

The lawyer and human rights activist Bryan Stephenson is an advocate of proximity to suffering. "We cannot change global injustice if we isolate ourselves in places that are safe and removed and disconnected," Stephenson says. "To change the world, we are each going to have to find ways to get closer to people who are living on the margins of society." It's one thing to talk about schools without functional bathrooms. It's another thing to work in one. The commonality among the activists whose stories I've told here—Sara Goldrick-Rab, Rebecca Sibilia, Simon Cataldo—is that they all stepped outside the bubble within which they'd been raised. I have been transformed by a career spent working with brilliant students of ordinary means.

Living in the high noon, without ever seeing the midnight, promotes a sort of blindness. When you live in the suburbs and your children attend wealthy schools, it's easy to tell yourself that you've earned your place, that your family deserves its privileged status. Elite colleges reinforce this belief. Few pause and wonder what other kids would do if they were granted the same access to tutors and lacrosse coaches. It's easy, too, to say that poor students deserve their fates, that public college students drop out because they're less intelligent or shiftless. Almost no one bothers to learn that these young men and women are the hardest working people in American society.

Nobody is immune from this blindness. Even the faculty at elite colleges fall victim to it, though they surely know better. "The part that I struggle with the most," Goldrick-Rab says, "is that I have some extraordinary colleagues who I know believe in all the right things, but they work at these places and they stay there and I don't believe they're doing enough. How can you fight for the people when you're standing tip-top way above them in the clouds?" John Friedman says that he makes a point of asking elite educators what they make of his data. "Everyone agrees that this is something we should care about," he told me. "But they differ in their expectation of how hard they need to try at this before they could credibly claim to themselves, 'Look, I did what I could here.'" I concluded each of my interviews by asking my subject what they made of their own college's efforts to promote social mobility. These were social scientists at the most elite colleges and universities who had dedicated their careers to studying inequality. Almost everyone rationalized their institution's efforts in the way Friedman described, metaphorically throwing up their hands and saying nothing more could be done. No one was willing to go on the record criticizing their college.

What makes this affliction so insidious is that one rarely has the experience of doing harm. The mechanisms that fuel educational apartheid in America are excesses of kindness—scholarships for athletes, tuition relief for upper-middle-class families, loyalty by alumni to their college, doing right by the kids in affluent, white communities. The faculty, administrators, and alumni of elite colleges are all the more likely to fall prey to the heuristic biases Leanne Son Hing taught us about because their subjective, psychic experience is of doing good. Faculty teach their students to reason critically. Alumni give money to their alma maters and help current students make connections. These acts feel good. Helpful. Their lack of proximity to suffering—living only in the high noon—relieves them of the obligation of thinking of those who are excluded from those classrooms and networks.

With apologies to Michael Wang and the plaintiffs in the Students for Fair Admissions lawsuit, I don't believe that Harvard intends to discriminate against Asian American applicants. No one in the admissions

office is moo-hoo-hooing with evil glee, as perhaps they did in excluding Jews a century ago. They are, rather, unmotivated to disturb their
historical relationships with prep schools or the expectations of their
alumni and faculty or to do any of the uncomfortable things that would
be required to significantly increase opportunity, including acknowledging the reality that college admissions are a zero-sum game.

The blindness leads us to confuse generosity with justice. Ford Foundation president Darren Walker explains that generosity is principally
about the donor. "When you give money to help a homeless person, you
feel good," Walker explains. "Justice is a deeper engagement where you
are actually asking, 'What are the systemic reasons that put people out
onto the streets?'" Justice requires consideration of both the good and
the harm caused by a gift. Donating $1.8 billion to Johns Hopkins is
generous but not just. Helping your pal from the country club's neph-
ew or the smart kid in your Yale freshman seminar land a summer
internship is generous but not just. Lavishing Ivy Leaguers with fellow-
ships and study abroad opportunities is generous but not just. This is
challenging. "Generosity makes the donor feel good," Walker explains.
"Justice implicates the donor."

Complicating the challenge is that justice almost certainly requires
affluent whites to accept less than they historically have. "If we, the beneficiaries of a system that perpetuates inequality, are trying to reform
this system that favors us," Walker says, "we will have to give up something." Michael Sarbanes agrees. "There's a tremendous need for a more
morally rigorous and challenging conversation among white people,"
he says. The Brookings Institution's Richard Reeves says simply, "We
need more downward mobility from the top."

Reeves says that he's ruined dinner parties by making this argument.
I get it. Years ago, when I first started researching and writing about
these issues, I presented some of what I'd learned about legacy preferences to someone I knew from Manhasset who'd gone to an Ivy League
college. When I finished, she asked, "How much money do I have to
give for my children to get noticed by the admissions office?" Lauren
Rivera says the single question she most often gets is from parents asking how to land their kid a job at McKinsey or Goldman Sachs.

Justice does not require accepting less for your child. Parents want the best for their kids, as they should. My argument does not implicate the children of legacies or donors or faculty—or anyone who exploited legitimate pathways to admissions. Rather, it's an indictment of the institutions that legitimated those pathways in the first place.

Justice does require that all of us with a connection to elite institutions condemn those inequitable pathways, regardless of the small, indirect cost it might impose on our children. It's a modest ask. "Whites need to embrace taking a smaller share of the economic pie," Sarbanes says. "It's not the case that they have to take a smaller share of the happiness."

Justice requires, too, that elite colleges take less than they historically have. They should because it's the right thing to do. By their stated mission, and by virtue of the extensive taxpayer support that they have received and continue to receive, universities have an obligation to act as forces for the common good—to serve as genuine engines of social mobility that provide opportunity to a genuinely diverse student body, not to reinforce class stratification and engage in tokenism. But if they won't do this because it's the right thing to do, then they should do it because their survival depends on it. Our survival depends on it.

If the faculty and leaders of elite colleges continue to hoard, the damage will be incalculable. The academy's expansive, independent thinking on the widest range of issues that bear on improving the human condition—subjects as diverse as physics, economics, and criminal justice—has driven American hegemony. Today, that position is threatened by skepticism about science and the objectivity of elites. But how can anyone be expected to continue to follow the academy's leadership when the nation's top colleges and universities have been so thoroughly exposed as bastions of inequality—when the average Harvard professor makes over $250,000 per year, and the average Harvard student comes from a family making more than twice that?

The precarity of this position has led the academy to engage in an excess of virtue signaling and to become overly involved in culture wars, which have very little to do with bettering humanity. "One of the reasons that you have this extreme woke radicalism at places like

Swarthmore and Yale is because those rich institutions scream hypocrisy," Leon Botstein says. Faculty, he argues, are the most complicit. "Their liberal rhetoric—their willingness to sign every petition—hides their collusion with the college and university's desire to maintain their endowments."

Ultimately, ethical questions boil down to a simple dichotomy of rationalizations between those who defend the status quo as deserved and those who think we have a greater obligation to help others. It's impossible to preach charity while hoarding. The elite academy has the authority of a profligate nun. "The faculty make pious claims about social justice, but they will accept no action that risks their security," Botstein says.

The hypocrisy engenders antipathy. Of the many hateful mechanisms Donald Trump exploited on his pathway to the presidency, none was quite so effective and damaging as his denunciation of elites, a ploy the University of Pennsylvania graduate borrowed from Adolf Hitler. In connection with social media, this scheme undermines truth itself and poses an existential threat to American democracy. Trump's rhetoric resonates because it is, at bottom, true. Even before coronavirus, Walker said, "Social mobility, the ability for a person to climb from poverty to security as I did, had all but disappeared." Walker, who was born in a charity hospital in Lafayette, Louisiana, raised by a single mother, and attended the University of Texas on a Pell Grant, has dedicated the entirety of the Ford Foundation's funding to combatting inequality. "Inequality contributes to a hopelessness and cynicism that undermines our shared ideals and institutions, pits us against one another, and drives communities further apart," Walker says. "That's why I am worried about our democracy, deeply and for the first time in my life."

Inequality in America cannot be meaningfully addressed without elite colleges and universities doing their bits. "The challenges that our nation is facing are just huge right now," Cappy says. "They intersect with what's happening with the economy, with our history, and with our diversity, all of those things are working to make it just incredibly complicated to work collectively for the public good. But elite schools have gone from being kind of neutral to reinforcing privilege in our society and that's really hurting us. It seems to me that higher ed just has to do more."

So, dear reader, I call upon you to act as an agent of change. To fight within your residential and academic communities to soften borders and create opportunity. To change the narrative about merit. To inhabit the reality that neither affluence nor poverty are deserved. To fight hoarding and reject tokenism. To be generous and just. To know the midnight. To demand that the entirety of the hundreds of billions of dollars raised by elite institutions with the support of Americans be used to fuel the American Dream, not to thwart it. To demand that your alma mater and community change, not in twenty-five years, but today. Because, as President Kennedy asked:

If not you, who?

If not now, when?

ACKNOWLEDGMENTS

A few weeks ago, I sat down with Brianne to discuss her future. Despite all the effort that she'd put into studying for the LSAT, and her excellent performance on the test, I urged her to consider taking a gap year. Brianne skipped eleventh grade. At twenty, she's young to be graduating from college. Some data, and my own experience, suggest that older students do better in graduate school. Furthermore, she, like tens of millions of students, had been cheated out of a normal college experience by the pandemic. I thought Brianne might enjoy doing a fellowship or a congressional internship or teaching English in a foreign country. The particulars didn't matter that much. Just something where her mind could grow and she could explore the world and decompress a bit from a stressful four years. The key question was what would be meaningful and enjoyable to her.

"What do you daydream about?" I asked.

Brianne thought for a moment before answering. "I've never allowed myself to dream about my own life," she said.

Of the many senses in which I understand my own privilege, none is quite so profound as the license that I've been given to do what Brianne has been denied—to dream about my own life. Two years ago, I set out to examine the role that elite colleges play in shaping American society and what lessons my own experiences might offer about opportunity in the United States. A book begins as a dream. I'm grateful to everyone who helped make this particular dream of mine a reality.

Thanks to the hundreds of students, scholars, and educators who spoke with me in the course of researching this book. I learned from each and every interview. I was particularly emboldened by my conversations with Kirsten Hextrum, Sara Goldrick-Rab, and Amy Binder. Special thanks to Amy for introducing me to several of the people you've met in these pages and for her friendship.

I expect that my affection for John Jay is obvious at this point. I'm grateful for the chance to serve an institution committed to advancing social justice. I'm particularly indebted to Dara Byrne and Charles Davidson for sharing their experiences with me. They are among the most extraordinary of my extraordinary colleagues.

My friend and agent, Stephanie Steiker, has been a steadfast champion of this book since its conception. I could not imagine a better steward of it than the incomparable Tara Grove and everyone at The New Press. Thank you all.

My gratitude to my family is boundless. My parents, Matt and Sherry, always put my education above everything else. The time my father spent tutoring me in math and coaching me in bowling are among the happiest memories of my life. No one has been more supportive of my writing exploits than my mom.

Thanks to Eamon and Suria Vanrajah for sharing their own college experiences with me and for abiding many dinnertime conversations about the subjects covered here.

My baby girl, Mattie Rajah-Mandery—now impossibly twelve years old—is the joy of my life and my inspiration. My heartfelt apologies to her for the many jokes she's already had to endure about her father ending her chances of going to an elite college. For my own jokes, I offer no apologies.

This book simply would not be possible without my wife, Valli Rajah-Mandery. Her sociological imagination suffuses this work. We've discussed every idea in these pages so thoroughly that this book is as much hers as my own. I'm grateful for her brain and her love.

Finally, thanks to my students. It's almost impossible for me to imagine that I've been teaching in one way or another for more than twenty-five years. Somehow, after all that time, I'm still thrilled each time I enter a classroom and learn something new every day. I'd like to offer my thanks to three sets of students in particular.

After the 2016 presidential election, I taught an ethics class at Appa-

lachian State University as part of my own effort to reconcile the ran-
cor of discourse in America with the civility I experienced in my own
classrooms—even when discussing the most emotionally charged
ethical issues. The students at App were extraordinary, and I thought
the class might offer some lessons about dialoguing across difference.
Several of the students—including my friends Jackson Cooter, Sienna
Lafon, and Gaby Romero—agreed to let me profile them for a Politico
article. Their openness led me to conceive for the first time of the sort of
immersive journalism that you've read here.

My second set of thanks go to ten beloved John Jay students who read
a draft of this book as part of a seminar on opportunity in America.
My heartfelt thanks to Tige Anderson, Rafia Islam, Eqra Muhammad,
Maddy Mullen, Brianne Ortiz, Brendin Skakel, Sydney Spellman, Liz
Torres, Hannah Williams, and Amanda Zhu.

Finally, thanks to the students who allowed me to share their stories with you. Abdoulaye, Nico, Brianne, Hannah, Michael, Brianna,
Denisse, Krystle, Ed, and Brendin each shared my dream of explicating
the ways that elite colleges shape segregation in America and the walls
that we've built around our communities to restrict social mobility.

Here's to a nation in which the capacity to dream is equally available
to all.

RECOMMENDED READING

Armstrong, Elizabeth A., and Laura T. Hamilton. *Paying for the Party*. Harvard University Press, 2013.

Avery, Christopher, Andrew Fairbanks, and Richard J. Zeckhauser. *The Early Admissions Game*. Harvard University Press, 2009.

Binder, Amy J., Daniel B. Davis, and Nick Bloom. "Career Funneling: How Elite Students Learn to Define and Desire 'Prestigious' Jobs." 89 *Sociology of Education* 20–39, 2016.

Bowen, William G., and Derek Bok. *The Shape of the River*. Princeton University Press, 1998.

Carnevale, Anthony P., Peter Schmidt, and Jeff Strohl. *The Merit Myth: How Our Colleges Favor the Rich and Divide America*. The New Press, 2020.

Chetty, Raj, John N. Friedman, Emmanuel Saez, Nicholas Turner, and Danny Yagan. *Mobility Report Cards: The Role of Colleges in Intergenerational Mobility*. No. w23618. National Bureau of Economic Research, 2017.

Ciocca, Christina. *Organizational Effects on Bachelor's Degree Completion for the New Majority*. Columbia University, 2019.

Clotfelter, Charles T. *Unequal Colleges in the Age of Disparity*. Harvard University Press, 2018.

Cottom, Tressie M. *Lower Ed: The Troubling Rise of For-Profit Colleges in the New Economy*. The New Press, 2017.

Ehrenreich, Barbara. *Fear of Falling: The Inner Life of the Middle Class*. Pantheon, 1989.

Espeland, Wendy Nelson, and Michael Sauder. *Engines of Anxiety: Academic Rankings, Reputation, and Accountability*. Russell Sage Foundation, 2016.

Gaztambide-Fernández, Rubén A. *The Best of the Best: Becoming Elite at an American Boarding School*. Harvard University Press, 2009.

Golden, Daniel. *The Price of Admission: How America's Ruling Class Buys Its Way into Elite Colleges—and Who Gets Left Outside the Gates*. Broadway Books, 2007.

Goldrick-Rab, Sara. *Paying the Price: College Costs, Financial Aid, and the Betrayal of the American Dream*. University of Chicago Press, 2016.

Guinier, Lani. *The Tyranny of the Meritocracy: Democratizing Higher Education in America*. Beacon Press, 2015.

Hagerman, Margaret A. *White Kids*. New York University Press, 2018.

Hextrum, Kirsten. *Special Admission: How College Sports Recruitment Favors White Suburban Athletes*. Rutgers University Press, 2021.

Jack, Anthony Abraham. *The Privileged Poor*. Harvard University Press, 2019.

Kahlenberg, Richard D. *The Future of Affirmative Action: New Paths to Higher Education Diversity After* Fisher v. University of Texas. The Century Foundation, 2014.

Karabel, Jerome. *The Chosen: The Hidden History of Admission and Exclusion at Harvard, Yale, and Princeton*. Houghton Mifflin Harcourt, 2005.

Khan, Shamus. *Privilege: The Making of an Adolescent Elite at St. Paul's School*. Princeton University Press, 2012.

Kozol, Jonathan. *Savage Inequalities: Children in America's Schools*. Crown, 1991.

Kozol, Jonathan. *The Shame of the Nation: The Restoration of Apartheid Schooling in America*. Crown, 2005.

Lemann, Nicholas. *The Big Test: The Secret History of the American Meritocracy*. Macmillan, 2000.

Lukas, J. Anthony. *Common Ground: A Turbulent Decade in the Lives of Three American Families*. Vintage, 1986.

Markovits, Daniel. *The Meritocracy Trap*. Penguin, 2019.

Massey, Douglas, and Nancy A. Denton. *American Apartheid: Segregation and the Making of the Underclass*. Harvard University Press, 1993.

Massey, Douglas S., Len Albright, Rebecca Casciano, Elizabeth Derickson, and David N. Kinsey. *Climbing Mount Laurel*. Princeton University Press, 2013.

Mullen, Ann L. *Degrees of Inequality: Culture, Class, and Gender in American Higher Education*. Johns Hopkins University Press, 2011.

Owen, David. *None of the Above: The Truth Behind the SATs*. Rowman & Littlefield, 1999.

Putnam, Robert D. *Our Kids: The American Dream in Crisis*. Simon and Schuster, 2016.

Rivera, Lauren A. *Pedigree: How Elite Students Get Elite Jobs*. Princeton University Press, 2016.

Roth, Alvin E. *Who Gets What—and Why: The New Economics of Matchmaking and Market Design*. Houghton Mifflin Harcourt, 2015.

Rothstein, Richard. *The Color of Law: A Forgotten History of How Our Government Segregated America*. W. W. Norton, 2017.

Sandel, Michael J. *The Tyranny of Merit: What's Become of the Common Good?* Farrar, Straus and Giroux, 2020.

Sharkey, Patrick. *Stuck in Place: Urban Neighborhoods and the End of Progress toward Racial Equality*. University of Chicago Press, 2013.

Stevens, Mitchell L. *Creating a Class*. Harvard University Press, 2007.

Synnott, Marcia Graham. *Student Diversity at the Big Three: Changes at Harvard, Yale, and Princeton Since the 1920s.* Routledge, 2017.

Tough, Paul. *The Years That Matter Most: How College Makes or Breaks Us.* Houghton Mifflin Harcourt, 2019.

Warikoo, Natasha K. *The Diversity Bargain.* University of Chicago Press, 2016.

Wilder, Craig Steven. *Ebony and Ivory: Race, Slavery, and the Troubled History of America's Universities.* Bloomsbury, 2013.

NOTES

Epigraph

vii **"Until you do, who will?"** "I want you to make a difference" is from p. 381 of *The Guardians: Kingman Brewster and the Rise and Fall of the Progressive Establishment* by Geoffrey Kabaservice. It was published by Henry Holt and Co. in 2004.

Introduction

xiv **the angst that affluent, suburban parents feel** Barbara Ehrenreich discusses class anxiety throughout her book *Fear of Falling: The Inner Life of the Middle Class*, published by Pantheon in 1989.

xiv **"This knowledge, however tacit"** Patricia McDonough discusses the wind that chills the bones of suburban parents who dread downward mobility on p. 433 of her article "Buying and Selling Higher Education: The Social Construction of the College Applicant," which appeared in the *Journal of Higher Education*, vol. 65, no. 4 (July–August 1994).

xiv **a near-perfect protection from falling** Harvard and CUNY's graduation rates are from their websites. On expenditures per student, an invaluable resource is www.howcollegesspendmoney.com, a website maintained by the American Council of Trustees and Alumni, an independent, nonprofit organization.

xiv **dropout rate for poor college students** The national data on the effect of family income on college completion comes from Martha J. Bailey and Susan M. Dynarski's 2011 NBER Working Paper 17633, "Gains and Gaps: Changing Inequality in the U.S. College Entry and Completion." It's available at https://www.nber.org/system/files/working_papers/w17633/w17633.pdf.

xiv **investment in public education dwindles** On diminishing public support for public colleges, see David Leonhardt's article "America's Great Working-Class Colleges" in the *New York Times*, January 18, 2017. Former Vassar president Catharine Bond Hill also discusses the issue in her April 4, 2019, plenary address to the American Council on Education, "The Market, the American Dream, or Dreams of the Lottery." A text is available at https://thekeep.eiu.edu/cgi

/viewcontent.cgi?article=1833&context=jcba. It can also be seen at https://www
.youtube.com/watch?v=TC-5xXih7ns.

xv **growing income inequality in America**   On income inequality, Thomas
Piketty and his colleagues Emmanuel Saez and Gabriel Zucman report that the
top 1 percent earn 20.2 percent of national income while the bottom 50 percent
earn 12.5 percent in their article "Distributional National Accounts: Methods and
Estimates for the United States." The article appeared on pp. 553–609 of the *Quarterly Journal of Economics*, vol. 133, issue 2 in May, 2018. Piketty and Saez examine
the history of income inequality in America in their article "Income Inequality in
the United States, 1913–1988," also in the *Quarterly Journal of Economics*, vol. 188,
issue 1, p. 1 (February 2003).

xv **In a global ranking of social mobility**   The global social mobility rankings are from the January 2020 Davos report "The Global Social Mobility Report
2020 Equality, Opportunity and a New Economic Imperative." It's available at
http://www3.weforum.org/docs/Global_Social_Mobility_Report.pdf.

xv **The American Dream is fading**   The intergenerational income data is
from figure 3 on p. 6 of Leonard Lopoo and Thomas DeLeire's 2012 book *Pursuing the American Dream: Economic Mobility Across Generations*, published
by Pew Charitable Trusts. The race disparities are from figure 15 on p. 20. On
intergenerational mobility over time, see Xi Song, Catherine G. Massey, Karen
A. Rolf, Joseph P. Ferrie, Jonathan L. Rothbaum, and Yu Xie's article "Long-Term
Decline in Intergenerational Mobility in the United States Since the 1850s" in the
Proceedings of the National Academy of Sciences of the United States of America
(January 7, 2020), https://www.pnas.org/content/117/1/251.

xv **had linked declines in social mobility**   Leanne Son Hing, Anne E. Wilson, Peter Gourevitch, Jaslyn English, and Parco Sin summarize the negative consequences of income inequality in their 2019 *Daedalus* article "Failure to Respond
to Rising Income Inequality: Processes That Legitimize Growing Disparities," vol.
148, issue 3. The summary appears on p. 105, with citations on p. 127.

xv **responsibility our alma mater bore**   Emily Hanford offers a good
overview of the role colleges have played in fraying the American Dream in her
podcast and accompanying article "Are America's Colleges Promoting Social
Mobility?" *APM Reports*, April 23, 2018. It is available at https://www.apmreports
.org/episode/2018/04/19/american-colleges-promoting-social-mobility.

xv **So, we bet dinner**   My friend and I settled our bet using data from the
Harvard Crimson's survey of the entering class of 2017. Family income data is
available here: https://features.thecrimson.com/2013/frosh-survey/admissions
.html. The Chetty and Friedman data first appeared in July 2017 in a National
Bureau of Economic Research Working Paper 23618, "Mobility Report Cards:
The Role of College in Intergenerational Mobility" (hereafter, "Mobility Report
Cards"), which they co-authored with Emmanuel Saez, Nicholas Turner, and
Danny Yagan. It's available at https://www.nber.org/system/files/working_papers
/w23618/w23618.pdf.

xvii **hundreds of millions they spend every year**   Niall McCarthy discusses lobbying expenditures by petroleum giants in his March 25, 2019, *Forbes* article "Oil and Gas Giants Spend Millions Lobbying to Block Climate Change Policies." On carbon emissions, see Ron Bousso and Shadia Nasralla's article "Shell's 2020 Carbon Emissions Fall on the Back of Fuel Sales Drop," *Reuters*, March 11, 2021.

Chapter 1

10 **first major quantitative study**   Alan C. Kerckhoff discusses Blau and Duncan's work, and the history of social mobility research generally, in his article "The Current State of Social Mobility Research." It appeared in vol. 25, issue 2 of the *Sociological Quarterly* in spring 1984, pp. 139–53.

11 **So began a friendship**   My account of the origin story of Chetty and Friedman's partnership is based upon my interview with Friedman, supplemented by Paul Tough's account of their relationship on pp. 14–19 of his book *The Years That Matter Most: How College Makes or Breaks Us*. It was published by Houghton Mifflin Harcourt in 2019.

12 **grading institutions on their "mobility rate"**   The mobility report cards first appeared in the NBER working paper referenced in the introduction. The effect of the differential impact of attending an elite college on rich and poor students is discussed on p. 2 and again on pp. 19–21.

12 **if a college admitted 5 percent**   Sarah Reber and Chenoah Sinclair sort the data by middle-class mobility, which they define as students from the middle-income quintile who move up at least one quintile, in their May 19, 2020, paper "Opportunity Engines: Middle-Class Mobility in Higher Education." It was published by the Brookings Institution and is available at https://www.brookings.edu/research/opportunity-engines-middle-class-mobility-in-higher-education.

13 **suggested before in other research**   Earlier research on access to elite colleges includes David Karen's paper "Changes in Access to Higher Education," which appeared in issue 75 of *Sociology of Education* in 2002 at pp. 191–210. Marcia Graham Symnott focused on Harvard, Yale, and Princeton in her 2013 book *Student Diversity at the Big Three: Changes at Harvard, Yale, and Princeton Since the 1920s* (Transaction Publishers).

13 **Nationally, about a third of students**   The national data on representation of low-income students at public and private colleges is from Richard Fry and Anthony Cilluffo's May 22, 2019 report for the Pew Research Center, "A Rising Share of Undergraduates Are From Poor Families, Especially at Less Selective Colleges."

14 **picture emerged from Chetty and Friedman's research**   David Leonhardt was among the first to report on Chetty and Friedman's research in his January 18, 2017, *New York Times* article "America's Great Working-Class Colleges." All the Opportunity Insights data is publicly available on their website at https://opportunityinsights.org/data.

15 **Table 2** Table 2 excludes U.T. Brownsville, which ceased operations in 2015; Franklin Career Institute, which closed in 2016; and International Career Development Center, which closed the same year.

Chapter 2

19 **even more true than when we were there** Six-year graduation rates are from Harvard's and Yale's websites.

20 **one of the most comprehensive studies** Christina Ciocca Eller first presented her research on CUNY in her dissertation "Organizational Effects on Bachelor's Degree Completion for the New Majority." It was published in 2019 by ProQuest Dissertations Publishing and is available at https://www.proquest.com /openview/31eda70976423bdd12c315ad860e9f19/1?pq-origsite=gscholar&cbl= 18750&diss=y.

22 **America's disinvestment in public universities** The Center on Budget and Policy Priorities data comes from Michael Mitchell, Michael Leachman, and Matt Saenz's October 24, 2019, paper "State Higher Education Funding Cuts Have Pushed Costs to Students, Worsened Inequality." It's available at https:// www.cbpp.org/sites/default/files/atoms/files/10-24-19sfp.pdf. David Leonhardt graphically illustrates Mitchell and his colleagues' findings in "America's Great Working-Class Colleges." John Bound, Breno Braga, Gaurav Khanna and Sarah Turner explore the effects of these cuts in their NBER Working Paper 25945, available at https://www.nber.org/papers/w25945.

22 **Student support costs money** The data on student services expenditures is from the *Chronicle of Higher Education*'s February 16, 2020, article "Colleges That Spend the Most Per Student on Student Services." Data on overall spending is from www.howcollegesspendmoney.com.

25 **These disparities** The Upshot has a terrific graphic representation of the effect of family income on college attendance in the January 18, 2017, issue of the *New York Times* in an article titled "Some Colleges Have More Students From the Top 1 Percent Than the Bottom 60. Find Yours." The 77-fold disparity between the likelihood of rich and poor children attending an Ivy is from Mobility Report Cards.

25 **earliest available data on the socioeconomic status of** Ora Edgar Reynolds's *The Social and Economic Status of College Students* was published in 1927 by Teachers College at Columbia University. Charles Clotfelter discusses the history of research on the socioeconomic status of college students on pp. 64–69 of his 2017 book *Unequal Colleges in the Age of Disparity*. It was published by the Belknap Press of Harvard University Press.

25 **influence of parental income** David Karen's findings appear in his 2002 article "Changes in Access to Higher Education," in vol. 75 of the *Sociology of Education* on pp. 191–210.

27 **Stagnation requires two conditions**   Richard Rothstein's characterization of income stagnation is from p. 153 of *The Color of Law: A Forgotten History of How Our Government Segregated America*. It was published by W. W. Norton in 2017.

Chapter 3

29 **a riveting episode**   The *This American Life* episode is no. 534, "A Not-So-Simple Majority." It aired on September 12, 2014.

30 **the overwhelming majority of winners**   Statistics for Marshall winners can be found at https://www.marshallscholarship.org/the-scholarship/statistics-and-resources.

32 **Ivy League transcripts into Monopoly money**   The grade inflation metaphor comes from Tom Lindsay's March 30, 2019, *Forbes* article "The 'Other' College Scandal: Grade Inflation Has Turned Transcripts into Monopoly Money."

34 **Access to extreme affluence**   Chetty and Friedman discuss upper-tail mobility in Section V.E of Mobility Report Cards at pp. 34–35. See especially table II and online appendix figure IVB. Paul Tough summarizes this data on pp. 17–18 of *The Years That Matter Most*.

35 **delivered the keynote address**   You can see Scalia's speech at https://www.c-span.org/video/?285480-1/justice-scalia-judicial-review. Adam Liptak covered the speech in his May 11, 2009, *New York Times* article "On the Bench and Off, the Eminently Quotable Justice Scalia." Scalia's speech is also discussed in a Season 4 episode of Malcom Gladwell's podcast *Revisionist History* titled "The Tortoise and the Hare." Gladwell uses Scalia's speech as a launching point for discussing the absurdity of the LSAT's time constraints. As part of his answer to Christina Stutt's question, Scalia cites Jeffrey F. Sutton—who is today chief judge of the U.S. Court of Appeals for the Sixth Circuit—as one of his best clerks. Scalia inherited Sutton from retired justice Lewis F. Powell, but says that he never would have selected him on his own. "I wouldn't have hired Jeff Sutton," Scalia told the audience. "For God's sake, he went to Ohio State!" Sutton is an example of a long-thinker—a tortoise in Gladwell's formulation.

38 **made that the focus of her study**   Rivera's book *Pedigree: How Elite Students Get Elite Jobs* was published in 2015 by Princeton University Press. Jasmine's comment that "number one people go to number one schools" appears on p. 36. Bill's lament that Stanford is "just too far" appears on p. 32. Some of the biographical details of Rivera's life come from pp. 133–42 of *The Years That Matter Most*. Amit expresses his desire for a friend on p. 93 of *Pedigree*.

39 **the longstanding *Times* columnist**   Frank Bruni's book *Where You Go Is Not Who You'll Be: An Antidote to the College Admissions Mania* was published in 2016 by Grand Central Publishing.

Chapter 4

44 **"we were concerned about the schools"**   Michael J. Petrilli's 2012 book
The Diverse Schools Dilemma: A Parent's Guide to Socioeconomically Mixed Public Schools was published by the Thomas Fordham Institute. The quote from the
book—"They had a mixed reputation and lackluster test scores, largely due to their
diverse population of students"—appears on p. 3.

44 **bought a house in Bethesda**   The statistics on Bethesda are from
the U.S. Census Bureau Quick Facts: https://www.census.gov/quickfacts
/bethesdacdpmaryland.

46 **higher, "macro" level of segregation**   Lichter lays out his theory of
macro-segregation in his 2015 paper "Toward a New Macro-Segregation? Decomposing Segregation within and between Metropolitan Cities and Suburbs." Co-authored with Domenico Parisi and Michael C. Taquino, it appeared in vol. 80 of
the *American Sociological Review* on pp. 843–73.

47 **splintering based on economics**   Bischoff and Reardon's data comes
from their article "Residential Segregation by Income, 1970–2009." It appeared
in *Diversity and Disparities: America Enters a New Century*, a volume edited by
John Logan, which was published by the Russell Sage Foundation in 2014. Robert
Putnam has an accessible presentation of their work on p. 38 of his 2016 book
Our Kids: The American Dream in Crisis. It was published by Simon & Schuster. Bischoff discusses school district fragmentation in her 2008 article "School
District Fragmentation and Racial Residential Segregation: How Do Boundaries
Matter?" It appeared in vol. 44, issue 2 of the *Urban Affairs Review* on pp. 182–217.

47 **concerted cultivation**   Annette Lareau's research on how suburban families choose schools appeared in chapter 6, "Schools, Housing, and the Reproduction of Inequality," in her 2014 edited volume *Choosing Homes, Choosing Schools:
Residential Segregation and the Search for a Good School*. It was co-authored with
Kimberly Goyette and published by the Russell Sage Foundation. Maria Krysan
and Kyle Crowder report similar findings in their study of Chicago area schools,
Cycle of Segregation: Social Processes and Residential Stratification. It was published in 2017 by the Russell Sage Foundation. Lareau's quote on the blowback
faced by middle-class parents who send children to diverse schools is from an
interview she gave to Michael Petrilli. It appeared on p. 7 of *The Diverse Schools
Dilemma*.

48 **places that feel comfortable and safe**   In a series of studies, Courtney
Bonam of University of California, Santa Cruz, has found that white Americans
hold strong negative stereotypes of Black neighborhoods even if they aren't explicitly racist. From the presence of a Black family, many infer that a neighborhood
is "impoverished, crime-ridden, and dirty," though they refrain from making
similar assumptions about a white family in a similar house. An excellent introduction to Bonam's work is her 2018 article "Invisible Middle-Class Black Space:

Asymmetrical Person and Space Stereotyping at the Race–Class Nexus." The article, which was co-authored with Caitlyn Yantis and Valerie Jones Taylor, was published in vol. 23 of *Group Processes & Intergroup Relations* on pp. 24–47.

48 **famously dilapidated school buildings**   Mike Debonis wrote about the history of H. D. Woodson High School in his article "End of an Error." It appeared in the February 22, 2008, issue of *Washington City Paper*, available at https://washingtoncitypaper.com/article/235941/end-of-an-error.

49 **started playing with census data**   All of Sara Hodges's amazing maps and EdBuild's reports are available at www.edbuild.org. To watch student poverty spread like a virus, visit http://viz.edbuild.org/maps/2015/student-poverty-timelapse. Another useful source on inequities in school funding is the Center for American Progress's 2012 report *The Stealth Inequities of School Funding: How State and Local School Finance Systems Perpetuate Inequitable Student Spending*. It was written by Bruce D. Baker and Sean P. Corcoran and is available at https://www.americanprogress.org/issues/education-k-12/reports/2012/09/19/38189/the-stealth-inequities-of-school-funding.

51 **tony St. George neighborhood**   St. George's efforts to create their own school district were covered by Adam Harris in his article "The New Secession," which appeared in the May 20, 2019, issue of *The Atlantic*.

51 **by creating a "parcel tax"**   On the history of the parcel tax, see the Piedmont School District website: https://www.piedmont.k12.ca.us/district-info/budget/parcel-tax. They're quite proud of their efforts to "preserve and maintain important educational programs and services in the schools."

52 **this often excludes unofficial spending**   The data on PTA spending is from pp. 167–68 of *Our Kids*.

52 **"keeping our tax dollars here"**   Mayor Stan Hogeland's quote about keeping Gardendale, Alabama, tax dollars "here with our kids" appears, among other places, in Emma Brown's August 26, 2016, *Washington Post* article "A Southern City Wants to Secede From Its School District, Raising Concerns about Segregation."

53 **known as the Black achievement gap**   James S. Coleman's study was originally published in 1966 by the U.S. Department of Health, Education, and Welfare, Office of Education, under the title *Equality of Educational Opportunity*. It is officially report no. OE-38001 and is available at https://files.eric.ed.gov/fulltext/ED012275.pdf. Gregory J. Palardy has a useful overview of the study in his August 2013 article "High School Socioeconomic Segregation and Student Attainment." It appeared in vol. 50 of the *American Education Research Journal* on pp. 714–54. Elizabeth Evitts Dickinson explores the history of Coleman's work in her article "Coleman Report Set the Standard for the Study of Public Education." It appeared in the winter 2016 issue of *Johns Hopkins Magazine*.

53 **have reconceptualized the gap**   For an introduction to the opportunity gap, see Prudence Carter and Kevin Welner's 2013 edited volume *Closing the Opportunity Gap: What America Must Do to Give Every Child an Even Chance.* It was published by Oxford University Press.

53 **Coleman's findings**   Lichter discusses peer effects in his article "Poverty and Inequality Among Children." It appeared in vol. 23, issue 1 of the *Annual Review of Sociology* on pp. 121–45. Caroline Hoxby's study on peer effects was published in 2000 by the National Bureau of Economic Research under the title *Peer Effects in the Classroom: Learning from Gender and Race Variation.* Reardon and Bischoff write that between the 1970s and early 2000s, the test-score gap between rich and poor students increased by about 40 percent. This research appeared in their 2011 article "Income Inequality and Residential Segregation," which appeared in vol. 116, issue 4 of the *American Journal of Sociology* on pp. 1092–1153. Former Harvard president James B. Conant, whom you'll meet momentarily, also discussed the issue in his 1961 book *Slums and Suburbs: A Commentary on Schools in Metropolitan Areas.* It was published by McGraw Hill.

53 **consistent findings in research on education**   Gary Orfield and Susan E. Eaton's observation that the relationship between concentrated poverty and academic results is "one of the most consistent findings in research" appears on p. 53 of their 1997 book *Dismantling Desegregation.* It was published by The New Press.

53 **grit and optimism**   Angela Duckworth's research on the importance of "softer" traits is summarized in her 2016 book *Grit: The Power of Passion and Perseverance.* It was published by Scribner.

Chapter 5

55 **upon Harvard for its 1946 commencement**   William M. Blair covered the 1946 Harvard Commencement for the *New York Times* in his June 7, 1946, article "Harvard Honors Go to Fighting Forces: Harvard Honors Our Military Leaders." It appeared on p. 26. It was later covered in an unsigned *Harvard Crimson* article "Graduates Participated in Unusual Commencement," which was published on June 4, 1996.

55 **Harvard's president, James Conant**   Jerome Karabel discusses James Conant's views on social mobility and the threat of communism on pp. 157–61 of his definitive history of admissions at the Big Three, *The Chosen: The Hidden History of Admission and Exclusion at Harvard, Yale, and Princeton*, which was published by Houghton Mifflin in 2005. "The Russian experiment" quote appears on p. 160. It's also accessibly discussed in Louis Menand's review of James G. Hershberg's book *James B. Conant: Harvard to Hiroshima and the Making of the Nuclear Age*, which was published by Knopf in 1993. Menand's review, titled "The Quiet American," appeared in the July 14, 1994, issue of the *New York Review of Books.* Conant's fear of communism is also discussed in Jacqueline A. Newmyer

and David S. Stolzar's June 7, 1999, *Harvard Crimson* article "Class of 1949 Witnesses Prelude to Anti-Communist Hysteria."

56 **time machine to go back to Cambridge** On the differences between Harvard in 1946 and today see pp. 21–23 of *The Chosen*.

58 **true devotee of testing** Nick Lemann's discussion of Henry Chauncey appears on pp. 3–16 of *The Big Test: The Secret History of the American Meritocracy*. It was published by Macmillan in 2000.

60 **The pitchman** David Owen's profile of John Katzman and his partner, Adam Robinson, appeared in the March 1985 issue of *Rolling Stone* under the title "Adam and John Say Put Your Pencil Down." Nick Lemann discusses Katzman and the rivalry between Princeton Review and Kaplan on pp. 227–31 of *The Big Test*.

61 **teach you the SAT** "This isn't school" is from p. 120 of David Owen's book *None of the Above: The Truth Behind the SATs*, which was republished in 1999 by Rowman & Littlefield. The original version was published in 1985 by Houghton Mifflin under the title *None of the Above: Behind the Myth of Scholastic Aptitude*.

62 **College Board president George Hanford** Owen details his hilarious efforts to engage George Hanford of the College Board on p. 132 of *None of the Above*.

63 **renounced his own work** Brigham's statement that the "native intelligence hypothesis is dead" appears on p. 34 of *The Big Test*.

63 **united in opposition to a test** Charles Murray advocated against the SAT in his March 7, 2012, *New York Times* op-ed "Narrowing the Class Divide." He wrote about the SAT more extensively in an article for the July/August 2007 issue of *The American*, the journal of the American Enterprise Institute, titled "Abolish the SAT." It's available at https://web.archive.org/web/20110101113633/http://www.american.com/archive/2007/july-august-magazine-contents/abolish-the-sat.

63 **In 1948, shortly after ETS** The 1948 *Scientific Monthly* article titled "The Mismeasurement of Mental Systems (Can Intelligence Be Measured?)," was authored by W. Allison Davis and Robert J. Havinghurst. It's discussed on p. 66 of *The Big Test*.

63 **Conant himself had suspected** Nick Lemann discusses Conant's suspicions that the SAT might really be an achievement test on p. 38 of *The Big Test*. On p. 47, he asks whether Conant's blindness was "touchingly naïve, or willfully naïve, or just unpardonably naïve."

64 **showed that the test was coachable** David Owen reports that ETS fired Pike on p. 100 of *None of the Above*.

64 **the organization responded** The "attack on truth itself" quote appears on p. 20 of *None of the Above*. It, and the populist attacks on ETS, are also discussed on p. 221 of *The Big Test*.

64 **it released data showing**   The SAT data is reported, among other places, on p. 231 of *Unequal Colleges in the Age of Disparity.*

64 **how much tutoring**   Claudia Buchmann uses the term "shadow educa-tion" in her article "Shadow Education, American Style: Test Preparation, the SAT and College Enrollment." It was co-authored with Dennis J. Condron and Vincent J. Roscigno and appeared in 2010 in vol. 89, issue 2 of *Social Forces* at pp. 435–61. Buchmann finds that kids from families making over $50,000 are about twice as likely to hire a tutor as those who don't. The effect is almost cer-tainly higher at higher income levels. In the *Harvard Crimson*'s 2018 survey of incoming freshmen, 36.8 percent of students from families making over $500,000 per year reported having a private admissions counselor. Among families making less than $40,000 per year, the rate was 17.8 percent, almost certainly bolstered by nonprofits targeting low-SES, minority kids. For freshmen coming from families making between $80,000 and $125,000 per year, the rate was merely 7.5 percent. The survey is available at https://features.thecrimson.com/2018/freshman-survey /makeup. Daniel Engber discusses the effect of courses in his April 3, 2019, *Slate* article "Does SAT Prep Actually Work?"

64 **the College Board looked at the data**   Paul Tough discusses students who underperform and overperform their high school average on the SAT on pp. 174–75 of *The Years That Matter Most* and in the accompanying notes.

65 **They're nonprofits**   The College Board's tax filing is available at Pro Publica: https://projects.propublica.org/nonprofits/display_990/131623965 /01_2020_prefixes_06-13%2F131623965_201812_990_2020012717070895.

65 **"We know that the best predictor"**   Thomas Leblanc made his boast to Valerie Strauss, which she reported in her March 19, 2019, *Washington Post* article "Is It Finally Time to Get Rid of the SAT and ACT College Admissions Tests?"

66 **Bowdoin proudly boasts**   Bowdoin's policy is from its website: https:// www.bowdoin.edu/admissions/our-process/test-optional-policy/index.html.

66 **proposals to narrow the income gap**   Susan Dynarski lays out her pro-posal in a February 8, 2018, article for Brookings.edu titled "ACT/SAT for All: A Cheap, Effective Way to Narrow Income Gaps in College." It's available at https: //www.brookings.edu/research/act-sat-for-all-a-cheap-effective-way-to-narrow -income-gaps-in-college.

67 **looked at ten million SAT-takers**   Joshua Goodman presented his data on students retaking the SAT in NBER Working Paper 24945, "Take Two! SAT Retaking and College Enrollment Gaps." It was co-authored with Oded Gurantz and Jonathan Smith and is available at http://www.nber.org/papers/w24945. Jacob Vigdor and Charles Clotfelter also researched the issue. Their findings are pre-sented in their 2003 article "Retaking the SAT," which appeared in vol. 38, issue 1 of the *Journal of Human Resources* on pp. 1–33.

67 **performance on the ACT**   The ACT data is available at https://www.act
.org/content/dam/act/unsecured/documents/R1604-ACT-Composite-Score-by
-Family-Income.pdf.

67 **The ACT has always allowed super-scoring**   The ACT's decision to let
students sit for individual sections of the exam was reported by Chris Quintana
for *USA Today* in his October 8, 2019, article "ACT Test Changes Could Mean
Higher Scores, Especially for Wealthy Students."

68 **only entity that has ever denied this**   Lemann discusses ETS's denial of
the superiority of high school grades on p. 86 of *The Big Test*.

68 **DePaul University asked admitted students**   DePaul's experiment with
relying solely on high school grades is discussed on pp. 176–78 of *The Years That
Matter Most*.

69 **her college preparation is typical**   The AP disparity data is from the College Board's "10th Annual AP Report to the Nation," February 11, 2014. It's from
the Civil Rights Data Collection of the U.S. Dept. of Education and covers the
2009–2010 school year. It's also discussed on p. 168 of *Our Kids*. The Government
Accountability Office reports on massive disparities in the offering of calculus in
its October 2018 report "K-12 Education: Public High Schools with More Students
in Poverty and Smaller Schools Provide Fewer Academic Offerings to Prepare for
College."

73 **a marketplace approach**   Katzman discusses his vision for the SAT in his
June 1, 2020, article for *Inside Higher Ed* "What a New Test Needs to Have."

73 **special accommodations for test taking**   The *Wall Street Journal*'s study
of extra time for exams was reported by Douglas Belkin, Jennifer Levitz, and
Melissa Korn in their article "Many More Students, Especially the Affluent, Get
Extra Time to Take the SAT." It appeared on May 21, 2019. See also Dana Gold-
stein and Jugal K. Patel, "Extra Time on Tests? It Helps to Have Cash," *New York
Times*, July 30, 2019.

73 **special accommodations for test taking**   Jon Marcus reported on grade
inflation for the *Hechinger Report* in his August 16, 2017, article "The Newest
Advantage of Being Rich in America? Higher Grades."

Chapter 6

77 **"Stickball" was developed**   Thomas Vennum Jr. has a short, accessible
history of lacrosse at https://www.brooklynlacrosse.org/lacrosse-history. His book
American Indian Lacrosse: Little Brother of War was published by Smithsonian
Institute Press in 1994. Jane Claydon's short history, "Origin of Men's Lacrosse," is
available at https://worldlacrosse.sport/about-world-lacrosse/origin-history.

79 **Among the myths of college in America** The best source for data on participation in college sports is the NCAA, which maintains an extensive demographics database. It can be accessed at https://www.ncaa.org/about/resources /research/ncaa-demographics-database. Figures 1 and 2 are drawn from this database.

83 **an indictment of higher education** *Special Admission: How College Sports Recruitment Favors White Suburban Athletes* was published by Rutgers University Press in 2021. Hextrum discusses pay-to-play sports in chapter 3. The data point on the dearth of physical education classes in lower-income urban communities appears on p. 105.

84 **no physical education classes** The data on physical education offerings is from Don Sabo and Phil Veliz's study *Go Out and Play: Youth Sports in America*. It was published by the Women's Sports Foundation in 2008 and is available at https://eric.ed.gov/?id=ED539976. According to the Aspen Institute's Project Play, in 2018, 22 percent of kids ages six to twelve in households with incomes under $25,000 played sports on a regular basis, compared to 43 percent of kids from homes earning $100,000 or more. Kids from low-income homes are more than three times as likely to be physically inactive. The report is available at https://www .aspeninstitute.org/wp-content/uploads/2019/10/2019_SOP_National_Final.pdf. The National Women's Law Center found that schools where more than 90 percent of the students are white have about twice as many sports opportunities as schools where less than 10 percent of the students are white. Their report, *Finishing Last: Girls of Color and School Sports Opportunity*, is available at https://www .aspeninstitute.org/wp-content/uploads/2019/10/2019_SOP_National_Final.pdf.

84 **pay to play** The Aspen Institute's Project Play reported on p. 14 of its 2019 report that families spent an average of $693 per year on sports. The most expensive annual costs were ice hockey ($2,583), skiing/snowboarding ($2,249), gymnastics ($1,580), lacrosse ($1,289), and tennis ($1,170). Some parents reported spending over $20,000 a year in one sport. Rowing was not part of the survey.

85 **High School Teams and Roster Spots** The data in Table 8 is from pp. 203–204 of *Special Admission*.

87 **the only money-making programs** The data on the finances of college sports again comes from an extensive database maintained by the NCAA. It can be accessed at https://www.ncaa.org/about/resources/research/finances -intercollegiate-athletics.

88 **special, less rigorous academic pathways** Sean Gregory covered the North Carolina scandal for *Time* in his October 13, 2017, article "North Carolina Academic Fraud Decision Exposes College Sports Hypocrisy."

88 **one thousand times the rate** Peter Arcidiacono, Josh Kinsler, and Tyler Ransom presented their research on athletic preference at Harvard in 2019 in NBER Working Paper 26316, "Legacy and Athlete Preferences at Harvard." It's available at https://www.nber.org/papers/w26316. The 1,000 times multiplier for

athletes rated four was reported by Saahil Desai in his article "College Sports Are Affirmative Action for Rich White Students." It appeared in the October 23, 2018, issue of *The Atlantic*.

Chapter 7

91 **he wanted to go to Harvard** For background on Michael Wang, see Esther Wang's October 13, 2018, *BuzzFeed* article "About Michael Wang: Michael Wang Didn't Get into Harvard. He Thinks It's Because He's Asian"; Arrington Luck's October 17, 2018, article in the *Williams Record* "Michael Wang '17 Takes Part in Advocacy Related to Anti-Asian Discrimination Lawsuit"; Hua Hsu's October 15, 2018, article in the *New Yorker*, "The Rise and Fall of Affirmative Action"; and Katie Reilly's March 12, 2019, *Time* article "As the Harvard Admissions Case Nears a Decision, Hear From 2 Asian-American Students on Opposite Sides."

94 **Arcidiacono testified** Peter Arcidiacono's expert report in *SFFA v. Harvard* is available at https://samv91khoyt2i553a2t1s05i-wpengine.netdna-ssl.com /wp-content/uploads/2018/06/Doc-415-1-Arcidiacono-Expert-Report.pdf.

97 **U.S. District Court Judge Allison Burroughs** Judge Burroughs's Findings of Fact and Conclusions of Law are available at https://www.clearinghouse .net/chDocs/public/ED-MA-0002-0008.pdf. Senior admission officer Charlene Kim's testimony, "it's not what I know our office to be," appears on p. 30.

95 **After CNBC reported** The CNBC report on Ivy Coach's fees can be viewed at https://www.youtube.com/watch?v=OcgI6T7pPNo. Ivy Coach responded to CNBC in a May 13, 2018, blog post titled "Fees of College Consultants." It's available at https://www.ivycoach.com/the-ivy-coach-blog/college-admissions /fees-college-consultants. Kathianne Boniello reported the $1.5 million fee that Ivy Coach charged Vietnamese mom Buoi Thi Bui in her February 10, 2018, *New York Post* article "Mom Agreed to Give Consultant $1.5M to Help Kids' College Admissions: Suit."

96 **incoming Harvard freshmen** Data on Harvard freshmen and private counseling is from the 2020 *Harvard Crimson* freshman survey. It's available at https://features.thecrimson.com/2020/freshman-survey/makeup.

96 **Ivy Coach said** Ivy Coach commented on Wang in a June 10, 2015, blog post titled "A Misinformed Ivy-League Applicant." It's available at https://www .ivycoach.com/the-ivy-coach-blog/college-admissions/a-misinformed-ivy-league -applicant. Their comments on well-roundedness, including "ordinary's boring," appeared in a June 3, 2015, blog post titled "Well-Rounded College Applicants." It's available at https://www.ivycoach.com/the-ivy-coach-blog/college-admissions /well-rounded-college-applicants.

97 **the so-called "Jewish problem"** Jerome Karabel discusses the history of the "Jewish problem" on pp. 110–28 of *The Chosen*.

98 **indictment of America's exploding opportunity gap**   Bob Putnam writes about the extracurricular gap on pp. 174–83 of *Our Kids*. Putnam is drawing upon research he conducted with Kaisa Snellman, Jennifer M. Silva, Carl B. Frederick, and their paper "The Engagement Gap: Social Mobility and Extracurricular Participation Among American Youth," which appeared in the 2015 *Annals of the American Academy of Political and Social Science*. See also Snellman, Silva, and Putnam's 2015 paper "Inequity Outside the Classroom: Growing Class Differences in Participation in Extracurricular Activities," which appeared in vol. 40 of *Voices in Urban Education* in 2015. Other research includes Christina Theokas and Margot Bloch's paper "Out-of-School Time Is Critical for Children: Who Participates in Programs?" (Research-to-Results Fact Sheet No. 2006-20). See also Kristin Anderson Moore, David Murphey, Tawana Bandy, and P. Mae Cooper's research brief for Child Trends (no. 2014-13), "Participation in Out-of-School Time Activities and Programs."

98 **they found a similar pattern**   Elizabeth Stearns and Elizabeth J. Glennie research on extracurricular activities in North Carolina, "Opportunities to Participate: Extracurricular Activities' Distribution Across and Academic Correlates in High School," appeared in March 2010 in vol. 39 of *Social Science Research* at pp. 296–309.

98 **Model U.N. programs**   The Model U.N. program rankings are from bestdelegate.com, an education company that promotes participation in Model U.N. The rankings are available at https://bestdelegate.com/the-top-150-high-school -model-united-nations-teams-in-north-america-from-the-2017-2018-school -year.

100 **the quality of an applicant's college essay**   AJ Alvero, Sonia Giebel, Ben Gebre-Medhin, anthony lising antonio, Mitchell L. Stevens, and Benjamin W. Domingue described the relationship between essay content and income in CEPA Working Paper 21-03, "Essay Content is Strongly Related to Household Income and SAT Scores: Evidence from 60,000 Undergraduate Applications." It's available at https://cepa.stanford.edu/sites/default/files/wp21-03-v042021.pdf. CEPA is the Center for Education Policy Analysis.

100 **distinguishing excellences**   Elizabeth Heaton's post on distinguishing excellences appeared in the *Huffington Post* on August 10, 2017, under the title "What Kind of Hook Do I Need to Get Accepted to an Ivy League College?" It's available at https://www.huffpost.com/entry/what-kind-of-hook-do-i-need-to-get -accepted-to-an-ivy_b_597124f3e4b0545a5c30fec8.

101 **children born into low-income families can escape**   "A fantasy that we share" is from p. 183 of *The Color of Law*.

102 **Bial-Dale College Adaptability Index**   Rebecca Winters wrote about the Bial-Dale Index for the March 4, 2001, issue of *Time* in her article "Here Comes the Lego Test." Lani Guinier discusses the test extensively on pp. 63–73 of her

2015 book *The Tyranny of the Meritocracy: Democratizing Higher Education in America*. It was published by Beacon Press in 2015.

102 **notoriously bad at predicting job performance**   Research on the dangers of unstructured interviews includes Jason Dana, Robyn Dawes, and Nathanial Peterson's 2013 article "Belief in the Unstructured Interview: The Persistence of an Illusion." It appeared in vol. 8, issue 5 of *Judgment and Decision Making* on pp. 512–20. For an overview on the subject, see Allen I. Huffcutt's literature review "An Empirical Review of the Employment Interview Construct Literature." It appeared in 2011 in vol. 19, issue 1 of *International Journal of Selection and Assessment* on pp. 62–81. Lauren Rivera also discusses the issue on p. 283 of *Pedigree*.

Chapter 8

107 **Conley's memoir**   *Honky* was published by Vintage, an imprint of Penguin Random House, in 2001.

107 **examined data from the Panel Study of Income Dynamics**   Conley presented his research on the relationship between wealth and educational outcomes in a book chapter titled "The Why, What and How of Class-Based Admissions Policy." It appears in *The Future of Affirmative Action*, a volume edited by Richard Kahlenberg and published in 2014 by Century Foundation Press. Conley's dissertation research became a book-length treatment of wealth inequality, *Being Black, Living in the Red*. It was published in 1999 by the University of California Press. A more recent study by Breno Braga, Signe-Mary McKernan, Caroline Ratcliffe, and Sandy Baum also relied upon the PSID and found similar wealth effects to those Conley identified. "Wealth Inequality Is a Barrier to Education and Social Mobility" was published by the Urban Institute. It's available at https://www. urban. org/research/publication/wealth-inequality-barrier-education-and-social-mobility (2017). Another useful reference is Su Jin Jez's article "The Differential Impact of Wealth Versus Income in the College-Going Process," which appeared in vol. 55, issue 7 of *Research in Higher Education* on pp. 710–34 in 2014.

108 **Not all the difference in white and Black family wealth**   "But a good portion certainly is" is from p. 185 of *The Color of Law*. Rothstein discusses wealth inequality throughout the book. The cumulative effect of the deprivation of the opportunity of homeownership for Black families is the focus of chapter 11.

109 **Legacy evolved in the early twentieth century**   Jerome Karabel discusses the origins of legacy admissions on pp. 116–17 of *The Chosen*. Another useful source is Deborah L. Coe and James D. Davidson's 2011 article "The Origins of Legacy Admissions: A Sociological Explanation." It appeared on pp. 233–47 of the *Review of Religious Research*.

110 **The practice has been condemned**   The *Boston Globe* opposed legacy preference in its December 1, 2019, editorial "Time for Colleges to End Legacy Admissions." The *New York Times* editorial board came out against legacy

preferences on September 7, 2019, in "End Legacy College Admissions." I was five years ahead of them with my *Times* op-ed "End College Legacy Preference." It was published on April 24, 2014. The *Harvard Crimson* was ahead of everyone with its December 13, 2006, editorial "End Legacy Preference." The practice has also been condemned by the editorial boards of the *Hoya*, Virginia Tech's *Collegiate Times*, the *Amherst Student*, and the *Denton Record-Chronicle*.

110 **researchers at Princeton found**   The Princeton study finding a 160-point boost for legacies was conducted by Thomas J. Espenshade, Chang Y. Chung, and Joan L. Walling. It was first published in vol. 85, issue 5 of *Social Science Quarterly* at pp. 1422–46 in December 2004.

110 **The admission rate is about 42.2 percent**   Delano R. Franklin and Samuel W. Zwickel covered trial testimony on donor preference in their October 18, 2018, *Harvard Crimson* article "In Admissions, Harvard Favors Those Who Fund It, Internal Emails Show."

111 **notoriously high rates of legacy admissions**   Brandon Kochkodin disclosed legacy rates at Notre Dame and Baylor in a March 21, 2019, article for Bloomberg.com, "Notre Dame and Baylor Admit More Legacies Than Harvard and Yale."

111 **a particularly egregious offender**   The University of Virginia Admission Liaison Program can be accessed at https://alumni.virginia.edu/admission. Joseph Price discusses University of Virginia's scandalous record on legacy in his op-ed for *Inside Higher Ed*, "End Legacy Admissions." It was published on September 28, 2020.

115 **examined alumni giving**   Chad Coffman, Tara O'Neil, and Brian Starr explored the relationship between legacy preference and alumni giving in "An Empirical Analysis of the Impact of Legacy Preferences on Alumni Giving at Top Universities," a chapter in *Affirmative Action for the Rich*, which was edited by Richard Kahlenberg and published by The Century Foundation Press in 2010. The subject is also covered in Joe Pinsker's article "The Real Reasons Legacy Preferences Exist," which appeared in the April 4, 2019, issue of *The Atlantic*. Nick Anderson wrote about Johns Hopkins's experience with ending legacy in "Hopkins Says Scrapping 'Legacy' Preference Has Boosted Campus Diversity," in the January 13, 2020, issue of the *Washington Post*.

Chapter 9

123 **workforce after graduation**   Data on career choices at Harvard is from the *Crimson* senior survey. It's available at https://features.thecrimson.com /2020/senior-survey/after-harvard. Data on career choices at John Jay is from the six-month alumni survey. It's available at http://johnjay.jjay.cuny.edu/files /2013_Alumni_Survey_Final_Report.pdf. Data on Cal State LA career choices is

from their alumni demographic infographic, available at https://www.calstatela
.edu/sites/default/files/groups/Cal%20State%20LA%27s%20Strategic%20Plan
/alumni_v211.pdf. Berea data is from the college fact book, available at https:
//4efrxppj37llsgsbr1ye6idr-wpengine.netdna-ssl.com/ira/wp-content/uploads
/sites/27/2021/05/2020-2021FactBookOnline-1.pdf

123 **investment banks or consulting firms** The data point that 70 percent of
Harvard students apply to investment banks or consulting firms is from p. 54 of
Pedigree.

126 **the lion's share of her career** A great introduction to Amy Binder's
research is her article "Why Are Harvard Grads Still Flocking to Wall Street?"
which appeared in the September/October 2014 issue of *Washington Monthly.*
Other essential reading includes her article "Career Funneling: How Elite Students Learn to Define and Desire 'Prestigious' Jobs," which appeared in vol. 89,
issue 1 of the *Sociology of Education* in 2016 on pp. 20–39 and was co-authored
with Daniel B. Davis and Nick Bloom; "Industry, Firm, Job Title: The Layered
Nature of Early-Career Advantage for Graduates of Elite Private Universities," also
co-authored with Davis, which appeared in vol. 5 of *Socius* in 2019 on pp. 1–23;
and "Symbolically Maintained Inequality: How Harvard and Stanford Students
Construct Boundaries Among Elite Universities," which was co-authored with
Andrea R. Abel and appeared in vol. 92, issue 1 of *Sociology of Education* in 2019
on pp. 41–58.

126 **a Harvard alum named Kevin** Kevin's statement that he planned "to
study philosophy" is from "Why Are Harvard Grads Still Flocking to Wall
Street?"

127 **the baller lifestyle** Lauren Rivera talks about the baller lifestyle throughout *Pedigree.* See especially chapter 3, "The Pitch," on pp. 55–83.

127 **seize every opportunity** "At Harvard, you always want to seize every
opportunity you can" is from the same article.

128 **a Stanford student named Izzy** Izzy's statement that she'd "be a nothing" if she became a teacher is from p. 34 of "Career Funneling" and my interview
of Binder.

128 **corporate partnership program** Binder and Davis expose corporate
partnerships in their book chapter "Selling Students: The Rise of Corporate Partnership Programs in University Career Centers." It appeared in *The University
Under Pressure* by Elizabeth Popp Berman and Catherine Paradeise, which was
published by Emerald Group Publishing Limited in 2016.

129 **"a core company to us"** "We are not trying to make Microsoft a core
company to us" is from p. 411 of *Selling Students.*

129 **Bastian, a Harvard senior**   Bastian's statement that consulting or finance is a good job because "that's what the Office of Career Services has" is from p. 29 of "Career Funneling."

131 **Bates opened its Center for Purposeful Work**   You can read about the Center for Purposeful Work at https://www.bates.edu/purposeful-work.

131 **A student named Opal**   Opal's statement that Stanford "could do a much better job" cultivating interest in careers other than finance and consulting is from "Why Are Harvard Grads Still Flocking to Wall Street?"

Chapter 10

133 **a Princeton freshman named Tal Fortgang**   Tal Fortgang's essay was originally published in the *Princeton Tory* on April 2, 2014, under the title "Checking My Privilege: Character as the Basis of Privilege." It was republished by *Time* on May 2, 2014, under the title "Why I'll Never Apologize for My White Male Privilege."

134 **an editor at the *New Republic***   Katie McDonough's response, "'I'll Never Apologize for My White Privilege' Guy Is Basically Most of White America," was published in *Salon* on May 5, 2014.

134 **at Princeton's opening exercises**   A video of Princeton's 2013 opening exercises is available at https://mediacentral.princeton.edu/media/Opening+E xercises+2013A+A+University+Convocation/1_ktr640uw. The text of President Eisgruber's speech can be found at https://president.princeton.edu/blogs/opening -exercises-2013-princetons-honor-world.

135 **Stanford president John Hennessy**   The text of President John Hennessy's address at Stanford's September 22, 2000, freshman convocation is available at https://news.stanford.edu/news/2000/september20/convocation-927.html.

136 **self-taught sociologist named Michael Young**   Michael Young's *The Rise of the Meritocracy* was published in 1958 by Thames and Hudson.

137 **believes that they deserve their place**   Michael Sandel's *The Tyranny of Merit: What's Become of the Common Good?* was published in 2020 by Farrar, Straus and Giroux. "It means that those who are left behind deserve their fate" appears on p. 5.

137 **college-educated elites look down on**   Toon Kuppens, Russell Spears, Antony S. R. Manstead, Bram Spruyt, and Matthew J. Easterbrook find that highly educated people hold negative attitudes toward less-educated people but that the less educated do not show education-based intergroup bias. Their article "Educationism and the Irony of Meritocracy: Negative Attitudes of Higher Educated People Towards the Less Educated" appeared in vol. 76 of the *Journal of Experimental Social Psychology* in May 2018 on pp. 429–47.

137 **opens the door to populism**   *The Meritocracy Trap: How America's Foundational Myth Feeds Inequality, Dismantles the Middle Class, and Devours the*

Elite by Daniel Markovits was published by Penguin Press in 2019. "A deep and pervasive mistrust" is from p. 64.

138 **faith in the academy is eroding**   The data on perceptions of the academy is from Kim Parker's August 19, 2019, article for the Pew Research Center, "The Growing Partisan Divide in Views of Higher Education."

138 **white men without college educations**   Data on Donald Trump's advantage among non-college-educated white men and the characterization of them as "a key Trump base" is from William H. Frey's November 12, 2020, *Brookings* article "Exit Polls Show Both Familiar and New Voting Blocs Sealed Biden's Win."

138 **Sandel argues that belief in meritocracy**   "The more we think of ourselves as self-made" appears on p. 14 of *The Tyranny of Merit*.

138 **a student's capacity to collaborate**   "What's urgent for the world" is from p. 2 of Lani Guinier's *The Tyranny of Meritocracy: Democratizing Higher Education in America*. It was published in 2015 by Beacon Press.

138 **At a psychological level**   Mark Clifton discusses how meritocracy increases selfishness and discrimination in his March 8, 2019, *Aeon* article "A Belief in Meritocracy Is Not Only False: It's Bad for You." It's available at https://aeon.co/ideas/a-belief-in-meritocracy-is-not-only-false-its-bad-for-you. One mechanism for testing this relationship is so-called ultimatum and dictator games in which participants are asked to either propose or unilaterally determine a division of money between themselves and another player. As Clifton describes, social scientists have found that subjects acted more selfishly if they'd first played a fake game of skill and were told that they'd won. Another experiment similarly found that just playing a game of skill led participants to tolerate more unequal payments to other participants.

138 **At an organizational and sociological level**   MIT's Emilio J. Castilla and Indiana sociologist Stephen Benard find an association between meritocratic cultural beliefs in organizations and gender bias in their article "The Paradox of Meritocracy in Organizations." It appeared in 2010 in vol. 55, issue 4 of *Administrative Science Quarterly* on pp. 543–676. Castilla and Benard hypothesize that adopting meritocracy as a value convinces participants of their justness and makes them less inclined to reflect upon their own prejudice. Social psychological research includes Chunliang Feng, Yi Luo, Ruolei Gu, Lucas S. Broster, Xueyi Shen, Tengxiang Tian, Yue-Jia Luo, and Frank Krueger's article "The Flexible Fairness: Equality, Earned Entitlement, and Self-Interest," which appeared in vol. 8, issue 9 of *PloS One* in 2013, and Aldo Rustichini and Alexander Vostroknutov's article "Merit and Justice: An Experimental Analysis of Attitude to Inequality," which appeared in vol. 9, issue 12 of *PloS One* in 2014.

139 **similar dynamic in affluent suburbs**   "The false sense of superiority that segregation fosters" is from p. 197 of *The Color of Law*.

139 **the crushing demands meritocracy places**   The misery of life under meritocracy is arguably the central point of *The Meritocracy Trap.*

139 **Tufts professor Natasha Warikoo**   Natasha Warikoo presents her research on meritocracy at elite institutions in *The Diversity Bargain: And Other Dilemmas of Race, Admissions, and Meritocracy at Elite Universities.* It was published by University of Chicago Press in 2016.

140 **a teacher at St. Paul's**   Shamus Khan discusses his year at St. Paul's in *Privilege: The Making of an Adolescent Elite at St. Paul's School.* It was published by Princeton University Press in 2010.

140 **two years of ethnographic research**   Rubén A. Gaztambide-Fernández presents his research on the Weston School in *The Best of the Best: Becoming an Elite at an American Boarding School.* It was published by Harvard University Press in 2009.

141 **easily enhanced in experiments**   On the ease with which meritocratic beliefs can be primed, see Shannon McCoy and Brenda Major's 2007 article "Priming Meritocracy and the Psychological Justification of Inequality." It appeared in vol. 43, issue 3 of the *Journal of Experimental Social Psychology* on pp. 341–51. Other research on the stickiness and negative consequences of meritocratic beliefs includes Céline Darnon, Virginie Wiederkehr, Benoît Dompnier, and Delphine Martinot's 2018 article "'Where There is a Will, There is a Way': Belief in School Meritocracy and the Social-Class Achievement Gap." It appeared in vol. 57, issue 1 of the *British Journal of Social Psychology* on pp. 250–62. See also Chris Goode and Lucas Keefer's 2016 article "Grabbing Your Bootstraps: Threats to Economic Order Boost Beliefs in Personal Control," which appeared in vol. 35, issue 1 of *Current Psychology* on pp. 142–48.

141 **psychologist Allison Ledgerwood**   Allison Ledgerwood's research on people's willingness to work harder to prove that meritocracy is real is from her article "Working for the System: Motivated Defense of Meritocratic Beliefs." It was published in 2011 in vol. 29, issue 3 of *Social Cognition* on pp. 322–40. It was co-authored by Anesu N. Mandisodza, John T. Jost, and Michelle J. Pohl.

141 **by a 71-to-21 margin**   Polling data on meritocratic beliefs is from the Economic Mobility Project, "Findings From a National Survey & Focus Groups on Economic Mobility." It's available at https://www.pewtrusts.org/~/media/legacy/uploadedfiles/wwwpewtrustsorg/reports/economic_mobility/emp20200920survey20on20economic20mobility20for20print2031209pdf.pdf.

142 **her final Harvard commencement**   The text of President Drew Faust's 2018 commencement speech is available at https://www.harvard.edu/president/speeches-faust/2018/2018-commencement-speech.

142 **Stanford's president Marc Tessier-Lavigne**   The text of President Marc Tessier-Levigne's 2019 commencement speech is available at https://news

.stanford.edu/2019/06/16/remarks-stanford-president-marc-tessier-lavigne-2019 -commencement-ceremony.

142 **Yale president Peter Salovey**   The text of President Peter Salovey's 2019 commencement speech is available at https://president.yale.edu/president /speeches/what-are-you.

142 **the content of commencement speeches**   Jenifer J. Partch and Richard T. Kinnier's research on commencement speeches is from their 2011 article "Values and Messages Conveyed in College Commencement Speeches," which appeared in vol. 30 of *Current Psychology* on pp. 81–92. Alice Robb covered the issue in her *New Republic* article "Your Commencement Speech Will Be Generic and Bland." It was published on May 16, 2014.

Chapter 11

144 **she's the sort of professional**   Julie McMahon profiled Joyce Suslovic for syracuse.com in her June 8, 2016, article "How Syracuse Teacher Joyce Suslovic Helped Generations of Students Find Their Voices." It's available at https://www.syracuse.com/schools/2016/06/37-year_syracuse_history_teacher _joyce_suslovic.html.

144 **Known to her students as "Miss S"**   You can check out J-Sus's rap to the class of 2020 at https://cnycentral.com/news/local/scsd-teacher-raps-to-the-class -of-2020-and-goes-viral.

148 **Suslovic's interviewer was Anthony Abraham Jack**   Paul Tough profiled Tony Jack on pp. 109–12 of *The Years That Matter Most*. Additional biographical details, including Gulliver Prep's mandatory office hours, are from Lory Hough's profile of Jack, "Poor, but Privileged." It appeared in the summer 2017 issue of *Harvard Ed. Magazine* and can be found at https://www.gse.harvard.edu/news/ed /17/05/poor-privileged.

149 **a widely acclaimed 2019 book**   *The Privileged Poor: How Elite Colleges Are Failing Disadvantaged Students* was published by Harvard University Press in 2019.

149 **Jose, a talkative senior**   Jose's statement, "We come here, we're so alive and full of hope," appears on p. 43.

150 **Elise, a white junior**   Elise's statement, "When I need help, I don't have anyone else to turn to," appears on p. 122.

150 **Forced to perform janitorial services**   Jack's observation that "hiring poor students to clean the toilets in rich students' dorm rooms is not a way to break down class boundaries" is from p. 23.

150 **Harvard encouraged poor students**   William's explanation of the pressure to pursue a selfish career appears on pp. 46–48 of *The Privileged Poor*.

151 **calls this the "hidden curriculum"** The phrase "hidden curriculum" first appears on p. 86 of *The Privileged Poor*. Douglas S. Massey, Camille Z. Charles, Garvey Lundy, and Mary J. Fischer explore the different characteristics that students begin college with and trace how these factors connect to their academic performance in *The Source of the River: The Social Origins of Freshmen at America's Selective Colleges and Universities*. It was published by Princeton University Press in 2003.

151 **Doubly Disadvantaged don't have that experience** Jack's observation that faculty and administrators "remain authority figures who should be treated with deference" appears on p. 82.

151 **Shaniqua, a doubly disadvantaged Black woman** Shaniqua's statement that "when you're poor and you're homeless, you get used to taking what is given" appears on p. 93.

151 **a prescriptive and descriptive matter** Jack's observation that the Doubly Disadvantaged have "strong faith in the idea of meritocracy" is from p. 127.

152 **holding those two ideas** Ezra Klein interviewed Tressie McMillan Cottom on April 13, 2021, on his podcast *The Ezra Klein Show*. A transcript of their conversation is available at https://www.nytimes.com/2021/04/13/podcasts/ezra-klein-podcast-tressie-mcmillan-cottom-transcript.html.

155 **the rate of Black admissions** Shaun Harper's observations are from his September 25, 2017, keynote address to the National Association for College Admission Counseling's annual conference. It can be viewed at https://www.youtube.com/watch?v=zcUkalvq0LA.

155 **the consistency of these statistics** The data on race diversity is from Priceonomics Data Studio, "Ranking the Most (and Least) Diverse Colleges in America." It's available at https://priceonomics.com/ranking-the-most-and-least-diverse-colleges-in.

155 **Kiki, a Princeton student** Tough's profile of Kiki appears on pp. 121–27 of *The Years That Matter Most*. Her observation that she'd only met about a dozen low-income Black students in her freshman class is from p. 121.

156 **Another reason to be pessimistic** Paul Tough summarizes the evidence on how elite colleges have treated boosting socioeconomic diversity as a game on pp. 117–21. The data on colleges' distorted behavior around the Pell threshold is also discussed by Doug Lederman in his January 28, 2019, article for *Inside Higher Ed*, "Underrepresented Students, Underrepresented Consequences." Catherine Rampell also covers the issues in her January 24, 2019, *Washington Post* article "Colleges Have Been Under Pressure to Admit Needier Kids. It's Backfiring."

156 **were effectively cherry-picking** Hoxby and Turner published their research in 2019 in NBER Working Paper 25479, "Measuring Opportunity in U.S. Higher Education."

157 **first noted this pattern**   Guinier and Gates's observation about the dearth of third-generation Black families is from Sara Rimer and Karen W. Arenson's June 24, 2004, *New York Times* article "Top Colleges Take More Blacks, but Which Ones?"

158 **Imani, a Black undergraduate at Brown University**   Imani's characterization of the cultivating elite and a commitment to diversity as "a fundamental contradiction" is from p. 56 of *The Diversity Bargain*.

Chapter 12

162 **the majority spent no money**   Sara Goldrick-Rab's findings on alcohol spending and consumption are from chapter 5, footnote 3 of *Paying the Price: College Costs, Financial Aid, and the Betrayal of the American Dream*, which was published by the University of Chicago Press in 2016. The footnote appears on p. 300. The accompanying text, about the drinking habits of a student named Tyler, is on p. 125.

162 **found the same thing**   Elizabeth A. Armstrong and Laura T. Hamilton's *Paying for the Party: How College Maintains Inequality* was published by Harvard University Press in 2013. "I don't know how this project has become so much about class" is from p. xii.

163 **Armstrong and Hamilton call this**   The phrase "party pathway" first appears on p. 15 of *Paying for the Party*. Armstrong and Hamilton's frame traces back to Murray Sperber—Kirsten Hextrum's mentor—who argued in a 2000 book, *Beer and Circus: How Big-Time College Sports Has Crippled Undergraduate Education*, that colleges had made a tacit bargain not to ask much of rich students. *Beer and Circus* was published by Henry Holt in 2000.

163 **It is the college experience**   Jenny Stuber observes that affluent students see networking as the most important part of college in her book *Inside the College Gates: How Class and Culture Matter in Higher Education*. It was published by Lexington Books in 2011.

164 **evolved to satisfy that expectation**   "The social and academic infrastructure of the university seemed tailor-made for a particular type of affluent" appears on p. xii of *Paying for the Party*.

164 **Hannah landed an internship**   Hannah's story appears on p. 138.

165 **wrote in her field notes**   "I always feel like the biggest loser" appears on p. 102.

165 **the college briefly banned**   John S. Rosenberg covered Harvard's decision to rescind the final-club ban in "Harvard Single-Gender Social-Club Rules Rescinded." The article appeared in the June 30, 2020, issue of *Harvard Magazine*.

165 **sparked a massive backlash**   Brianna Suslovic's anti-final-club op-ed "Dismantle Final Clubs Now" appeared in the April 1, 2015, issue of the *Harvard*

Crimson. It was co-authored with Jordan T. Weiers. Suslovic also wrote a column about the ensuing backlash, titled "Open Up," which appeared in the November 6, 2015, issue of the *Crimson.* The quote, "club members told me," is from this piece.

166 **a luxury rehab facility in Florida**   Seaside Palm Beach's warning to affluent parents can be found at https://www.seasidepalmbeach.com/addiction-blog/highest-risk-teen-alcoholism-found-upper-class-families.

167 **In a 2015 study**   The 2015 National Survey on Drug Use and Health was conducted by the Substance Abuse and Mental Health Services Administration. The findings can be accessed at https://www.samhsa.gov/data/sites/default/files/NSDUH-DetTabs-2015/NSDUH-DetTabs-2015/NSDUH-DetTabs-2015.pdf.

167 **heavy episodic drinking**   A summary of the CDC research on binge drinking is available at https://www.cdc.gov/alcohol/fact-sheets/binge-drinking.htm.

167 **teenagers from affluent families**   The British study of 120,000 teenagers was covered in, among other places, *The Guardian*'s December 9, 2015, article "Affluent Teens Twice as Likely to Drink Regularly, Study Finds." Teensavers, an organization dedicated to treating adolescent substance abuse, discusses the relationship between wealth and alcoholism among teenagers in a February 26, 2000, article "Family Income Affects Teenage Drinking." It's available at https://www.teensavers.com/post/family-income-affects-teenage-drinking.

167 **the malaise of wealthy youth**   Connor Fritchley discusses the relationship between "affluenza" and drinking in an August 7, 2014, article for the Connecticut Health I-Team, "Privilege, Free Time May Fuel Suburban Teen Drinking." It's available at http://c-hit.org/2014/08/07/privilege-free-time-may-fuel-suburban-teen-drinking.

167 **A Manhattan Institute study found**   The January 1, 2004, Manhattan Institute study, "Sex, Drugs, and Delinquency in Urban and Suburban Public Schools," was written by Jay P. Greene and Greg Forster. It's available at https://www.manhattan-institute.org/html/sex-drugs-and-delinquency-urban-and-suburban-public-schools-5907.html.

168 **as one subject told Rivera**   "Working at Starbucks or mowing lawns" is from p. 105 of *Pedigree.*

168 **explains how overcoming disadvantage**   Malcom Gladwell's *Outliers: The Story of Success* was published by Little, Brown and Company in 2008.

168 **successful poor students**   Lauren Rivera discusses the resilience of poor students on p. 282 of *Pedigree.* Rivera is drawing upon Edith Chen and Gregory Miller's 2012 article "Shift and Persist Strategies: Why Being Low in Socioeconomic Status Isn't Always Bad for Health," which appeared in vol. 7 of *Perspectives on Psychological Science* on pp. 135–58. The finding that low-SES students are more likely to sacrifice for the group is from Michael Kraus, Stéphane Côté, and Dacher Keltner's 2010 article "Social Class, Contextualism, and Empathic Accuracy." It appeared in vol. 11 of *Psychological Science* on pp. 1716–23.

169 **laundering scheme**   Mitchell Stevens used the term "laundering privilege" in *Creating a Class: College Admissions and the Education of Elites*. It was published by Harvard University Press in 2009.

169 **Berkeley's Zeus Leonardo**   "The world belongs to them" is from p. 112 of Zeus Leonardo's book *Race, Whiteness, and Education*. It was published in 2009 by Routledge.

Chapter 13

174 **Almost all are professors**   Scott Jaschik has an excellent overview on the political orientation of college faculty in his article "Professors and Politics: What the Research Says." It appeared in the February 27, 2017, issue of *Inside Higher Ed*.

174 **73 percent of faculty**   Data on the political preferences of Harvard faculty is from Lucy Wang, Like W. Xu, Brian P. Yu, and Phelan Yu's May 2, 2018, *Harvard Crimson* article "Eighty-Eight Percent of Surveyed Harvard Faculty Believe Trump Has Done a 'Very Poor' Job as President."

174 **survey of 479 sociology professors**   Data on the political leanings of sociologists is from Jeremiah B. Wills, Zachary W. Brewster, and Gerald Roman Nowak's 2019 article "Students' Religiosity and Perceptions of Professor Bias: Some Empirical Lessons for Sociologists." It appeared in vol. 50, issue 1 of the *American Sociologist* on pp. 136–53.

174 **at least as liberal**   The data on the political attitudes of Harvard students is from the *Harvard Crimson* senior survey of the class of 2020. It's available at https://features.thecrimson.com/2020/senior-survey/national-politics.

175 **the measures are milquetoast**   Scott Jaschik reported on the Stanford Faculty Senate's resolution on legacy preference in his article "Is Stanford Letting In Too Many Wealthy Students?" It appeared in the February 16, 2021, issue of *Inside Higher Ed*.

177 **system justification is the idea**   John T. Jost and Mahzarin R. Banaji first wrote about system justification in their article "The Role of Stereotyping in System-Justification and the Production of False Consciousness." It appeared in 1994 in vol. 33, issue 1 of the *British Journal of Social Psychology* on pp. 1–27.

178 **shows that the opposite is true**   The best introduction to Leanne Son Hing's research is her 2019 *Daedalus* article "Failure to Respond to Rising Income Inequality: Processes That Legitimize Growing Disparities." Another entry point is her 2011 article "The Merit of Meritocracy," which appeared in vol. 101, issue 3 of the *Journal of Personality and Social* on pp. 433–50. It was co-authored with D. Ramona Bobocel, Mark P. Zanna, Donna M. Garcia, Stephanie S. Gee, and Katie Orazietti.

178 **The leading rational-choice model**   The Meltzer-Richard Model is from their October 1981 paper "A Rational Theory of the Size of Government." It appeared in vol. 89, issue 5 of the *Journal of Political Economy* on pp. 914–27.

178 **Some of these mechanisms** Daniel Kahneman's *Thinking, Fast and Slow*
was published by Farrar, Straus and Giroux in 2011.

180 **Harvard economist Benjamin Friedman** Benjamin M. Friedman's *Religion and the Rise of Capitalism* was published by Knopf in 2021.

180 **participants in a study worked harder** Alison Ledgerwood, Anesu N.
Mandisodza, John T. Jost, and Michelle J. Pohl wrote about motivated defense
of meritocracy in their 2011 article "Working for the System: Motivated Defense
of Meritocratic Beliefs." It appeared in vol. 29, issue 3 of *Social Cognition* on
pp. 322–40.

180 **Eighty percent of Stanford seniors** The data on Stanford students' perception of fairness is from Data Team 94305, "The Class of 2020 by the Numbers,"
which appeared in the June 14, 2020, issue of the *Stanford Daily*. It's available at
https://www.stanforddaily.com/2020/06/14/the-class-of-2020-by-the-numbers.

181 **a remarkable behind-the-scenes look** Michèle Lamont's *How Professors Think* was published by Harvard University Press in 2010. Montclair State
University professor Patricia A. Matthew is one of many observers who have
noted that the purportedly objective metrics of the academy work to systematically disadvantage professors of color. Matthew's article "What Is Faculty
Diversity Worth to a University?" appeared in the November 23, 2016 issue of
The Atlantic.

181 **a memoir of a year and a half** Mitchell Stevens's *Creating a Class: College
Admission and the Education of Elites* was published by Harvard University Press
in 2007.

182 **Another part, Stevens says** Mitchell Stevens's quote is from Joe Pinsker's
article "The Real Reason That Legacy Preferences Exist," which appeared in the
April 4, 2019, issue of *The Atlantic*.

183 **About half of this total** MacKenzie Scott's donation to Texas A&M
International University and the size of the school's endowment prior to her gift
were reported by Julia Wallace in her December 15, 2020, article for the *Laredo
Morning Times*, "TAMIU Received $40 Million Donation from MacKenzie Scott,
Essentially Doubling the School's Endowment."

184 **elite universities continue to fundraise** Michael Bloomberg's gift was
announced on November 18, 2018, in a press release issued by the Johns Hopkins
University Office of Communications titled "Michael Bloomberg Makes Largest
Ever Contribution to Any Education Institution in the United States." It's available at https://releases.jhu.edu/2018/11/18/michael-bloomberg-makes-largest
-ever-contribution-to-any-education-institution-in-the-united-states.

184 **Malcolm Gladwell tweeted** Malcolm Gladwell recounts the events leading up to his conversation with John Hennessy, and the conversation itself, in season 1, episode 6 of his podcast *Revisionist History*. A transcript of the episode, "My
Little Hundred Million," is available at https://www.simonsays.ai/blog/my-little

-hundred-million-with-malcolm-gladwell-s1-e6-revisionist-history-podcast
-transcript-e1942c633432.

184 **the most egregious example** The phrase "dream hoarding" is from
Richard V. Reeves's book *Dream Hoarders: How the American Upper Middle Class
is Leaving Everyone Else in the Dust, Why That Is a Problem, and What to Do
About It.* It was published by Brookings Institution Press in 2018.

185 **empathy can lead us** Paul Bloom's *Against Empathy: The Case for Rational Compassion* was published by Random House in 2017.

Chapter 14

186 **Shortly after ten o'clock** You can watch the June 27, 2019, Democratic
debate at https://www.youtube.com/watch?v=cX7hni-zGD8. A transcript is available at https://www.nbcnews.com/politics/2020-election/full-transcript-2019
-democratic-debate-night-two-sortable-topic-n1023601.

188 **busing wasn't always a bad word** For an overview of the history of busing, see David Frum's *How We Got Here: The 70's, The Decade That Brought You
Modern Life (For Better or Worse).* It was published by Basic Books in 2000. Many
scholars have noted the myriad ways in which southern schools failed Black students even after busing. These include Jarvis Givens, Ruby Sales, Sonya Ramsey,
Vanessa Siddle Walker, Gary Orfield, and Susan Eaton.

189 **As J. Anthony Lukas recounts** Tony Lukas's *Common Ground: A Turbulent Decade in the Lives of Three American Families* was published by Vintage in
1986.

189 **reaction made Boston's seem quaint** Joyce A. Baugh discusses the
response to Judge Roth's decision on pp. 118–19 of her history *The Detroit Busing
Case: Milliken v. Bradley and the Controversy over Desegregation.* It was published
by the University Press of Kansas in 2011.

190 **Discussing *Milliken v. Bradley*** For background on *Milliken*, see Nikole
Hannah-Jones's article "It Was Never About Busing" in the July 12, 2019, issue of
the *New York Times*, and Elissa Nadworny and Cory Turner's July 25, 2019, NPR
article "This Supreme Court Case Made School District Lines A Tool For Segregation."

195 **There was state action in *Milliken*** John Michael Geise wrote about the
NAACP Legal Defense Fund's strategy in *Milliken* in his 2008 dissertation "*Bradley v. Milliken*: The Failure of Idealism." It's available at https://deepblue.lib.umich
.edu/bitstream/handle/2027.42/63940/geise_john_2009.pdf;sequence=1.

190 **Joe Biden perceived the same mood** Jason Sokol covered Joe Biden's
record on busing in his August 4, 2015, *Politico* article "How a Young Joe Biden
Turned Liberals Against Integration."

190 **Warren Burger didn't care** Bob Woodward and Scott Armstrong discuss the internal debate at the Supreme Court over *Milliken* on pp. 340–43 of their

seminal history of the Burger Court, *The Brethren: Inside the Supreme Court*. It was published by Simon & Schuster in 1979.

191 **Harvard Law School professor Martha Minow**   Martha Minow's statement that *Milliken* marked "the beginning of the end" of serious efforts at segregation is from "*Brown* at 60 and *Milliken* at 40," which appeared in the Summer 2014 issue of *Harvard Ed. Magazine*.

191 **NYU's Patrick Sharkey**   Patrick Sharkey reported his findings in "Neighborhoods and the Black-White Mobility Gap." The article was published by Pew Charitable Trusts in July 2009 and is available at https://www.pewtrusts.org /~/media/legacy/uploadedfiles/wwwpewtrustsorg/reports/economic_mobility /pewsharkeyv12pdf.pdf.

192 **disadvantage could hardly be more concentrated**   Eliza Shapiro reported on segregation in New York City public schools in her March 26, 2019, *New York Times* article "Segregation Has Been the Story of New York City's Schools for 50 Years." John Kucsera and Gary Orfield wrote a report on the issue in 2014 for the Civil Rights Project. *New York State's Extreme School Segregation Inequality, Inaction and a Damaged Future* is available at https://www.civilrightsproject .ucla.edu/research/k-12-education/integration-and-diversity/ny-norflet-report -placeholder/Kucsera-New-York-Extreme-Segregation-2014.pdf.

192 **sixty public schools in eleven states**   "I simply never see white children" is from p. 10 of Jonathan Kozol's *The Shame of the Nation: The Restoration of Apartheid Schooling in America*. It was published by Crown in 2005. See also Kozol's article "Overcoming Apartheid" on p. 26 of the December 19, 2005, issue of *The Nation*.

192 **"it would be indistinguishable"**   "If you took a photo of the typical classroom" is from Kozol's December 14, 2005, interview with Elizabeth Gehrman for the Harvard Graduate School of Education. "Shame of the Nation" is available at https://www.gse.harvard.edu/news/05/12/shame-nation.

192 **By 2010, this exposure had declined**   Rothstein's statement that "high average achievement is almost impossible to achieve in a low-income, segregated school" is from p. 197 of *The Color of Law*.

192 **more than 15,000 school boards**   "More decentralized than in any other advanced nation" is from p. 97 of *The Big Test*. Research on local control of school boards includes Deborah Land's 2002 article "Local School Boards Under Review: Their Role and Effectiveness in Relation to Students' Academic Achievement" on p. 230 of vol. 72, issue 2 of the *Review of Educational Research*, and Jeffrey R. Henig and Wilbur C. Rich's book *Mayors in the Middle: Politics, Race, and Mayoral Control of Urban Schools*, which was published in 2004 by Princeton University Press.

194 **remarkable piece about a wealthy district**   Annette Lareau's research on "Kingsley," co-authored with Elliot Weininger and Amanda Cox, was published

on pp. 1–46 of vol. 120, issue 1 of *Teachers College Record* under the title "Parental Challenges to Organizational Authority in an Elite School District: The Role of Cultural, Social, and Symbolic Capital." Lareau and her colleagues summarized their findings in their June 24, 2018, *New York Times* op-ed "How Entitled Parents Hurt Schools."

194 **the instinct to hoard** The data on PTA funding disparities is from Catherine Brown, Scott Sargrad, and Meg Benner's article "Hidden Money: The Outsized Role of Parent Contributions in School Finance." It was published by the Center for American Progress on April 8, 2017.

194 **Cardozo Law School professor Michelle Adams** Michelle Adams's quote is from an interview she gave to the podcast *Integrated Schools*. The episode, titled "Not In My Suburbs: *Milliken v. Bradley* @ 45," is available at https://integratedschools.org/podcast/not-in-my-suburbs-milliken-v-bradley-45-bonus.

196 **is modern redlining** "Moving from an urban apartment to a suburban home" is from p. 179 of *The Color of Law*. Richard Kahlenberg discusses the urgency of zoning reform in his April 19, 2021, *New York Times* op-ed "The 'New Redlining' Is Deciding Who Lives in Your Neighborhood."

196 **willful blindness to unapologetic, overt racism** The account of Cambridge evictions is from p. 26 of *The Color of Law*. The account of University of Chicago evictions and President Hutchins's quote are from p. 105.

196 **MIT historian Craig Steven Wilder** Craig Steven Wilder's characterization of early colleges as "the third pillar of a civilization based on bondage" is from p. 11 of *Ebony and Ivory: Race, Slavery, and the Troubled History of America's Universities*. It was published by Bloomsbury in 2013.

196 **Maryland Jesuits sold 272 slaves** Rachel Swarns reported on Georgetown's involvement with the slave trade in the April 16, 2016, issue of the *New York Times* in an article titled "272 Slaves Were Sold to Save Georgetown. What Does It Owe Their Descendants?"

196 **brought eight slaves to campus** Professor Wilder's research on Dartmouth and Columbia is summarized in Jennifer Schuessler's October 18, 2013, *New York Times* article "Dirty Antebellum Secrets in Ivory Towers."

196 **consider the curious case** The account of Salazar and Jaquette's disparate experiences with high school recruiting—or lack thereof—is from Jaquette's op-ed "State Universities Say They Want Diversity but Recruit Well-Off, White, Out-of-State Students." It appeared in the March 12, 2020, issue of the *Los Angeles Times*.

197 **where colleges invest their recruiting time** Karina Salazar and Ozan Jaquette's research, co-authored with Crystal Han, was published under the title "Coming Soon to a Neighborhood Near You? Off-Campus Recruiting by Public Research Universities" in the May 2021 issue of the *American Educational*

Research Journal. It's available at https://journals.sagepub.com/doi/full/10.3102 /00028312211001810.

197 **the rate is 63.3 percent**   The percentage of suburban Harvard students is from the *Harvard Crimson*'s survey of the class of 2024. It is available at https:// features.thecrimson.com/2020/freshman-survey/makeup.

Chapter 15

198 **a transformative figure**   Michael Lewis discusses his admiration for his high school baseball coach Billy Fitzgerald in *Coach: Lessons for the Game of Life* (W. W. Norton, 2005) and in Season 2 of his podcast *Against the Rules* in an episode titled "Don't Be Good, Be Great."

198 **Lewis's bestseller**   *Moneyball: The Art of Winning an Unfair Game* was published by W. W. Norton & Company in 2004.

199 **Play changed too**   Tom Verducci wrote about the tedium of baseball in his March 17, 2021, *Sports Illustrated* article "MLB Can't Wait Any Longer to Fix Its Pace of Play Crisis."

200 **most expensive project ever proposed**   The account of Wendy Espeland's experiences with the Orme Dam project are from her 1998 book *The Struggle for Water: Politics, Rationality, and Identity in the American Southwest.* It was published by University of Chicago Press.

201 **how the rankings were affecting law schools**   Espeland and Sauder's research on law schools is from their 2016 book *Engines of Anxiety: Academic Rankings, Reputation, and Accountability.* It was published by the Russell Sage Foundation Press. For an accessible introduction to their research on law schools, see their 2009 article "Rating the Rankings" in vol. 8, issue 2 of *Contexts* on pp. 16–21. For an introduction to Espeland's work on commensuration, see her book chapter, co-authored with Stacy Lom, "Noticing Numbers: How Quantification Changes What We See and What We Don't." It appears in *Making Things Valuable,* edited by Martin Kornberger, Jan Mouritsen, Lise Justesen, and Anders Madsen (Oxford University Press, 2015). Espeland and Sauder discuss the negative impact that rankings have on diversity in a 2009 law review article "How Rankings Affect Diversity," published in vol. 18, issue 3 of the *Southern California Review of Law and Social Justice* at pp. 587–608.

202 **their first rating of American colleges**   The history of the *U.S. News & World Report* rankings is from p. 10 of *Engines of Anxiety* and pp. 71–74 of Jeffrey Selingo's 2020 book *Who Gets In and Why: A Year Inside College Admissions,* published by Scribner. The profile of Morse also draws upon Richard Leiby's profile, "The *U.S. News* College Rankings Guru," in the September 9, 2014, issue of the *Washington Post.*

203 **basically their entire business model**   Support for my claim that rankings constitute the bulk of the *U.S. News* business model comes from, among

other sources, Thomas Heath's April 28, 2013, *Washington Post* article "Value Added: *U.S. News & World Report* Returns to the Ranks of Profitability."

203 **so doing causes incalculable harm** Michael Sauder wrote about the dangers of creating zero-sum games and how commensuration can affect status systems in his 2006 article "Third Parties and Status Position: How the Characteristics of Status Systems Matter." It appears on pp. 299–321 of vol. 35 of *Theory and Society.*

205 **Shortly after she became president** Cappy's efforts to improve socioeconomic diversity at Vassar were covered by Kerry Hannon in her June 22, 2016, *New York Times* article "At Vassar, a Focus on Diversity and Affordability in Higher Education."

206 **Gladwell's interview with Cappy** You can listen to "Food Fight," the second of the three-part *Revisionist History* miniseries on socioeconomic diversity and college at https://www.pushkin.fm/episode/food-fight. A transcript is available at https://www.simonsays.ai/blog/food-fight-with-malcolm-g ladwell-e5-s1-revisionist-history-podcast-transcript-113601722d87.

206 **producing a world-class dining experience** Bowdoin's presentation of food: https://www.bowdoin.edu/campus-life/dining/index.html and https://www .bowdoin.edu/dining.

206 **Bowdoin howled** Bowdoin's defense that it only offers two lobster dinners per year is from a July 14, 2016, press release titled "Bowdoin Responds to Malcolm Gladwell's 'Food Fight' Podcast" It's available at http://community .bowdoin.edu/news/2016/07/bowdoin-responds-to-malcolm-gladwells-food-fight -podcast.

207 **tracked a representative sample** The results of the Education Longitudinal Study were published in the U.S. Department of Education report *The Condition of Education 2015.* The authors include Grace Kena, Lauren Musu-Gillette, and Jennifer Robinson. It's available at https://nces.ed.gov/pubs2015/2015144 .pdf.

208 **fell victim to the "halo effect"** The story about Princeton's phony business program and the halo effect is from NPR's Anya Kamenetz's September 13, 2016, article "New College Rankings Are Out: NPR Ed Rates the Rankings!"

210 **my extensive efforts to interview Morse** Here's the full account of my efforts to speak with Bob Morse: I began by emailing Morse to ask for an interview. The *U.S. News* communications manager, Madeline Smanik, intercepted the email and asked me about my book. I explained the topic and said that I was interested in the origin of the rankings and how they'd decided to calculate social mobility in the way they had. After a month, I'd received no reply. Katzman told me that he knew Morse and offered to make an introduction. Shortly thereafter, Katzman told me that Morse would speak with me and that I should email him again. I did. Smanik then replied to my earlier email and said they were "unable

to accommodate an interview at this time." Smanik also said, however, that they "would be happy to fact-check anything related to *U.S. News*."

I said that I'd prefer to engage with Morse in a thorough, thoughtful conversation, but if these were the rules, I'd abide by them. I asked four "factual" questions. A few weeks later, I received a reply from Smanik, passing along "Bob's responses." It was like receiving a communique from the Pope! (Albeit not an entirely satisfying one.) They were responses—just not to the questions I'd asked. They felt more like replies to the questions they wish that I'd asked.

For example, my first question was whether Bob and *U.S. News* agreed that virtually all the factors used to rank colleges are strongly, positively associated with the wealth of schools and their students? Bob replied, "Among our top 50 ranked National Universities, the average six-year graduation rate of Pell students was an impressive 89 percent—only a few percentage points lower than the average graduation rate of their students not awarded Pell Grants." Morse's argument effectively was that elite colleges graduated the few poor kids they let in almost as often as the rich kids.

My second question was whether—given that faculty resources and financial resources per student were tied to institutional wealth by their terms—could *U.S. News* cite any evidence that these resources were associated with positive learning outcomes for students? Bob told me there was "no shortage of social science literature" linking small classes to positive learning outcomes. Of course, that doesn't explain why Harvard needs to pay its professors an average of a quarter million dollars per year. Not to worry. Bob said, "With faculty salaries, there are also numerous studies linking teacher compensation toward the ability for institutions to attract and retain faculty." In other words, to hire and keep the type of faculty that will make the institution attractive to rich kids, Harvard needs to pay its faculty a small fortune.

Third, I asked whether capping the social mobility multiplier at 0.5 for schools that have greater than 50 percent Pell recipients effectively amounted to a penalty on schools that admit majority poor students. Bob answered that based on graduation data they'd collected, "enrolling more Pell students beyond a certain amount was no longer disadvantageous to achieving a higher graduation rate among Pell students." I'm offering a $100 prize to the first person who can explain that in English. I'm sure it doesn't translate to, "You're right, schools that let in lots of poor kids have it harder."

My final question was whether they could confirm that the overwhelming majority of *U.S. News* revenue comes from rankings, as has been reported in various outlets. Smanik intercepted this one. "*U.S. News* does not publish those numbers," she wrote, "and so we are unable to accommodate this request." I resisted the temptation to reply and say that Smanik apparently did not understand the distinction between "unable" and "unwilling."

209 **that a one-rank improvement**   The data point that a one-rank improvement can lead to a 1 percent increase in applications is from Michael Luca and Jonathan Smith's article "Salience in Quality Disclosure: Evidence from the *U.S. News* College Rankings." It was published as Harvard Business School Working Paper 12-014 on September 27, 2011, and is available at https://hbswk.hbs.edu/item/salience-in-quality-disclosure-evidence-from-the-u-s-news-college-rankings. Of course, the flip side of Luca and Smith's finding is that a drop in ranking can lead to a decline in applications.

210 **Almost everyone in higher ed**   The list of critics of the *U.S. News* rankings is too long to recount. Influential pieces include Malcolm Gladwell's "The Order of Things," which appeared in the February 14, 2011, issue of the *New Yorker*; Valerie Strauss's September 12, 2018, *Washington Post* article "Analysis: *U.S. News* Changed the Way it Ranks Colleges. It's Still Ridiculous"; Scott Jaschik's September 10, 2018, article "*U.S. News* Says it Has Shifted Rankings to Focus on Social Mobility, But Has It?" for *Inside Higher Ed*; Cappy's April 8, 2014, *Inside Higher Ed* article "A Call for President Obama;" and The College Solution article "15 Reasons to Ignore *U.S. News & World Report*'s College Rankings," available at https://www.thecollegesolution.com/15-reasons-to-ignore-u-s-news-world-reports-college-rankings.

210 **"almost a parody of real research"**   Leon Botstein's characterization of the *U.S. News* rankings as "one of the real black marks" in the history of higher ed is from Alex Kuczynski's August 22, 2001, *New York Times* article "'Best' List for Colleges by *U.S. News* Is Under Fire."

210 **modest efforts to buck the system**   The accounts of *U.S. News*'s harsh treatment of non-compliers are from former Reed president Colin Diver's November 2005 *Atlantic* article "Is There Life After Rankings," and former Sarah Lawrence president Michele Tolela Myers's March 11, 2007, *Washington Post* article "The Cost of Bucking College Rankings." Myers's comparison of bucking the rankings to "universal disarmament" is from her *Washington Post* piece.

212 **jibe with people's preconceptions**   Mel Elfin's statement that the MVP shouldn't be a "utility player hitting .220" is from Nicholas Thompson's September 1, 2000, *Washington Monthly* article "Playing With Numbers."

Chapter 16

215 **Vanderbilt came in tenth**   Vanderbilt's positive diversity ranking is from https://www.collegefactual.com/rankings/diversity/

216 **what C. Wright Mills called "the power elite"**   *The Power Elite* was published in 1956 by Oxford University Press.

217 **Whatever limited progress has been made**   My summary of the AGB data on diversity among college board members draws upon Vicki W. Kramer

and Carolyn T. Adams's report "Increasing Diversity on the Boards of Colleges and Universities, Association of Governing Boards," which was published in September/October 2020. It's available at https://agb.org/trusteeship-article /increasing-diversity-on-the-boards-of-colleges-and-universities. Kramer and Adams's principal focus is diversity. Paul Fain reported AGB's 2010 findings on race diversity in his *Chronicle of Higher Education* article from November 29 of that year, "Diversity Remains Fleeting on Colleges' Governing Boards, Surveys Find." A more recent survey based upon a random sample of 1,300 trustees found that 87 percent of respondents were white and 60 percent were male. The *AGB 2018 Trustee Index* is available at https://agb.org/wp-content/uploads/2019/01 /report_2018_index.pdf.

217 **only 5 percent of the trustees are Black**   The USC data is from Charlotte Pruett's article "USC's Leadership Is Still Less Diverse Than Its Student Body." It was published by USC Annenberg Media on September 19, 2018.

217 **Included ten white men and one white woman**   The composition of UNC-Chapel Hill's board is from Martha Quillin and Kate Murphy's article "New Trustees Join UNC-Chapel Hill Board. Will They Bring the More Diverse Ideas Students Want?" It appeared in the July 3, 2021, issue of the *(Raleigh) News & Observer.*

217 **Randy Dumaling, an undergraduate at Fordham**   Sami Umani reported Randy Dumaling's findings in the July 7, 2020, issue of Fordham's newspaper, *The Observer.* The article is titled "Student Says #LookUpStepDown to a Predominately White Board of Trustees."

218 **"it isn't far-fetched to assume"**   Raquel Rall's inference that race is not a "top-of-mind issue" when boards make decisions is from her October 22, 2020, *Inside Higher Ed* opinion piece "Governing Boards and Race."

218 **data bears out Rall's intuition**   Data on the age, tenure, and political leanings of board members is from the *AGB 2020 Trustee Index: Concern Deepens for the Future of Higher Education*, 2020. It's available at https://agb.org/wp -content/uploads/2020/01/AGB_2020_Trustee_Index.pdf. While trustees may serve for a long time, they often have little or no training for their jobs, as Jon Marcus reported in his April 30, 2015, article for the *Hechinger Report* "Once Invisible, College Boards of Trustees Are Suddenly in the Spotlight."

219 **how universities manage their endowments**   The best source for data on college endowments is the May 4, 2018, Congressional Research Service report "College and University Endowments: Overview and Tax Policy Options." The report was authored by Molly F. Sherlock, Jane G. Gravelle, Margot L. Crandall-Hollick, and Joseph S. Hughes. It's available at https://fas.org/sgp/crs /misc/R44293.pdf. The report includes data on endowment returns, payouts, and the concentration of endowment wealth.

219 **the ten largest endowments**   The endowment ranking is from Danielle Douglas Gabriel's February 29, 2022, *Washington Post* article "College Endow-

ments Aren't Piggy Banks. But Some Experts Say Wealthy Schools Could Spend More."

220 **Yale draws down 5.25 percent**   John Geanakoplos explained the Yale's spending rule, particularly as it applied to the pandemic, in a June 2020 report to Yale's Faculty Senate. It's available at https://fassenate.yale.edu/sites/default/files /files/Reports/The%20Yale%20Endowment%20Spending%20Rule%20and%20 the%20COVID-19%20Crisis(1).pdf.

220 **promoted a notion of intergenerational fairness**   James Tobin laid out his views on endowment spending in his article "What Is Permanent Endowment Income?" It was published in May 1974 in vol. 64, issue 2 of the *American Economic Review* on pp. 427–32. The "guardians of the future" quote is from p. 427. For a critical view of elite colleges' endowment conservativism, see Paul Jansen's article "Rethinking Endowment Payout in Higher Education" in the *Forum for the Future of Higher Education*. It's available at http://forum.mit.edu/articles /rethinking-endowment-payout-in-higher-education.

221 **During the pandemic**   Catherine Thorbecke reported on endowment spending during the pandemic in her April 25, 2020, article for *ABC News* "Why Coronavirus-Battered Universities May Not Be Able to Use Their Endowments." Ellen M. Burstein and Camille G. Caldera also reported on the issue in their March 19, 2020, *Harvard Crimson* article "COVID-19 Leaves Harvard in 'Grave' Financial Situation, Experts Say."

221 **Ted Cruz and Josh Hawley shamed Harvard**   Renee Morad reported on Ted Cruz and Josh Hawley's criticism of Harvard for accepting CARES Act money in her April 21, 2020, *Forbes* article "Harvard Under Fire For Accepting Nearly $9 Million In Coronavirus Relief Funds."

221 **University of Pennsylvania's Peter Conti-Brown**   Peter Conti-Brown's observation that "universities use their endowments as a symbol of prestige" is from "Scarcity Amidst Wealth: The Law, Finance, and Culture of Elite University Endowments in Financial Crisis," which appeared in vol. 63, issue 5 of the *Stanford Law Review*, beginning at p. 699, where the quoted language appears.

221 **Law professor Victor Fleischer**   Victor Fleischer's observation that more money goes to endowment managers than students is from his August 19, 2015, *New York Times* op-ed "Stop Universities From Hoarding Money." Fleischer proposed that Congress require universities with endowments over $100 million to spend down at least 8 percent of their endowment every year.

221 **the largest share of its endowment**   The data on how Harvard spent its endowment money is from the Harvard University Financial Report, Fiscal Year 2020. It's available at https://finance.harvard.edu/files/fad/files /fy20_harvard_financial_report.pdf. Abigail Johnson Hess reported on Harvard's endowment spending in her October 28, 2019, CNBC.com piece "Harvard's Endowment is Worth $40 Billion—Here's How It's Spent."

222 **claims about its critics**   "There is a common misconception" is from p. 10 of Harvard University Financial Report, Fiscal Year 2019. It's available at https:// finance.harvard.edu/files/fad/files/fy19_harvard_financial_report.pdf.

224 **John Stuart Mill called out**   John Stuart Mill's characterization as irrational the idea of making a "dead's man's intentions for a single day" immortal is from p. 6 of "The Right and Wrong of State Interference With Corporation and Church Property," a chapter of his 1868 book *Dissertations and Discussions*, which was published by W. V. Spencer.

Chapter 17

227 **the overwhelmingly white, local school district**   Data on relative spending in South Euclid and Beachwood is from the Ohio Department of Education. Detail on district expenditures is available at https://reports.education.ohio.gov /report/report-card-data-district-expenditures-detail.

228 **a summer program for veterans**   Kathleen J. Sullivan wrote about Stanford's Veteran Accelerator Program in her August 17, 2018, article for *Stanford News* "Summer Studies at Stanford Give Military Veterans an Academic Boost."

229 **Amherst demanded his "family contribution"**   Goldrick-Rab wrote about the problems with expected family contributions in a September 27, 2016, article for *The Atlantic*, "How Financial Aid Betrays the Modern Family."

231 **determine the extent of the problem**   Goldrick-Rab discusses the various definitions of food insecurity in a 2019 paper co-authored with Nicholas Freudenberg and Janet Poppendieck, "College Students and SNAP: The New Face of Food Insecurity in the United States." It was published in vol. 109, issue 12 of the *American Journal of Public Health* at pp. 1652–58.

231 **Wisconsin colleges confirmed the result**   The HOPE Lab published the results of its study of Wisconsin students in its January 13, 2016, report "What We're Learning: Food and Housing Insecurity Among College Students: A Data Update from the Wisconsin HOPE Lab." It's available at http://bit.ly/2dHI8L1.

231 **findings have been replicated many times**   Subsequent research on food insecurity notably includes the Government Accountability Office's December 2018 report "Food Insecurity: Better Information Could Help Eligible College Students Access Federal Food Assistance Benefits." It's available at https://www .gao.gov/assets/gao-19-95.pdf.

231 **Thirty-nine percent of CUNY students**   On food insecurity at CUNY, see Nicholas Freudenberg's April 2011 report "Food Insecurity at CUNY: Results from a Survey of CUNY Undergraduate Students." It's available at http://bit. ly/1MkQ2Vx.

231 **the rate is 40 percent**   Suzanna Martinez and her colleagues reported on food insecurity at the University of California in a July 11, 2016, report

"Student Food Access and Security Study." It's available at http://regents
.universityofcalifornia.edu/regmeet/july16/ e1attach.pdf.

231 **it's 59 percent**   Megan Patton-Lopez and her colleagues detailed food
insecurity at Western Oregon University in their report "Prevalence and Correlates of Food Insecurity Among Students Attending a Midsize Rural University in Oregon." It's available at http:// ir.library.oregonstate.edu/xmlui/bitstream
/handle/1957/45177/PattonLopez_JNEB_ foodinsecurity_11414.pdf.

232 **surveyed students at thirty-four colleges**   Students Against Hunger's
report "Hunger on Campus: The Challenge of Food Insecurity for College Students" was authored by James Dubick, Brandon Mathews, and Clare Cady. It was
published in October 2016 and is available at http://studentsagainsthunger.org
/wp-content/uploads/2016/10/Hunger_On_Campus.pdf.

232 **For the past five years**   The Hope Center published the results of its
follow-up study in its 2020 report "#RealCollege 2020: Five Years of Evidence
on Basic Needs Insecurity." It's available at https://hope4college.com/realcollege
-2020-five-years-of-evidence-on-basic-needs-insecurity.

232 **nearly 10 percent of Middlebury students**   Molly Babbin, Bella Pucker,
and Grace Weissman reported Molly Anderson's findings about food insecurity at Middlebury in their April 16, 2020, article for the *Middlebury Campus*
"COVID-19 Exposes Long-Existing Patterns of Student Food Insecurity."

232 **22 percent of students**   The data on food insecurity at Cornell is from
Alexa Davis's December 17, 2015, *Forbes* article "Food Insecurity on Campus: Is
Your Ivy Leaguer Starving?"

232 **76 percent of students on financial aid**   The data on food insecurity at
Dartmouth is from "Scope of Food Insecurity at Dartmouth: A Report by the
2018–2019 Student Assembly." It's available at https://static1.squarespace.com
/static/5b397fa0e2ccd1b58ab7a317/t/5c5b37e1c83025ca9dd8f300/1549481953264
/Food+Insecurity+Report+-+Fall+2018-5.pdf.

232 **Breaks from school are a particular problem**   Tony Jack wrote about the
problem of food insecurity during breaks from school in his March 18, 2018, *New
York Times* op-ed "It's Hard to Be Hungry on Spring Break." Charlotte Susser also
wrote about the issue in her July 14, 2019, *Study Breaks* article "How Dining Hall
Closures Lead to Food Insecurity and What Can Be Done About It." It's available
at https://studybreaks.com/college/dining-halls-closures.

232 **found that only one in five colleges**   "There's always famine during
spring break" is from p. 165 of *The Privileged Poor*.

233 **exacerbated the problem**   The Hope Center's report on hunger during the pandemic, "#RealCollege During the Pandemic," is available at https:
//hope4college.com/wp-content/uploads/2020/10/Hopecenter_RealCollege
DuringthePandemic_Reupload.pdf.

233 **less than 5 percent of the students**   The data on Thomas Jefferson High School is from Lisa Rab's April 26, 2017, *Washingtonian* article "Does the No. 1 High School in America Practice Discrimination?"

234 **tells the story of how six undergraduates**   *Paying the Price: College Costs, Financial Aid, and the Betrayal of the American Dream* was published by the University of Chicago Press in 2016.

234 **declined precipitously over the past half century**   The data on Pell Grant purchasing power is from p. 19 of *Paying the Price*. The U.S. Department of Education also reported on the issue in its August 2019 report "Data Point: Trends in Ratio of Pell Grant to Total Price of Attendance and Federal Loan Receipt."

236 **Goldrick-Rab offers commonsensical ideas**   You can read Goldrick-Rab's proposals at https://hope4college.com/realcollege-federal-policy-agenda -2021/. She expands upon her school lunch proposal in an April 25, 2016, policy brief co-authored with Katharine Broton and Emily Brunjes Colo, "Expanding the National School Lunch Program to Higher Education." It's available at https: //hope4college.com/wp-content/uploads/2018/09/Wisconsin-HOPE-Expand -Lunch_Program.pdf.

237 **only 46 percent of undergraduate aid**   The National Association of State Student Grant and Aid Programs data is from their 2017 survey, available at https: //www.nassgapsurvey.com.

237 **As Paul Tough reports**   The observation that more aid goes to families making over $100,000 than to families making under $20,000 is from p. 162 of *The Years That Matter Most*. Tough cites David Radwin and his colleagues' report *2015–16 National Postsecondary Student Aid Study (NPSAS: 16): Student Financial Aid Estimates for 2015–16*. It was published by the National Center for Education Statistics in 2018.

238 **Let colleges agree to stop paying merit aid**   Scott Jaschik reported on Cappy's proposal to end merit aid in his March 11, 2019, *Inside Higher Ed* article "A Call for Policy Changes to Improve Access." Cappy expounded upon her ideas in an April 2, 2015, interview with Paul Glastris and Daniel Luzer for *Washington Monthly*, "Can an Elite School Do Right by Poor Students? A Conversation with Vassar President Catharine Bond Hill."

239 **Robert Litan, the attorney-economist**   Robert Litan detailed the history of the congressional antitrust exemption in his July 20, 2021, opinion piece for the *New Republic*, "Why Does Congress Let the Ivy League Operate as a Monopoly?"

240 **Bowdoin went on to emphasize**   Bowdoin's "commitment to meeting the full financial need of all admitted students" is from their July 14, 2016, press release "Updated: Bowdoin Responds to Malcolm Gladwell's 'Food Fight' Podcast." It's available at http://community.bowdoin.edu/news/2016/07/bowdoin -responds-to-malcolm-gladwells-food-fight-podcast/

240 **not really blind to the financial circumstances** Several astute observers have reported that students who don't need financial aid are more likely to get in. Paul Tough discusses the issue on pp. 153–67 of *The Years That Matter Most*. Ron Lieber covered it in his March 16, 2019, *New York Times* article "One More College Edge." Steve Cohen wrote about it for *Forbes* on September 29, 2012, in "The Three Biggest Lies in College Admission."

241 **As Nick Lemann puts it** Nick Lemann's observation that "the connection between family money and higher education was never truly severed" is from p. 140 of *The Big Test*.

Chapter 18

243 **On September 8, 2008** A complete transcript of the Grassley-Welch roundtable is unavailable, but several of the participants published their remarks. Former Amherst president Tony Marx's remarks are available at https://www .amherst.edu/amherst-story/president/past_presidents/marx/statements/node /64808. Former Princeton President Shirley Tilghman's remarks are available at https://www.aau.edu/sites/default/files/AAU%20Files/Key%20Issues /Taxation%20%26%20Finance/Test-Tilghman-Endowments-09-08-08.pdf. University of Tennessee law professor Iris Goodwin's remarks are available at https://papers.ssrn.com/sol3/papers.cfm?abstractid=1268999. A complete list of participants is available at https://welch.house.gov/media-center/press-releases /grassley-welch-release-participant-list-mondays-college-endowment. Peter Welch's opening statement is available at https://welch.house.gov/media-center /press-releases/welch-opening-statement-college-endowment-roundtable-sen -grassley-0. Excerpts of Senator Grassley's comments from the end of the roundtable, including his questions for the university leaders, are from a summary issued by the National Association of College and University Business Officers on September 1, 2008, titled "Endowment Roundtable Addresses Impact of Mandatory Payouts." It's available at https://www.nacubo.org/News/2008/9/Endowment -Roundtable-Addresses-Impact-of-Mandatory-Payouts. While Senator Grassley's opening remarks are unavailable, he published an op-ed titled "Wealthy Colleges Must Make Themselves More Affordable" in the *Chronicle of Higher Education* on May 30, 2008, a little more than two months before the roundtable. Libby A. Nelson covered Senator Grassley's focus on endowments for *Inside Higher Ed* in her December 9, 2011, article "Hoarding Assets?" Anne Kim also reported on the Grassley-Welch roundtable in her October 4, 2017, *Atlantic* article "The Push for College-Endowment Reform." Neither Senator Grassley nor Representative Welch responded to my requests for an interview.

244 **the Congressional Research Service estimated** The Congressional Research Service data is from its May 4, 2018, report "College and University Endowments: Overview and Tax Policy Options." It was written by Molly F.

Sherlock, Jane G. Gravelle, Margot L. Crandall-Hollick, and Joseph S. Hughes. It's available at https://sgp.fas.org/crs/misc/R44293.pdf.

244 **placed the figure above $20 billion**   Charlie Eaton's estimate is from his November 10, 2017, *New York Times* op-ed "How Elite Colleges Hide their Cash." For greater detail, see Eaton's January 2018 research brief for the Hass Institute, "The Ivory Tower Tax Haven," available at https://belonging.berkeley.edu/ivory-tower-tax-haven.

244 **James Conant had argued**   Conant's belief that elites would "later serve the taxpayer" is from p. 50 of *The Big Test.*

244 **Approximately one hundred schools**   Data on endowment per student is from the 2020 NACUBO-TIAA Study of Endowments. It's available at https://www.nacubo.org/Research/2020/NACUBO-TIAA-Study-of-Endowments.

244 **This list included Amherst**   Amherst reported an 11.6 percent return over twenty years in a 2009 press release, "Better Than Expected." It's available at https://www.amherst.edu/amherst-story/magazine/issues/2009fall/collegerow/endowment.

245 **law professor John Colombo**   John D. Colombo offers a history of the college tax exemption in his 1993 law review article "Why is Harvard Tax-Exempt? (And Other Mysteries of Tax Exemption for Private Educational Institutions)." It appeared in vol. 35 of the *Arizona Law Review*, beginning on p. 841. Emily J. Levine and Mitchell L. Stevens discuss the history in their November 30, 2017, *New York Times* op-ed "The Right Way to Fix Universities." Also see Oksana Koltko's 2009 law review article "Chasing Profits—Disregarding Values: Legal Persona of Elite Schools and Their Destructive Tax-Exempt Status," in vol. 42 of the *John Marshall Law Review*, beginning on p. 1073.

246 **a slave trader**   Whether Eli Yale was a slave trader depends on one's definition of the term. Yale certainly profited at least indirectly from slave trading, as Joseph Yannielli details in his November 1, 2014, Yale digital history "Elihu Yale was a Slave Trader." It's available at https://web.archive.org/web/20141108031612/http://histi3.commons.yale.edu/2014/11/01/elihu-yale-was-a-slave-trader/. Former Yale professor Steven Pincus emphasizes that Eli Yale never owned slaves, as reported by Valerie Pavilonis for *Yale News* in her June 28, 2020, article "Cancel Yale? Not Likely."

246 **invested nearly the entire endowment**   John R. Nofsinger discusses Yale's investment in Eagle Bank on p. 85 of his book *Investment Blunders of the Rich and Famous—and What You Can Learn from Them.* It was published by Financial Times Management in 2002. David F. Swensen also discusses the investment on pp. 59–60 of *Pioneering Portfolio Management: An Unconventional Approach to Institutional Investment*, which was published by Free Press in 2009.

246 **The so-called "Yale model"**   Alan Ruby reported on the shift in Yale's investment strategy in his May 15, 2021, article for *University World News* "University Endowment Models: A Tale of Two Missions."

246 **ten thousand acres of California vineyard**   Libby Nelson reported on Harvard's wine portfolio in a January 27, 2015, article for Vox "Why Harvard Owns 10,000 Acres of California Vineyards." It's available at https://www .vox.com/2015/1/27/7924109/harvard-endowment-vineyards. John Schoen observed that the ability of schools with the biggest endowments to attract the best advisers and make alternative investments is part of why they're able to generate higher returns and makes it all the less likely that the wealth gap will close over time. Schoen's article "Why Does a College Degree Cost So Much?" was published by CNBC.com on June 16, 2015. It draws upon an April 16, 2015, Moody's report "Wealth Concentration Will Widen for U.S. Universities." It's available at https://www.moodys.com/login?Return Url=http%3a%2f%2fwww.moodys.com%2fresearchdocumentcontentpage .aspx%3f%26docid%3dPBM_1000885.

246 **were using offshore havens**   Normal Silber and John C. Wei detailed their allegations in their 2015 article "The Use of Offshore Blocker Corporations by U.S. Nonprofits: Should the Blockers Be Blocked?" It appeared in vol. 6 of the *Nonprofit Policy Forum* beginning on p. 353. Joshua Humphreys and a team of researchers had raised concerns about elite colleges "chasing speculative returns" in the "shadow banking system" in a 2010 report issued by the Tellus Institute at the Center for Social Philanthropy, "Educational Endowments and the Financial Crisis: Social Costs and System Risks in the Shadow Banking System." The report is available at http://www.croataninstitute.org/documents/Educational -Endowments-and-the-Financial-Crisis-2010.pdf.

246 **were revealed to be partners**   *New York Times* reporter Stephanie Saul reported on Columbia's, Dartmouth's, and Johns Hopkins's involvement with blocker corporations in her November 8, 2017, article "Endowments Boom as Colleges Bury Earnings Overseas."

247 **Rothstein calls out the IRS**   Rothstein says "we have a right to expect the IRS to have been especially vigilant" when nonprofits promote segregation on p. 102 of *The Color of Law.*

248 **Harvard attracted $918 million**   Harvard grant support data is from its 2020 financial report, available at https://finance.harvard.edu/files/fad/files /fy20_harvard_financial_report.pdf. Kris Snibbe also reported on Harvard's federal support in his March 1, 2020, *Harvard Gazette* article "With Federal Funds, Harvard Helps Drive Local Economy." Yale grant support data is from: https://provost.yale.edu/budget/data-glance. Stanford data is from https://budget .stanford.edu/sites/g/files/sbiybj9886/f/budgetplan2021-22.pdf.

248 **Yale Law School professor Yair Listokin**   Yair Listokin argued that the IRS should stop treating alumni contributions as tax deductible in a May 10, 2021, op-ed for *Inside Higher Ed* "It's Time for the IRS to Question Legacy Admissions."

249 **A *New York Times* analysis**   The *New York Times* analysis of Black representation at one hundred top colleges was written by Jeremy Ashkenas, Haeyoun

Park, and Adam Pearce. The article, "Even With Affirmative Action, Blacks and Hispanics Are More Underrepresented at Top Colleges Than 35 Years Ago," appeared in the August 24, 2017, issue.

249 **recently published research**   The Ithaka S+R report "College and University Endowments: In the Public Interest?" is dated May 22, 2018. It was authored by Sandy Baum, Cappy, and Emily Schwartz, and is available at https://doi.org/10.18665/sr.307377.

249 **nonprofits in name only**   The *Boston Herald* characterization of elite colleges as nonprofits in name only is from an unsigned editorial "Colleges Owe a Lot to City," in the August 4, 2018, issue.

249 **co-founder of the Debt Collective**   Astra Taylor argued that "universities are becoming billion-dollar hedge funds with schools attached" is from an article with the same title, which appeared in the March 8, 2016, issue of *The Nation*.

250 **elite schools have come to view**   Peter Conti-Brown's statement that an elite university's endowment is a "symbol of status and prestige" is from his 2011 article "Scarcity Amidst Wealth: The Law, Finance, and Culture of Elite University Endowments in Financial Crisis." It appeared in vol. 63 of the *Stanford Law Review* beginning on p. 699.

250 **an air of resignation**   Cappy's lament that "the incentives aren't there" is from her interview with Paul Glastris and Daniel Luzer in the April 2, 2015, issue of *Washington Monthly*.

250 **dropped by about $1 billion**   The data on Pell Grant expenditures is from the Congressional Budget Office publication *Baseline Projections, Pell Grant Program*. It's available at https://www.cbo.gov/system/files/2021-02/51304-2021-02-pellgrant.pdf.

250 **Cappy proposes**   Cappy laid out her Pell Grant proposal in a December 23, 2000, opinion piece in *The Hill*, "Supporting Broad-Access Colleges and Increasing Opportunity at Selective Colleges Are Not Mutually Exclusive." It was co-authored with Martin Kurzweil.

251 **Congressman Tom Reed**   Rick Seltzer described Congressman Reed's proposal in his May 12, 2016, article for *Inside Higher Ed* "Lawmaker with the Idea Higher Ed Leaders Hate." Matt Willie proposed limiting the tax exemption to schools that do not allow tuition to outpace inflation in his 2012 law review article "Taxing and Tuition: A Legislative Solution to Growing Endowments and the Rising Costs of a College." It appeared in issue 5 of the 2012 *BYU Law Review* beginning on p. 1665.

251 **The existing excise tax generates**   The data on the total revenue generated by the Trump excise tax is from Michael Katz's August 28, 2020, article in *Chief Investment Officer*, "White House Regulatory Office Reviews Endowment Tax." It's available at https://www.ai-cio.com/news/white-house-regulatory-office-reviews-endowment-tax.

251 **Elite colleges have responded negatively**   Cornell's response to Representative Reed's proposal, including their claim that the congressman "doesn't seem to understand the endowment," was reported by Rick Seltzer in the May 12, 2016, edition of *Inside Higher Ed* in his article "Lawmaker with the Idea Higher Education Leaders Hate." Director of government relations for the American Council on Education Steven Bloom's statement that ACE wouldn't be "interested in negotiating over the terms of the bill to make it less bad" is from the same article.

252 **elite colleges found money**   Mae Quinn's observation that colleges freed up money to fight the Trump excise tax is from her 2019 law review article "Wealth Accumulation at Elite Colleges, Endowment Taxation, and the Unlikely Story of How Donald Trump Got One Thing Right." It appeared in vol. 54 of the *Wake Forest Law Review* beginning on p. 451. Quinn discusses the flexibility in Harvard's, Washington University's, and Brown's endowments specifically, and elite college endowments generally, on pp. 464–66 and 475–76. Professor Quinn's article also includes a comprehensive history of early efforts at understanding wealth accumulation at elite colleges on pp. 458–61.

252 **a diatribe about elite colleges**   Jose DelReal and John Wagner covered Donald Trump's Chester, Pennsylvania, speech in their September 22, 2016, *Washington Post* article "Trump Tests New Message on College Affordability, A Key Issue for Clinton." A transcript and C-SPAN's video of the event are available at https://www.c-span.org/video/?415738-1/donald-trump-campaigns-chester -township-pennsylvania.

253 **"I've gotten increasingly incensed"**   Malcolm Gladwell's August 22, 2015, interview with NPR's Scott Simon for *Weekend Edition Saturday* is published as "In Elite Schools' Vast Endowments, Malcolm Gladwell Sees 'Obscene' Inequity," and is available at https://www.npr.org/2015/08/22/433735934/in-elite -schools-vast-war-chests-malcolm-gladwell-sees-obscene-inequity.

Chapter 19

256 **But that's not the whole picture**   The calculation of Brendin's chances of getting into Princeton as a regular applicant draws upon a variety of sources: Princeton published its aggregate admission rate in a March 28, 2018, press release, "Princeton Offers Admission to 5.5 percent of Class of 2022 Applicants." Liam O'Connor wrote a pair of articles for the *Daily Princetonian* that included data on legacy and athletic preference rates. "Pulling Back the Veil: The Truth about Princeton Admissions" was published on June 23, 2020. "Ivy League Athletics Are the New 'Moneyball'" was published on October 10, 2019. On recruited athletes, see also Martin Kessler's June 26, 2020, article for WBUR "Accelerating Their Advantage: How White Students Use College Sports to Get (Further) Ahead." It's available at https://www.wbur.org/onlyagame/2020/06/26/russell -dinkins-brown-track.

257 **introduced the "A-B-C" system**　Christopher Avery, Andrew Fairbanks, and Richard Zeckhuser recount the history of early admissions on pp. 19–42 of their book *The Early Admissions Game: Joining the Elite*. It was published by Harvard University Press in 2003.

258 **changed with the Common Application**　Anne Kim wrote about the problems with the Common App in her October 17, 2016, article for *The Atlantic* "How the Internet Wrecked College Admissions." The article includes data on the number of applications filed. Allison Pohle also reported on the average number of applications in her March 16, 2021, article for the *Wall Street Journal* "Is it Harder to Get Into College in 2021?"

258 **recommends that students apply to**　IvyWise's recommendation is from its website: https://www.ivywise.com/blog/how-many-colleges-should-you-apply-to.

258 **Visits send a strong signal**　Chris Avery and Jonathan D. Levin discuss the strength of the signal sent by applying early in NBER Working Paper 14844, "Early Admissions at Selective Colleges." It was published in April 2009 and is available at http://www.nber.org/papers/w14844. Brian Gawor discusses the relationship between college visits and yield in his May 12, 2015, blog for *Education Insights*, "Understanding the Impact of FAFSA Filing and Visiting Campus on College Student Yield Rates." It's available at https://www.ruffalonl.com/blog/enrollment/understanding-impact-fafsa-filing-visiting-campus-college-student-yield-rates.

258 **a team led by Chris Avery**　Chris Avery presents his data on college visits on pp. 58–62 of *The Early Admissions Game*.

259 **likens to Martian Blackjack**　The "Martian Blackjack" analogy is from chapter 3 of *The Early Admissions Game*.

259 **Stanford economist Al Roth**　Al Roth's observation that a market is dysfunctional "if you have to hire a guide" and Mark Sklarow's observation that "anxiety is off the charts" are from Anne Kim's October 17, 2016, *Atlantic* piece.

259 **Thirty years ago**　The estimate of the number of college counselors is from Michelle Fox's March 18, 2019, article for CNBC.com "The Business of College Advisors is Booming. Here's How to Navigate the Consulting Process." Sklarow also discusses how the numbers have changed over time in Anne Kim's *Atlantic* piece.

260 **couldn't end them on their own**　Karen Arenson reported on Yale's flirtation with ending early decision in a December 13, 2001, *New York Times* article "Yale Proposes That Elite Colleges Abandon Early-Decision Admissions." It includes President Levin's fear that Yale would be "seriously disadvantaged" if it acted on its own. Jocelyn Lippert also covered the issue for the *Yale Daily News* in an April 22, 2002, article "The Waiting Game on Early Decision."

260 **announced that Harvard would stop**　Lee Hudson Teslik covered Harvard's decision to end early admission in a September 15, 2006, *Newsweek* article

"Why Harvard Ended Early Admission." *Harvard Magazine* covered the reversal of the decision in an unsigned article from the May/June 2011 issue titled "Reenacting Early Action."

260 **Over the course of his career** For anyone interested in getting to know the charismatic Al Roth, great places to start are *Who Gets What—And Why* (First Mariner Books, 2015) and the autobiographical essay he penned for the Nobel Prize committee. It's available at https://www.nobelprize.org/prizes /economic-sciences/2012/roth/biographical. Other profiles include Susan Adams, "Un-Freakonomics," (*Forbes*, July 22, 2010) and Phyllis Cramer, "New Nobel Prize Winner Designed City's HS Admissions System," (*Chalkbeat New York*, October 15, 2012).

261 **granting colleges an antitrust exemption** The legality of ending early admissions and Cappy's support for an antitrust exemption are discussed in Jeffrey Selingo's April 27, 2018, *Atlantic* article "The Best Ways to Fix College Admissions Are Probably Illegal."

262 **class sizes should double** Daniel Markovits proposed doubling admitted class sizes in an opinion piece in the September 12, 2019, issue of *Time*, "American Universities Must Choose: Do They Want to Be Equal or Elite?"

262 **points to satellite campuses** David Kirp's proposal is from his April 6, 2021, *New York Times* op-ed "Why Stanford Should Clone Itself." Jonah S. Berger proposed increasing Harvard's class size in an opinion piece for the *Harvard Crimson*, dated February 12, 2021, "The Case for Increasing Undergraduate Enrollment."

262 **related a story to *Freakonomics*** Cooper's comments are from *Freakonomics* episode 456, "How to Fix the Hot Mess of U.S. Healthcare." A transcript is available at https://freakonomics.com/podcast/healthcare-costs.

263 **rejected the idea** Justice Burroughs's conclusion that eliminating ALDCs would "have no meaningful impact on racial diversity" is from p. 120 of the district court decision.

263 **leading proponent of "top class rank"** David Orentlicher's top class rank proposal is laid out in "Economic Inequality and College Admissions Policies." The article appeared in vol. 26, issue 1 of the *Cornell Journal of Law and Public Policy* in fall 2016, beginning on p. 101.

264 **transformed the institution** The concentration of high schools in the University of Texas system is discussed in Mark C. Long, Victor Saenz, and Marta Tienda's article "Policy Transparency and College Enrollment: Did the Texas Top Ten Percent Law Broaden Access to the Public Flagships?" It appeared in vol. 627 of the *Annals of the American Academy of Political and Social Science* in 2010 on pp. 82–105.

264 **a similar concentration of wealth** Meg P. Bernhard discusses the concentration of high schools among Harvard students in her December 13, 2013, *Harvard Crimson* article "The Making of a Harvard Feeder School."

265 **found that many Texas families**   Julie Berry Cullen presented her research on parental strategic decision making under a top-rank choice model in her article "Jockeying for Position: Strategic High School Choice Under Texas' Top Ten Percent Plan." Co-authored with Mark C. Long and Randall Reback, the article appeared in vol. 97 of the *Journal of Public Economics* in 2013, beginning on p. 32.

265 **any student from an approved school**   The history of Harvard's "top-seventh" plan is discussed on pp. 171–72 of *The Chosen*, p. 21 of *The Early Admissions Game*, and in the unsigned, ironically titled April 12, 1935, *Harvard Crimson* article "Top Seventh Plan Will Not Carry Favoritism." For insight into President Lowell's complicated past, see Shera S. Avi-Yonah and Delano R. Franklin's article "Renovated Lowell House Will Not Display Portrait of Controversial Former University President Abbott Lawrence Lowell" in the March 26, 2019, issue of the *Harvard Crimson*.

265 **conducting a lottery among applicants**   The idea of a lottery among qualified applicants has a long history. On p. 207 of *The Big Test*, Nick Lemann reports that Supreme Court justice William O. Douglas considered proposing a lottery as a solution to the problem of affirmative action in *DeFunis v. Odegaard*, an early challenge to affirmative action at University of Washington Law School, which reached the Supreme Court in 1974 but was set aside as moot. Among others, Michael Sandel offers support for a lottery on p. 184 of *The Tyranny of Meritocracy*, as does Natasha Warikoo in *The Conversation*, January 8, 2019.

265 **Clark University's engagement**   Lani Guinier tells the Clark University story on pp. 46–56 of *The Tyranny of the Meritocracy*.

266 **Outstanding performance in junior college**   Support for community college as a predictor of success includes Barbara K. Townsend, Nancy McNerny, and Allen Arnold's 1993 article "Will This Community College Transfer Student Succeed? Factors Affecting Transfer Student Performance." It appeared in vol. 17, issue 5 of the *Community College Journal of Research and Practice*, beginning on p. 433.

266 **That year, Princeton announced**   Princeton touted its community college transfer program in a May 6, 2020, press release titled "Princeton Offers Admission to 13 Transfer Students in Third Year of Reinstated Program." It's available at https://www.princeton.edu/news/2020/05/06/princeton-offers-admission-13-transfer-students-third-year-reinstated-program. Harvard's transfer numbers are laid out in Benjamin E. Frimodig and Truelian Lee's February 4, 2018, *Harvard Crimson* article "'A Second Freshman Year': Harvard's Transfer Students."

Chapter 20

271 **the inspiration of Jill Wrigley**   The best evidence of how Jill Wrigley conceptualized Collins Streamside is a book chapter that she co-authored with

Mila Kellen Marshall and Michael Sarbanes. Titled "Coming Home to Common Ground in Stressed Communities: Intentional Civic Engagement in the Collins Avenue Streamside Community of Southwest Baltimore," the chapter appears in *Grassroots to Global: Broader Impacts of Social Ecology*, a volume edited by Marianne E. Krasny and published by Cornell University Press in 2018.

274 **Dutch geographer Louise Meijering's** Louise Meijering's definition of an intentional community as "challenging the norms of society" is from her article "Intentional Communities in Rural Spaces." Co-authored with Paulus Huigen and Bettina Van Hoven, the 2007 article appears on pp. 42–52 of vol. 98, issue 1 of *Tijdschrift voor Economische en Sociale Geografie* (*Journal of Economic and Human Geography*). It's available at doi:10.1111/j.1467-9663.2007.00375.x.

275 **"When the walls are down"** Thurman's views are laid out in *The Luminous Darkness: A Personal Interpretation of the Anatomy of Segregation and the Ground of Hope*, which was published by Harper & Row in 1965. The quoted language appears on p. 91.

276 **conditioning federal financial aid** The educational reformer Michael Dannenberg offers a similar proposal to Katzman's idea of conditioning federal aid on diversity in his August 12, 2019, blog post, "Ideas to Make College Fairer," https://edreformnow.org/blog/ideas-to-make-college-fairer.

276 **dangers of obsessing with perfection** Bill Burnett discusses "the unattainable best as the enemy of all available betters" around the six-minute mark of his amazing TedX talk in connection with Dysfunction Belief #3—Be the Best Version of You. You can find the talk at https://www.youtube.com/watch?v=SemHh0n19LA. Also check out Burnett and Dave Evans's book *Designing Your Life: How to Build a Well-Lived, Joyful Life*, published by Knopf in 2016.

277 **largest nonprofits in the United States** The ranking of nonprofits by assets is from CauseIQ, "Largest Nonprofits by Assets in 2019." It's available at https://www.causeiq.com/insights/largest-nonprofits-by-assets.

277 **five times the estimated value** The valuation of America's parks is from Julie Seger's article for the National Parks Foundation "Beyond a Visit: How We Value National Parks." It's available at https://www.nationalparks.org/connect/blog/beyond-visit-how-we-value-national-parks. Bouree Lam also discussed the valuation in a July 19, 2016, piece for *The Atlantic*, "How Much Are America's Parks Worth?"

277 **twice the value** The value of U.S. gold reserves comes from the Bureau of the Fiscal Service, "Status Report of U.S. Government Gold Reserve." It was issued by the U.S. Department of the Treasury on July 31, 2020.

Postscript

279 **Kennedy started slowly** A transcript of Kennedy's Amherst speech is available through the JFK Library at https://www.jfklibrary.org/learn/about-jfk/historic-speeches/remarks-at-amherst-college-on-the-arts. A

two-minute video clip is available on YouTube at https://www.youtube.com /watch?v=D2W4vLKo8DU. Neil Bicknell, Roger Mills, and Jan Worth-Nelson collected a series of their classmates' recollection of the speech and some related scholarly work in an edited volume, *JFK: The Last Speech*. It was published by Mascot Books in 2018. Naomi Shuman wrote about the origins of the book, and a related documentary film, in a June 22, 2018, piece for *Amherst Magazine* "The Speech That Shaped Their Lives."

279 **Income inequality has grown more severe**   The income distribution data is from https://courses.lumenlearning.com/suny-microeconomics/chapter /income-inequality-measurement-and-causes/ and https://www.statista.com /statistics/203247/shares-of-household-income-of-quintiles-in-the-us.

282 **Obama administration made a trove of data**   Rothstein discusses the Obama administration's Affirmatively Furthering Fair Housing regulation on pp. 200–01 of *The Color of Law*. Julie Hirschfeld Davis and Binyamin Appelbaum also covered the rule in their July 8, 2015, *New York Times* article "Obama Unveils Stricter Rules Against Segregation in Housing." Ashraf Khali covered the repeal in a July 23, 2020, article for AP Top News, "HUD Revokes Obama-Era Rule Designed to Diversify the Suburbs."

282 **redress America's history of residential segregation**   Rothstein lays out his remedies on pp. 202–07 of *The Color of Law*. Rothstein's pessimism is principally directed at repurchase programs and direct subsidies. He notes that New Jersey and Massachusetts have enacted "fair share" measures based on income. The New Jersey rule is based on a 1975 state supreme court decision, *Southern Burlington County N.A.A.C.P. v. Mount Laurel Township*, which read into the New Jersey Constitution an affirmative requirement that the state and municipalities use their zoning power to promote the production of low- and moderate-income housing. The sociologist Douglas Massey and his colleagues discuss the positive effects of a project built in a New Jersey suburb of Philadelphia as a result of the *Mount Laurel* decision in *Climbing Mount Laurel: The Struggle for Affordable Housing and Social Mobility in an American Suburb*. It was published by Princeton University Press in 2013.

283 **advocate of proximity to suffering**   Bryan Stevenson discussed proximity in his conversation with NBA guard J.J. Redick on episode 45 of Redick's podcast, *The Old Man and the Three*, starting at the 15:30 mark. His quote is from a speech to Boston College students, described in Megan Kelly's article "Stevenson Counsels 'Proximity' to the Marginalized," published in *The Heights* on June 4, 2020.

285 **generosity is principally about the donor**   Darren Walker discusses the ethics of philanthropy in his book *From Generosity to Justice: A New Gospel of Wealth* (Ford Foundation, 2019). A good introduction to his work is Lesley Stahl's interview, "Darren Walker: How the Head of the Ford Foundation Wants to Change Philanthropy," *60 Minutes*, April 4, 2021. A transcript of Stahl's conversa-

tion with Walker is available at https://www.cbsnews.com/news/darren-walker
-ford-foundation-60-minutes-2021-04-04.

285 **The Brookings Institution's Richard Reeves**   Richard Reeves is quoted
saying "we need more downward mobility from the top" on p. 72 of *The Merit Myth*.

285 **accept less than they historically have**   Walker says "we will have to give
up something" in his June 25, 2020, *New York Times* op-ed "Are You Willing to
Give Up Your Privilege?"

285 **he's ruined dinner parties**   Richard Reeves talks about ruining dinner
parties on p. 60 of *Dream Hoarders*.

285 **question she most often gets**   Rivera reports her experiences with parents on p. 277 of *Pedigree*.

286 **when the average Harvard professor makes**   Data on professorial salaries is from https://thebestschools.org/magazine/highest-paid-college-professors
-america.

287 **the entirety of the Ford Foundation's funding**   The Ford Foundation's
commitment to combatting inequality is reported, among other places, in the
June 12, 2015, *Philanthropy News Digest* article "Ford Foundation to Refocus
Grantmaking on Inequality."

INDEX

Page numbers followed by "f" and "t" refer to figures and tables, respectively.
Page numbers followed by "n" refer to notes.

on sports, 89–90
on top-end mobility, 34, 35
Friedman, Thomas, 30
Fritchley, Connor, 320n
Frost, Robert, 279, 280, 283
Frum, David, 323n
Fund for Wisconsin Scholars, 230–31, 236
funding. *See also* financial aid
   disparities, between school districts, 51–52
   federal-state partnership, 237
   of public colleges, 267
fundraising. *See* endowments; legacies

Gabriela, 29, 30
Garcia, Donna M., 321n
Gardendale, Alabama, 52, 303n
Garfield, James, 136
Garrity, Arthur, 189
Gates, Bill, 185
Gates, Henry Louis, 157, 319n
Gawor, Brian, 340n
Gaztambide-Fernandez, Ruben A., 140, 316n
Geanakoplos, John, 331n
Gebre-Medhin, Ben, 310n
Gee, Gordon, 214, 216
Gee, Stephanie S., 321n
Gehrman, Elizabeth, 324n
Geise, John Michael, 323n
geographic diversity, 113
Georgetown University, 19
George Washington University, 233
G.I. Bill, 57, 59, 228, 257
Giebel, Sonia, 310n
gifts, 222
Gladwell, Malcolm, 320n, 329n, 339n
   and Bowdoin College, 206, 240
   on endowments, 184, 253
   and Hennessy, 267, 322n
   on LSAT, 301n

on overcoming disadvantage, 168
Glastris, Paul, 334n, 338n
Glazer, Nathan, 153
Glennie, Elizabeth, 98, 310n
Goering, Susan, 273
Goldrick-Rab, Sara, 162, 230–32, 233–37, 240, 241, 284, 319n, 332n, 334n
Goldstein, Dana, 307n
Goode, Chris, 316n
Goodman, Joshua, 67, 306n
Goodwin, Iris, 335n
Gorsuch, Neil, 30
Gourevitch, Peter, 298n
governing boards, 216, 217–18, 224, 329–30n
Goyette, Kimberly, 302n
graduate indebtedness metric (*U.S. News & World Report* ranking), 209
graduation rate performance metric (*U.S. News & World Report* ranking), 209
graduation rates, 19, 20, 22–23, 82, 189
Graham, Frank, 55
grants, 234, 241
   Fund for Wisconsin Scholars, 230
   Pell Grants, 156, 184, 206–7, 209, 234, 250–51, 267, 328n, 334n, 338n
   research, 248
Grassley, Chuck, 243, 244, 253, 335n
Gravelle, Jane G., 330n, 336n
Greek life, 123, 164–66
Greene, Jay P., 320n
Greenpeace, 176–77, 179
Gregory, Sean, 308n
Griffin, Robert, 190
Groening, Matt, 61
Gu, Ruolei, 315n
Guinier, Lani, 64, 138, 157, 265–66, 310–11n, 315n, 319n, 342n

management consulting firms, 127,
167–68, 181
Mancuso, Frank, Jr., 71
Mandisodza, Anesu N., 316n, 322n
Manhasset, New York, xiv, 67, 86, 193,
195, 274
Manstead, Antony S. R., 314n
Mao Zedong, 91
Marcus, Jon, 307n, 330n
marketplace approach to testing, 73
Markovits, Daniel, 137–38, 262, 341n
Marshall, Mila Kellen, 343n
Marshall, Thurgood, 190
Marshall Scholarship, 30–31
Martinez, Suzanna, 332n
Martinot, Delphine, 316n
Marx, Bernard, 136
Marx, Karl, 200–201
Marx, Tony, 245, 335n
Mason, Derek, 216
Massey, Douglas S., 157, 318n, 344n
Mather, Cotton, 245–46, 247
Matthew, Patricia A., 322n
McCarthy, Niall, 299n
McCoy, Shannon, 316n
McDonough, Katie, 134, 135, 314n
McDonough, Patricia, xiv, 297n
McKernan, Signe-Mary, 311n
McMahon, Julie, 317n
McNerny, Nancy, 342n
Meijering, Louise, 274, 343n
Menand, Louis, 304n
Mencken, H. L., 271
merit aid, 237–38, 334n
meritocracy, 135–36, 151, 315–16n,
322n
in American culture, 140
belief in, 140–41, 143, 154, 180, 181
and beliefs about others, 137
collective merit, 139–40, 159
and commencement speeches,
141–42

and discrimination, 138–39
faith in meritocratic admissions,
139, 140
high school graduation speeches,
142–43
and institutional critiques, 175
and mistrust in institutions, 138
and morality, 138
overestimation of, 181
parenting styles and meritocratic
beliefs, 140
peer review, 181
and Republican politicians, 138
and social-dominance orientation,
181
and system justification, 180
term, descriptive usage of, 136–37
term, prescriptive usage of, 136
METCO program, 75, 193
Metzenbaum, Howard, 238
Middlebury College
racial diversity in, 156
students, food insecurity among,
232
middle class, 104, 152
mobility, 299n
parents, 47
Midwest University, 162–65
Mifflin, Houghton, 304n, 305n
Mill, John Stuart, 152, 224, 332n
Miller, Gregory, 320n
Milliken v. Bradley, 190–91, 194–95,
197, 282, 323–24n
Mills, C. Wright, 216–17, 224
Mills, Roger, 344n
Minow, Martha, 191, 324n
MIT, 238
admission process, 115–16
endowments, 117
stability rate of, 26
students, family income of, 117
upward mobility of, 117, 118

private admissions counselors, xiv, 96, 306n
Privileged Poor students, 149, 154
professional college advisors, 259
property taxes in California, 51
Pruett, Charlotte, 330n
PTAs, 52, 194
public education, xiv
  careers, 123
  separate but equal doctrine, 191
public service careers, 122, 123, 131, 248–49
Pucker, Bella, 333n
Putnam, Robert, 98, 175, 302n, 310n

quarter-section blocks (census data), 46
Quillin, Martha, 330n
Quinn, Mae, 252, 339n
Quintana, Chris, 307n

Rab, Lisa, 334n
race, 148, 186–87. *See also* Asian Americans; Black Americans; class
  Brown v. Board of Education, 187–89
  color-blindness, 157–58
  diversity, 44, 66, 97, 112, 155–56, 263
  and governing boards, 217, 218
  and lacrosse, 78
  Milliken v. Bradley, 190–91, 194–95, 197, 282, 323–24n
  and poverty, 191–92
  and power, 158
  representation in college athletics, 79f
  representation in selected sports, 80, 80f
  and slavery, 196
  stereotypes, 302n
racism, 81

cultural, 157
housing policies, 108
Southern Strategy, 189
stereotypes, 162
Radwin, David, 334n
Rall, Raquel, 217–18, 330n
Rampell, Catherine, 318n
Ransom, Tyler, 308n
Ratcliffe, Caroline, 311n
rational-choice model, 178
Rawls, John, 139
#RealCollege initiative, 232
Reardon, Sean, 46, 53, 302n, 304n
Reber, Sarah, 299n
Redick, J. J., 344n
Reducing Excessive Debt and Unfair Costs of Education (REDUCE) Act, 251
Reed, Tom, 251, 338n
Reed College, 203, 210, 211, 212
Reeves, Richard, 184–85, 194, 285, 345n
Reilly, Katie, 309n
Republicans, 138, 189, 282
research function of colleges/universities, 248
residential segregation, xvi, xviii, 108, 189, 195, 197, 282
Reynolds, Ora Edgar, 25, 300n
Rhee, Michelle, 49
Rice, Condoleezza, 39
Rich, Wilbur C., 324n
Rivera, Lauren, 37–38, 87, 285, 301n, 311n, 313n, 320n, 345n
  on baller lifestyle, 127
  on career choice, 128
  on elite jobs, 38, 39, 127, 137, 167–68
Robb, Alice, 317n
Robinson, Adam, 305n
Robinson, Jennifer, 327n
Romney, George, 281–82

ABOUT THE AUTHOR

Evan Mandery, a Peabody and Emmy Award winner, is a professor at the City University of New York and the author of seven prior books. He has written for the *New York Times* and Politico and has appeared on the Today Show, CNN, and NPR's *Fresh Air*. His journey as a Harvard alum publicly challenging legacy admissions at elite schools led him to write *Poison Ivy: How Elite Colleges Divide Us* (The New Press). He lives in Montclair, New Jersey, with his partner, Valli Rajah-Mandery, a sociologist. They have three children.

PUBLISHING IN THE
PUBLIC INTEREST

Thank you for reading this book published by The New Press. The New Press is a nonprofit, public interest publisher. New Press books and authors play a crucial role in sparking conversations about the key political and social issues of our day.

We hope you enjoyed this book and that you will stay in touch with The New Press. Here are a few ways to stay up to date with our books, events, and the issues we cover:

- Sign up at www.thenewpress.com/subscribe to receive updates on New Press authors and issues and to be notified about local events
- Like us on Facebook: www.facebook.com/newpressbooks
- Follow us on Twitter: www.twitter.com/thenewpress
- Follow us on Instagram: www.instagram.com/thenewpress

Please consider buying New Press books for yourself; for friends and family; or to donate to schools, libraries, community centers, prison libraries, and other organizations involved with the issues our authors write about.

The New Press is a 501(c)(3) nonprofit organization. You can also support our work with a tax-deductible gift by visiting www.thenewpress.com/donate.